Dramatists in Revolt

The New Latin American Theater

The Texas Pan American Series

Dramatists in Revolt

The New Latin American Theater

Edited by Leon F. Lyday & George W. Woodyard

University of Texas Press, Austin and London

The Texas Pan American Series is published with
the assistance of a revolving publication fund
established by the Pan American Sulphur Company.

Library of Congress Cataloging in Publication Data
Main entry under title:

Dramatists in revolt.

(The Texas pan-American series)
Bibliography: p.
Includes index.
1. Latin American drama—History and criticism—
Addresses, essays, lectures. I. Lyday, Leon F.,
1939–   II. Woodyard, George W.
PQ7082.D7D7   1976   862   75-16078
ISBN 0-292-71510-2

Second Printing, 1977

TO BETTIE AND ELEANOR

Contents

Preface

The present volume is intended as an introduction to the contemporary theater in Latin America presented through studies on individual playwrights. The editors have chosen this approach rather than a thematic or country-by-country one because they consider virtually all the major themes and dramatic currents in recent Latin American theater to be present in one or the other of these writers. Further, they believe that by concentrating on a limited number of dramatists, and by having the production of each essayed by a critic familiar with his or his country's theater, much greater depth is afforded than would otherwise be possible.

While the dramatists included in the study doubtless rank among the most significant in Latin America today, Carlos Solórzano (Guatemala and Mexico) and a number of other playwrights, such as Sergio Vodanović (Chile), Wilberto Cantón (Mexico), Elena Garro (Mexico), Francisco Arriví (Puerto Rico), and Demetrio Aguilera-Malta (Ecuador and Mexico) have also made exceptional contributions. However, since comprehensive essays on each of these dramatists—except Vodanović—are already available, they are not presented here. In the case of Vodanović, an essay was originally planned but regrettably was not forthcoming.

The editors would like to give thanks to the eleven colleagues who contributed to the volume. We also pay homage to the fifteen playwrights herein treated, for they have provided us all with material for many pleasurable and stimulating hours of reading and reflection.

Introduction

The decade of the sixties witnessed a surge in popularity in Latin American prose unparalleled in the literary history of that area. The novel, which into the 1950s was considered, albeit wrongly, to be largely regionalist in scope and of relatively little universal consequence, by 1970 had emerged as a major force in world literature, and writers such as Jorge Luis Borges, Gabriel García Márquez, Julio Cortázar, and João Guimarães Rosa were both highly acclaimed and widely translated. An equally significant, though less spectacular, metamorphosis from the regionalist to the universal occurred in Latin American drama during the same period, and the playwrights discussed in the present volume rank among the leaders in effecting this change.

Drama, of course, has long been a viable art form in Latin America. There is ample evidence, including a few extant plays, of some type of the theater among the pre-Columbian Indian civilizations, and for much of the colonial period religious orders in Spanish America and Brazil found the theater an effective medium for Christian indoctrination. Profane drama also began to take hold in the sixteenth century and came to the fore with such playwrights as the Mexicans Juan Ruiz de Alarcón (1580?–1639) and Sor Juana Inés de la Cruz (1648–1695), and the Peruvians Juan del Valle y Caviedes (1645–1697?) and Pedro de Peralta Barnuevo (1664–1743).

With the nineteenth century came Romanticism and *costumbrismo*, movements during which a great many plays were written in Mexico, Argentina, Colombia, and Brazil, but from which only a few significant playwrights emerged. Prominent among these were the Brazilians Luis Carlos Martins Pena (1815–1848) and Antônio Gonçalves Dias (1823–1864), the Peruvian Manuel Ascensio Segura (1805–1871), and the Mexican José Peón y Contreras (1843–1907).

Around the turn of the century a distinct movement sprang up and flourished, both in Brazil and in many parts of Spanish America. Much like Spain's *género chico*, this movement was characterized chiefly by a new kind of *costumbrista* theater and by other light forms, such as revues and operettas. The leader in Brazil was Artur Azevedo (1855–1908), while in the River Plate area, where the tradition was especially strong, Florencio Sánchez (1875–1910) was the acknowledged master. Several plays by these two dramatists, particularly Azevedo's *A Capital Federal* and Sánchez's *Barranca abajo*, have borne the test of time and are still quite playable today.

For most of the second and third decades of the twentieth century the theater in Latin America was relatively moribund. A few playwrights from this period, almost all of them creators of social or thesis dramas, are worthy of note, nonetheless. Among these are the Chileans Armando Moock (1894–1942) and Acevedo Hernández (1886–1962), the Uruguayan Ernesto Herrera (1886–1917), the Cuban José Antonio Ramos (1885–1946), and the Colombians Antonio Alvarez Lleras (1892–1956) and Luis Enrique Osorio (1886–1966).

The period between 1928 and 1943 is extremely important to Latin American drama, for it was during those years that a new consciousness of and concern for theater developed in almost all the countries with a significant literary tradition. Theatrical groups sprang up in many of the capitals, and there was renewed interest in so-called serious drama, with emphasis on trends and techniques of the contemporary European and American stages. In Mexico, for example, the Grupo de los Siete (1923) set Pirandello, Chekhov, O'Neill, and others as their models. Two subsequent organizations, the Grupo de Ulises (1928) and the Teatro Orientación (1932–1934 and 1938–1939), also followed universalist tendencies but, with the leadership of Celestino Gorostiza (1904–1967) and Xavier Villaurrutia (1903–1950), did much to foment the new Mexican theater as well.

In Cuba the Teatro de la Cueva group was founded in the early 1930s, as was the Teatro del Pueblo in Argentina. The Brazilian theater, which had lain virtually dormant since just after the turn of the century, came awake with a start in 1932 with the production of Joracy Camargo's (1898–1973) then highly controversial *Deus lhe Pague*. This and other works by Camargo, along with plays by Nelson Rodrigues (1912) and the technical advances introduced by the exiled Polish director Zbigniew Ziembinsky, served to revitalize Brazil's theater, which since the 1940s has been one of the best in Latin America.

In 1940, under the leadership of the playwright Emilio Belaval (1903), the Areyto group was founded in Puerto Rico to further theatrical activity, while in Chile the now famous ITUCH (Instituto de Teatro de la Universidad de Chile) and TEUC (Teatro Experimental de la Universidad de Chile) were established in 1941 and 1943 respectively.

These various groups and organizations, some of them short-lived and others of longer tenure, all served to encourage young dramatists and to promote theater in general, and, largely because of this stimulation, the 1940s and early 1950s witnessed a substantial upswing in dramatic activity. Of the playwrights who held sway during this period, several must be ranked among the foremost in the history of Latin American dramaturgy. Among them are Rodolfo Usigli (1905), the Mexican psychological and historical dramatist whose career spans the past four decades but whose best works remain *El gesticulador* (1937) and *Corona de sombra* (1943); Xavier Villaurrutia, the Mexican intellectual playwright whose *Invitación a la muerte* (1940) is considered one of the masterpieces of the theater in Spanish America; Samuel Eichelbaum (1894–1967), the Argentine psychological dramatist particularly noted for works such as *Un guapo de novecientos* (1940) and *Un tal Servando Gómez* (1942); Conrado Nalé Roxlo (1898–1970), the Uruguayan humorist best known for his fantasy *La cola de la sirena* (1941) and the farcical *Una viuda difícil* (1943); and Nelson Rodrigues (1912), the Brazilian naturalistic playwright whose *Vestido de Noiva* (1943), because of its daring theme and scenographic originality, marked a major turning point in that country's theater.

The five playwrights just mentioned, along with others, such as Mexico's Celestino Gorostiza and Salvador Novo (1904–1974), and Puerto Rico's Manuel Méndez Ballester (1909), very effectively ushered Latin America's theater into an unparalleled two decades of dramatic production and excellence and an accompanying swell in critical interest. These two decades, extending from the early 1950s to the present, constitute what may be termed the contemporary movement in Latin American theater. This movement began with the maturation of Brazil's Jorge Andrade, Mexico's Emilio Carballido, Argentina's Carlos Gorostiza, and several others, all of whom have continued to produce over the past twenty years.

While contemporary drama in Latin America is perhaps best characterized by its diversity—in type and in theme—the playwrights who have created this drama are united by a spirit of revolution, both in terms of aesthetics and often of sociopolitical values as well. Out of this revolutionary spirit has come a new order of message plays, incorporating such major European trends as existentialism, the theater of the absurd, and the theater of cruelty and of ritual. Surrealistic drama and the farce also continue to be found, but even here a new level of artistry is discernible.

The thesis play has a long and often uninspiring tradition in Latin America. This new generation of dramatists, however, has incorporated expressionistic devices and techniques in order to break the bonds of straightforward realism. The thematic variety possible within the category of thesis drama is virtually endless. Puerto Rico's René Marqués, in *La carreta* and *La muerte no entrará en palacio*, is extremely nationalistic, for example, while Chile's Egon Wolff, in *Los invasores* and *Flores de papel*, and Argentina's Osvaldo Dragún, in *Y nos dijeron que éramos inmortales* and other plays, pit new social and moral values against the old. Brazil's Alfredo Dias Gomes, meanwhile, has concerned himself with the conflict between individual liberty and structured society in such plays as *O Pagador de Promessas* and *O Santo Inquérito*, whereas Plínio Marcos, also from Brazil, has depicted the life of society's marginalia—prostitutes, pimps, petty thieves—in *Dois Perdidos numa Noite Suja*, *Navalha na Carne*, and several additional works.

Existentialism, through Sartre and Camus, has had strong influence in Latin American literature and has found its dramatic expression in such works as *La zona intermedia* by Carballido, *Las manos de Dios* by Carlos Solórzano (Guatemala and Mexico), *Juicio final* by José de Jesús Martínez (Panama), and *Funeral Home* by Walter Béneke (El Salvador).

Following the lead of Ionesco, Beckett, Adamov, and others, various Latin Americans have also written plays in the absurdist vein. The most successful of these has been the Chilean Jorge Díaz, whose early works, such as *Requiem por un girasol*, *El cepillo de dientes*, and *El velero en la botella*, reveal a close kinship with the writings of Ionesco. Antón Arrufat (Cuba), René Marqués, and Elena Garro (Mexico) have also employed in their works comparable techniques of fragmentation, distortion, and linguistic play.

The theater of cruelty and of ritual, inspired by Artaud and Genet, has also left its mark. *Los siameses* and *El campo* by Griselda Gambaro (Argentina) and Cuban José Triana's masterpiece *La noche de los asesinos* are brutal pieces designed to shock and at times sicken the audience into an awareness of the savagery and barbarity existing in modern society.

Several writers have found farce to be an appropriate vehicle for criticizing the maladies of the societies in which they live and work. Agustín Cuzzani is a leader in this tradition, with *Una libra de carne*, *El centroforward murió al amanecer*, and *Sempronio*, although various other playwrights have also experimented in this form, among them Emilio Carballido with his *Silencio, pollos pelones* and Dias Gomes with *Odorico, o Bem Amado*. These two writers are also known for their occasional experimentation with surrealistic forms, as in *La hebra de oro* and *O Santo Inquérito*.

One cannot, of course, speak solely in terms of playwrights and literary movements, for the production on stage, involving interpreters and directors, is the essence of theater. And herein lies the major problem for most Latin American dramatists, past and present. Only a relatively few major cities—Rio, São Paulo, Buenos Aires, Santiago, Lima, Mexico City, and possibly two or three others— have legitimate theatrical seasons, and even in these it is and has been commercially expedient to present a fare weighted with European and American hits. Thus, even playwrights from countries represented by these few cities have difficulty in getting their works staged, while those from other countries only rarely see true commercial productions of their plays. Additionally, dramatists and entrepreneurs in several countries are faced with severe political censorship. Many playwrights also find it difficult to encounter publishers for their works, and almost nowhere does there appear to be ample market to warrant large printings of plays that do manage to reach press.

In spite of these many problems, there has been encouraging progress on several fronts in recent years. A major advance has been the initiation of annual national or international theater festivals in at least a dozen Spanish American cities. Although in these festivals works by major European and American playwrights are occasionally staged, a large majority of the presentations are works by Latin Americans, and the participating dramatic companies, many of them university groups, are almost without exception from Latin America. Thus, these festivals function as a much-needed forum for dramatists and acting companies alike.

Critical interest in Latin America's theater has also increased markedly over the past two decades. There are by now a goodly number of journals devoted exclusively to this theater. Yet another favorable sign has been the translation of plays into English as well as other Eastern and Western European languages. This, in turn, has facilitated the presentation, within the past few years, of works by José Triana, Alfredo Dias Gomes, Jorge Díaz, and several other top-ranked playwrights in the international theater capitals—New York, London, Paris, or Madrid. These and other dramatists are also being staged, in increasing numbers, by amateur and university groups in the United States and in certain European countries as well.

The theater in Latin America has, in summary, made great strides over the past twenty years. The playwrights represented in this volume continue to be active, while new talent is constantly being added. Vicente Leñero, Mexico's novelist turned dramatist, has developed very effectively the documentary drama, following the tradition of Brecht and Peter Weiss, in such plays as *Pueblo rechazado* and *El juicio*. Others who have used a similar form are Julio Ortega (Peru) in *Mesa Pelada*, a highly poetic and diversified account of the death of the guerrilla leader Luis de la Puente Uceda, and Fernando González Cajiao (Colombia) in *Huellas de un rebelde*, a medieval mystery-style documentary about the young Latin American rebel priests following Camilo Torres's example. Much of the theater continues to have a committed viewpoint; political and social injustices predominate in many parts of the Latin world. The multiple forms of repression are a part of this reality, which induces writers and creative artists to deal with these problems in whatever ways they can. Where some self-censorship is not operational, the government often takes explicit steps to impede the production of "subversive" plays. The promoters of the Third World movement many times have abandoned the commercial theater in favor of productions in the streets and barrios in order to bring a message to the people for whom even the minimal cost of a theater ticket is prohibitive. Many writers have adopted a radical stance in exposing these problems, in which the spectacular or shocking aspects of form reflect the theme. Manuel J. Arce (Guatemala) has captured the public's attention with *Delito, condena y ejecución de una gallina*. Julio Mauricio (Argentina) in *Un despido corriente* and Antonio Larreta (Uruguay) in *Juan Palmieri* have posed similar problems in slightly more conventional format. As a part of this movement, the development of the *creación colectiva* has become common; where texts have not been available or suitable, groups of dedicated people have developed their own. *El asesinato de X* is a creative effort by eight young Argentines that exposes brutality and repression in a very direct manner. The danger, of course, is that a radical work will have little transcendent value if its agitprop aspects outweigh considerations of aesthetics or if it is too closely tied to a particular incident or point in time. A case in point is *El avión negro*, a collaborative work by four Argentines (Roberto Cossa, Germán Rozenmacher, Carlos Somigliani, and Ricardo Talesnik) predicated on Perón's future return to Argentina; in passing from the realm of myth to reality, the play loses some of its appeal.

In any event, from this vantage point, the future of the theater in Latin America looks promising, a condition that has been helped by the international attention it has both sought and received and that has brought about new levels of sophistication in playwrighting and in production.

L.F.L. and G.W.W.

Part One

Spanish American Dramatists

1. The Theater of Antón Arrufat

Frank N. Dauster

Antón Arrufat is, with José Triana, one of the leading exponents of the nonrealistic drama in Cuba. Born in Santiago in 1935, he lived in Havana from 1947 to 1957, when he emigrated to New York; since his return to Cuba in 1959, Arrufat has held a number of literary and dramatic positions. One of his major preoccupations is the search for a dramatically coherent fusion of contemporary innovations with the traditional forms of the *teatro bufo*, the popular theater comparable to the Spanish *género chico* or the *sainete orillero* of the Río de la Plata. It may seem curious that Arrufat should be so concerned with a form that is, at least superficially, trivial. But the roots of the contemporary movement are to be found in strange places; it is no more startling to find Arrufat influenced by the *bufo* than to observe his European and North American contemporaries entranced by Buster Keaton, W. C. Fields, or the Marx brothers. Uruguayan and Argentine playwrights are turning again to their own *sainete orillero*, with its cast of toughs, poor working girls, and pimps, in a search for the expression of contemporary problems. If the turning to odd quarters of the past is, for those dramatists loosely characterized as absurd, a result of the "sense that the certitudes and unshakeable basic assumptions of former ages have been swept away, that they have been tested and found wanting,"[1] then for Arrufat it is a very different thing. He seeks significance rather than rejecting it; if the *bufo* is a very merry joke, it is also a source for a new evaluation of the Cuban people. In this reconciliation of traditional dramatic forms with cosmopolitan tendencies, we find an analogy to the very profound wish for a reconciliation of the two in human terms. This is no hollow harking to a dead past, but a serious effort to identify and salvage that part of the past which is valid today and always.

Arrufat's own comments on the *bufo* are enlightening: ". . . we have again established contact with our own reality, we are observing again for ourselves, and in so doing we have stumbled on the *bufo*, which did the same in its own moment."[2] "The *bufos* tried to begin again, to observe the reality that surrounded them; instead of imitating the results of an established culture, they began where the theater began, little grotesques and farces; they created the theater again among us, as though it had not existed in any other part of the world."[3]

This humorous deformation of reality in the effort to re-create the most essential aspects of it is precisely what so attracts Arrufat, and his essay on the *bufo* is almost a description of his own concerns as a practicing dramatist. He writes: "I observe that the Cuban intelligence proceeds by leaps, associates badly, goes from witticism to witticism, now an irony, a brilliant idea, like a chaos that cannot be organized in a coherent and systematic way; and all this ends in a lot of uproar, the faltering sentences begin, the silences, the gestures that try to rescue the disorder, to help the unexpressed idea, and finally someone tosses off a joke, and laughter undermines the importance of what someone was trying to state or explain."[4]

This zigzagging, illogical character that he stresses, with its digressions into pure verbiage, its sudden silences and trailing, unresolved situations, is very close to Arrufat's method of construction; the sudden and violent oscillation from apparent seriousness to triviality is the theme of his first play, *El caso se investiga* ("The case is investigated"). Performed unsuccessfully in 1957, the work had a lengthy run in 1963. The subject is a thoroughly anti-Cartesian murder investigation. The principals are conspicuously attired: the Inspector in a striped suit and patent leather shoes, the widow Eulalia in a lacy white robe, her sister Amelia in a party gown of the 1920s. Each time Amelia passes there is a fanfare; the stage directions specify that the play be acted "como una comedia vertiginosa de Mack Sennett, o como un dibujo animado."[5] On several occasions the characters break into dance, ranging from a grotesque ballet to the *guaracha* appropriately and gruesomely entitled "Los carniceros" ("The butchers").

The entire play is a series of *non sequiturs*; the widow, her sister, and the maid all attempt to throw suspicion on each other, with obvious malevolence, and Eulalia, coquettish for all her sixty years and new bereavement, forgets entirely that there has been a murder and that she has discovered the body. The Inspector is constantly diverted by a discussion of remedies for insomnia or a dialogue on the art of definition, which somehow leads to a circular conversation on the proper time to eat *guanábana* fruit. The aimless pattern of the investigation, the meandering conversations and casual attitudes, the leaps from logic to blind illogic are interrupted by an agitated canasta game, and the whole is a minuet of contradictions and blind alleys.

There is about all this, of course, an air of Ionesco and his hilarious portrayals of the meaninglessness of man's relation to man. Such statements as Eulalia's "¡La justicia es la justicia!", which provokes the Inspector's admiring "¡Usted lo ha dicho! ¡Nunca oí definición tan exacta!"[6] recall the purposeful insanity of *The Bald Soprano* or the devastating annihilation of all hope of communication of *The Chairs*. The logic of illogic, a coherent series of associations that lead to utter chaos, is a favorite technique of Ionesco and is at the root of *El caso se investiga*. A closer antecedent, however, is Virgilio Piñera's *Falsa alarma* ("False alarm"), written in 1948 and first staged in 1957. Also a murder investigation, it anticipates several elements of Arrufat's play: the decay of logic, the disruption of anything resembling normalcy, and a final solitary Murderer waltzing alone to *The Blue Danube*, uncertain whether he has been the victim of an elaborate joke, betrayed by his own memory, or gone mad entirely. This latter is also an anticipation of *El vivo al pollo* ("Long live life") and *La zona cero* ("The zero zone"). *El caso se investiga* is more coherent than *Falsa alarma* in that the illogicality is less abrupt; rather than erupting almost without preparation, it is inherent from the beginning. Further, the final dance of *El vivo al pollo* has an important dramatic meaning of an entirely different sort, and the climactic scene of *El caso se investiga* is of a piece with it. The Inspector's accusation of Eulalia is followed by a finale that reduces all pretense of reason to chaos: "Eulalia saca un cartucho grande en forma de mitra color violeta y lo coloca en la cabeza del inspector. Amelia se coloca junto a él y remeda grotescamente un paso de ballet. Música de fanfarria. Eugenia se adelanta con una cámara fotográfica antigua de paño negro, un aparato de luz de magnesio y retrata el grupo. Fogonazo y deflagración. Telón rápido."[7] This is no lonely dance but a denial of all logic and all reason, a rejection of all possibility of the solitary waltz of incipient comprehension or even the desire to comprehend.

Underlying *bufo* reminiscences and a vision of justice similar to that of Ionesco and Piñera is a theme that becomes the dominant motive of almost all Arrufat's later work: man's immersion in time. The characters are totally subject to its action; the sisters operate by schedule, to the extent of having assigned themselves alternate days for serving coffee and having a "minute of despair" and a "minute of contradiction." Amelia is deaf from 7 to 11 A.M. They are obsessed by memory; the dead Fernando had a master file in which all his memories were classified, and one evening each week he opened the envelopes for that period and savored the memories contained therein. The sisters are anguished at each new wrinkle, and Eugenia suddenly appears dragging an invisible chain. Abruptly, the three women curse the dead man in a savage parody of the Litany, which ends in final dissolution.

El caso se investiga is a kaleidoscope of the incoherence and fatality of man's existence, tied always to a chain of mortality whose other end is tugged by an invisible enemy. It is a highly theatrical and surprisingly effective work, given its author's youth and the occasional blurring of focus. In its emphasis on man's illogical reactions in the face of death, it anticipates the later works.

Arrufat's second play, the one-act *El último tren* ("The last train"), was written in 1957 and first performed in 1963, although a version known as *Los días llenos* ("The full days") served as libretto of an opera performed in 1962. Superficially, it is a vignette of two people living in the stultifying atmosphere of the province, whose engagement has dragged on for so many years that it is now only pretense. They are both a bit ridiculous and a good deal old-fashioned; Martel is mortally bored, and Alicia knows it. Their relationship is important only to her; Martel has set up a home for his mistress and her children with him, while he is Alicia's last hope of evading spinsterhood. Her life is the house and the relationship with Martel; his is the alien world of business, his club, and his mistress, and they touch only tangentially.

But one night the aimless chatter of their stagnant relationship breaks. Determined to force a wedding date or a separation, Alicia drives them both into honesty. They both speak the truth, and both recognize that whatever they had held in common had been lost. When Martel refuses to commit himself, Alicia summons her remnants of courage and dignity and bids him leave, which he does with alacrity. But habit is binding; stammering, he returns for his forgotten cane, and soon Martel, Alicia, and her sister are again seated, as on so many Mondays and Thursdays, for dinner and a game of cards. The last train has passed definitively, and all that remains is the desperate illusion of routine.

The same obsessive theme of fatal time pervades *El último tren*; the characters have all been betrayed by a time that slipped past without seeming to do so. But the fault is also theirs; they have clung to routine because it gave a façade of stability, and they have refused to be reminded. For an instant of pitiless vision, after her desperate gamble has lost, Alicia recognizes herself: "¿Quieres saber la verdad? Soy una mujer fracasada que no quiere reconocerlo. (*Exaltada, furiosa de repente*) ¡Mírame! Mírame al fin tal como soy. Cuando el día amanezca ésta es la mujer que verás. (*Se quita el maquillaje, se despeina*) Soy aun más vieja de lo que tú pensabas. Si pudiera mostrarte las arrugas del pecho, de los muslos. ¡Pellejo!"[8] But this is too much to bear, and Alicia slides again, almost without effort, into the routine that gives form to her existence. It would be stretching the point considerably to suggest that this is tragedy, and yet Alicia transcends the simple drama of customs. Alicia reproduces in miniature Fergusson's threefold tragic sequence of purpose, passion, and perception. Just for a moment in her pointless existence, she recognizes herself and her world for the futile things they are; just for a moment she is of the tragic mold. But the moment passes; Alicia is not of the fiber to live with this pitiless knowledge, and she turns her back on it. Her life is so deadened that, when the last train does pass, she is anaesthetized beyond hope of being faithful to her resolve. The sacrifice is too great, and she returns to the empty rite.

El vivo al pollo, Arrufat's only three-act play to date, was first staged in 1961. Any effort to understand it in orthodox terms is doomed, since it is a complex updating of the *bufo* and was inspired directly by one of the most famous and most staged of the *bufos*, the Robreño brothers' *El velorio de Pachencho* (1901, "Pachencho's wake"); its title is from the proverb "el vivo al pollo y el muerto al hoyo," "long live life, and into the dirt with the dead." The play deals with the distress of the newly widowed Matilde at her husband's death and her decision to have him embalmed in order to retain him forever at her side. For a good deal of the play, the embalmed Vicente is on stage, and the characters are required, in Matilde's presence, to treat him as though he were still alive. The work ends as Matilde becomes the business partner of the embalmer Ramad, and Vicente is now their prize advertising display.

Aside from the macabre humor, *bufo* elements abound. There is a good deal of music, such as the burlesque sung to the tune of the traditional *Mambrú se fue a la guerra* ("Mambrú went off to war") by Vicente's secretary Octavio and the chauffeur Guillermo. Anyone familiar with the heroic origins of *Mambrú* and its universality as a children's song will recognize the double-edged burlesque. The ending of the play is in the same vein, a blending of satire with the traditional *fin de fiesta*. Also *bufo* in origin is the contrast between the distinct and often antagonistic worlds of the servants and the bourgeoisie. This is consistently expressed through different modes of language; Migdalia and Guillermo speak far more colloquially than does Matilde, while Octavio straddles the two worlds. In Matilde's presence, he is discreet and self-effacing, but in her absence, he opens his collar, steals cigars and brandy, and engages in crude discussions with Guillermo. It is a mark of Matilde's change that Octavio becomes increasingly open with her during the latter part of the play. Several characters are directly from the *bufo*, notably the seamstress Migdalia and the embalmer Ramad, whose careful diction, pompous sobriety, and burlesque appearance place him in the line of the stock figure of the *negro catedrático*.

The play revolves about Matilde's inability to accept Vicente's death. This unreal atmosphere extends to nearly all the characters; only Octavio is completely practical about his employer's death. Even the daughter Rosita and her fiancé Rogelio, although appalled by Matilde's behavior, are unable to resist the tempting sofa, and only the horror of Vicente's physical presence at last deters Rosita. There is, finally, the macabre, even gruesome, aspect; all doors and windows must be kept closed, with the result that the heat is intolerable. A spilled glass of water provokes a frenzy, lest it reach the highly susceptible Vicente; a buzzing fly throws Matilde into panic.

Matilde has refused to accept death and is engaged in a determined struggle to defeat it on its own terms: time. Whatever we may think of this resolution, she has achieved what she set out to do. There is a basic and, I believe, deliberate ambiguity in Arrufat's attitude toward Matilde. The primary trick of having the embalmed cadaver on stage while the others treat him as though he still lived teeters perilously close to third-rate horror, or worse, the ludicrous. Yet Arrufat avoids both these dangers. The farcical nature of the play prevents the audience from taking too seriously what it is seeing. In other words, the audience and the characters are in the same position, unable to take Vicente's death very literally, although for different reasons. Matilde is slightly ridiculous at all times, but she is never a distasteful or grotesque figure. Her ultimate happiness may be due partly to the financial windfall of her new business venture, but it is above all due to the double fact that she has defeated death on its own terms—even more, she will help others to do the same—while herself becoming reconciled to life. A tarnished triumph, if you will, but a triumph all the same. She is, manifestly, a futile and pathetic figure, but at the same time she is strangely gallant and very much alive. In her unreasoning fear, she resorts to a solution that is at best impractical, and Arrufat, like the audience, laughs at her and her inability to recognize life for what it is. At the same time, that part of all of us which would have us be immortal, in spite of our bravado and our intellectual recognition that it is impossible, warms to this absurd gallantry. She has defeated death in the conquest of her own fear. She is no longer afraid to live, and so, perhaps, she will not be afraid to die.

Calvert Casey pointed out Arrufat's true debt to the *bufo* in an article on *El velorio de Pachencho*.

There is a Creole way of seeing death. Rarely, in Mexico or in Cuba, is death treated with melancholy. In Haiti, Guedó, the most festive of the gods of the Radá pantheon, a sort of mocking divinity, is the lord of the cemeteries. In the Congo rites of Cuban folklore, death is a happening which is not lamented and which is celebrated in style. In popular songs we treat the matter of our own death with a festive irony which would be inconceivable in other cultures. "If I die on the roadway / don't throw me flowers." We would reject as sentimental the self-pitying complaints of the inevitability of death, common in other latitudes.[9]

Arrufat has captured this in an irreverent laugh at life and death. It is significant that the work ends in a joyous dance. For all the traditional nature of this final scene, it is literally what Northrop Frye has called "the integration of society,"[10] which he posits as the basic theme of the comic. Matilde has been reintegrated into the society of the living, and simultaneously this society has achieved a deeper coherence in its joyous celebration of life. Casey sensed this when he commented on the final moments of any *bufo* production: "If the final rumba is not indicated, it is included anyway, for the audience must go out dancing. It is demanded by tradition, which ordered that all unite and forgive each other in the great ending to the party."[11] And Arrufat himself has stated that "all or almost all the *bufo* pieces end with the unity of all: whites, blacks, Chinese, rich, poor, they all dance reunited at the end. All returns to order and harmony."[12] Susanne Langer has called the comic action "the upset and recovery of the protagonist's equilibrium, his contest with the world and his triumph."[13] If Matilde's equilibrium is still far from stable and her triumph foreordained to be fleeting, she has, just for the moment, won another skirmish in mankind's war against time. And the obvious debt of the *bufo* to ancient comic forms is not restricted to such figures as Octavio, who is clearly a remote derivation from the wily slave, or traditional figures, such as the *negro catedrático*, a black pseudo-savant, a classic example of the *alazón* or impostor. Vicente's final entrance, followed by the joyous dance of life, is a kind of burlesque epiphany: "The ritual pattern behind the catharsis of comedy is the resurrection that follows the death, the epiphany or manifestation of the risen hero."[14]

A more pessimistic mode pervades the one-act *La repetición* ("The repetition"), first played in 1963. The play is simple; on the two levels of a lower-class house live the Girl, whose room is pathetically adorned with flowers, and the Woman, where all is absolutely identical but more faded, more worn. After an uneventful dialogue between the two, underlining the younger woman's fading but still living hope and the older Neighbor's struggle with poverty and hopelessness, a door-to-door Salesman arrives. Soon, the two young people are in love. Within the play's realistic structure, Arrufat has masked his characters to underline his meaning. In the last brief scene, the Salesman and the Girl descend the stairs on their way to a dance. They stop at the Neighbor's apartment, where they exchange masks with the latter and her husband. The Girl, now masked as the Neighbor, transformed into a repetition of her, repeats the identical words of our first encounter with the latter. The hope of the preceding scenes has been blasted, and the cycle is complete. Time has again worked its evil, and as life begins again with a new Girl on the second floor, we know that it is destined to drag out a sorry existence until it, too, ends in defeat.

Although *La repetición* has effective moments, it appears to suffer from serious weaknesses. The simple use of masks is not enough to overcome the realistic structure and popular dialogue, and the last sudden reversal is too swift, too close to trickery to be entirely convincing. It is almost as though Arrufat had found himself creating for his characters a future that he, intellectually, felt to be impossible, and so, unable to change the characters, he grafted on a rapid shock ending. There is good use of aimless, mechanical repetition of movement by the Girl, and the dialogue is swift and comic, but the result is a little too syllogistic.

Written in 1958 and still unperformed, *La zona cero* is a strange and ambiguous work. In it, Arrufat abandoned entirely the realistic approach and comic structures of his earlier plays. Two of the three long scenes consist of an interminable, complex canasta game between a mysterious host, Raimundo, and three guests, Reinaldo, Teresa, and Delia. The middle scene is a flashback, showing the arrival of the three, who are acquainted neither with their host nor with each other. Guests or prisoners, Reinaldo and Teresa finally plot with Gómez, Raimundo's butler, to kill their host-jailer. But they have made a fatal error; Gómez degenerates into near lunacy, and they are driven into yet another round of canasta.

The point of the play is obscure. The near viciousness with which the three guests-inmates-prisoners behave toward each other in their apparent limbo echoes Sartre's *Huis Clos*, but they are less well defined. They have none of the weakness become evil of Sartre's dwellers in Hell. Indeed, it is not at all certain that they are dead, although this is the most likely interpretation. In their pointlessness and frustration, they are close to the empty world of Krapp or Vladimir and Estragon. But the play is not sufficiently focused for us to know whether these are suicides, which is hinted, whether they are in some limbo to which their frivolity and passive evil have brought them, or whether this is some mad parable of man's normal discourse. It may well be a portrait of the sterility of the wealthy, but it is far from social propaganda. Who is Raimundo? Certainly he is no avenger, unless we consider the eternal repetition of canasta a suitable punishment. The broken maunderings of Gómez are hardly a call to action; his increasing insolence and unintelligibility only add to the enigma. If this is a portrait of a social class designed as agitational propaganda, it is a flawed portrait indeed. It is far more convincing to accept these doomed people as simply that—individuals who represent the frivolity and frustrated sensuality, the indulgence of this endless round of sterility. This is heightened by the final moments, as the card players are slowly encased by a lowered glass covering while a slow rain of dust covers the stage. The characters remain, permanently frozen in their own sterility. It seems unlikely that Arrufat has intended more than a portrait of the total absence of meaning among those best able, because of their wealth, to give direction to their own lives and to society.

Even in this provocative and baffling work, Arrufat's obsessive concern with time is visible; the canasta game is spiced with ambiguous comments on morality, life and death, and, always, time. The players are terrified of forgetting what day it is in this strange land without clocks or calendars, and so they impose an arbitrary chronological order in the absence of a true one. But this missing "true" order is no less arbitrary than that invented by the characters. In other words, we, who order our lives in days, minutes, hours, and seconds, are as hagridden by time as are Teresa, Delia, and Reinaldo. Whatever social or metaphysical visions may have informed Arrufat's concept of the play, it is again the chain of time that gives it coherence. We are in time and of it, and without it we cannot function properly. Simultaneously, it congeals our spirits.

In 1965, Arrufat premiered *Todos los domingos* ("Every Sunday"), written one year earlier. With *El vivo al pollo*, it is his best work to date. The action takes place in the home of Elvira, a wealthy woman, presumably in her early forties, who is totally confined to a wheelchair and dependent on her nurse-companion Alejandrina. Twenty years earlier, Elvira had been abruptly abandoned by her fiancé, for reasons that, like her ailment, are left unexplained. She has fallen into the custom of paying young men of the neighborhood to come to her home dressed in clothing identical to that of the vanished fiancé, and together, the two re-enact literally her happiest afternoon, the one prior to the disappearance. This obsessive ritual has become difficult; it is no longer easy to find young men willing to play the role exactly according to a fixed script. The neighbors murmur darkly, and the process is complicated by the need, for unspecified reasons, to find a different man each time. The latest, moreover, is different from the others. He resembles the missing suitor to a remarkable degree; he also becomes extremely fond of Elvira and finally prevails on her to permit him to return the following Sunday, to play the role again. This is the first time such a second visit has been allowed, and Alejandrina mutters darkly of possible consequences. The second performance leads finally to his break with the rite and a declaration of his love for Elvira, and then to an open clash with Alejandrina, who kills him with a pair of scissors as Elvira cackles madly in her chair.

The pattern of these repeated performances is fixed and invariable, to the point that they have come to form a rigid ritual, but a ritual that is, until the climactic moment, devoid of meaning. The formalized structure, even to the performance from a script, the ritual costumes, the setting (the house is transformed into a terrace café, and various local types, even a fortuneteller or soothsayer, are hired to repeat endlessly, every Sunday at five o'clock, their identical words and actions), the sense that this all stands for something larger, some meaning that gives shape and sense to the otherwise empty rote—all these are characteristics of the ritual. There is an air of menace; Alejandrina and Elvira constantly slash at each other's frayed nerves. Further, at each performance, Alejandrina hides behind a curtain, armed with a large pair of scissors, presumably to protect Elvira from assault and theft. The mood is heightened by Alejandrina's obvious horror that Elvira will permit a second visit and by the nagging question about Elvira's insistence on repeating that one afternoon. It is not enough for her to protest that she lives on her memories and must replenish constantly the exactness of the moment. The order of the ritual is too formal, the precision too exact. It is only when the young man playing the Fiancé breaks his role to propose marriage that the climax of this frozen pattern also breaks free. At first, Elvira can only suspect that he wants her money, and bitterly she offers him valuable jewels, which he refuses, as he refuses the payment for his afternoon's performance. Alejandrina is malevolent, fighting against what seems to be the Fiancé's romantic, if somewhat illusory, love for Elvira and his wish to free her from Alejandrina's domination. He offers her the real world: "Elvira, detrás de estas paredes está el mundo, la vida, el domingo que empieza. Salgamos. Iremos juntos a ese parque del que hablamos, aún queda un poco de sol. Después tendremos la noche, la alegría. Yo me basto para hacerla feliz."[15]

Elvira appears almost to accept, but at the critical moment her dark angel speaks: "Déjala en paz. Vete de una vez. Eres un trago amargo, un tipejo. ¿La ibas a cargar como yo la he cargado durante treinta años? Ella sola no podría levantarse de la cama. Todas las mañanas tiene que llamarme, que esperar a que yo la levante y le acerque la silla. ¡Si la vieras en cama, con las piernas inertes como una muñeca de goma, así!"[16]

And the horrified Fiancé watches as Alejandrina lifts Elvira's skirt from the crippled, dead, unmoving legs. The two women burst into demoniacal laughter, and we realize that Elvira's near acceptance has been, at least in part, a deliberate bait to lead him into his declaration, preparing the way for the final humiliation and surrender before the expiatory sacrifice. They shriek obscenities at him as he kneels supplicating, until Alejandrina rapidly steps to him and sinks the scissors in his back. To Elvira's tired question, "¿Entonces, es esto lo que yo quería?"[17] Alejandrina's only answer is to remark that dinner is served, and Elvira strews petals on the corpse before being wheeled off. The ritual is complete, and all the years of impotent dress rehearsal have been fulfilled; the scapegoat has paid for the crime.

But *Todos los domingos* is not a neat little package to be neatly tied up, explained away, and disposed of. Elvira's motivations are complex: the young man is simultaneously a stand-in for the fiancé, whose sin must be expiated, and for reality, which Elvira cannot accept, and perhaps he is even, obscurely, the vicarious victim of her hatred of her own deformity. The relationship with Alejandrina becomes even more provocative. Alejandrina is devoted to Elvira to the point of performing for her all the gross details of daily existence, including the physiological, as she leeringly tells the young man; she is devoted even to the point of murder. Yet the two women are participants in a love-hate relationship reminiscent of the ambivalence of the maids in Genet's *Les bonnes*. They rage at each other and threaten to end the relationship. From the opening moment when Elvira threatens, then pleads with Alejandrina not to leave her simply sitting in the chair, and Alejandrina menaces Elvira with a second abandonment, their obscure relationship is colored by this dependence and by Alejandrina's odd independence, which is never resolved by the simple act of leaving, of which she speaks constantly. Only with the final murder, when the dual relationship of accomplices and enemies is resolved, is the link between them somewhat clarified. Each has achieved her goal; Elvira has had revenge, and Alejandrina has eliminated the threat to her position of power. They both live vicariously—Alejandrina through the power of her hold over Elvira, and Elvira through the memories of her love affair and now, at last, her vengeance. But even this is not enough. Was Alejandrina's anger and fear of the second visit simply a reaction to her possible loss of privilege and power, or a horrified realization that the ritual was preparing to burst out of the frozen, artificial ending? Is this indeed the last and only sacrifice, or will the same bloody drama be played out again?

Again, Arrufat's characters are frozen by time and memory. Elvira lives preoccupied by time; for her, as for Matilde, time has stopped, retreated, in order that one fatal moment may cease to have existed. Unlike Matilde, however, Elvira is neither gallant nor pathetic. Once her revenge is achieved, she is spent; the illusion has died and been replaced by guilt with which she must live until, perhaps, the ritual begins again. Arrufat is obsessed by time's influences on man-within-time. Elvira's ritual playacting, the desperate cocktail party chatter of *La zona cero*, the embalming of Vicente, the futile dreams of the Salesman and the Girl, the interminable game of cards in *El último tren*, the neosurrealistic behavior of *El caso se investiga*, are all efforts to forget the corrosive effect of time and to forge an illusion that a dreadful past or a problematical future are of no consequence. The dream is almost always deliberate and self-induced, frequently conscious, and almost invariably a failure. But they cling to their dream because it is all they have.

This recurrent theme is expressed dramatically in a series of diverse styles and forms: the *bufo* in *El vivo al pollo* and *El caso se investiga*, the delicately developed realism of *El último tren*, the realistic framework and use of masks and stylized setting in *La repetición*, the spiritual no man's land of *La zona cero* expressed through the incoherence and vacuity of the characters' actions, and, finally, the ritual of cruelty and revenge of *Todos los domingos*. They have in common the vision of man in time; they celebrate the triumph of life, however evanescent the triumph and however ludicrous the man who would defeat death, while they simultaneously strip away our pretense of illusion to show us the darkest corners behind the struggle.

Arrufat's most recent play, *Los siete contra Tebas*, ("The seven against Thebes") marks a considerable departure, both formal and thematic, for him. Closely patterned after Aeschylus's *Seven Against Thebes*, it received the 1968 Premio de Teatro José Antonio Ramos of the Unión de Escritores y Artistas de Cuba and was published the same year by UNEAC. The play provoked extreme controversy within the jury; the published version includes the customary statement of the jury, composed of Adolfo Gutkin, Ricardo Salvat, Juan Larco, José Triana, and Raquel Revuelta, a minority statement by Revuelta and Larco disagreeing with the award, and a lengthy introduction, signed by the Comité Director de la Unión de Escritores y Artistas de Cuba, denouncing the play's ideological content. The introduction, like the minority statement, is expressly political and denounces the play's alleged ambiguity with regard to the Revolution. The source of the uproar is the work's reference to Playa Girón and to the fact of the considerable numbers of Cubans living abroad, presumably hoping one day to return to the island. The play has clear relevance to this context; however, the import of the play is perhaps not entirely what the committee suspected.

Los siete contra Tebas is so closely based on the Aeschylan model that it is sometimes more adaptation than original work. Arrufat added the Adivino and turned Aeschylus's Soldier into the Two Spies, who have the same dramatic function. He deleted Antigone, Ismene, and the Herald, who were in any case somewhat extraneous in Aeschylus and, according to Philip Vellacott, were added by an unknown emendator some fifty years after Aeschylus's death.[18] Much more important, and forming the core of the difference between the two plays, Arrufat focuses his play on the conflict of the two brothers. His Etéocles' opening speech is based on the Greek model, but unlike Aeschylus, Arrufat mentions Polinice immediately, setting the stage for the conflict that looms throughout the play. The short speech by the Adivino heightens tension by announcing that omens predict an enemy attack that night, whereupon the Two

Spies report on the enemy encampment with a gusto and gore based on the original, but again referring directly to Polinice. The result of all this is that, unlike the original, in which the confrontation erupts suddenly and disastrously, in the Cuban version it is a growing menace throughout. Etéocles is constantly aware that he may be forced to face his brother in battle.

> Que estos hogares no se derrumben
> bajo el golpe enemigo. Que el polvo
> de sus piedras no se disperse en el viento.
> Si es necesario
> que enfrente a mi hermano Polinice,
> si es necesario, sea.
> Estoy dispuesto.
> Me entrego a la causa de Tebas.[19]

This sense of barbarous splendor is heightened by the speeches of the six valiants and the individual speeches of the chorus, but the key element is the appearance on stage of Polinice. The Aeschylan play was written in 467 B.C., and is formally classified within Old Tragedy, whose conflict was essentially internal and which utilized primarily one character and the chorus. "The essence of Old Tragedy was the solitary hero facing his own destiny or playing out an inner drama of his own soul—like Pelasgus. Pelasgus is not more solitary than Eteocles and Prometheus; Eteocles does not grapple with Polyneices but with himself—not because Aeschylus was hampered by his small cast, but because he did not want Polyneices."[20]

But Arrufat specifically *did* want Polinice, whose shadow hovers over Thebes until his entry under a flag of truce. The brothers rehearse in verbal combat the savage duel that is to lead to their double slaughter. Finally, recognizing that their encounter is inevitable, Polinice leaves, and the remainder of the play is devoted to long choral sequences establishing and describing the battle and lamenting over the bodies. This section is too long and too verbal, and the dramatic impact is diffused; the thrust of the play is contained in the powerful *agon* between the two brothers.

It is, apparently, this *agon* that has created the opposition to the play. Polinice, in his brother's words, has delivered himself "a otras gentes . . . / y con ellos vienes a tu tierra natal."[21] But Polinice in turn points out that Etéocles has betrayed their sworn pact:

> Pacté contigo gobernar un año
> cada uno, compartir el mando
> del ejército y la casa paterna.
> Juraste cumplirlo. Y has roto

el juramento y tu promesa.
Solo gobiernas, solo decides,
solo habitas la casa de mi padre.[22]

And Etéocles himself recognizes the justice of this claim but defends himself:

Rectifiqué los errores de tu gobierno,
repartí el pan, me acerqué a los pobres.
Sí, es cierto, saqueé nuestra casa.
Nada podrás encontrar en ella. Repartí
nuestros bienes, repartí nuestra herencia,
hasta los últimos objetos, las ánforas,
las telas, las pieles, el trigo, las cucharas.
Está vacía nuestra casa, y no alcanzó
sin embargo para todos.
Sí, es cierto, profané un juramento.
Pero no me importa. Acepto esa impureza,
pero no la injusticia.[23]

The encounter builds until it is a series of short, sharp statements, defining the positions and making clear that the brothers are past all possibility of reconciliation. The climactic encounter follows:

Polinice. —Sólo tú sabes, Etéocles. Sólo tú sabes. Tú decides lo que está
bien o mal. Repartes la injusticia, mides el valor de los hombres.
¡Sólo tú eres libre en Tebas!

Etéocles. —Pero el pueblo está en las murallas. Pero el pueblo está dispuesto
a tirar contra tu ejército.[24]

And Etéocles recognizes clearly his own situation; with tragic insight he perceives the nature of his mission:

Mi vida se realiza esta noche y se cumple.
Polinice nos despierta con una luz atroz:
Implantar la justicia es un hecho áspero
y triste, acarrea la crueldad y la violencia.
Pero es necesario. Esta es la última
claridad que alcanzo en esta noche última.
Recuérdenlo: es necesario.
En vuestras manos frágiles dejo
esta certeza.
La paz vendrá después, aplacado el furor.
Recuérdenlo: es necesario.

De algún modo detendremos la injusticia
en el mundo: de un golpe, de una patada,
de un alarido.
¡Adiós, mujeres![25]

This is hardly the counterrevolutionary Trojan horse that the writers of the introduction see in *Los siete contra Tebas*; rather, it is a vision of the tragic nature of the struggle of Etéocles and the Cuban people, which he represents, caught in the dilemma of injustice on the one hand and violence on the other. But beyond this, *Los siete contra Tebas* differs from *Seven Against Thebes* in a far more fundamental fashion than has been observed. Of the Greek model, Vellacott says, "Unlike the *Oresteia*, however, it bears no hopeful message of 'redemption from within'; the curse exhausts itself only with the extinction of the family."[26] But in Arrufat, although the family is extinguished, the conflict leaves a message of hope and redemption: that this final tragic onslaught is perhaps the necessary consequence of necessary but drastic measures and that it will be the last. *Los siete contra Tebas*, in final analysis, is firmly within the tradition of tragedy, one of whose ancient themes is the vision of the extirpation of old hatreds and the growth of a newer and sounder society.

NOTES

1. Martin Esslin, *The Theatre of the Absurd* (Garden City, N.Y.: Doubleday Anchor Books, 1961), p. xviii.
2. "Charla sobre teatro," *Casa de las Américas* 2, no. 9 (November–December 1961): 96. This and all subsequent translations from the Spanish are my own.
3. "El teatro bufo," *Revista Unión*, nos. 3–4 (September–December 1962), p. 63.
4. Ibid., p. 62.
5. ". . . like a dizzying Mack Sennett comedy, or an animated cartoon" (*Teatro* [Havana: Ediciones Unión, 1963], p. 11).
6. "Justice is justice!" "You said it! I never heard such an exact definition!" (ibid., p. 12).
7. "Eulalia takes out a large cylindrical cartridge in the form of a violet mitre and places it on the Inspector's head. Amelia stands next to him and grotesquely apes a ballet step. Fanfare. Eugenia steps forward with an ancient camera, with a black cloth and a hand magnesium flare and takes the group's picture. Flash and explosion. Rapid curtain" (ibid., p. 34).
8. "Do you want to know the truth? I am a failure as a woman, and I don't want to recognize it. (*Impassioned, suddenly furious*) Look at me! Look at me as I am at last. When the day comes, this is the woman you will see. (*She takes off her makeup, musses her hairdo*) I am even older than you thought. If I could show you the wrinkles on my breasts and thighs—skin and bones!" (ibid., p. 102).
9. Calvert Casey, "El velorio de Pachencho," *La Gaceta de Cuba*, 12 April 1963.
10. Northrop Frye, *Anatomy of Criticism* (New York: Atheneum, 1966), p. 43.

11. Casey, "El velorio de Pachencho."

12. "El teatro bufo," p. 66.

13. Susanne Langer, *Feeling and Form* (New York: Charles Scribner's Sons, 1953), p. 331.

14. Frye, *Anatomy of Criticism*, p. 215.

15. "Elvira, beyond those walls is the world, life, the Sunday that begins. Let's go out. We'll go together to the park we talked about, there is still a little sun. Later, we will have the whole night, happiness. I'm enough to make you happy." All references to *Todos los domingos* are to an unpublished manuscript.

16. "Leave her alone. Get out of here. You're useless, bad news. Are you going to carry her around the way I have for thirty years? She can't even get out of bed by herself. Every morning she has to call me, to wait until I lift her up and get her chair. If you saw her in bed, with her legs still as a rubber doll, like this!"

17. "Is this what I wanted, then?"

18. Philip Vellacott, "Introduction," *Prometheus and Other Plays* (Baltimore: Penguin Books, 1961), p. 16.

19. May these homes not fall
under the enemy blow. May the dust
of their stones not be dispersed on the wind.
If it is necessary
that I face my brother Polyneices,
if it is necessary, so be it.
I am ready.
I deliver myself to the cause of Thebes.　　　　　[*Los siete contra Tebas*, p. 31]

20. H. D. F. Kitto, *Greek Tragedy* (Garden City, N.Y.: Doubleday Anchor Books, 1954), pp. 33–34.

21. ". . . to other people . . . / and you come with them to your native land" (*Los siete contra Tebas*, p. 69).

22. I agreed with you to govern one year
each, to share the command
of the army and our father's house.
You swore to fulfill it. And you have broken
the oath and your promise.
You alone govern, you alone decide,
you alone dwell in the house of my father.　　　　　[Ibid., p. 74]

23. I corrected the errors of your government,
I shared the bread, I approached the poor.
Yes, it is true, I sacked our home.
You will find nothing in it. I shared
our goods, I shared our heritage,
to the least thing, the amphoras,
the cloths, the skins, the wheat, the spoons.
Our house is empty, and even so
it was not enough for all.
Yes, it is true, I profaned an oath.
But I do not care. I accept that impurity.
But not injustice.　　　　　[Ibid., p. 78]

24. *Polinice*. Only you know, Etéocles. Only you know. You decide what is right or wrong. You share the injustice, you measure the value of men. Only you are free in Thebes!

Etéocles. But the people are on the walls. But the people are ready to fight against your
army.   [Ibid., p. 78.]
  25. My life is realized this night, it is fulfilled.
      Polinice wakes us with an atrocious light:
      Implanting justice is a harsh thing
      and sad, it brings cruelty and violence.
      But it is necessary. This is the last
      clarity that I achieve in this last night.
      Remember this: it is necessary.
      In your fragile hands I leave
      this certainty.
      Peace will come after, when the furor has calmed.
      Remember this: it is necessary.
      In some way we will stop injustice
      in the world: with a blow, with a kick,
      with a scream.
      Farewell, women!   [Ibid., pp. 83–84]
  26. Vellacott, *Prometheus and Other Plays*, p. 14.

2. The Theater of Emilio Carballido:

Spinning a Web

Eugene R. Skinner

Emilio Carballido has proved to be one of Mexico's most accomplished writers. He has published outstanding works in both the dramatic and narrative genres, beginning with *La zona intermedia* (1948) and extending to his recent short novel *El sol* (1970). His work has been recognized nationally and internationally through literary awards, fellowships, tenure of academic positions, and critical studies.[1] His dramatic career coincides with the rapid growth of Mexican theater following World War II, and Margaret S. Peden has identified Carballido's major contribution as the introduction and consistent implementation of "a kind of theatre that may be called fantastic, poetic, surrealistic—or simply non-realistic . . . plays that transcend the specifically realistic and restrictively Mexican to achieve a theatre that can be called modern contemporary and universal."[2] The majority of his plays employ twentieth century Mexico as a scenario; however, this specific reality serves primarily as the raw material from which he fashions a universal image of man. The aim of this study is to define that image, outline its development, and relate it to the techniques employed in its representation. Emphasis will be given to five plays. *La zona intermedia* and *Rosalba y los Llaveros* exemplify tendencies in his earliest works. *La hebra de oro* marks a significant change in his representation of reality, which is further developed in *Silencio, pollos pelones, ya les van a echar su maíz* and *Yo también hablo de la rosa*.

La zona intermedia (*The Intermediate Zone*), Carballido's first published work, affords a concise allegorical image of man. The action of this one-act *auto*, a variant of the traditional morality play concerning Final Judgment, takes place in a spiritual limbo in which the final disposition of "inhumans" is determined. The First Assistant of the Intermediate Zone formulates the distinction between human and inhuman: "Potential, *and* man. He must choose between one thing and another, realizing the worthwhile, rejecting what is not worthwhile. He has a powerful weapon, pain, and he polishes it with the tears of his decisions. . . . Man can close his ears to his vocation for something worthy, or something unworthy. He can live between two worlds. He can do evil or good incidentally, unconsciously, like a weak little animal. Then he is lost. He has ceased to be a man." (*The Intermediate Zone*, pp. 129–130).[3] This concept reveals a basic existentialist position: human existence is equated with potentiality. Unlike an animal that simply *is*, man exists and must create his own being through a process of conscious election. These decisions are made in anguish and suffering, face to face with his ignorance and his limitations. The failure to accept fully this responsibility results in an inhuman existence.

Four mortals are brought into the Zone: the Critic, the Woman, the Little Man, and the Virgin. Each has become an effective theatrical image of an aspect of inhuman existence. These images occupy the extremes of two conceptual axes:

	REASON	FEELING
Active	Critic	Woman
Passive	Little Man	Virgin

All four modes of behavior preclude an authentic existence. Later a fifth character, the Nahual, enters the Zone.

The image of the Critic corresponds to the active overevaluation of a single aspect of human potentiality. He has spent his life criticizing with "impartial reason" the creations of others. With the detachment of an immortal observer, he imposes a rational order on reality that results in his separation from creative participation in existence. He assumes the form of the works that he has judged, a ridiculous mixture of cubist painting and sculpture. Towards the end, he is devoured by the Nahual.

The Woman is characterized as having a mixture of human and feline features. She represents overevaluation of feeling, specifically libidinous desire, which imposes a subjective view on the world converting others into mere objects for satiating her passion. She confesses: "I lost everything human. I was no longer a woman; I was a walking sore, a beast, anything except a woman. I wanted to tear him to pieces" (*The Intermediate Zone*, pp. 133–134). Recognizing that her lover suffered a passion equal to her own, she repents her inhuman condition and finally is considered worthy to proceed to Final Judgment.

The Little Man is old, short, fat, timid, and vacillating. His subservient behavior suggests a defense mechanism against the violence of the world. Within the context of the play, he stands at the opposite extreme to the Critic: whereas the Critic imposed a rational order on the world, the Little Man accepts and bows before any order or will that he encounters. His hiding behind convention results not only in an inauthentic existence, but it also fails to protect him from the world. The Devil asks him if the idea of going to Hell "displeases" him, and he cannot refuse the invitation. Using empty formulas of excessive courtesy, he attempts to avoid conflict and suffering. The Devil simply has him bodily carried off to Hell, and, as he exits, the Devil labels him "amorphous matter," an unrealized potentiality.

The Virgin enters dressed in white and carrying a lily. She, like the Little Man, has avoided active participation in existence. Her life remains uncontaminated, removed from the consciousness of human limitations and indifferent to the desire to overcome these limitations. She has become a passive reflection of nature. She remains in the Intermediate Zone, to fade away slowly and without suffering like the inanimate flower that she has become.

The Nahual is neither human nor inhuman, but rather a curious anachronism: a Mexican Adam before the Fall, completely unconscious of good and evil. His body—half coyote and half human—suggests that his image is fabricated from elements of the Aztec trickster figure, Ueuecoyotl, and from elements of the biblical Adam. His entrance into the Zone is caused by having eaten the Little Man and been unable to digest the crucifix that his victim had been wearing. The act is symbolic of his confrontation with an institutionalized system of values —good vs. evil—that stands in opposition to his previous mode of existence, which was governed by the less abstract polarity of pleasure vs. pain. A further transformation occurs when he ingests the Critic, who tastes like "green apples." The Nahual becomes ill, suffers, and is transformed into the "New Man," Adam after the Fall. Then he is given the opportunity to return to Earth and to create his own human existence.

This contemporary adaptation of the morality play provides a series of images central to the development of Carballido's theater and his most explicit evaluation of the human situation. Of the four mortal types of inauthentic existence, only the Woman possesses any redeeming value. Since she represents libidinous desire, it is evident that the playwright recognizes the primacy of this vital force. With only minor modification, he allows her to proceed to Final Judgment. The other three mortals (Critic, Little Man, and Virgin) are fixed types, incapable of transformation, and are condemned. The Nahual-New Man becomes the central and exemplary figure by virtue of the immensity of his transformation and the degree to which he integrates the other four images. The immortal Nahual, as Ueuecoyotl, is as libidinous as the feline Woman and, as the free-running lightning bolt, is as indifferent to human suffering as is the Virgin of the Flower. During his transformation to the New Man, he physically incorporates the two masculine figures: the Little Man with his crucifix, representing consciousness of an order superior to his own desire, and the Critic, or rational censor of the creative act. Finally, the New Man is returned to Earth where he will embark upon the process of self-creation, elections made in anguish, aware of both his limitations and of his responsibility for these actions, which will realize his potentiality.

Rosalba y los Llaveros ("Rosalba and the Llaveros"), a three-act comedy written within two years of *La zona*, reveals another early tendency in Carballido's theater. Whereas *La zona* is a play of stylized masks that projects within a realm of fantasy archetypal problems of the human situation, *Rosalba* is a comedy of manners providing a realistic depiction of more fully developed characters in a specific context. The action occurs in Otatitlan, Veracruz during the Festival of the Santuario in 1949. The apparent object of ridicule is provincial family life, and the conflict revolves about the differences between the traditional, closed life style of the province and the progressive, open life style of the metropolis. Aurora Llavero de Landa and her daughter Rosalba arrive from Mexico City to visit the family of Aurora's brother, Lorenzo Llavero. Their entrance in the first scene serves to disrupt the strained equilibrium of the provincial family, and, as Rosalba probes the family's unresolved conflicts, the situation increases in complexity, reaching a chaotic climax at the end of act II. Act III provides the necessary scenes of recognition and final resolution.

The major characters are Lorenzo's son, Lázaro Llavero, the victim of traditional values, and Rosalba, the incarnation of progressive values. Lázaro, at the tender age of twelve, had fathered a child by the servant Luz. Ostracized by the family, which projected upon him their repressed libidinous desires, he has internalized their attitude toward sex to the extent that his psychological growth has been arrested. Now, at the age of twenty-six, he works in his father's pharmacy without receiving wages, and he is unable to relate to women in any but a guilt-ridden manner. The stage directions indicate his arrested ego development: "Podría pasar por guapo si no fuera arratonado para moverse. Se ve más joven que su edad."[4] By act II, scene 5, Rosalba has helped Lázaro consciously confront his situation, reject the guilt feelings imposed upon him by the family, and decide to assert his independence. This is the turning point, but further complications arise.

Rosalba, a student of Freudian psychology, at first appears as the light of reason and objectivity necessary to probe the dark recesses of the Llavero family. However, even in the first act there are indications that her analytic approach is exaggerated as she relates how she carried out a detailed clinical study on her own mother for a class in psychopathology (act II, scene 18). Later, Lázaro points to her shortcomings:

> Lázaro. —Sí, mira, tratas todo sobre esquemas, lo resuelves con
> principios nuevos, tuyos, pero son principios, ¿no? Y es lo
> mismo. Quitas los viejos principios para dar nuevos. Vaya, ¿cuál
> es la diferencia?
>
> Rosalba. —¡Lázaro! ¿Eres anarquista?
>
> Lázaro. —No sé. Te he dicho que no le pongo nombres a las cosas.
>
> Rosalba. —Sí eres, Lázaro, pero no actúas, no te rebelas. ¿Por qué?[5]

Lázaro, through his failure to objectify his inner feelings, is unable to act. Conversely, Rosalba, through her excessive rationalization, is decisive, but she ignores vital aspects of the situation and is equally unable to cope with it. Frequently her actions are counterproductive.

By act II, scene 31, Rosalba's intervention has alienated Felipe, fiancé of Lázaro's sister Rita. Rosalba, thinking that Rita did not want to marry Felipe, had convinced him that Rita is insane. Now that Felipe has decided to leave, Rita is disconsolate. Not only has Rosalba misconstrued the situation, but she has also misappropriated Rita's prerogative to decide her fate. The budding relationship between Rosalba and Lázaro is also threatened. She finds out that Luz is pregnant and that Lázaro is again suspected to be the father (act II, scene 23). She does not even ask Lázaro if he is the father of the expected child but demands that he apologize to Luz and ask her to remain so that Azalea (Lázaro's daughter by Luz) will have a mother. Azalea takes Rosalba to task, and now even Rosalba begins to suspect that her intervention has been counterproductive.

In act III, scene 12, it is revealed that Lázaro is not the father of the unborn child. He rebels against Lorenzo for suggesting, at Rosalba's instigation, that he marry Luz. Later Lázaro declares that he is leaving home and demands his back wages from his father. Now that Lázaro has asserted his independence, Rosalba comes to accept that her clinical approach has been overevaluated and that she is in love with Lázaro. Their union is prepared by two transformations: his ego is strengthened to the point of being able to free itself from the confining irrational guilt feelings and thus enter actively and consciously into a meaningful relationship with a woman; conversely, Rosalba's discovery of the irrational has allowed her to open herself to something beyond her own ego and form a human relationship with others. For Rosalba, this union produces a "physiological happiness." She has awakened to the emotional aspect of human love, and this puts her in a harmonious relationship with the physical world in general.

Rosalba is fundamentally a comedy of manners, and its treatment of provincial life can be classified as psychological realism. The central conflict involves two antagonistic attitudes towards sex: an irrational repression of sexual desire that impedes the development of a human relationship and a clinically detached approach that also frustrates the creation of a human bond. The first represents a situation in which the ego's development is arrested; the second indicates an overevaluation of the ego.

This conflict is given form in the two main protagonists and is reinforced by other techniques. The surname Llaveros conveys the repressive attitudes of the provincial family, the ones who lock up the sexual instinct. Their house is described as a "vicious circle," the confining circle that Lázaro must break. His father Lorenzo, the comic tyrant, repeatedly commands that the windows be closed. Rosalba, at the end of act II, shouts through the window for the police. Although she is able to bring these repressed conflicts to consciousness, she alone cannot resolve them. However, her cry elicits the necessary assistance in a most unexpected form: Nativitas.

Nativitas, also known as Encarnación de la Cruz, is the only figure in the comedy who approaches the mythological plane. However, her behavior is justified realistically through her characterization as an insane *curandera*. In act I, scene 5, she enters dressed in men's clothes with a red camellia behind her ear. She recites an incantation to rid the house of evil spirits, offers sacramental sweets to the family, and departs. Rosalba's reaction is excessively strong. Here, Nativitas functions primarily as a grotesque mirror for Rosalba, who, with her normal clinical detachment, diagnoses Nativitas's exhibitionism as originating in a frustration of sexual desire. Still, she does not recognize the analogy with her own situation until act II, scene 20. Having confessed that she is really timid, that she considers herself ugly, that her audacious behavior is a compensation for her underevaluation of herself as a woman, she adds: "Hago teatro para los demás, a veces para mí sola, no puedo evitarlo."[6] Like Nativitas, Rosalba tries to draw attention to herself by putting on a show, playing to the hilt her role of the liberated modern woman.

At the beginning of act III, Nativitas appears for the second time. At this point her basic function is to clarify the conflict and foreshadow the eventual union of Rosalba and Lázaro. Illuminated by the full moon, she peers through the window where Rosalba was sitting at the end of act II. Now attired in white sheets, the old *curandera* throws lighted fireworks through the window, awakening everyone in the house and announcing the beginning of the Festival of the Santuario. Next, she offers the following incantation: "¡Guerra a Lucifer y a los leones paganos! ¡Dios nos libre del mal inocente que aseguran que reinando está! Se casa el rey con la reina mora que a veces canta y a veces llora. Cruz, cruz, cruz. Confiad en la Santísima Encarnación de la Cruz."[7] War is to be waged against Lucifer and the pagan lions, against the rebellious ego (Rosalba), and against the destructive libidinous forces (Luz). The "innocent evil" that has plagued the house is precisely the inability to cope with these two forces. Now, a solution is proposed: the marriage of the king (Lázaro) and the Moorish queen (Rosalba). The triple repetition of "cross," a traditional symbol of union and wholeness, conveys that the marriage is imperative.

Nativitas herself is the Incarnation of the Cross (masculine in act I, scene 5 and feminine in act III, scene 1) and has given birth to a cat, another feline symbol of the libido. It is significant that Nativitas's cat is caged, for this indicates that the libido is no longer destructive. In act III, scene 5, it is revealed that Nativitas gives birth at every full moon and that the last time her "child" was a rat. Thus, she becomes the mother of both Lázaro ("mousy") and Rosalba ("kitten"). She functions both as a mirror for the dramatic action and as a fertility figure representing the source of all creation.

It was the locking up on this vital source of energy that produced the original limiting situation, the stagnation of life in the Llavero family. Rosalba begins the process of liberation, but her distortion of the rational principle creates a new limiting situation, the chaos at the end of act II. Nativitas supplies the synthesis necessary for the creative release of this energy: the formation of meaningful human bonds in which recognition is given to both the rational and irrational forces. Under the sign of the cross, a union can be achieved, not as something static or limiting, but rather as a dynamic equilibrium capable of change and new creativity.

La hebra de oro (*The Golden Thread*) also conveys this image of man as a complex of rational and irrational forces, but it marks a turning point in the development of Carballido's drama. In contrast to *La zona intermedia*, basically a morality play, *La hebra de oro* is a variation on the mystery play, specifically the *auto* of resurrection. It is more closely aligned with the primitive ritual of the cyclic regeneration of vegetation than with the allegorical form of the morality play based on a rational conceptualization of ethical values. *La hebra de oro* achieves a greater integration of man and the cosmos. Human potentiality and natural forces are brought together under a single term: energy. Thus, beginning in the late 1950s, Carballido's theater combines a more complex concept and representation of reality.

In a letter to Peden, Carballido himself has recognized the significance of *La hebra de oro*: "'The Thread' is quite important to me; it was the first time I attempted to join a realistic treatment with an imaginative one . . . . Before, I wrote works of one genre or the other, but never mixed together."[8] While *La zona intermedia* depicts an imaginary world and *Rosalba* a realistic environment, they both differ from *La hebra de oro* in their separation of the two approaches to drama. *La hebra de oro* effects an interpenetration of the two approaches and produces a more fluid image of reality, in which both the external and the internal facets of the characters are physically projected on the stage.

The realistic context in which the *auto* begins and ends is the hacienda of Ixtla, Mexico in the year 1953. The hacienda belongs to Silvestre Sidel, who has been missing for a number of years. Adela Sidel, Silvestre's paternal grandmother, and her accomplice Rafael have brought Silvestre's maternal grandmother, the ailing Leonor Luna, to the hacienda with the intention of having Leonor die there and taking over Silvestre's estate for themselves.

A basic opposition is established between the two grandmothers: Adela is cold, calculating, and insensitive; Leonor represents maternal compassion. At first Adela is the dominant force, but already in the first act Leonor assumes the initiative as her maternal instinct is awakened. Sibila's child is ill, and Salustio, the *mayordomo* of the estate and Sibila's father-in-law, maintains that nothing can be done for the child because it is possessed by evil spirits. In order to be allowed to care for the child, Leonor must prove to Salustio that she has power over the forces of evil. Therefore, she improvises a ritual against the powers of death.

Leonor's incantations at the end of act I literally open the doors to the supernatural world. First, a radio turns on by itself, emitting bursts of static until the wave lengths of the natural and supernatural realms are brought into tune. Then, a door, sealed by two boards in the form of a cross (X), mysteriously opens. This door parallels the symbolism employed in *Rosalba*. There, Rosalba called for help through a window, and the necessary assistance appeared in the figure of Nativitas. Here, the door, another opening connecting two regions, is reinforced by the sign of a cross, the intersection of opposites. On one side of the door is the living room of the hacienda, the region of consciousness, and on the other side are dark, cavernous passages and a subterranean spring, symbolic of the subconscious. Thus, the opening of the door marks the eruption of the subconscious, or the dream world, into the realm of consciousness, and the Man in the Caftan enters to direct the fantastic episode.

However, the following scenes do not represent a normal dream within the mind of an individual. All the characters present before the fantastic episode (Adela, Leonor, Sibila, the Child, Salustio) are also present after its conclusion, and all of them experience the same events. Also, the natural elements participate in the fantastic episode, specifically the rain and the sprouting of the corn. Thus, this part of the play is more closely related to the collective participation of ritual than to the individual character of dreams. This fantastic episode constitutes the greater part of the play (act II, scene 1 to act III, scene 5) and on the psychological level serves to exteriorize subconscious facets of the major characters through the re-enactment of events from the past. Thus, instead of a linear development of a conflict, the play consists of a series of recognition scenes that provide an opportunity to reveal and evaluate human behavior.

Adela, born of a poor family, married a wealthy man who suffered from asthma. The marriage was a failure emotionally and financially. She had married for money, but when her husband died he left everything to his son. Adela has an inferiority complex, is paranoiac, and never has established an authentic relationship with anyone. Closed within her own ego, insensitive to the feelings of others, she is alone and ill. Her accomplice Rafael has left, and the only person that cares for Adela is Leonor.

Leonor is very compassionate, but, because of her traditional education, she suffers a physical aversion to sex. After Silvestre's parents died, she raised her grandson. Having internalized the traditional attitude towards sex, she tended to impose it on Silvestre and caused him to flee the hacienda. The Man in the Caftan, playing the role of the young Silvestre, accuses Leonor of not having allowed him to fulfill his desires. Her attitude towards sex impeded the development of Silvestre's ego. Still, her protective maternal instinct saves her, renewing her will to live as she cares for Sibila's child.

Sibila functions as an antithesis to Leonor. She represents animal passion, dominated by immediate physical pleasure, and thus she is analogous to the Woman in *La zona intermedia*. She engaged in intercourse with Silvestre before he left the hacienda. Since then, she has had three children by the *mayordomo's* son, all of which have died. The maternal instinct is completely absent. Although she abandons her child and runs off with her new lover Rafael, her fate is still in question: both the Devil and her Guardian Angel are seen hovering overhead as she rides off.

The Man in the Caftan, with the aid of his female assistant Mayala, directs the enactment of these recognition scenes. He has a double function: he is the mimetic author of the fantastic episode, directing and commenting upon these scenes, and he himself is a fictional character, enacting the role of the lost grandson Silvestre. In the latter role, he re-creates his own death, lamenting not having realized himself fully: "But I am no longer I, he, Silvestre, but the other, my frustrated possibilities, my nonbeing, the reflection of my broken potentials" (*The Golden Thread*, p. 115).[9] This disjointed farewell, as his unfulfilled desires disintegrate into the void, serves as an exhortation to Leonor. His death returns her to an active role, and reciprocally she gives him a new existence. Picking up the child abandoned by Sibila, Leonor exclaims: "And you, baby, you're not going to cry. You're going to live. You're going to be named Silvestre and you'll have lots of friends, and since you're a little lame, you're not going to be able to get away" (*The Golden Thread*, p. 118). The child's lameness underscores the masculine principle's ultimate dependency on the feminine.

La hebra de oro is not structured upon a linear development of a conflict between realistically delineated characters. Instead, a rythmic pattern of death and regeneration is employed, effecting a sympathetic relationship between the human and cosmic planes. Leonor Luna (feline and lunar characteristics are usually evident in Carballido's libidinous figures) represents the feminine generative principle. At the beginning of act I she is dormant and weak. The reappearance of her lost grandson Silvestre, who is related to seed and rain during the fantastic episode, brings in the masculine fecundating principle. His entrance, death, and absorption awaken Leonor's maternal instincts and finally in act III she gives "birth" to a new Silvestre. In the last scene, this process is given explicit visual expression by the sack of corn: "Something has burst forth in the sack of corn. It has been rising slowly since the beginning of the scene. Now it can be seen clearly: it is stalks of corn, many of them, which stretch upward while Leonor sings" (*The Golden Thread*, p. 119).

Beginning with *La hebra de oro*, these physical effects are fundamental to Carballido's representation of reality.[10] Rather than an illusion of reality like *Rosalba* or a conceptualized fantasy like *La zona intermedia*, his theater becomes magically real: a rhythmic flux of physical sensations that create an archetypal reality. The distinction between reality and illusion is further attenuated in the fantastic episode in which fictional characters (Adela, Leonor, Sibila) represent themselves in their "true" identities; a mimetic author (Man in the Caftan) directs the play within a play, comments upon it, and he himself enacts a fictional role (Silvestre). The total effect of these techniques, which find varied expression in Carballido's later works, is to involve the audience in the spectacle in a more direct and more active manner.

La hebra de oro also develops several images that reveal Carballido's increasingly more complex view of reality. With the threads of his existence—time, space, energy—man fashions his life. "It's like spinning the threads of the spider webs we always have around us" says the Man in the Caftan (*The Golden Thread*, p. 79). The abstract concept of potentiality employed in *La zona intermedia* has become metaphor: a web, fragile and complex, a myriad of interrelated elements spun together as one plays out his existence. The "golden thread" is the spiritual thread that binds our web to that of our fellow man and gives continuity and meaning to our existence. Yet, these threads are not distinct from cosmic forces: energy existing everywhere, taking a multitude of forms, changing, growing, disappearing, and reappearing in the most unexpected ways. The Man in the Caftan may be considered the unfulfilled desires of Silvestre, returning as a spirit to direct the fantastic episode. Still, he returns via a radio magically tuned to a wave length that is spiritual but differing from ordinary radio waves only in frequency. The sky, seen through the living room window of the hacienda, appears as a spider web modeled on a painting by the Mexican artist Tamayo. Thus, the human and the cosmic planes interpenetrate and are united under the image of a complex and ever-changing web of energy.

Since *La hebra de oro* Carballido's plays have generally depicted a struggle for the liberation of vital creative forces, and the form employed has been the comedy or farce. In his earlier works, the disruptive force was associated with an exaggeration of ego or with traditional mores, represented by specific individuals and within the context of the family. In his later works, this force becomes an institution or society in general.

The one-act farce *Silencio, pollos pelones, ya les van a echar su maíz* ("Quiet, you mangy mutts, you'll get your bone") is an excellent example of Carballido's didactic social theater, presenting a vivid image of social conditions and clearly delineating causal factors. Although political and economic realities are treated, the main object of satire is the institutionalization of charity in the Social Welfare Agency. Charity, while apparently ministering to the needs of the poor, has only a cosmetic effect. It leaves unexplored the causes of poverty and serves to perpetuate the existing system that is based on a dominant-subordinate relationship. Formally the play combines elements of popular satire and epic theater. There are twenty-one characters portrayed by eight actors. Two actors serve as two choruses, providing musical commentary in the popular ballad or *corrido* form. Including transitional devices, there are thirty-six different scenic events with prop and costume changes made in view of the audience. Because of the number of scenes and the frequent transition from representation to commentary, the total effect is not that of illusion but of a rhythmic movement that requires an active, critical response by the audience.

For analytical purposes the farce can be divided into three parts: prologue, story, epilogue. In the prologue, the actors enter uniformly dressed, wearing placards (actor A, B, C; actress A, B, C; chorus D, E). After preliminary banter about the underdeveloped status of Mexican theater, they create the setting of the story through song, maps, and posters. Finally they don, over their uniforms, the costumes of the characters.

The story, an adaptation of Carballido's short story "La caja vacía" ("The empty coffin"), consists of three major segments. The action of the first segment occurs in a small rural village of Veracruz during the present. Because of the abject poverty in which Porfirio and his family exist, he decides to sign up with some North Americans who collect a wild herb and process it into medicine. A poster, pointing out that 14.4 percent of the state's economically active population works as braceros, directs attention to the economic causes of this situation. Later, at the North American camp, the relationship between the gringo and the Mexican is revealed. The employer, feeling morally superior, labels all the workers cheats. Porfirio, distrusting the gringos' jerry-built tram that crosses to the forest where the plants are gathered, attempts to swim the river. The choruses and characters narrate how he is swept away by the swift current. The final scene depicts the villagers' reaction to the news. Porfirio's death leaves his mother, wife, and daughter completely destitute. One woman, who last year had received government assistance to bury her mother while her husband was laboring in the United States as a bracero, suggests that Porfirio's wife Domitila contact Leonela.

The second segment of the story entails a flashback of one and a half years, and the setting shifts to the state capital. The first scene introduces the central character of the play, Leonela, childless and a widow now for eight years. She runs the Refugio Guadalupano, a private mission for the poor. The name of the mission and a conspicuous portrait of the Virgin of Guadalupe externalize the maternal nature of her role. Leonela's relationship with the poor, however, emphasizes the negative characteristic of dependency as opposed to the nourishing and liberating aspect. Another important motivational factor is the sense of moral superiority that she derives from her role.

Events soon set in motion the revelation of the contradictions inherent in the institution of charity and in the character of Leonela. Her nephew Eustaquio, whom she had raised as her own child, is the government party's candidate for state governor. Short, rapid scenes satirize the rhetoric of the campaign, the fraudulent elections, and the division of the spoils. As assuredly as the electoral process represents no threat to the establishment and the government party, Leonela's appointment as director of social welfare will not eradicate the causes of poverty nor even alleviate the situation of the poor. At first Leonela demands that her staff allow the indigents to present their requests in person. This individualistic approach is countered by Berta, a young professional social worker:

"También hay problemas de grupos, no sólo individuales."[11] Berta serves as a rational foil to Leonela as the latter strives to fulfill through a state agency her earlier maternal role. Now, with increased funds and authority, the nature of this role becomes evident:

> *Leonela.* —. . . ¡Me encanta el don de mando! *(Se queda seria)* ¡Hasta miedo me da... lo fácilmente que me brota![12]

Although at this time she directs her efforts against the forces of bureaucracy, the satisfaction derived from the exercise of power reinforces the dominant-subordinate relationship that characterized her attitude toward the poor.

After less than two months in office, a decisive conflict occurs. The "leftist press" has exposed how the showers she sent to a remote village that lacked running water ended up in the hands of a hotel enterprise, criticized her use of the Virgin's portrait in a state office, and ridiculed the governor whom Leonela insists on addressing with the diminutive Tiquín. Realizing that she is a political liability, the governor orders her to remove the Virgin's portrait, limit her activities to bureaucratic forms, and stop treating him as a child. Denied the supports of her positive self-image, she begins to exercise her power in a vindictive manner. In the Welfare Office, she fires her loyal secretary Clementina and labels the poor as ignorant and undeserving of her love.

The third segment returns to the plot begun in the first segment. The scenario now includes both Leonela's office and the rural village. As the unsuccessful search for Porfirio's body continues, Domitila presents her request for assistance. Leonela, now in her second year in office, refuses to provide money for Porfirio's wake. However, Berta, more responsive to Domitila's needs, volunteers to investigate the case. Berta's arrival in the village causes the North Americans to offer Berta 250 pesos so that they will not be implicated in Porfirio's death. She passes the money on to Domitila.

Back in the capital, the following exchange captures the opposing attitudes toward the poor:

> *Leonela.* —. . . Me hacían creer que era yo buena: idiota, eso era yo. Mi tiempo, mi dinero, todo tirado al pozo. Quisiera yo juntarlo otra vez: abriría mi Refugio de nuevo, nada más para darme el gusto de echarlos a empujones. ¿No les gusta vivir así como viven? ¡Pues que ellos mismos hagan algo!
> *Berta.*   —Tal vez vayan a hacerlo... nunca se sabe.[13]
> *(Casual)*

Leonela, who had always considered the poor as children incapable of doing anything for themselves, now completely rejects them. Berta, on the contrary, views the poor not only as equals but also as the potential agents for changing the existing system. She rebels against Leonela's refusal to supply additional assistance by sending the most expensive casket she can find.

During Porfirio's wake, the major complication arises from the presence of the luxurious coffin. Aside from the absurd contrast with the humble surroundings, there is no corpse. The death of the ninety-year-old Dalia furnishes a happy resolution. The casket fulfills its normal function, and Porfirio's widow receives a few pesos from Dalia's relatives.

In the epilogue, the actors remove the costumes of the characters and in their commentary make it clear that "No queremos caridad, / sólo queremos justicia."[14] This is followed by a series of petitions, ranging from an increased subsidy for the theater to the release of political prisoners, and ends with the response of the authorities:

> Todos. —¡Silencio, pollos pelones,
> ya les van a echar su maíz![15]

The disrespect and unresponsiveness to the just demands of the actors parallels the reaction to the people by the dominant groups within the play: social (Leonela), political (Eustaquio), economic (North Americans). This repetition within the nonfictional frame (prologue, epilogue) underscores the didactic intent and reinforces the fact that the representation is an accurate reflection of reality. Although the solution is not explicitly given, it is clear that justice, not charity, is required, and that if justice is not forthcoming within the system, the people will become the agents for changing the system.

Yo también hablo de la rosa (*I Too Speak of the Rose*) synthesizes earlier thematic concerns and technical achievements of Carballido. This one-act masterpiece further elaborates the concept of human existence as a complex web of interrelationships through a fusion of realistic and poetic techniques, as in *La hebra de oro*. Also, it delineates the repressive effects of ideologies and institutions through popular satire and alternating scenes of commentary and representation, as in *Silencio, pollos pelones, ya les van a echar su maíz*. Finally, it succeeds in realizing both an explicit statement on the function of theater and an exemplary model of total theater.

The action occurs in Mexico City during the present, and the central realistic event is the derailment of a freight train by two adolescents, Toña and Polo. The technique and structure of the play focus the spectator's attention on the process of interpretation rather than on the event itself. There are eighteen basic scenes with twenty-nine characters portrayed by thirteen actors. Transitions are fluid and rapid, effected by lighting and the commentary of the Medium and the Newsboy.

The initial scene establishes a nonrealistic atmosphere. A spot comes up on the Medium, dressed in peasant costume. In her monologue, she conjures up an image of her heart. The heart, like the rose of the play's title, symbolizes human existence, complex and fragile, but also precise and powerful. The Medium herself is an objectification of the social function of theater. In the final lines of her monologue, she outlines the following process: events are perceived and images formulated, and the latter are then communicated and contemplated. The artist provides a representation of the people and their surroundings, an image that is physical and integral as opposed to the abstract and fragmentary analyses employed by scientists and politicians to manipulate reality. With each appearance the Medium's costume becomes increasingly lighter in color until the pure white of the final scene. This externalizes the process of clarification through which art succeeds in transcending the chaos of diverse partial visions in a total concrete image.

During a blackout following the monologue, the event is first presented sensorially: the sound of the derailment, silence, lightning flashes; then the Newsboy: "Get your papers now! Delinquents derail a train!" (*I Too*, p. 294).[16] Although apparently a neutral medium for the news, he varies his salespitch according to the version he is vending. The Medium, however, remains constant in her refusal to offer a limited fragmentary interpretation.

Scene 2 provides a realistic representation and employs a linear progression: street scene, derailment, effects of the derailment. The behavior of the young truants is spontaneous. They steal some coins from a public telephone, and then they decide to buy some candy. Their encounters with the Candy Vendor, the Old Woman selling *jícama*, and the young mechanic Maximino develop a contrast between human relationships motivated by self-interest and, in the latter case, mutual respect. Later, at the dump, Toña and Polo give their remaining coins to a Scavenger. Objects that they find, scrap iron and flowers, are seen as gifts for their friend Maxi. In an unpremeditated gesture, they roll a metal tub filled with concrete onto the train tracks. The brief tableau (din of the crash, lightning, Toña and Polo awed by the wreck) suggests the import of the change effected by their actions.

In scene 3 the Medium reads from a Bestiary. Diverse interpretations of human existence are illustrated by animal images. They range from the canine guardian of physical integrity and property rights, the cat watching over man's spiritual integrity, the hen, fish, butterfly, and snake, to the bee that knows "*all* about solar energy and light. Things we don't suspect!" (*I Too*, p. 306). The latter most closely approaches the dramatist's concept of man as an intricate web of interrelationships based upon cosmic energy.

The next five scenes provide brief interpretations of and reactions to the derailment. Commenting upon the newspaper report, a Gentleman identifies poverty as the cause of delinquency. A Lady agrees: "Oh, yes, their poverty's something awful. But they didn't say anything about the trunk murder, huh?" (*I Too*, p. 306). Even if the cause is identified, there is no active response, only the passive consumption of journalistic sensationalism. The Teacher uses the newspaper to illustrate the "dangers of idleness." She, too, refuses to accept any responsibility or attempt to alleviate the problem. Two University Students react with greater sympathy, revealing perhaps a desire to rebel against society. All three responses, however, contrast with that of Maxi. Informed by phone that his friends have been arrested, he immediately requests that his employer give him money and time off so that he can go to the aid of the adolescents. Scene 8 shifts to the dump where the Scavengers and others reap the fruits of the wreck, carrying off sacks of food.

Scene 9 returns to the Medium. She narrates a story that is enacted by two dancers. Living in different towns, they both receive the same command in a dream: to dance and pray *together* at the sanctuary near the house of their brother. They meet in mid-route and, confused by the ambiguous dream, celebrate the rite at the place of their encounter. Each returns home, feeling he has only half-fulfilled the command. The anecdote reflects the image of human existence presented by the play. Man has no foreknowledge of the consequences of his actions. Therefore, primary emphasis is placed upon the process: contradictions should be faced and choices made in a spirit of solidarity with others.

The next seven scenes supply additional interpretations, and the basic opposition is human-vs.-inhuman response. First, we see Toña's mother preparing food and clothing to take to her daughter, and then Polo's mother visits him in prison. Both mothers are confused and vacillate in assigning blame. However, they do reveal a human maternal concern for their children's welfare and establish an obvious contrast with the two following scenes, which employ more elaborate distancing techniques. Both are introduced by the Newsboy: first, he hawks a Freudian analysis holding up papers covered with Rorschachlike ink blots and, later, a Marxist interpretation carrying papers printed in red on black. Each scene includes a narrator (Professor One, Professor Two) who comments upon his version as it is presented by Toña and Polo. The result is the satire of two opposing overrationalizations: the first exaggerating the repression of the libido in the individual, the second stressing the exploitation of the proletariat under capitalism. The three following scenes underscore the inhumanity of the preceding ones by focusing upon the mutual bond of love. Maxi visits Toña in prison. He had come to free his two friends by paying their fines. This is impossible because the derailment has resulted in a half-million-peso "crime." That the real crime is poverty is implied by Toña's expression of solidarity with her fellow inmates, who have violated society's laws in order to live. Toña and Maxi embrace as he vows to carry only Toña's picture in his wallet. What had begun as idol worship on her part and friendship on his part ends in love. A scene at the dump develops a similar bond on the collective level. Here, it assumes a more popular and realistic form, as four Scavengers (two male, two female) celebrate around a fire with food, drink, and song. The earthy language of the songs contrasts strongly with the dehumanizing terminology of analysis employed by the two Professors. The scene concludes with the same gesture as the preceding one: the two couples embrace. Scene 16 returns to the Toña-Maxi plot. On the telephone at the garage, he breaks his engagement with his previous girlfriend and thus prepares the way for his future union with Toña.

Scene 17 restates the theses of the two Professors, adds a third, and requires the audience to make a choice. The Announcer illustrates the theses with three projected images and offers a magnificent prize to those who select the correct interpretation. In addition to the Freudian and Marxist rationalizations (rose petal and rose respectively), we have the weblike fiber of a rose petal seen under a microscope. This is the Medium's image, "primal matter" that is also "energy." The latter thesis destroys the former: there is no rose, no petal, only "a fusion of miraculous fictions. . . . Without the least possibility of rational explanation." (*I Too*, p. 328).

In the transition to the final scene, the Newsboy carries parchmentlike papers imprinted with magical signs and offers *all* the news. This introduces the Medium, now dressed in white, who gives her version. The previous representations by Toña and Polo, commented upon by the two Professors, were basically satires of exaggerated rationalizations, whereas the final scene achieves the total physical effect of ritual. The street scene included by the Professors is eliminated and dramatic intensity heightened as the Medium narrows the focus to the dump, where the change effected by the derailment occurs. As Toña and Polo enter, she explains: "They are changing into all that surrounds them" (*I Too*, p. 328). Their dance harmonizes with and evokes the creative potential of the cosmos. The flowers respond as a Feminine Chorus in a liturgy: "I have strength . . . / I have promise . . ." (*I Too*, p. 329). The dump itself begins to glow from within, and the Medium adds: "With rhythms such as these we summon and arouse fertility" (*I Too*, p. 329). After the derailment, all the characters in the play embrace, kiss, dance, at first chaotically and finally in a chain, with precise and complex movements. A change from sterility to fertility occurs on all levels: Toña and Polo pass from adolescents to adults (she marries Maxi, he gets his own garage), the situation of the poor shifts temporarily from lack to abundance, and the cosmos itself participates in this realization of creative potential.

Now, instead of commenting upon the representation, the Medium addresses a question to the characters:

Medium. —And now, what about that light from that star—extin-
(Asking in the guished for so many years?
manner of
a teacher)

Toña.·   —. . . It kept flowing into the telescope . . . but all it meant
to say . . . all it meant to reveal . . . was the humble existence of the hairy hunter, who was drawn by his friend,
the painter, on the walls of an African cave. [*I Too*, p. 331]

This exchange provides, within the play, a statement on the function of art.
The artist produces an image that persists long after the event or person represented ceases to exist. The sole function of the artist is to affirm, through an
integral objectification, the existence of his contemporaries as a complex web of
creative potential. Thus, the web becomes an image not of entrapment but of
liberation, transcending, through a complex yet precise physical representation, the limits imposed by analytical rationalizations of human existence. The
play itself is an exemplary realization of this concept of drama, and it clearly
demonstrates how greatly Carballido has enriched the allegorical image of man
expressed in *La zona intermedia*.

NOTES

1. An excellent bibliographical source on Carballido is George W. Woodyard and Leon
F. Lyday's "Studies on Latin American Theatre, 1960–1969," *Theatre Documentation*
2 (Fall 1969–Spring 1970): 49–84. More recent items include: Oswaldo A. López's
"Crítica de la realidad social mexicana en obras representativas de Emilio Carballido"
(Ph.D. dissertation, University of Pittsburgh, 1973); Mary Vázquez-Amaral's "*Yo
también hablo de la rosa*: Un estudio crítico," *Revista de la Universidad de México* 27,
no. 5 (January 1973): 25–29; Joseph F. Vélez's "Tres aspectos de *El relojero de
Córdoba* de Emilio Carballido," *Explicación de textos*, nos. 1–2 (1973), pp. 151–159;
and his "Una entrevista con Emilio Carballido," *Latin American Theatre Review*,
7, no. 1 (Fall 1973): 17–24.
2. *The Golden Thread and Other Plays*, trans. Margaret S. Peden (Austin: University
of Texas Press, 1970), p. xi.
3. *La zona intermedia*, in *Teatro mexicano contemporáneo*, no. 26 (Mexico City: Unión
Nacional de Autores, 1951). The translations provided in the text are from *The Golden
Thread and Other Plays*, and the title of the play and page numbers will be indicated in
parentheses following the quotation.
4. *Rosalba y los Llaveros*, in Carballido, *Teatro* (Mexico City: Fondo de Cultura
Economica, 1960), pp. 151–247. All references to this play are from this edition. Translations provided in the notes are mine: "He could pass as handsome if he were not so
mousy. He looks younger than his age" (*Rosalba*, p. 167).
5. *Lázaro*. Yeah, look, you treat everything schematically, you decide everything by
new principles, yours, but they're principles, right? It's all the same. You do away with
old principles to put up new ones. Come on, what's the difference?

Rosalba. Lázaro! You're an anarchist!

Lázaro. Could be. I've told you I don't label things.

Rosalba. Yes you are, Lázaro, but you don't do anything, you don't rebel. Why? [*Rosalba*, p. 187]

6. "I put on a show for others, sometimes even for myself; I can't avoid it" (*Rosalba*, p. 241).

7. "War against Lucifer and the pagan lions! God save us from the innocent evil that prevails. The king marries the Moorish queen who sometimes sings and sometimes cries. Cross, Cross, Cross. Have faith in the Holy Cross Incarnate" (*Rosalba*, pp. 222–223).

8. *The Golden Thread and Other Plays*, p. xiii.

9. *La hebra de oro: Auto sacramental en tres jornadas* (Mexico City: Universidad Nacional Autónoma, 1957). The translations provided in the text are from *The Golden Thread and Other Plays*, and the title of the play and page numbers will be indicated in parentheses following the quotations.

10. Margaret S. Peden, "Theory and Practice in Artaud and Carballido," *Modern Drama* 2, no. 2 (September 1968): 132–142.

11. *Silencio, pollos pelones, ya les van a echar su maíz*, in *Teatro mexicano, 1963*, ed. Antonio Magaña Esquivel (Mexico City: Aguilar, 1965). All references to this play are from this edition. Translations provided in the notes are mine: "There are also collective problems, not only personal ones" (*Silencio*, p. 137).

12. *Leonela*. . . . I really enjoy ordering people about! (*She becomes serious*) It even frightens me—how easy it is for me! (*Silencio*, p. 139).

13. *Leonela*. . . . They made me believe I was good: an idiot, that's what I was. My time, my money, everything wasted. I wish I had it again: I'd open the mission again, just to have the pleasure of booting them out. Don't they like living like they do? Well let them do something for themselves!

 Berta. (*Casually*) Perhaps they will—you never know.   [*Silencio*, p. 151]

14. *Everyone*. We don't want charity,
   we just want justice.   [*Silencio*, p. 159]

15. *Everyone*. Quiet, you mangy mutts,
   you'll get your bone!   [*Silencio*, p. 160]

16. *Yo también hablo de la rosa*, in *Teatro mexicano del Siglo XX* (Mexico City: Fondo de Cultura Económica, 1970), V, 235–275. The translations provided in the text are from William I. Oliver's translation *I Too Speak of the Rose*, in *The Modern Stage in Latin America: Six Plays*, ed. George W. Woodyard (New York: E. P. Dutton & Co., 1971). The shortened title of the play and page numbers will be indicated in parentheses following the quotation.

3. The Spectacular in the Theater

of Agustín Cuzzani

Alyce de Kuehne

There are two periods to be considered in the production of the Argentine playwright Agustín Cuzzani. The first includes a cycle of four *farsátiras* written from 1953 to 1958 and compiled in his volume of *Teatro* in 1960.[1] These farces, all successfully produced—*Una libra de carne* (1954), *El centroforward murió al amanecer* (1955), *Los indios estaban cabreros* (1958), and *Sempronio* (1960)—are destined for heterogeneous audiences. They especially cater to popular taste in that each one establishes what the author calls a *situación-espectáculo*—a "theatrical-fantastic" kind of conflict carried to irrational extremes. In each case the result is a caricatural deformity of reality, in which man is depicted as victim of his fellow men.

The second period marks a conscious deviation in spirit, as well as in form and technique, judging from *Para que se cumplan las escrituras* (1965), the initial play of what is apparently Cuzzani's recent trend toward a more complex level of dramatic composition. While this drama is conceived in the vein of modern tragedy, it coincides with the *farsátiras* in the sense that it, too, depicts man as victim, not necessarily of other human beings, but of something as abstract and elusive as Destiny, captured nevertheless in the concrete form of a unique Computer that foretells the future.

An analysis of Cuzzani's entire production will demonstrate that, in addition to his gift for assimilating techniques compatible with popular theater, his thematic inspiration has resulted from literary sources as varied as classical and vanguard theater, the Bible, mythology, history, and science. It will likewise show why scholars like Carlos Solórzano consider the theater of Cuzzani, one of Latin America's foremost playwrights, to be of lasting value.[2]

With the following quotation from *The Merchant of Venice*, Cuzzani recognizes his debt to Shakespeare[3] for a theme that he has nevertheless adapted to his own ideology, with twentieth-century expressionism and elements of the absurd:

> A pound of man's flesh taken from a man
> Is not so estimable, profitable neither,
> As flesh of muttons, beefs, or goats.   [Act I, scene 3]

This epigraph establishes the unifying motif of the four *farsátiras*: the degradation of the human species. The Argentine dramatist is inspired by the scene of The Trial (act IV, scene 1). The merchant, having defaulted in the payment of his debt to Shylock, is brought to trial by the Jewish usurer, who now demands fulfillment of the terms of the pact signed by the merchant: the forfeiture of one pound of the debtor's flesh. In *Una libra de carne* ("A pound of flesh"), Cuzzani mocks Justice even before the trial begins. The courtroom scenery and props eloquently foreshadow the verdict. The judge's "throne," the desk of the prosecution adorned with the Greek mask of comedy and that of the defense with the mask of tragedy, all proclaim that Shakespeare's tragicomedy will be turned into a tragic farce.

The two classical antagonists are radically changed in *Una libra de carne*. The Venetian merchant who owns a fleet of ships becomes, in Cuzzani's version, a meek, downtrodden clerk exploited by a large commercial firm. Shakespeare's Shylock is a victim of anti-Semitic persecution and therefore basically motivated by hate and a desire for vengeance against the merchant who has insulted him. Cuzzani's Tomás Shylock García has no such motives for his cruelty; unscrupulous and fraudulent, he tricks his victim into the absurd contract, knowing that he has nought to gain but 450 grams of worthless human flesh.[4] The classical religious-racial conflict emerges with sociological implications as a contemporary protest against the injustice of the economic class system.

In a unified way, the whole play is structured in one continuous act that focuses entirely on Elías Beluver's defeat in the proverbial "rat race" (*corretaje*). The Trial is transformed into a spectacle intensified with the additional dimensions of time and space afforded by theatrical expressionism. Flashbacks literally throw light upon different aspects of the life of the accused, victim of a nagging wife, slave-driving bosses, quack doctors, hounding creditors, and, finally, of Tomás Shylock García. Were these dramatizations conceived as a serious imitation of reality, the whole process depicting the systematic ruin of a human being would be a modern tragedy. Cuzzani achieves quite the contrary, however, with hilarious caricature and absurd metaphors. For example, just before the trial commences, the expectation of the public is compared to that of a theater at curtain time.

La Señora.   —¿Qué dan hoy?

La Nena.   —¿Es divertido papito?

El Señor.   —Lo de hoy no es tan interesante. Sólo el simple caso de un deudor que no ha pagado. Se llama proceso por defraudación.

Rentista.   —¿Oyeron? Se trata de un caso de...

Corredor.   —¡No oí nada! Está prohibido. (*Agita el manual*)

Coro del Jurado.   —¡Pro-hi-bi-do! ¡Pro-hi-bi-do! ¡No escuchemos, no
(*Tapándose los oídos*) escuchemos!⁵   [P. 27]

The defendant is exhibited in a cage. While this expressionistic device is not original—O'Neill uses it in *The Hairy Ape*—Cuzzani exploits the idea to the maximum by adding circus music to heighten the atmosphere of excitement. The little girl throws a cracker into the cage of the monster, thus consummating the *situación-espectáculo*. Beluver is condemned a priori by a subjective jury sympathetic toward Shylock García, the kindhearted "philanthropist."

The absurd prevails throughout. The monologues of the selfish wife are utterly ridiculous, the diagnoses of Beluver's malady preposterous, and the hypocrisy of the boss farcical and satirical:

Don Bonifacio. —. . . Créame que lo lamento profundamente. En
            dieciocho años que usted ha trabajado para la firma, hasta
            me había formado la costumbre de verlo haciendo letra
            gótica. . . . Pero... (*Lo palmea*) ¡La salud ante todo,
            Beluver! Nosotros no podemos, desgraciadamente, variar
            nuestras normas de trabajo. Y la letra gótica nos es
            imprescindible para la presentación y pulcritud de
            nuestros libros de comercio. . . . Pero si su médico le
            aconseja dejar este trabajo no seré yo quien le impida
            presentar su renuncia. (*Busca en su bolsillo*) Aparte de
            eso, yo he querido significarle el agradecimiento de
            nuestra firma por sus servicios. . . . ¡Oh, no es dinero,
            por supuesto! No iba yo a ofender a usted que es un amigo
            de la casa. Es una carta de recomendación para que
            encuentre trabajo. . . . Y ahora sí, mi querido Beluver,
            quiero darle una prueba más de afecto. *Como un padre
            a un hijo.* (*Pone su mano extendida sobre el hombro de
            Beluver*) Así. *Dios lo bendiga, hijo mío.*

Publico y Jurado. —¡Amén!⁶
(*A coro*)   [P. 42, my italics]

In this *farsátira*, choral chants are used to attain a variety of effects. The Public, reciting in unison, echoes the bigotry of the Jury or the lies of the Prosecution. The irrational role of this chorus is evidently a deviation from the traditional Greek chorus, which, in varying degrees, played an integral part in the ancient tragedy or comedy. Cuzzani's chorus of creditors, with an economy of action and dialogue, gives the impression of overwhelming numbers against the solitary Beluver. Collective clamor likewise produces an auditory impact, especially when the chanting degenerates into meowing and barking, as occurs when the creditors give chase to their prey. The overall choral effect serves to punctuate the silence of Beluver, who utters but one single word of despair during the entire play. His testimony is, in fact, all pantomime. Nevertheless, his woes are voiced by the superb Chorus of Passengers—*la caravana de los espantados* ("the caravan of the terrified")—which embodies the collective urban neurosis:

> *Coro de Pasajeros.* —¡Ahí viene! ¡No, no viene! ¡Sí, viene! ¡No, no viene!
> *(Inclinándose para*
> *ver si viene el ómni-*
> *bus)*

Uno.	—¡Con tal que no venga atrasado!
Coro.	—¡Que no venga atrasado!
Otro.	—¡Inventemos una excusa!
Coro.	—¡Una excusa! ¡Una excusa! ¡Esa nos conviene!
Otro.	—¡Diremos que nuestra suegra está enferma!
Otro.	—¡Que llegó un hijo del campo!
Otro.	—¡Que nuestras señoras están de parto!
Otro.	—¡Que tuvimos que ir al médico!
Otro.	—¡Nos citó la policía!
Otro.	—¿Y si dijéramos que el ómnibus venía atrasado?
Otro.	—¡Nunca! ¡Eso nunca!
Uno.	—¡Eso no lo cree ningún patrón!
Otro.	—¡Los patrones no creen nunca nada!

Coro. (Con terror) —¡Los patrones, los patrones, los patrones!

Uno. —¡El ómnibus! *(Mutis corriendo despavorido)*
(Asomándose)

Otro. —Es cierto. El ómnibus. ¡Allá, en aquella esquina! *(Mutis y corriendo)*

Otro. —Pero si la parada es aquí.

Otro. —No, no... Desde hoy la parada es allá. Nueva reglamentación. *(Todos corren despavoridos y mutis)*[7]

[P. 36]

The protagonist is thus mirrored in multiple fashion in these automatons of obsessive monologue.

There can be no mercy for the likes of Beluver; his flesh is chopped off as near as possible to his heart. This verdict constitutes a radical deviation from Shakespeare's happy ending achieved through the intervention of Portia, who disguises herself as a lawyer. She invokes a law by which the Jew would be condemned for attempted homicide should a drop of Christian blood be shed in the process of mutilation. Shylock promptly desists, and the merchant is spared. There is one direct, if distorted, reference to this incident in *Una libra de carne*. The defense, by way of protest, cites a "legal precedent" in an analogous case that occurred in Venice, in the time of "Judge Porcio." Even more absurd is the tardy endeavor of Shylock García to return the package of meat to the debtor: "No quiero nada. Que se guarde su maldita carne. Que se la ponga de nuevo en su sitio. . . . ¡Yo lo quería *como a un hijo!*" (p. 59, my italics).[8]

The absurd reaches a climax with the subsequent discovery that there is no longer any blood in Beluver's body. And so the "show" does have a happy ending for all but one perplexed spectator—designated "the Man"—who wonders what will now become of Beluver. His query is hastily dismissed:

> *Ujier.* —El procesado está en libertad. A la Justicia no le importa saber ni averiguar nada de la vida privada de las gentes. Son libres y responsables de sus actos.[9]   [P. 61]

Cuzzani makes a farce of the Sartrian precept by demonstrating that free, responsible choice is valid only as long as there is a free man capable of exercising it. Beluver is not an authentic man. There is only one character—"the Man"— who bears that label in the play. Beluver, the antihero, is what is commonly known as "a poor devil" (*un pobre diablo*). His name suggests an almost perfect anagram (interchanging *b* and *v*) of Belcebú (Beelzebub or Beelzebul), generally known as Satan, the prince of the fallen angels. Even though Beluver has the given name Elías (Elijah, one of the greatest biblical prophets), he, like the devil, is condemned to perpetual darkness, obliged to use medieval Gothic script on one job and dark clothes on the other. Everyone condescends to treat him as a "son," with false paternalism, comparable to the way a feudal lord treated his vassal or servant. This is further illustrated by the medieval liturgical elements in the "confession scene," when Beluver is "absolved" by Tomás Shylock García, who calls him "my son" (*hijo mío*) five times within one minute (p. 50). Finally, the very forfeiture of his flesh is inspired in practices of this nature that date historically from the Middle Ages, when, for example, a master could mutilate the body of his serf.[10] Cuzzani conceives capitalist society as a modern version of the feudal system.[11]

In *El centroforward murió al amanecer* ("The centerforward died at dawn"), certain elements of *Una libra de carne* persist, as often occurs in works of a cycle. There are, for example, some choral chants, mainly the cheering of the soc-cer fans. On the other hand, in *El centroforward*, the individual debtor expands into a collective entity, a soccer club whose enormous debt is not to be settled with a mere package of human flesh but with a whole human being, cartoned, sealed, and delivered to the new owner. The absurd assumes even greater proportions in this three-act *farsátira*, more complex in every way than the pre-ceding one. Again, Cuzzani leans heavily on Shakespeare, not for a modified version of a character but to avail himself of his most famous protagonist, Hamlet. He manages this by exploiting the Pirandellian concept of the "char-acter," as defined in *Six Characters in Search of an Author* and further elabora-ted in *Henry IV*, which treats the related question of a personage drawn from the historic past.

In *El centroforward*, Garibaldi, the great soccer player, is sacrificed at public auction by his bankrupt club. The purchaser, Ennésimo Lupus, is a sadistic capitalist who covets the player, not for another team but simply as a novelty for his collection of extraordinary human beings. Garibaldi will add the dimen-sion of sports to this unique collection representing art, science, and brute force. The catalogue includes such rare specimens as the legs of the famous young Nora Rodrigova, a ballerina who is now only on special occasions permitted to exhibit a few steps of ballet, lest she fall and hurt herself or deform her precious ex-tremities. The exact opposite of this delicate beauty is the beastlike mental re-tard King Kong, who had previously performed as a trained monkey in a circus. Another curious "item" of the inventory is the German physicist who amuses his intellectual solitude by fabricating little atomic bombs. But without a doubt, the most bizarre acquisition of the eccentric collector is Hamlet. Once, fol-lowing the performance of the Shakespearean masterpiece, Lupus had capri-ciously resolved to own, not the flesh and blood mortal who portrayed the title role of *Hamlet*, but rather the original "character" perpetuated by Shakespeare in his play.

The influence of the Italian playwright Pirandello on the Argentine Cuzzani is evident. On distinguishing between the literary character and the real actor, Cuzzani recognizes the difference established in *Six Characters in Search of an Author* between the fictitious being or image created in the mind of the author, and the cerebral form that an individual assumes (like a superstructure) in an effort to *appear to be* the character he is portraying. By using the Shakespearean hero, Cuzzani assures universal recognition of his "character." Moreover, Ham-let is timeless in so far as he expresses the difference between life (the struggle to survive) and death (the seduction of peaceful sleep). The young Prince of Den-mark is compatible with vanguard theater, since he expresses the anguish of im-prisoned man, even though his very nature makes him a target for existentialist speculation. He is egocentric, uncommunicative, suspicious, insincere, and in-decisive.

The basic distinction between Cuzzani's "character" and that of Pirandello is that the latter is permanently crystallized in a work of art and is therefore immortal. The actor-Hamlet, however, can never be that unique creature conceived by Shakespeare—in the same way that the "six characters" were born as characters (as opposed to human actors) in the mind of their creator, Pirandello. With his mask, the pseudocharacter can simulate the eternal youth of Hamlet, thus concealing the ravages of time, but he will ultimately perish like all mortals. Unlike the "six," frustrated in their search for an author who will solve their conflict, this solitary pseudocharacter complacently accepts the imposed role. He has no human conflicts, for he is isolated from his fellow-actors. With no decisions to make, he is relieved of his moral responsibility as an existential being. Finally, while Pirandello's "six" long to know the denouement of their drama, Hamlet's impostor knows that to "live" the last act of his tragedy means to die—poisoned by Laertes. Therefore, like the authentic Hamlet, he prefers to prolong the period of meditation.[12] He is the puppet symbol whose human essence has been devoured by the Wolf (*lobo*): Lupus is comparable to the blood-sucking vampires denounced in *Una libra de carne*.

Garibaldi is the anti-Hamlet, for whom the grotesque world of Lupus is not a refuge, but a zoo. If at first he reacts like an animal in a cage, his solitude—unlike that of the beast—provokes introspection. Pirandello maintained that one distinction between man and beast is that man can both live and see himself live at the same time. Garibaldi becomes aware of the absurdity of his life when he sees himself in the surrealistic fragments of a dream. He suffers. This marks the initial transition (end of act II) of his becoming an authentic man, as opposed to all the other irrational beings. Hence, the underlying significance of the animal symbolism throughout the play. An example of this is apparent in the early scene with Dr. Cassassola Cordero,[13] the evasive shyster lawyer who "guarantees" to save the centerforward from the auction block, where the soccer player is, notwithstanding, subsequently sold to Lupus. The animal concept is carried to its ultimate consequences when Lupus proposes to exploit the candid love of the centerforward and the ballerina, thereby combining the excellence of both, in order to produce a superior human breed. When the athlete rebels, the tyrant threatens to "mate" the ballerina with King Kong. The centerforward, motivated for the first time in his life by an ideal, strangles Lupus.

The animal theme is reinforced by the degeneration of language as the tool of communication, an aspect frequently treated in existentialist literature and demonstrated in the theater of the absurd. In this play, it is illustrated by ugly bird cries in the monotonous "dialogue" cawed by the so-called Crow-Lawyers (*Abogados-Cuervos*), Crow-Judges (*Jueces-Cuervos*), and Crow-Chorus (*Coro de Cuervos*), all of whom had obviously preestablished the guilt of the centerforward, before the trial. In the final scene, the rope employed for the hanging of the criminal is generously provided through the courtesy of Cannis Company

Limited (given thus, in English). It is likewise significant that the rope manufacturer himself, Sr. Cannis ("Canine" or "Dog"), is the speaker at this event, who manages to address the public with the aid of an English-Spanish dictionary.

Structurally, this play resembles *Una libra de carne* in that the plot unravels in retrospect: it begins when the centerforward has already been condemned to the gallows. A vagabond finds the memoirs dropped by the prisoner from his cell window. He reads them aloud, addressing the people in the audience as though they were the bloodthirsty spectators assembled in anticipation of the show-within-the-show (the hanging). In one scene there is even a third plane of reality: the surrealistic dream of Garibaldi, who himself functions on an expressionistic plane in flashbacks that, in turn, depend on the basic "present" reality of the vagabond. At the very end, at the break of dawn, the first two levels converge in time and space when the centerforward "actually" appears on the scene just prior to his execution.

The sunrise heralding a new day for humanity at the end of *El centroforward* is a recurring symbol in *Los indios estaban cabreros* ("The Indians were indignant").[14] It establishes the theme of act I, entitled "Los indios al sol" ("The Indians in the sun"), which is the candid optimism of three Indians of pre-Columbian Mexico who aspire to reach their sun-god—not through sacrifice and worship, but through physical encounter—in order to tell him personally about the poverty and suffering of the people. Unlike the foregoing *farsátiras*, which pivot around a kind of Brechtian narrator, this play exemplifies another technique equally or more effective in breaking the conventional enchantment of the theater. This device, also favored by Brecht, is the deliberate anachronism.

A modern street sign clashes with the primitive setting of a fifteenth-century marketplace. A verbal edition of the News Bulletin is prepared by "Agencias Tinahuaquense Unida y Goldstein Limitada." The town crier announces the imposition of a new tax burden, this one pertaining to the beggars: ". . . Establece que dada la falta de bienes y propiedades los mendigos deberán juntar y entregar al recaudador oficial cada dos meses, una bolsa de piojos que serán sacrificados en holocausto a la divinidad. . . . Se recuerda a los que deseen enrolarse en el ejército . . . que el enrolamiento es completamente voluntario y que los que se nieguen a enrolarse serán enrolados por la fuerza, ya que la policía garantiza la libertad de enrolamiento" (p. 128).[15] Symbol of the despotism of the Emperor Axayaca is the policeman who significantly appears attired in a typically twentieth-century uniform.

After eight frustrated attempts at rebellion, the revolutionary leader, Prince Tupa, is convinced that he is in disfavor with the sun-god, who is being deceived by the lies of the priests. He therefore proposes to sail eastward in the company of a beggar, Tonatio, and a miner, Teuche, in search of the rising sun. In the absence of the exaggerated farce of the *situación-espectáculo* (which does not occur until the second act), Cuzzani achieves an overall effect of pathos and humor—combining a feeling of present-day anguish with a touch of the absurd—as may be summarily appreciated in the departure scene. Having given their messages to the three emissaries, the people send them off to the sun-god, chanting:

Todos. —¡Que no haya más guerras,
que no haya más llantos,
que todo sea amor…!

Mendigo II. —¡Tonatio! ¡Cuando llegues al Sol, mándanos unas bolsas de piojos importados, para el impuesto!

Todos. —¡Que no haya más llantos,
Que todo sea amor!
¡Que no haya más llantos,
que todo sea amor…!16   [P. 138]

Act II, "Los indios a la sombra" ("The Indians in the shadows"), concerns the eclipse of their hope of ever reaching the sun-god. They somehow end up in a village on the other side of the Atlantic, equally plagued with beggars, priests, and the very same policeman who had tyrannized them before. Instead of one despot, there are two: Isabel and Fernando. The Mexicans land in the net of a fisherman who plans to put the exotic fish on exhibition. His wife protests in vain: "Si tienen manos y cara y ojos y pelo y… ¡Válgame Dios! Y…" (p. 142).17 But when his daughter falls in love with the "tiniest of the fish," that is the cue to denounce them to the Holy Inquisition for witchcraft and heresy. Brought to trial in a huge sardine can, the three fish are finally declared innocent, since they lack immortal souls. However, since fish cannot long survive out of water, they must soon perish spontaneously or burn at the stake.

The prison scene contains satirical references to the past and present of both Spain and America. Illustrious philosophers and masters in letters and sciences (Arabs and a Jew among them) are the inmates who marvel that three mere delinquents, not scholars at all, should be imprisoned in Spain. Ben Benib's observation regarding the political chaos of Spanish America is no less disheartening: "Se les llama americanos del italiano 'amare i cani' porque la leyenda dice que esas gentes tienen la obligación de amar a los perros tiranos y déspotas que parece que por aquellas regiones abundan" (p. 159).18

A further observation may be made concerning the dawn as the recurring symbol of hope, which now becomes identified with Mariceleste, the daughter of the Spanish fisherman. Cuzzani's expressionistic lighting effects seek to enhance the symbolic meaning of the text. This act opens before dawn. The ensuing scenes cover a period of one month; yet they suggest a prolonged night, which comes to an end with the first appearance of Mariceleste at the break of dawn, the rays of which promptly illuminate the whole center of the stage. "Mari-cielo, Mari-mar, Mari-estrella," as young Teuche calls her with adoration, signifies for the Indians a new hope. As her name symbolically implies, she embodies the fused Christian-pagan religious concept destined to eclipse their inaccessible sun-god.

In the final act, "A la sombra de los indios" ("In the shadow of the Indians"), the Mexicans regain their human status, thanks to Mariceleste's intervention with Queen Isabel, at the very moment Her Majesty is deliberating the proposal of Christopher Columbus. The presence of the Indians precipitates her decision to equip the expedition to the west. She greedily anticipates the acquisition of the new lands and inhabitants. Just as Cuzzani turns the discovery of the Indies into the discovery of Europe by the Indians, he likewise shatters the traditional beliefs regarding events that culminated in Columbus's voyage to America. He begins by rendering Columbus himself a nebulous anachronism. The discoverer is dubious about his own nationality. While a number of historians agree that he is Genoese, he claims that "Fray Bartolomé de las Casas, Oviedo o el portugués Barros lo dudan, mientras Sabellius cree que soy un pirata irlandés llamado Colombo Junior y Antonio Palencia me confunde con el navegante francés Casanove Coullon y Salvador Madariaga da a entender que soy judío catalán... Ahora bien, no me haga mucho caso de todos modos, porque como dice Ruy de Pina, soy muy mentiroso. Le recomiendo que lea la obra de John Boy Tacher, titulada 'Christophers [*sic*] Columbus: His life, His Works, His Remains.' Edición Nueva York, 1903, que es bastante completa" (p. 171).[19] Informed that he has been provided with an Indian guide to guarantee his "discovery," Columbus confesses the frustration of his secret desire: "Yo quería navegar hacia occidente para llegar al horizonte y entrar en los cielos, llegarme a la Casa de Dios y contarle de mi propia boca los infinitos males y miserias que sufren las gentes de este mundo..." (p. 173).[20]

Prince Tupa voluntarily returns to his cell to await death, thus to become the first of the millions of Indians to be sacrificed to the conquering sword. In a final display of expressionism (reinforcing the theme of hope staged in the opening scene of the play), Tupa "hears" the great chorus of his people in America chanting and pleading at sunrise. The individual protest of the *centroforward* optimistically assumes revolutionary proportions.

Los indios estaban cabreros is Cuzzani's most ambitious attempt to create episodic action of epic stature. Like Brecht, he is not concerned with individual conflicts or psychological character development but rather with overall problems of humanity. Along Brechtian lines (*Mother Courage*), Cuzzani plots his action in a distant past so that the audience—thus removed from familiar circumstances—will more objectively draw parallels with prevailing situations in the present. However, in the event that the spectator should become emotionally involved in the action of the play, an occasional anachronism will serve to jolt him back to his critical attitude as a twentieth-century bystander.[21]

Sempronio is probably Cuzzani's most widely read play.[22] It is curious that this last *farsátira* should be the most conventional of all in structure: the three acts progress in linear chronological sequence. Such formal simplicity could well have bearing on the fact that this was originally a one-act play—later to be developed with greater depth and detail. For the first time Cuzzani situates, in a middle-class environment of Buenos Aires, an ideal family consisting of the parents, a son, and a daughter. While each is typical of his sex and generation, all live together harmoniously, quite oblivious of the proverbial "gap." Sempronio, a retired employee, is proud of the "bonds" that literally unite him, not only with his family, but also with his community. As an avid stamp collector, he has become radioactive as a result of licking Japanese stamps from Hiroshima and Nagasaki. His vibrant body not only is the source of energy for Susanita's radio but also generates power for Diego's club and labor union. No less significant is Sempronio's "contact" with the merry-go-round. He does all this for love, not money:

> Sempronio. —¡Cobrar! ¿Por qué cobrar? Si a mí no me cuesta nada. Al contrario, es una gran alegría sentirme unido por cables a tanta gente que trabaja, a tantos chicos que juegan. . . .[23] [P. 196]

Sempronio's blissful state of coexistence is abruptly terminated with the intervention of the oligarchy. And the degradation of human dignity, characteristic of all the *situaciones-espectáculos*, is consummated when The Most Supreme Commissioner of Atomic Energy solemnly takes possession of the "atomic battery" and proclaims Sempronio property of the nation, legalizing the expropriation with a provisional receipt for his wife. Again, the human being is negotiated like an object or an animal. In this case (unlike *Una libra de carne* or *El centroforward*) there is no question of a pending debt, and yet this senior citizen suddenly finds he "owes" it to his country to sacrifice his individual freedom to become an inventory item of the federal domain.

The dehumanized hero is classified as the deadly Element S.P. 49 H321 V/60 and isolated in a cell, in preparation for the great day he is to power an atomic bomb. In spite of a nutritious diet fortified with creamed stamps and other radioactive morsels, Sempronio fails to produce the explosion. The Commissioner's glorious dream of annihilating entire cities ("inhabitants and all") is only temporarily shattered, for he is determined to have this defective mechanism disassembled, rectified, and reconstructed. And Cuzzani makes of Sempronio an even more hilarious "spectacle" when he has him hoisted on a truck and towed away like an old wreck.

Altisimo Comisionado. —No se discute con las licuadoras o con las máquinas
de afeitar. Se las repara. . . . ¡Yo soy el que da
las órdenes! A los hombres y a las cosas. Les
digo: ¡Funcionad! ¡Y ellos, a funcionar![24] [P. 215]

In his vehement satire of dictatorial tyranny, Cuzzani stretches the element of
farce to the limit, but no more than Ionesco or Beckett. Like them, he seeks
irrational means to express artistically—not realistically—the irrational aspects
of man's contemporary existence. The dramatic form, geared to the content,
intensifies the total effect of absurdity.

Sempronio, hopelessly "discharged" from the Atomic Commission, is sent
home. But once restored to the congenial environment of family and friends, his
current—neutralized in contact with hate and destruction—is automatically
"turned on." As Susanita plugs her radio into him and Olga connects her iron-
ing cord and the carousel music mingles with the hubbub of the factories, it becomes evident that Sempronio's generating power is Love, metaphorically
dramatized by this network of cables and wires that communicates man in his
work and play. Cuzzani's genius lies in the strength of this metaphor—comparable to many by Ionesco—on which rests the weight of the entire play. The
message is simple enough: LOVE MAKES THE WORLD GO ROUND. Hence, the
symbolic significance of the merry-go-round, which, in spite of its absurd gyra-
tions, can nevertheless be a source of human joy. If the message strikes some
critics as banal or inadequate, this can hardly be said of the theatrical means by
which Cuzzani shows that love, as an end in itself, is a powerful antidote for
existential anguish and the problem of communication.

The mere fact that Cuzzani presents any solution at all disqualifies him as an
orthodox advocate of the theater of the absurd. Ionesco's *Les chaises*, for
example, is a superb treatment of the problem of human communication, but
the theater of the absurd, characteristically pessimistic, does not attempt to
solve problems. Another significant difference between Cuzzani and Ionesco is
that the latter's ambiguity of metaphor and dialogue makes him accessible only
to a sophisticated minority. Meanwhile, Cuzzani, especially in his cycle of
farsátiras, is committed to popular theater and to the task of spelling out what
he is trying to convey to his heterogeneous public. This is obvious—all too
obvious for the more sensitive reader or theatergoer—at the end of *Sempronio*
when the Commissioner attempts to repossess the hero, defended now by the
townspeople, who stage a massive attack. Their loving "arms" consist only of the
word *Love*, which they hurl at all the destructive elements of dehumanization.

In answer to the critics and scholars who have censured this "artificial message" (*mensaje postizo*), as they call it, he explains that the technique is of classical origin: "Esta inevitable caída en la verdad-brusquedad que los griegos lla-
maban Aleteia, permite precisamente ese tremendo efecto del hablar puro y

simple un personaje al público, al final de la farsa. La verdad así emitida, invariablemente produce una sacudida eléctrica en el auditorio."[25]

Although *Sempronio* was written almost fifteen years ago, its message has never been more appropriate than at the present time, in that it encompasses the sentiments and revolutionary attitudes of the younger generations regarding the two issues on which they have taken a firm stand: war and love, including the fraternal love of humanity.

Para que se cumplan las escrituras ("In order that the Scriptures may be fulfilled"),[26] which marks a turning point in the creative genius of Cuzzani, revolves ad infinitum around a parody of the thirty-third year in the life of Christ. The broad satire and low comedy of the *farsátiras* give way to a more subtle, ironic treatment of the theme, revealing affinities with the Brechtian theater, rather than with the aesthetic of the absurd. Notwithstanding, Cuzzani persists in exploiting the same vein of ingenuity that labels his farces. A computer that can predict the future is as imaginative as a human being who can generate atomic energy. Just as Sempronio is dehumanized to the status of a mechanical device, so the machine in this play is elevated to a superhuman sphere: it is endowed with an electronic "brain" capable of the psychic powers traditionally attributed to the Prophets as divine intermediaries. Obviously, the premises of both plays rely on the elastic reality of a science-fiction world. However, in *Para que se cumplan las escrituras*, rather than deliberately deform reality, Cuzzani merely "stretches" our imagination regarding the already incredible accomplishments and potential of cybernetics.

By way of epigraph, Cuzzani precedes the play with passages from Luke telling how Christ, in the synagogue of Nazareth, was given the Book of Isaiah—one of the four collections of Hebrew prophecies—from which He read the following verses predicting glad tidings for the lowly and poor:

> 18—El Espíritu del Señor es sobre mí, por
> cuanto me ha enviado,
> para dar buenas nuevas a los pobres,
> me ha enviado para calmar a los heridos
> en el corazón.
> Para pregonar la Libertad a los sometidos
> y luz a los cegados.[27]

The above quote-within-a-quote (Cuzzani quotes Luke, who quotes Isaiah's prophecy) is not only the key to the theme of *Para que se cumplan las escrituras*, but also a clue to its structural complexity as a play-within-a-play.

In another epigraph to the play, Christ announces the arrival of the Messianic era: "Y [Cristo] comenzó a decirles: 'Hoy se ha cumplido esta escritura.'"[28] These words have significant bearing on the title of the play, as will be subsequently demonstrated. The Book of Isaiah (first part) likewise prophesies the birth of a child whose symbolic name is Immanuel: "Behold a virgin shall conceive and bear a son" (Isa. 7:14). Manuel, the protagonist of *Para que se cumplan las escrituras*, is the symbolic reincarnation of Christ in the Atomic Age, in which the Machine replaces successively the artisan, the gifted human biblical prophet, and, finally, God Himself.

The drama opens with the assassination of Manuel by machine gunners. His body, sustained in vertical position by a computer in the form of a cross, is discovered by Lucas. When Marcos, Mateo, and Juan appear on the scene, he asks them what has happened. The four of them proceed to enact the events culminating in Manuel's "crucifixion," thus motivating the subordinate level of drama, which (in Pirandellian fashion) contains the primary plot. This emerges as a continuous, unified flashback in chronological sequence, with only momentary reminders that a play-within-a-play is evolving, as when the "evangelists" make minimal scenery changes (in rudimentary Brechtian style), or when the two levels of reality coincide, as occurs when Juan is too inebriated to do the drunk scene (p. 37). Regardless of the different parts these narrator-actors take in the course of the dramatization, it becomes apparent that they invariably retain their personal traits and keep their original names. Mateo, for example, is addicted to the Bible, whether he takes the role of a retired employee or that of an ambitious professor; he preaches the ancient precept of man's humble obedience. On the other hand, Juan is the skeptic who deplores the history of subjugation to prophecies and other superstitions that have long inhibited man's freedom to act in the present. But he is just as nauseated by the French existentialists and their postulate of free choice. As for the future, he claims that the Computer can at best "discover" it: "El futuro está en la barriga del pasado. Eso sí es donde entra Heráclito de Efeso" (p. 39).[29] Juan tauntingly invokes the fatalism of the ancient Greek philosopher whose hypothesis—forerunner of the Nietzschean doctrine of "eternal recurrences"—explains cosmic life as an eternal fire that alternately engenders and consumes the world in infinite, regular cycles. "Todo coexiste en lo redondo que no empieza ni termina" (p. 40).[30] Marcos's capitalistic rationale typecasts him in the role of cashier or treasurer. Finally, Lucas portrays the innocuous socialist, preoccupied like Manuel with the redemption of Humanity. In short, these four "evangelists" symbolize universal attitudes in a composite society.

There exists still another level of expressionistic reality of a most subtle nature. On an idealistic or spiritual plane, the remaining characters appear *spontaneously*—each reliving his own participation (not a role) in the parody-within-the-play—the most important of which is Manuel.[31] Pedro, Tomás, and Kery (the three wise Magi or magicians) are the inventors of the novel *macchina speculatrix*, which predicts that they will surrender their complex mechanism to the carpenter-vagabond Manuel, who is furthermore "destined" to become a public enemy, ultimately to be destroyed together with the Computer on April 17 at 3:00 P.M. The scientists have no choice: to ignore the prediction would only discredit their electronic prophet—transformed into a kind of monster of Destiny, of which they are now mere slaves.

The artisan Manuel is amused by the "precious tool" whose calculations have nevertheless overlooked one essential factor: "La libertad! El hombre no es un mecanismo ciego, una cifra en una computadora! Sería gracioso que yo no pudiera hacer lo que se me dieran las ganas porque las estadísticas se oponen!" (p. 47).[32] But months of intensive computer training convert the artisan, awed by the infallibility of this machine, which, like God, holds all the answers. He rebukes the unscrupulous who would turn his Prophet Machine into a profit machine for commercial speculation, instead of seeking the answer to man's suffering: Is there any hope for humanity? What is the destiny of mankind? He defiantly pulls the master control that combines all data pertaining to man's knowledge throughout the centuries. "El velo del tiempo rasgado para que nosotros sepamos hoy todo lo que vendrá y la razón por la cual yo debería morir" (p. 59).[33] Cuzzani appeals to every imaginable resource of lighting and sound effects to build up the climactic moment devised to mirror the epigraph preceding the play. Manuel reads the Computer's message (as Christ read the prophecy of Isaiah) conveying glad tidings to the poor:

> *Manuel.* —Bienaventurados los pobres, porque de ellos es el mundo de mañana. . . . Bienaventurados los que siembran, porque ellos recogerán las mieses. . . . ¡Ay de quién levante cercos y amuralle jardines! . . . El fin de toda noche y el acabamiento de toda angustia por causa del hombre terminará en breve, y en la paz y el sosiego del tiempo, los hijos del hombre conocerán el amor.[34]
>
> [P. 67]

Manuel admonishes the covetous: "Esto es un templo y no un mercado!" With this metaphor—the Computer Lab equated to a temple—Cuzzani consummates the parallel with the epigraphic content referring to Jesus in the synagogue when He announced that the Messianic era had begun.

An anonymous enemy threatens to destroy both Manuel and the Computer unless he retracts the prophecy of social revolution. By this time the roles of the man and the machine are completely reversed. Manuel is a mechanical puppet at the command of the deified Computer. He is obsessed by the "other Manuel" of electronic conception who must die to redeem an "absurd world": "Quizá tú me ordenes: . . . ¡Muere para que todos sean dichosos y bienaventurados! ¡Muere para que se cumplan las escrituras!" (p. 73).[35]

In an orbit all her own, Estrella nevertheless forms a part of the spiritual constellation of characters who appear in the spontaneous manner previously described. More than the "star" that her name signifies—Estrella initially appears as the "lucky star" of the three Magi-inventors, and subsequently she aspires to be the "guiding star" of the Christ figure—she is, above all, a mouthpiece for the author. Convinced that man is not inevitably bound by Destiny (statistics), she uses an argument compatible with the "new humanism" of the 1960s, which, reacting against a computerized society, advances the theory that certain elements of human interaction escape calculation. Estrella takes love, for example—inspired by so many incalculable human details (often "silly" ones) that defy statistics—to show Manuel that human liberty does exist: "Si quieres preguntarme qué seguridad tengo, yo te contestaré simplemente que estoy segura porque te quiero, ¿me entiendes?" (p. 60).[36] It is fitting that cybernetic procedure be refuted by an enamored female. Especially for Cuzzani, love—with its inestimable virtues—would intensify woman's natural intuitive perception. Estrella does, in fact, fail when she tries the psychological approach by instigating a party with pizza and wine to toast Manuel's decision to live. She has inadvertently prepared his "last supper," for the would-be redeemer resolves to die—but twenty-four hours earlier than predicted, thanks to Kery (a reluctant Judas of Kerioth), who agrees to persuade the enemy to eliminate the rebel at once.

With significant variations resulting from a change in perspective, the "crucifixion" scene—part of which was initially viewed on the audience side of a closed curtain, at the beginning of the play—is now repeated in dramatic context, revealing the identity of the three gunmen. They are Marcos, Mateo, and Juan. The curtain falls when Lucas arrives asking what has happened, just as he "really" did at the beginning. This, of course, would be the cue for the whole representation to begin anew—that is, another interminable play-within-a-play-within-a-play, which would theoretically spiral to infinity.

The circular architecture of the drama reflects the cyclical course of life and events presupposed in its contents. This philosophical concept of history is, in fact, the premise on which the whole fantasy evolves. The hypothetical invention of a computer that compares, combines, and relates all existing statistical data could conceivably foretell the future only on the assumption that everything recurs in infinite cycles. Like his compatriot Jorge Luis Borges, Cuzzani exploits that theory of time according to which eternal repetitions are not identical (as Nietzsche would have them), but analogous. In the opinion of Borges, of all the possible means of interpretation, this is "el menos pavoroso y melodramático, pero también el único imaginable,"[37] and he cites Heraclitus of Ephesus as an exponent of this theory. Borges likewise mentions, in his short story "Tema del traidor y el héroe" ("Theme of the traitor and the hero"), the question of transmigration of souls. This does not imply that either of the two Argentine writers upholds these beliefs. For Borges, they provide a source of inspiration for his literary caprice. For Cuzzani, perpetual repetitions are compatible with the epic approach to drama, concerned more with transcendental themes embracing all mankind than with individual-oriented plots. Circular time annihilates the uniqueness of personality. If, as Borges points out in his essay "El tiempo circular" ("Circular time"), the number of perceptions and experiences that man can have is finite, then similar individuals and analogous destinies exist and will be repeated ad infinitum. This view explains why Cuzzani has each of the "evangelists" identify with a particular type of person, whose role he portrays while maintaining his own traits. On the other hand, also demonstrated in *Para que se cumplan las escrituras* is the example of a saint who could be an assassin in another rebirth. Finally, Manuel's aspirations and destiny, analogous to Christ's, might well be interpreted as a case of transmigration of the soul—a belief most prevalent in India but also acceptable to Plato.

Like the *farsátiras*, *Para que se cumplan las escrituras* fulfills a requisite of present-day drama: it is highly theatrical. Even though the social content continues to express concern for the common man, *Para que se cumplan* is not popular theater. Cuzzani, in this last play, achieves a complexity of dialectic concepts, symbolism, and structure, far removed from the grasp of any but an elite audience. The theme of existential choice versus cyclical destiny is illustrated in an ingenious, if irreverent, manner, with biblical figures projected into a contemporary medium of social crisis paralleling antiquity. The effect is similar to that sought by Brecht, with his use of the documentary past to draw parallels with the present. On one level of interpretation, the Computer may be seen as the super symbol of mechanization, substituting both God as the traditional center of the universe and man as the homocentric ideal of existentialism. The artisan Manuel becomes subservient to the machine, which becomes his God, his cross, and ultimately the instrument of his death (*machine* gun). But all this is only incidental to what Cuzzani is trying to say.

Manuel's death is a concession to the two concepts confronted throughout the play: the obedience of man (Mateo says, "¡Aceptar y resignarse cada uno con su cruz y el destino de dolor que le toque!" p. 79.)[38] and responsible, free choice. Manuel *accepts* his predetermined death so that the prophesied redemption of mankind will also be fulfilled. But by *choosing* to die one day ahead of schedule, he proves that man is not a mere puppet manipulated by Destiny: "Yo ordeno acelerar todo el proceso! Yo adelanto el día de la bienaventuranza y la felicidad prometida" (p. 91).[39] Obviously, his reasoning is fallacious. The Computer, so precise in spelling out the exact hour of Manuel's death, fails to even approximate the date of triumph for the poor. The world of "tomorrow" (*el mundo de mañana*), as the ambiguous prophecy calls it, when considered from the perspective of infinite time, could well be another 3,000 years away (the time elapsed since Isaiah's prophetic glad tidings). Hence, the day by which Manuel proposes to reduce the suffering of humanity would be at best an infinitesimal gain. But the most flagrant fallacy is that, in demonstrating that at will he *can* alter the date of his death, Manuel invalidates the prophetic machine, and the whole illusion is shattered. Cuzzani's message is woven into the fabric of the plot, rather than appended at the end of the play, as occurs in the *farsátiras*. The message is not cut and dry. Nevertheless, the inconclusive title is a clue: *Para que se cumplan las escrituras*—"In order that the Scriptures may be fulfilled"—man must throw off his slavish attitudes of resignation and seek the means by which to accelerate the promised felicity of mankind so that Manuel will not have died in vain.

NOTES

1. *Teatro* (Buenos Aires: Editorial Quetzal, 1960). All subsequent citations from the four *farsátiras* will refer to this edition, page references being indicated in parentheses or brackets. All translations from the Spanish are my own, except for the biblical translations in notes 27 and 28.

2. Carlos Solórzano, *Teatro latinoamericano en el siglo XX* (Mexico City: Editorial Pormaca, 1964), p. 142.

3. Shakespeare, in turn, was indebted to others for the pound-of-flesh theme, which was considerably exploited in different languages centuries before *The Merchant of Venice*. For an account of numerous and varied pre-Shakespearean versions of this plot—in verse, prose, and drama—see Bernard Grebanier, *The Truth about Shylock* (New York: Random House, 1962), chap. 4.

4. In the historic antecedents of this theme, the question of motivation was ignored. Grebanier observes that "in most of the versions of the pound-of-flesh theme, even when the creditor is not a Jew—as very often he is not—no reason is advanced for the cruelty" (Grebanier, *The Truth about Shylock*, p. 105).

5. *The Lady*. What are they giving today?

The Little Girl. Is it good, daddy?

The Gentleman. Today's program isn't all that good. Just an ordinary case of a debtor who hasn't paid. It's called fraud.

Landlord. Did you hear that? It's a case of—

Broker. I didn't hear a thing! It's prohibited. (*He shakes the manual*)

Chorus of the Jury. (*Putting their hands over their ears*) Pro-hib-it-ed! Pro-hib-it-ed! Don't let's listen, don't listen!

6. *Don Bonifacio*. . . . Believe me, I am deeply sorry. In the eighteen years that you have worked for this company, I had even grown accustomed to seeing you make Gothic letters. . . . But—(*He pats him on the back*) One's health above all, Beluver! Unfortunately we cannot change our working rules. And Gothic script is indispensable for the beautiful presentation of our commercial books. . . . But if your physician advises you to leave this job, I shall not be the one to keep you from turning in your resignation. (*He searches in his pocket*) Aside from that, I would like to express to you the gratitude of our firm for your services . . . Oh, no, it's not money, of course! I wouldn't dream of of-

fending you, a friend of the house. It is a letter of recommendation so that you can find a job. . . . And now, my dear Beluver, I do want to show you a further proof of love. *Like a father to a son.* (*He puts his hand on Beluver's shoulder*) Thusly. *God bless you, my son.*

    Public and Jury. (*In chorus*) Amen!

    7. *Chorus of Passengers.* (*Leaning over to see if the bus is coming*) There it is! No, no, it isn't! Yes, it's coming! No, no, it isn't!

    A Passenger. As long as it doesn't come late!

    Chorus. We hope it doesn't come late!

    Another. Let's make up an excuse!

    Chorus. An excuse! An excuse! That's what we need!

    Another. We'll say our mother-in-law is sick!

    Another. That a son arrived from the country!

    Another. That our wives are giving birth!

    Another. That we had to go to the doctor's!

    Another. We got a citation from the police!

    Another. And if we just said that the bus came late?

    Another. Never! That, never!

    A Passenger. No boss would ever believe that!

    Another. Bosses never believe anything!

    Chorus. (*Terrified*) Bosses, bosses, bosses!

    A Passenger. (*Looking out*) The bus! (*He runs off horrified*)

    Another. That's right. The bus. Over there, on that corner! (*Running off*)

    Another. But the bus stop is here.

    Another. No, no—beginning today the stop is over there. New ruling. (*All run off scared to death*)

    8. "I don't want anything. Let him keep his damned flesh. Let him put it back in its place. . . . I loved him *like a son!*

    9. *Usher.* The defendant has been freed. The Law doesn't care to know or try to find out anything about the private lives of the people. They are free and responsible for their acts.

    10. Grebanier, *The Truth about Shylock*, p. 101.

    11. *Una libra de carne* has been one of Cuzzani's most successful plays and has been translated, edited, or presented in Argentina, Spain, Bolivia, Uruguay, France, Czechoslovakia, Russia, Poland, East Germany, and Israel.

    12. Striking similarities between Cuzzani's actor-Hamlet and the protagonist of Pirandello's *Henry IV* are brought to light in my article "Hamlet y el concepto del 'personaje' pirandelliano en una farsa de Cuzzani," *Cuadernos Americanos* 28 (January–February 1969): 208–218.

13. Observe the customary use of two last names: Dr. Hunt Lamb (literally Caza-sola [mente] Cordero: He-hunts-only Lamb).

14. *Cabreros* (Amer.): *encabritados, enojados* ("mad," "indignant").

15. "[The tax] stipulates that whereas beggars have no tangible or intangible property, they shall collect and submit to the tax authorities, every two months, a bag of lice, which will be sacrificed in holocaust to the divinity. . . . Those who wish to enlist in the army are reminded . . . that enlistment is entirely voluntary and that those who refuse to enlist will be enlisted by force, since the police guarantee liberty of enlistment."

16. *All.* Let there be no more wars,
   let there be no more tears,
   let all be love!

   Beggar II. Tonatio! When you get to the Sun, send us a few bags of imported lice, for the tax!

   All. Let there be no more tears,
   let all be love!
   Let there be no more tears,
   let all be love!

17. "But if they have hands and face and eyes and hair and—Oh my God, and—!"

18. "They are called Americans from the Italian 'amare i cani' ["to love dogs"] because legend has it that those people have the obligation of loving the dog tyrants and despots who apparently abound in those regions."

19. "Fray Bartolomé de las Casas, Oviedo, or the Portuguese Barros doubt it, while Sabellius believes that I am an Irish pirate named Colombo Junior, and Antonio Palencia has me confused with the French navigator Casanove Coullon, and Salvador Madariaga makes it known that I am a Catalan Jew. Well, don't pay very much attention to me anyway, because, as Ruy de Pina says, I'm a big liar. I recommend that you read John Boy Tacher's work entitled 'Christophers [*sic*] Columbus: His life, His Works, His Remains.' New York, 1903, which is quite complete."

20. "I wanted to navigate westward in order to reach the horizon and enter the heavens, present myself in the House of God and tell him with my own mouth the infinite misfortunes and misery suffered by the people of this world."

21. Cuzzani follows *Los indios estaban cabreros* with an extensive epilogue— "Epílogo para críticos y bachilleres"—designed to show the logic behind this work of fantasy based on historic fact, legend, mythology, and biblical prophecy. The copious footnotes enumerating his references contain profound observations concerning various aspects that he claims the critics neglected to mention. Thus does he dismiss the Buenos Aires critics. As for the scholars, the Argentine dramatist leaves them little to ponder. If indeed he has gone to great pains to search into the past, he apparently feels that it would be quite pointless for scholars to "re-search." He therefore puts all his cards on the table and at the same time eliminates possible censure for certain changes he has made in his play. For example, he attributes to the Emperor Axayaca the despotism that actually corresponds to Moctezuma in 1491. The lice tax levied on beggars (a historical fact) likewise corresponds to Moctezuma's reign. Referring to the very axis of his plot, the Indian voyage to Spain that practically coincides with Columbus's discovery of America, Cuzzani insists: ". . . resulta lo más armónico, lógico y natural, si arrancamos de muy antiguas leyendas y mitologías hebreas, egipcias babilónicas, griegas, así como aztecas, mayas, toltecas o de todo el nahuac" (p. 179). "[The Indian voyage to Spain] is a most harmonious, logical, and natural

assumption, if we take into account ancient legends and Hebrew, Egyptian, Babylonian, Greek, as well as Aztec, Mayan, and Toltec mythologies."

22. *Sempronio* is included in Carlos Solórzano's anthology of plays: *El teatro hispano-americano contemporáneo*, 2 vols. (Mexico City: Fondo de la Cultura Económica, 1964) I, 17–62.

23. *Sempronio*. Charge! Why should I charge? It doesn't cost *me* anything. On the contrary, it's a great joy to feel united by cables to so many people who work, to so many kids at play. . . .

24. *Most Supreme Commissioner*. You don't have to discuss with electric blenders or shavers. They get repaired. . . . I'm the one who gives the orders! To men and to things. I say: Work! And they start working!

25. "Balance y confidencia del autor," in *Teatro*, p. 13. "This inevitable coming down to reality with abruptness, which the Greeks called Aleteia, is precisely what causes that tremendous impact when the character speaks to the public in a pure and simple way, at the end of the farce. The truth thus stated invariably produces an electric shock in the audience."

26. *Para que se cumplan las escrituras* (Buenos Aires: Editorial Quetzal, 1965). All subsequent citations from this play will refer to this edition.

27. "18—The Spirit of the Lord is upon me, because he hath anointed me to preach the gospel to the poor; he hath sent me to heal the brokenhearted, to preach deliverance to the captives, and recovering of sight to the blind." (St. Luke 4:18).

28. "And he began to say unto them, 'This day is this scripture fulfilled in your ears' " (St. Luke 4:21).

29. "The future is in the belly of the past. Now that's where Heraclitus of Ephesus comes in."

30. "Everything coexists in a circle that neither begins nor terminates." Cuzzani makes the most of the fact that the Fourth Gospel, attributed to the Apostle John, was written at Ephesus, probably to show the spiritual affinity or coexistence of his modern "evangelist" Juan with the ancient Greek philosopher Heraclitus of Ephesus and his hypothesis of cyclical time.

31. This is a legitimate Pirandellian device. In *Six Characters*, a seventh character spontaneously appears when needed by the other six to act out a scene of their story. However, Manuel's case is somewhat different in that he is already dead at the beginning of the play.

32. "Liberty! Man is not a blind mechanism, a mere digit in a computer! It's ridiculous to think that I couldn't do whatever I felt like doing just because the statistics show otherwise!"

33. "The veil of time rent so that we may know today what will come to pass and the reason why I ought to die."

34. "Blessed are the poor, for theirs is the world of tomorrow. . . . Blessed are those who sow the seed, for they shall reap the fields of grain. . . . Woe be to him who puts up fences and walls in gardens! . . . The end of all darkness and the termination of all anguish caused by man will soon come to pass, and in the peace and quiet of time, the sons of man shall know love."

35. "Perhaps you command me: . . . Die so that all men may be joyful and blessed! Die so that the Scriptures may be fulfilled!"

36. "If you want to ask me what assurance I have, I'll simply answer that I am sure because I love you, do you understand that?"

37. ". . . the least frightful and melodramatic, but also the only one imaginable." (Jorge Luis Borges, "El Tiempo Circular," in *Cuentos de Jorge Luis Borges* [Godfrey, Ill.: Monticello College Press, 1958], IV, 15).

38. "To accept and to resign himself each one with his cross and the destiny of grief which befalls him!"

39. "I order the whole process to be accelerated! One day ahead of time, I bring about the promised happiness and good fortune."

4. Jorge Díaz and the Liturgy of Violence

George W. Woodyard

Within the past few years, a great deal of attention has been given to the relationship of violence to the arts.[1] The novel is characterized by black humor, poetry has its guerrilla tone, film has reached new levels in assaulting our sensibilities with atrocities previously only suggested, and television has invaded the privacy of the home, bringing with it the horrors of bloodshed and war. That violence exists in the theater may be taken as another reflection of the spirit of our times. The supposition is that violence on the stage captures the horrors of our existence, thereby warning us to effect change by some other means than violence itself. If the public can be shocked out of a sense of complacency and into a state of greater awareness, then some feeling of commitment to action against a degenerating moral climate may be induced. Jorge Díaz himself has commented on this aspect of his theater, a phenomenon that he attributes to the violence he sees in the moral and natural order of the universe:

> I believe the phenomenon is captured almost in one word, "contrasts." I feel my possibilities of expressing a Latin American reality through the contrast between an absurd reality and the certainty that there exists an internal logic of events that is rejected by this absurd reality, in social as well as in cultural and economic aspects. . . . For me these contrasts are of such an extreme violence that they produce the absurd in dramatic form. And the second part of this idea is the great violence of nature. I feel in a vague way, which I cannot explain, the impact of nature, of this volcanic earth—hard, but in constant change. The violence of an extreme nature, which overcomes the possibilities of domination, or of comprehension, of man. These concepts of violence that I feel are basic to my theater. I have betrayed myself at times because it is difficult to be always consistent with oneself; nevertheless, I must say that I feel the Spanish American theater is a theater of violence, of contrast.[2]

While the common denominator of Díaz's plays may be the various forms of violence, it is the correlation of the themes and techniques that mold and elevate them into a general aesthetic. From his very early plays, Díaz shows his concern about the problems of personal interrelationships. His characters tend to be insensitive to the needs or feelings of others. Each individual, Díaz suggests, lives in a world of his own creation, oblivious to the reality of the world that surrounds him. This indifference to the feelings of others within an immediate sphere of reference creates friction and anxieties that manifest themselves, eventually, in violent forms: first in callous indifference, then ostracism, which can lead to physical violence, even murder and, on an apocalyptic level, to world destruction. In order to capture indifference, Díaz uses aspects of humor and irony, special effects (lighting, movement, sound and music, staging), and especially language.

The importance of language in the contemporary theater cannot be stressed too much. In the twentieth century, the discrepancy between a tangible reality and language sufficient to express it has been the touchstone of novelists, poets, and dramatists alike. Since James Joyce, the language of the novel has been altered radically. One of the most significant features of the theater of the absurd is its radical use of language. Instead of filling a logical capacity of man's ability to communicate his thoughts and emotions, the theater of the absurd is characterized by a lack of logic and an insufficiency to communicate this reality. At the same time we are bombarded by the noise pollution of the age—radio, television, endless commercials, and certain kinds of music.

The techniques that have come to characterize Díaz's works were already evident in his early plays. In *El cepillo de dientes* (1961, "The toothbrush")[3] the two characters, El and Ella, play out a ritual in the game of life. In order to escape the monotony of their existence, they invent situations, presumably with daily variations, which culminate in violence. Díaz calls them "náufragos en el parque de atracciones"—two lonely, isolated beings in a circus-like world. Like tangential circles, their lives turn and overlap through marriage, but like the *tíovivo* of the circus, it is a merry-go-round existence with bizarre emotional experiences, cyclical in action as well as in structure.

In act I the action follows the couple through a sequence of scenes that emphasize their failure to communicate, culminating in his discovery that she has used his toothbrush, the ultimate symbol of his individuality, to whiten her shoes. Infuriated, he "kills" her. She returns in act II, disguised as the cleaning woman. The sequence continues, this time culminating in a violent sexual scene, followed by her "killing" him. In a final scene, they have survived, to repeat the game on another day.

The question of identity, symbolized by the toothbrush, manifests itself through various techniques of language and scenic effects. The dichotomy in their life styles is apparent from the beginning: the stage set is furnished, left and right, with contradictory furniture styles, a feature that produces tension even before the action begins. After the death of Ella at the end of act I, the set is rotated 180 degrees; the inversion implies a reversal and provides a clue to the subsequent action. At the moment of sexual encounter, the couple's differences are minimized; in the violence of the scene they destroy objects without being aware of it. From that point until the end of the play, the progressive destruction of the set indicates that it has served its symbolic function and is no longer important to a metaphoric statement of their differences. The final stage effects rely on lighting to focus on the exteriorization of their emotional states; the lighting of the funeral candelabra signals the end of this cycle. On the next day they will rise, phoenixlike, to repeat the cycle.

These staging effects, including the music (her jazz and his tangos), serve to intensify in symbolic form their individual differences explicit in the dialogue. Different kinds of linguistic and rhetorical phenomena support this theme. Their "dialogue" generally consists of two intercalated monologues. On occasion, the two characters talk in absurd fashion without being aware of a completely different point of reference (e.g., "cream" used for the face or for coffee). They coin words (*muérdago, mandrágora*) to insult each other when the shock value of traditional language seems insufficient. They use expressions from foreign languages with exotic sounds for certain phonetic effects. They invent proverbs that imitate the rhythm and syntax of the language but that are essentially meaningless. They use dictionary definitions to define complex realities. Throughout, the language has a deliberately clichéd quality that imitates the mechanization of contemporary life. The opening scene from a radio soap opera sets the tone for this vacuous language, characterized by commercials and slogans. This linguistic foreplay points up the inadequacy of conventional language to express a complex reality. The epitome of such absurdity is the attempt at the end of the play to reduce the complexities of human experience to a single word ("una palabra bien sencilla que lo explica y lo arregla todo").[4] The intervention of the outside world destroys the attempted moment of perfection, and the response echoes the opening word of *Ubu Roi*—"mierda."

The question of communication ultimately goes beyond this level, however. The two characters fail to communicate, but not always or simply because they lack the necessary means. Actually, they are involved in a very elaborate game in order to avoid communication. The rules are mutually understood: they write letters to each other by way of the newspaper, they talk at each other and each fails to listen. What is the function of these elaborate devices? They seem to constitute a defense system to conceal fear. Real communication involves a giving of self, a revealing of the soul, a lowering of defenses to the point that another can penetrate to the essence of one's being. As Harold Pinter once said: "I feel that instead of any inability to communicate there is a deliberate evasion of communication. Communication itself between people is so frightening that rather than do that there is continual cross-talk, a continual talking about other things, rather than what is at the root of their relationship."[5]

Díaz achieves other interesting effects through irony. The anonymity of the relationship between these two married persons is reflected in their names—El and Ella. She cannot remember his name, and he uses several to identify her, all of which she rejects as improper. Consuelo, Mercedes, and Amelia, plus several others, are names that connote tenderness and compassion, an ironic usage that belies her destructive nature. The characterization through furniture and music are not, however, either pejorative or ironic—to suggest, for example, that he is old-fashioned and therefore out of tune with her world. They are rather symbols of personal preferences and therefore individual differences. (Both Spanish and Danish furniture were *de rigueur* in Chile in the early 1960s.) Several scenes do depend upon irony, however, for their effectiveness: El reads in the newspaper the account of a strangulation with a transistor radio antenna immediately after having strangled his wife in the same manner; he announces *his* pregnancy to the maid; the maid "discovers" the body of Ella in the bedroom as he sings a Gardel tango that mourns the loss of his loved one. A rather complex phenomenon occurs at the beginning of act II: for the theater audience, El's oblique references to Ella's death in his conversation with the maid would seem ironic, but a double irony emerges when it becomes apparent that the maid *is* Ella, following the rules of the game. The reader of the play does not share in this nuance, since the stage directions reveal the maid's identity. A related feature is the distancing effect achieved by the characters speaking directly to the audience, acknowledging their presence (end of act I) or to the stage crew (end of act II), imploring them to stop dismantling the set.

Díaz combines these techniques in a coordinated system in which the language is appropriate to the situation. The result is a very funny play; the humor is sometimes grotesque, sometimes linguistic, sometimes situational, but the effectiveness of communicating the message is undeniable. Díaz's characters may suffer from an incapacity to communicate, but Díaz himself does it very ably.

In the same year (1961) Díaz premiered another play with a cyclical structure, *Requiem por un girasol* ("Requiem for a sunflower"). The setting is a funeral home for domestic animals, of which Sr. Linfa is the proprietor. Linfa is a grotesque figure who sustains himself economically and emotionally on death. He says: "Es reconfortante ver cómo las cosas se pudren inexorablemente. Cada grieta que descubro en las cosas me hace revivir."[6] Birth and the regenerative elements of nature do not interest him; he is characterized by his fetish for used clothing (belonging to the dead), his name (colorless lymph fluid), his ghoulish materialism, and his unctuous mannerisms.

The play deals with life and death in a metaphorical sense. The fact that Linfa draws his sustenance from death precludes an interest in life; his consuming and morbid interest in death emphasizes his complete indifference toward the living. As the repulsive central figure of the play, Linfa stands as an indictment against his own position, which is suggested by a line from a poem by Vicente Huidobro found on the title page: "Cuida de no morir antes de tu muerte."[7]

In contrast to Linfa is the position represented by Manuel, Linfa's assistant. His value system is predicated on flowers, the simple pleasures of the country, and the excitement of becoming a father. When Linfa refuses his request for a salary advance, he responds to the music of a circus parade and quits his job. Frail and undernourished, weakened by protest, he collapses and dies at the end of act I, ironically at the moment that his son's birth is announced.

If act I serves to present Manuel in life, where he has a very low profile in comparison with Linfa, act II serves to regenerate his presence after death. The boy who replaces Manuel as the assistant is also named Manuel; Linfa begins the ritual of robotizing him, just as he had done earlier with Manuel. The boy exhibits traits of sensitivity similar to those of Manuel, including responsiveness to the distant sound of the circus music. Other scenes also serve to revive the memory of Manuel: Sebo, the junk dealer, returns the first Manuel's clothing to Linfa; in a spiritist scene they attempt to invoke the return of Manuel. At one point in the séance, in which the boy *is* Manuel, Linfa chides him: "La historia empieza ahora para ti, en el segundo acto."[8] The final scene of the play, in which Linfa concedes to provide a decent burial for Manuel (in a grotesque coffin designed for a giraffe), emphasizes even more his presence through the grief of the widow, the ceremony in the cemetery, the tombstone, and the ironic testimonial of Linfa in which his ubiquitous hypocrisy seems to betray him: "Pero Manuel vive y vivirá entre nosotros."[9] Thus, the vital force of Manuel, who his wife claims is only sleeping, stresses the affirmation of life as a cyclical process. Paradoxically, Manuel seems more dead than alive in the first act and more alive than dead in the second act, where his presence and his memory resuscitate others.

At the end the Linfas and the plastic-flower vendors of the world have ostensibly overcome, but on a subtler plane the symbolism bodes for an optimistic future. Manuel's child is to be named Girasol after the sunflower seeds that Manuel was constantly eating. Through the final scene it rains, giving precious life to germinate the flower seeds. Linfa, finally, is converted into a completely grotesque figure (ironically like a circus clown) to participate in another burial. The height (or perhaps, depth) of the ridiculous occurs when he dumps Manuel's body out of the coffin in order to give the coffin back to the giraffe. In an ontological sense, Linfa survives through the secret of the "grandes vicios"—that is, a complete lack of responsibility for his actions—but Manuel has the essence of life, which will result in a regenerative cycle.

El velero en la botella (1962, "The ship in the bottle") is a three-act play dealing with the problems of incommunication, insensitivity, and dehumanization. Young David is mute—an escape mechanism from a household in which talk is cheap but communication is priceless. His father is a ham-radio fan, and the two identical aunts (they are as "different as two drops of water") share each other's words as if they were sharing the same minimal I.Q. A marriage is arranged between David and Emiliana as a form of concubinage; her grotesque millionaire parents (Mr. and Mrs. Tudor) describe her as a Tudor-style commode. To describe Emiliana and to sell her as a piece of furniture is as dehumanizing as David's escape—as if he were a ship in a bottle. David is the victim of the others' egocentric desires, but the love of Rocío, the maid, enables him to overcome his affliction. Rocío, his link with the outside world, has a profound influence on him. He begins to reflect on his withdrawal and to consider facing up to life. "Pensaba ¿cómo se mete un velero en una botella? Ahora lo sé. Primero hay que salir de la botella."[10] When he succeeds in talking, however, he expresses his anger and the need for revenge. Desperately he tries to communicate with his father and aunts, who fail to respond (or even to understand him). In ultimate despair, David commits suicide.

The techniques of the language in this play are well suited to the theme. As in *El cepillo de dientes*, no real communication or personal identification takes place because the conversations exist on two or more levels at once. The language is characterized by clichés and slogans: the aunts are classic examples of patterned talk with overtones of a litany, while the father is attuned to the blips and squeaks of his radio rather than to the needs of his son. David, on the other hand, is overwhelmed by the power of the word. For him, "es como tener la clave de las cosas, la que abre todos los misterios."[11] In this archetypal system, naming the thing carries the power to cause it to happen. If "agua" releases a flood and "viento" a windstorm, then by analogy his one-word summation of reality for his father, "muerte," reflects the poison in his soul and is predictive of the end. Díaz's epigram for this play is again a line from Huidobro, which emphasizes the power of communication: "Tengo una palabra fabulosa en medio de la lengua."[12]

In 1963 Díaz premiered *El lugar donde mueren los mamíferos* (*The Place Where the Mammals Die*), a work dealing with the superficiality and egocentricity of personal motivations, amplified through the setting of a charitable organization.[13] The Instituto Ecuménico de Asistencia Total is in danger of extinction, since it has performed so well that no more poverty cases are to be found. At this point, however, the needs of the benefactors begin to exceed the needs of the indigent. A victim must be found in order to protect the integrity of the institution and to continue to salve the collective conscience of those for whom charity work represents an escape from valid social responsibilities. Chatarra, the very essence of poverty, is discovered by the Institute in the nick of time. Any doubt remaining about the Institute's motives is quickly dissolved—the interest is not in helping Chatarra but in self-adulation. After cursory interrogations about his life, the Institute personnel immediately begin to plan his elaborate coming-out ceremony. Act II is an extension and intensification of the process of annihilating Chatarra. During an absurd presentation of absurd gifts, his real need—food—is completely ignored. Some months later, the staff devises individual plans to continue the exploitation, one of which is to use him as a watchdog (reminiscent of Dragún's *Historias para ser contadas*). In desperation, Chatarra hangs himself. Once again, the life of the Institute is threatened, until the directors think to preserve Chatarra's body to use in weekly burial services, thus showing to the world their on-going concern for the needy.

This play is neither as rich in symbolism nor as subtle in nuance as the previous plays, but it does continue the irony, the grotesque humor and situations, the linguistic experimentation, and especially the preoccupation with a system of morality. Like his other characters, these demonstrate the same shallowness of character, the unthinking automatism, and the institutionaliza-tion of their activities. Justo and María Piedad carry on an illicit love affair, María Piedad and Asunta claw at one another with their catty comments, while Chatarra's needs, like those of Manuel in *Requiem por un girasol*, go unattended. In the dump where he lived he enjoyed laughter and companion-ship, but in his new "protected" state, he is bitterly unhappy, sacrificed to the system. The situation is identical to that of Sr. Linfa who manifestly derived life from the dead; in this case the Institute survives through the death of Chatarra. At the end of this play, when Arquímedes uncovers many new indigents, the Institute staff confirms its absolute perversion by showing no interest; they continue to focus on Chatarra, long since dead. That the death of Chatarra has had no emotional impact upon them is demonstrated structurally by the fact that the play ends as it began, with the essential difference that the subject of Justo's public lecture deals not with the dangers of contamination by the dung fly but rather by mammals, such as Chatarra, contaminated with poverty.[14]

The ritualistic aspects seen in the previous plays are even more pronounced in *La víspera del degüello* (1965, "The eve of the execution"), a short one-act play known also as *La vigilia del degüello* and subtitled *El génesis fue mañana*.[15] Unlike *Requiem por un girasol*, in which the symbolism holds out some hope for the future, in this *acto homicida* all hope is eradicated through a series of nihilistic attitudes and events. The play has an apocalyptic quality; the cataclysmic event that caused the destruction described by Hosanna and Custodio at the beginning of the play is repeated in microcosm in the rest of the work.

The bare stage represents the emptiness remaining after the total destruction of the world. La Pioja drags in rubble (*chatarra*), symbolic of the ruins of a materialistic society, in a visual image suggestive of a grotesque bird building a nest. She is pregnant, mysteriously and perhaps miraculously. At least we know that the only man remaining is impotent under Hosanna's influence. La Pioja conveys a savage, animalistic nature, full of passion and sexuality. She does not speak, but her presence increases the tension and serves as the catalyst to the action.

Hosanna, ludicrously dressed in a ravaged wedding gown, is a distorted bride; she is perhaps a parody of the Church (the bride of Christ), as well as a parody of the praise to God that her name suggests. Her motivation is to lead Custodio in search of Paradise, but her concept of morality fails to consider the reality of the world around her and is therefore useless. We would not expect more; when Custodio explains things to her, she understands the words but not the concepts. She is violent and provokes Custodio—because of her barrenness and envy—to murder the pregnant la Pioja. Custodio is somewhat enigmatic; at times he seems to be the existential man caught between normal emotional responses and Hosanna's warped sense of morality. His reluctance to kill la Pioja, however, is not on moral grounds but rather because he will lose his *chatarra*. Hosanna is able to convince him that this sacrifice will absolve them of guilt. After he kills la Pioja, who is the last chance for survival of the human race, he also kills Hosanna in a final fit of ironic justice. Nothing remains, except that he is now ironically the custodian of an empty baby carriage and a garbage dump of remains from a materialistic society.

The play is a grotesque parody of conventional morality, as Díaz sees it, in biblical and apocalyptic terms. The epigram from Genesis 1:5 is repeated in Custodio's final words: "Anocheció, y luego amaneció: primer día del mundo."[16] La Pioja is a procreative force, but she collects *chatarra* and is eventually destroyed by it, *chatarra* that Custodio was willing to put before the promise of human life (the repopulation of the world). The murder of la Pioja is performed as a religious sacrament, with aspects of liturgical service, followed by the blessing with the holy water. It is doubly ironic that Custodio uses the same bottle of holy water, now broken, in order to carry out the killing of Hosanna.

Time functions here in a curious manner. In *El cepillo de dientes* and *Requiem por un girasol*, time appeared to be cyclical. This play has an atemporal quality, or, perhaps, an ambivalent time aspect in which the two sides cancel each other. The action moves forward while the search for the origins of man continues in the past. Hosanna and Custodio cannot agree on how long ago something happened, yet Custodio relates, minute by minute, the details of his life. This ambivalence is captured in the subtitle, *El génesis fue mañana*. In this apocalyptic state, time has ceased to exist.

The aspects of violence and the concern about social injustices apparent in Díaz's dramaturgy reached new levels of artistic expression in *Topografía de un desnudo* ("Topography of a nude") written in 1965 and premiered in Havana in 1966.[17] Inspired by a historical incident involving the massacre of a group of Brazilian *favelados*, the play incorporates mixed media, complicated temporal sequences, and a documentary flavor.

The action of the play takes place in a garbage dump on the outskirts of town, inhabited by a group of slum dwellers. An investigation into the death by drowning of Rufo, the central figure, leads into a series of events that reveal his history and especially his relationship with the police. Educated and literate, Rufo is a classic misfit—the indigents consider him to be a stool for the police, yet he is killed for refusing to cooperate with the police in a plan to clear the slum area. Don Clemente, a powerful newspaper publisher, had bought the area for speculative purposes, and he manipulates the governor, the police force, and his own staff of reporters in order to accomplish his goals. The police corporal San Lucas is killed, ostensibly as an act of revenge by the indigents for the death of Rufo but actually by Clemente in order to incite the police into reprisals against the poor, who, ill-equipped to defend themselves against the superior forces of the police, are subsequently exterminated. Thus, don Clemente, having eradicated the nuisance, can proceed with his plan to improve the property with a housing development. The ruthlessness of his actions and his absolute indifference to the human suffering or loss of life involved set the tone of the play. Given the theme, the play might have degenerated into unmitigated propaganda, but Díaz's artistic handling of the technical aspects elevate it to a work of art.

The central image of the work is contained in the title itself, a curious juxtaposition of two apparently unrelated terms, but a study of the topography—that is, the superficial, impersonal level—leads eventually to a penetration of the events surrounding Rufo's violent death. In the process, the nudity correlates both with the revelation of the facts as well as with the degrading and humiliating treatment of Rufo. The play is one of strong contrasts in language, sound, movement, and especially lighting. The contrastive lighting (black and white) focuses spots on actors performing in a stark light while other actors witness events from the dark shadows and recesses of the stage. The slides and films, also in black and white, are not realistic depictions of the events or people but rather are designed with an expressionistic nature intended to evoke appropriate reactions in the audience (discomfort, sympathy, horror, etc.). While complementing the action on stage, the slides and films serve two basic functions: to facilitate the presentation of some scenes difficult to accomplish because of the physical limitations of the theater, and to heighten the emotional experience for the public, as these projections acquire an abstract quality that corresponds to their larger-than-life size.

Díaz's concern for time structure was earlier evident in *El cepillo de dientes*, *Requiem por un girasol*, and *La víspera del degüello*, but *Topografía de un desnudo* is his most accomplished example of this technique. The functionaries (*notario, meteorólogo, topógrafo*) comment on specific times and dates, both in chronological as well as astrological terms, but the more complex form embraces both a projection toward the past (memory and flashback) and a timeless state in which the dead can function. Rufo—his return is unexplainable in conventional terms—enjoys the greatest temporal mobility, since he can function in all levels simultaneously. Abelardo as a journalist stimulates the transition from present to past; his investigation serves as the catalytic element that leads to the discovery of Rufo's death in a way resembling a filmed sequence run backwards.

Thus, the slides and films play an integral role in that each segment of retrospective vision leads to an understanding and greater appreciation of the conglomerate of events.

Clemente promotes all the action of the play; at the moment of maximum tension, when Rufo accuses him of San Lucas's death, Clemente takes strong action: "Sé que ya habías muerto...¡pero te mataría otra vez si fuera necesario!"[18] That is, Clemente not only precipitated Rufo's death the first time, but also ironically he "kills" him a second time when he is threatened with exposure. Thus, the movement of the play is that of discovering the "naked" truth, accomplished through the tension between the present and the memory or obliteration of these people and events.

While *El cepillo de dientes* led us to see the absurdity of existence in a humorous vein and with room for personal interpretation, *Topografía de un desnudo* strikes us with the barbarism of the characters and the violence of their motives and actions. Rufo (a name for a dog) is completely dehumanized in his contacts, whether with his own social class or higher. He is stripped during the police investigation and forced to behave like a dog, so we are struck by the irony that others (especially la Teo) show greater indignation over the killing of Canela, his dog, than over Rufo himself. The irony of all the characters' names is striking: don Clemente, who shows nothing of clemency; San Lucas, who has little of the saint and much of the devil; la Teo and la Monja, Rufo's prostitute friends; Comandante Blanco, whose spirit is black, not white. The linguistic play of Díaz's earlier works has been suppressed here in favor of a more serious presentation. The media projections, including the sounds (the theme song of Rufo, the flow of the river, the dog barks, the shots—even the silence), reinforce our emotive responses. At the same time, Díaz introduces techniques both alienating and involving, which induce an intellectual reaction—the forms of direct address and the use of media.

Esquema para una indagación inútil, the subtitle, reveals the basic orientation of the play: the functionaries conduct a pointless investigation into Rufo's death, which reveals that the poor have been maligned and eventually eradicated in order to serve the ends of the rich. The poor achieve some level of understanding and attempt to resist, but too late. As Abel explains: "Pero cuando uno quiere empezar a gritar, ya es demasiado tarde y se encuentra cerrado en una campana de vacío."[19] If public apathy continues to predominate in the face of such atrocities, there is little hope for the future of mankind.

Jorge Díaz was born in Rosario, Argentina in 1930, the son of Spanish parents. He early became a naturalized Chilean and spent his formative years in and around Santiago, receiving his formal training in architecture. A long-time interest in the theater developed into a closer relationship and eventually a new career when he was asked to design the scenography for a local theater production. Since 1960 he has dedicated himself completely to the theater as playwright, director, actor, set designer, impresario, and lecturer. Overwhelmed by pressures and administrative duties, he fled to Spain in January of 1965, seeking the solitude that he considered essential to his writing. *Topografía de un desnudo*, written during his first year of residency in Madrid,[20] marks a second stage in his dramatic production. His disillusionment with the theatergoing public, their indifference, their disposition toward easy entertainment with laughter but their reluctance to examine issues or to make a commitment toward social improvement, caused him to modify his techniques if not the objectives of his dramaturgy. The sophisticated nature, the clever language, the highly structured designs, and the carefully integrated imagery and symbolism of his earlier plays is gradually replaced by more direct presentations. His cynicism appeared to increase in direct proportion to audience apathy. Whereas *El cepillo de dientes* is humorous *and* thought-provoking, the later plays, beginning with *Topografía de un desnudo*, tend to be more serious and straightforward, even didactic.

Introducción al elefante y otras zoologías ("Introduction to the elephant and other zoologies"), presented by the ICTUS theater group in May 1968, is a politically and socially committed piece, divided into segments in an episodic nature that focus on different aspects of and attitudes toward revolutionary behavior. Instead of characters within a drama, the dramatis personae are "actors" who fulfill certain roles—soldier, guerrilla, or other. Containing overtones of the documentary theater, the piece relies on simulated newscasts in order to give a flavor of authenticity to the events under consideration. Plot has generally been subordinated to theme.

Each segment is introduced by an appropriate sign; the common denominators are corruption, venality, and apathy. The various scenes are linked with certain Latin American revolutionary heroes—Che Guevara, Régis Debray, Camilo Torres, plus other lesser-known figures. In the first scene, two mercenaries kill their commanding officer after he takes money from a dead guerrilla and spends it on prostitutes, ignoring the pleas of a poverty-stricken old woman. The smooth transition from the machine-gun fire of the killing to the Telex news report of the event underscores Díaz's craft in scenic effects. Later, the President of the country is interrupted during his stirring national message by a telephone call from the United States, offering money, which he happily accepts.

The various scenes illustrate different aspects of the situation: the Latin American is generally seen with a subservient, bootlicking mien toward the omniscient Yankee, the omnipresent CIA, and the (once) omnipotent dollar. The North American is characterized as a Spanglish-speaking dolt who buys his way into power. Considerable attention is given to the technique of torture, including the description of a machine that not only clears away the blood and gore but also converts the cries of anguished torture into religious hymns. One crucial aspect of the torture scene is the reaction by the revolutionaries as they disintegrate into abulia. They discuss the problem, their obligation to intervene, the need for instant response; they quote Lenin, Marx, Castro, Debray, and others; they draft statements; they discuss the need for a subcommittee report—in short, they do nothing, until finally the cries of the tortured prisoner are no longer heard, and it is too late. A sign appears: "El Che Guevara ha muerto."[21]

The prevailing attitude on the part of the Latin Americans of the play is one of apathy, and most of the scenes illustrate this characteristic in one way or another. The Archbishop pleads for resignation, patience, complacency, submission to authority; one "actor" explains how he was promoted through the ranks until he became an executive with the International Development Bank, at which point he began to think in terms of his new "maturity"; the emasculated Puerto Rican conjures up a vision of the good life in New York, free of discrimination. The most telling moments come at the end of the play, first when the emissary of the President of the United States presents the average Latin American citizen with "La Orden de la Pasividad," and later when a group of actors onstage, pretending to form a part of the audience, remain seated during the résumé of the call to action.

The play speaks effectively to this issue—that is, that Latin America wastes away, ignoring the example of its revolutionary heroes, enslaved to North American political and economic policies, ignoring the needs of its people, while corruption, venality, and a willingness to accept economic assistance from the United States compromises its goals. Díaz is obviously trying to jolt the complacent public out of its own apathy and passivity by insisting on scenes with strong emotional impact. The integration of music captures the mood of each segment of the play, including the instructions that some social-message songs should be played in the lobby during intermission. The words are included, although not the music (guitar is specified). At the end of the play, the music functions on a double plane with the verses showing the imperialist attitude, while the *estribillo* invites consideration of the revolutionary movement. The play, although much less subtle than *Topografía de un desnudo*, presents an interesting mixture of techniques and succeeds in achieving a feeling of universality. It is not bound to a particular country or problem but rather speaks to the problems of the masses who have, for whatever reasons, failed to unite in the face of oppression and exploitation.

After the incursion into works seriously committed to an expression of the political and social climate of Latin America, especially vis-à-vis the United States, Díaz returns to the familiar form of the comedy in *Liturgia para cornudos* (1969, "Liturgy for cuckolds"). The play nearly defies description. Díaz's irrepressible humor surfaces again in this piece, replete with its black humor, exaggerations, distortions, and absurdist features. A clue to an interpretation of the play lies in a remark made by the principal character: "A menudo uno se pregunta hasta qué punto está interpretando la realidad correctamente."[22] Díaz stretches our imagination to new limits. The images multiply and are compounded in abstract forms, leaving the central dramatic question very much in doubt. The result is a collage, incorporating fragments from such varied sources as Sigmund Freud, Camilo José Cela, Chumy Chumez, Robert Rius, and modern-day commercials. In an interview, Díaz has admitted to a fanciful impulse when writing the play: "In this work I give free rein to a series of images, free associations, and humorous situations that seemed to me to be useful in untangling a series of communication problems between human beings and for the analysis of solitude. The work is interesting to me, not so much for the theme (which I really cannot pinpoint), but for the existence of a series of instinctive, subconscious clues."[23]

The play has a very visceral quality, evident not only in the title itself but also especially in the subtitle, *Regurgitación en dos flatos*, in which the "flatos" serve as acts. The language is both comical and pungent. Although the strength of the play lies in its affective nature, the scant story line involves two principal characters, Gala and Castor, who remind us of the lovable couple of *El cepillo de dientes*. Their primitive emotions and basic urges suggest a relationship with the characters from Valle-Inclán's *Retablo de la avaricia, la lujuria y la muerte*. Gala involves the various men (all played by the same actor) who pass through her life in increasingly explicit sexual terms. She first embraces the TV repairman; she plays striptease (in reverse) with the clergyman; she makes love to the meter reader in the coffin in which Castor has placed her after she has "died" during a cannibalistic love act. The play has a bit of everything—adultery, necrophilia, homosexuality—but in spite of these perversions, it is not offensive because of the humor, which succeeds in counterbalancing or even negating any serious purpose. Many of the scenes are patently absurd: at the beginning Gala goes into labor, and, when the TV repairman enters, the couple treat him as their newborn child. While Rosano is cuckolding Castor, the latter prays a very original litany before the offending couple.

Díaz's usual preoccupations with time, problems of communication, basic emotions, and violence are not lacking. The violence seems to surpass all previous manifestations in a macabre and ludicrous scene in which Gala and Castor, performing an autopsy on the fourth intruder (Apolo), drag his bloody entrails across the stage. Castor remarks: "Bien miradas las cosas, la violencia que contesta a la violencia genera siempre una nueva violencia."[24] While the end of the play contends that the work contains a serious social message, the ultimate effect is countermanded by the overall tone of levity. This is the case even though we can accept seriously Gala's (or Díaz's) admonition that working in a literacy program is more useful than dissipating one's energy in adultery or harassment of one's fellow man.

The search for adequate linguistic forms to express the ubiquitous problems of oppression, social injustices, and communication that dominated Díaz's works inspired him to write an essay on the subject, "La erosión del lenguaje."[25] After *Introducción al elefante*, he admitted a temptation simply to remain silent, since all the formulas of conventional language, while acceptable in a day-to-day existence, became intolerable for him in the theater. *Liturgia para cornudos* represented the effort to turn the mechanical quality of the previous expression—the intentional clichés of the early pieces had themselves become clichéd in this context—into a dehumanized language.

In 1969, Díaz achieved the ultimate in dehumanization (short of a completely nonverbal theater) by writing a very brief piece in "nonlanguage," that is, in "words" that correspond to the phonological requirements of Spanish, arranged in "sentences" with orthodox connectors that fulfill the obligations of normal Spanish syntactical patterns. *La orgástula* ("The orgastule") has, paradoxically, a sterile quality and a highly emotive quality at the same time, a contrast that produces tension and leads to a violent ending. The stage directions call for an absolutely white set—white walls and floor (which fuse together) and white dress for all the characters (the little boy in his period costume, the Nuns, and especially the two principal characters bound together in a continuous strip of bandage, like mummies). No color or movement distracts from the focus on the two characters (Man and Woman) who face each other in a strangely erotic scene, uttering "words" with connotations of sensuality through analogy with known words in Spanish or other languages. (Díaz notes that in "inventing" words, he accidentally duplicated existing words in Catalan, Italian, and Basque.) The stage directions also indicate tones ranging from the tender and affectionate through the confused and disconcerted to the passionate, urgent, and finally violent. After the culminating moment, which is marked by a piercing scream, the Boy unwraps the bandages to reveal that the Man and Woman have stabbed one another. The long silence following the build-up to the previous tension serves as a hiatus before the final anticlimactic Gregorian chant, entoned by the two Nuns and echoed by "un coro de voces blancas muy lejano."[26] Even the voices are *white* in this sterile atmosphere.

The ritualistic aspects of the work are evident in the stylized movements (or in the mummification), the unintelligible dialogue that relies on tonal and affective qualities, the sharp contrasts of the stark white set accented by the blood red of the knifings, and the violent screams followed by the mournful liturgy. These features produce an interesting experiment in the potential expression of primitive emotions without the trappings of conventional theater, but as a model for a new direction the play was not successful. As Díaz remarked: "Naturally the result was an entertaining and suggestive game but one impossible to repeat a second time. I was once again in the trap."[27]

La pancarta ("The poster") is another brief work in which Díaz continues to search for an adequate expression of contemporary problems. Written in 1970, this one-act play depicts the radical division between the social classes—the haves and the have-nots, the exploiters and the exploited. El Señor and la Dama discourse in stentorian tones about their revolutionary stance and the need for social reform. Simultaneously they ride their servants—literally, as if they were animals—a highly visible and dramatic action that negates completely their petty concessions to the servants' freedom and the feeble protestations that they are allowed. While the masters are distracted by the anarchical behavior of their children protesting the old social order, the servants have an opportunity to rebel, but they are unable to use it to good advantage. Instead of breaking the bonds of slavery, they merely attempt to enslave each other. "Lo único seguro es que después que alguien nos defiende termina montándose sobre nosotros."[28] The old cycle is thus repeated, just as Azuela presented it in *Los de abajo*; the underprivileged who do succeed in rising through the ranks undergo a change in their value system and become the oppressors in the new order. As in *Introducción al elefante*, the revolutionaries are ineffective, indecisive, uncertain of their goals, and therefore subject to further oppression. El Señor and la Dama manage to turn division and disorganization to their own advantage. Plácido, the servant, is true to his name: he follows the instructions of his master and is exploited even while trying to be rebellious.

The servants on all fours serve as a metaphorical statement of their subjugation, just as their attempt to rise to a standing position is indicative of their opposition. The play is deliberately open-ended, as the servant vacillates between standing in an expression of his free will or crawling at his master's command. In the final scene the four actors face the audience and sing, "¿Cómo terminar esta obra, amigos?"[29] suggesting at least the possibility for change. The violence "within the law and established order" condoned by el Señor culminates in the killing of one servant by the other in a final dramatic indication not only of their failure to collaborate in protesting the system but also of the reassertion of domination by the upper class. Although the ending is ambiguous, the division between the classes is amply illustrated by the techniques of the play. The servant parrots the master's words and ideas, jumbling the syntax in order to show the emptiness of the concepts to the downtrodden lower class. The posters give the servants the feeling of an important form of protest, but the slogans that they carry are engineered by the masters to render them completely ineffective. Díaz engages in his usual linguistic play (fourteen virtually consecutive words beginning with "sub-" emphasize the subjugation of the servants), and the verse sections provide musical interludes not only to entertain but also especially to deliver the social message through another dimension. The play is, in short, indicative of Díaz's total commitment to a radical theater, in which character presentation is minimal and expression of the central idea dominant.

Since 1970, Díaz has continued to maintain his position as social activist in the theater. As actor in and director of the Teatro del Nuevo Mundo, he has carried ideas of political and social reform throughout the hemisphere. His *Americaliente* ("Hotamerica") is a montage of sketches that comment on different aspects of Latin American social reality. The scenes include documentary presentations on the genocide of Indians in Brazil, student repression in Guatemala, political persecution in Paraguay, the militarization of Latin America, the role of the clergy, United States foreign policy in Latin America, and others. What the long-range effect of this political stance will be on his dramatic production, of course, remains to be seen, but for the moment his disposition toward writing has been significantly affected. As he explains: "Personally, great works do not interest me. The important thing is the present, to communicate with the community where I live, to clarify and illuminate zones of human behavior. . . . What seems critical to me now is to make a theater of urgency, of immediate testimony, as a commentary on reality. A functional and direct theater, which is tied to well-determined local events. To do this I use living material related to Latin America."[30]

Since his earliest plays, Díaz has dealt with the demeaning or dehumanizing elements that prevent the realization of a full life. Class conflicts and problems of personal communication impair the happiness of the individual and impede the acquisition of his goals. Discrimination and social injustices (i.e., the mistreatment of the poor and the exploitation of their freedoms and privileges for economic or political reasons) are recurring themes. The setting of his plays is often the garbage dump, a metaphor for life among the lower classes, and the resolution of the conflict is generally achieved through violence—murder or suicide. Within these frameworks, basic emotions and behavioral responses tend to acquire an archetypal quality that elevates the plays through liturgical expression to the level of ritual. Throughout his work, Díaz has shown himself to be an inveterate experimenter, constantly searching for new forms, scenic devices, and language to express his vision of the world and an ever-changing reality.[31]

NOTES

1. See, among others, Martin Esslin, "Violence in Modern Drama," in *Reflections: Essays on Modern Theatre* (New York: Doubleday, 1971), pp. 159–175.

2. José Monleón, "Diálogo con Jorge Díaz," *Apuntes*, no. 61 (August 1966), pp. 8–9. This and all subsequent translations from the Spanish, except note 11, are my own.

3. In *Teatro*, ed. José Monleón (Madrid: Taurus, 1967), pp. 113–152. Originally written as a one-act play, Díaz rewrote it in two acts as it appears in this edition.

4. ". . . a very simple word that explains and fixes everything" (ibid., p. 151).

5. Quoted from an interview with Kenneth Tynan in Martin Esslin, *The Theatre of the Absurd* (Garden City, N.Y.: Doubleday Anchor Books, 1961), p. 207.

6. "It is comforting to see how things inexorably rot. Every crevice that I find in things makes me revive" *(Teatro*, p. 158).

7. "Be careful not to die before your death" (ibid., p. 153). To the question, "What contemporary authors do you consider to have had the most influence on your work?" Díaz responded, "Vicente Huidobro" ("Tres jóvenes dramaturgos y un cuestionario, respuestas de Jorge Díaz," *Apuntes*, no. 61 [August 1966], p. 13). It is not surprising that Díaz would name his Chilean forebear as a major influence, since Huidobro (1893–1948) was one of the early vanguard poets to experiment with new linguistic forms.

8. "The story begins for you now in the second act" *(Teatro*, p. 186).

9. "But Manuel is living and will live among us" (ibid., p. 195).

10. "I was thinking, how do you put a ship in a bottle? And now I know. First you have to get out of the bottle" *(El velero en la botella* [Santiago, Chile: Editorial Universitaria, 1973], p. 62).

11. "It is like having the key to things, the one that opens all mysteries" (ibid., p. 61).

12. "I have a fabulous word on the tip of my tongue" (ibid., p. 53).

13. *The Place Where the Mammals Die*, trans. Naomi Nelson, in *The Modern Stage in Latin America: Six Plays*, ed. George W. Woodyard (New York: E. P. Dutton & Co., 1971), pp. 181–235.

14. Two other plays of this time period, not considered here, are: *Variaciones para muertos en percusión*, published in *Conjunto*, no. 1 (1964), pp. 17–48, and *El nudo ciego*, performed by ICTUS in 1965. The former is the treatment of alienation and commercialization as seen through the personnel of a Madison Avenue–type advertising agency; the latter is an experimental play based on the conflict of appearance and reality, achieved through a double script in which the audience hears one version from the stage and the other over the theater loudspeakers.

15. "The genesis was tomorrow" *(Teatro*, p. 91). In a slightly shortened version, the play is published under the title *El génesis fue mañana*, in *En un acto*, eds. Frank Dauster and Leon F. Lyday (New York: D. Van Nostrand Co., 1974), pp. 119–137.

16. "And God called the light Day and the darkness he called Night. And the evening and the morning were the first day" (King James Version).

17. *Topografía de un desnudo* (Santiago, Chile: Editora Santiago, 1967).

18. "I know you died—but I would kill you again if I had to!" (ibid., p. 80).

19. "But when you want to begin to shout, it is already too late and you find yourself trapped in a bell jar" (ibid., p. 70).

20. "Jorge Díaz: 7 años en España," *Primer Acto*, no. 137 (October 1971), p. 62. (An interview with *Primer Acto*.)

21. "Che Guevara is dead" *(Introducción al elefante y otras zoologías*, MS, personal files, p. 45).

22. "Frequently you ask yourself to what point you are interpreting reality correctly" *(Liturgia para cornudos*, MS, personal files, p. 57).

23. "Jorge Díaz: 7 años en España," p. 65.

24. "Everything considered, violence that answers to violence always generates a new violence" *(Liturgia para cornudos*, p. 57).

25. "La erosión del lenguaje," *Latin American Theatre Review* 4, no. 1 (Fall 1970): 74–78.

26. ". . . a very distant chorus of white voices" *(La orgástula*, in *Latin American Theatre Review* 4, no. 1 [Fall 1970]: 82).

27. "La erosión del lenguaje," p. 76.

28. "The only thing certain is that after someone defends us he ends up dominating us" (*La pancarta, Textos,* June 1972, p. 7).

29. "How do we finish this work, friends?" (ibid., p. 7).

30. "María Luz Mellón, interviewer, "Jorge Díaz regresa a Chile," *Madrid*, 29 September 1971, p. 12.

31. This study was supported in part by the General Research Fund of the University of Kansas.

5. The Theater of Osvaldo Dragún

Donald L. Schmidt

Among his Argentine contemporaries, none has excelled Osvaldo Dragún in the mastery of dramatic art. As Frank Dauster has observed, "In Osvaldo Dragún one can appreciate the maturity of a dramatist while he develops."[1] While his technical mastery is evident in works of both traditional and innovative forms, it is in the latter that Dragún has made his greatest contributions to the Latin American theater. His thematic interests have ranged widely, even into the period of Greco-Roman antiquity. He has, however, shown a predilection for the contemporary inhabitant of Buenos Aires, whom he sees as struggling against forces of repression that seek to mold him according to norms that are not his own.

Dragún's first full-length work, *La peste viene de Melos* ("The plague comes from Melos"), reinterprets a historical theme taken from ancient Greece.[2] First performed by the Teatro Popular Independiente Fray Mocho in 1956, it deals with a rebellion on the island of Melos against Athens in 416 B.C., growing out of a politico-economic intrigue. The island maintains its independence from Athens, which sets a bad example for other regions under the latter's imperialistic yoke. To resolve the problem, the Athenians devise a scheme that will justify an attack on the island to defend against a nonexistent "plague" alleged to originate there. In Athens, the military is supported by the merchants, who see the war as a lucrative business. In Melos, the merchants want peace, because war would damage the local economy; if necessary, they are willing to sacrifice the island's autonomy to avoid war. They ask Pitias, a well-to-do peasant, to serve as leader and to negotiate with the Athenians in the hope of gaining a compromise. Pitias, however, refuses to give in to the Athenians, who begin a siege that lasts nearly two years. In the end, Melos is reduced to ashes, and Pitias dies in combat, but he has won his victory, because the uprising has spread to other regions, portending the fall of Athens.

In his treatment of this historical episode, Dragún develops certain themes that come to dominate his future works. Among the most important is materialism and its effects on man. The merchants of both Melos and Athens have reduced all values to the terms of commerce. For them, war and peace are only significant to the extent that they can alter economic conditions. They are prepared to sacrifice honor, liberty, and the lives of others, because they are capable of struggling only "por una cosa, aunque sea pequeña, pero que pueda tocarse y encerrarse en un puño" (p. 76).[3]

Pitias and his working-class followers stand in vivid contrast to the merchants.

They stubbornly refuse to sacrifice their liberty and submit to imperialistic exploitation. They love the land with such intensity that they prefer to destroy it rather than have it fall into the hands of the Athenians. The moral conflict between peasants and merchants acquires revolutionary proportions during the siege, when the poor sack the homes of the merchants and aristocrats in search of food. Their behavior is not merely an irrational act of desperation but grows out of a sense of class identity. The latter is dramatized when Pitias disavows the role of master by freeing his slave, León. In the play's final tragic moment, León says to Pitias: "Un día me dijiste que era libre. Luego me enseñaste a defender mi libertad. Ahora, en el minuto de mi muerte, te digo gracias, Pitias" (p. 77).[4]

The telluric roots that support the world view of the ancient Greeks serves in *La peste viene de Melos* as the axis around which the class struggle revolves. The land is associated with creation and fecundity, reflected in maternal imagery: ". . . una tierra pequeña y profunda... de una bahía redonda y suave como el vientre embarazado de una mujer" (p. 23).[5] This association between the land and woman imparts to the latter a special role in the dramatic conflict. Alcibíades, governor of the materialistic and decadent empire, hates women precisely because he does not understand maternity, and he senses that he is violating it with his destructive war. Tisias, commander of the Athenian forces, feels an anguished need for a woman. For him, woman represents a creative force that he yearns for in the loneliness of his profession. Acanto reaches the depths of crass materialism when he tries to negotiate treason by means of his daughter's virginal body.

This alienation from and perversion of creative forces—telluric and maternal —is what distinguishes the merchant class from the working class and leads to the degeneration of human values. The lives and values of the merchant class are completely sterile, parasitic, and destructive. The ultimate perversion of values is symbolized when the Athenians cast into the sea the statue of Pallas Athena because, "Ya no nos sirve para nada" (p. 44).[6]

In contrast to the moral dissolution of the Athenians, Pitias and his followers hold firm to the belief that man's primary role is to cultivate the land. Man thus functions within an order that is dominated by creative forces. In this context it is significant that Pitias's is the only complete family unit appearing in the work. It represents the normal human order in harmony with natural forces.

In this cast of good and evil types, one character stands apart. General Cleómedes from the beginning opposes war waged for purely economic motives: "Preferiría la lucha limpia" (p. 26).[7] Unable to reconcile his military duty with his personal morality, he is finally driven to suicide.

The general's suicide, like nearly all other major events, occurs offstage. The exceptions are the deaths of Pitias and León, which both culminate and end the drama. This relative simplicity of visible events permits an economy of stage setting that becomes typical of Dragún's future works. By means of lighting, offstage sounds, and dialogue, he creates a reality far greater and more complex than the visual reality of setting.

The following year (1957), Dragún's second historical drama was performed. *Tupac Amarú* centers around the rebellion of José Gabriel Condorcanqui in 1780–1781. All elements of colonial society are represented among the characters, from the Visitor General Areche to the anonymous Indian slaves. From this array a complete picture of colonial decadence emerges within which Areche's grandiose aspirations are totally frustrated. The Visitor General's frustration heightens the dramatic tension surrounding his conflict with Tupac Amarú. While the latter suffers torture and martyrdom at the hands of Areche, he is clearly the moral victor.

This tragedy offers an excellent example of the integration of form and theme. Structure and all scenographic effects are coordinated so as to achieve a maximum of dramatic effect. In the first act Areche and colonial society are introduced, along with the constant ringing of bells. For Areche their monotonous peal has a foreboding quality, reminding him of a funeral. The unrest of the masses is also communicated by means of the lamentations, chants, and shouts that rise from the Plaza del Regocijo. The second act presents the trial in which Tupac Amarú and his wife, Micaela Bastidas, are condemned to death. It is the crisis in the conflict between authority and the rebel that sustains the dramatic force from the beginning. The town crier's announcement of the trial rises incessantly from the street, and the unrest of the masses continues. The divided stage of the third act (between the office of the Visitor General and the cell of the Inca Tupac Amarú) simultaneously reveals the final agony of the two heroes. The town crier's persistent announcement of the death sentence, coupled with an approaching storm, heightens the sense of foreboding that culminates with the deaths of Areche and Tupac Amarú at nearly the same moment. Symbolically, the storm represents the wrath of God at the assassination of the Inca. The symbolism is carried further when the wind scatters his ashes, converting him into a mythic redemptive figure.

Besides its formal qualities, *Tupac Amarú* makes an important contribution to its historical theme by recasting it in contemporary terms. While it forcefully dramatizes the conflict between a decadent colonial system and the oppressed masses, it adds an existentialist dimension to that conflict. The Visitor General Areche considers power to be an absolute value, and to protect it he betrays the word of Commander Flores, he lies to the Indians, and he traps the Creole Felipe Roldán. Like Nietzsche's "superman," he respects no moral value, because in aspiring to power he is "beyond good and evil." Tupac Amarú and his wife, on the other hand, achieve self-realization through the exercise of free choice. The first to speak at their trial, Micaela formulates her responses in clearly existentialist terms: "Tuve que decidir. Muchas veces tuve que decidir"

(p. 49).[8] When asked if she repents, she answers: "No. Porque yo decidí. Y si pudiendo decidir otra cosa, decidí ésta, no tengo de qué arrepentirme" (p. 50).[9] At one point she even affirms that in the act of decision she felt herself to be God.

This independent spirit profoundly disconcerts the Visitor General, who becomes progressively more excited. Micaela's serenity contrasts with Areche's distress and betrays the moral victory that she is winning. Dramatic tension is heightened when Tupac Amarú is brought before the court. Although he is blind and bloodied from torture, his spirit is unbroken. Dialogue between the Inca and Areche soon crystallizes the fundamental difference between them:

Areche. (Suave) —¿Qué ambicionabas? ¿Poder? ¡Yo ambiciono poder! ¿Y tú?

Tupac Amarú. —Yo fui más ambicioso que usted. Quise que creyesen en
    mí. Que cuando les dijera que ya no eran esclavos se
    lanzaran a la conquista de su tierra...[10]   [P. 56]

The moral strength of the Inca deeply impresses the Visitor General: "Soy el vencedor. Pero si me ves perderme en la tormenta, pínchame con tu espada y recuérdame que soy el vencedor" (p. 65).[11] His ambivalent sense of victory leads Areche to the recognition that among those who surround him, only one is his equal: "¡No debí hacerte matar, indio! Sólo tú me hiciste siempre compañía... ¡No debí hacerte matar! Debí tomarte de la mano y pasear contigo por el mundo" (pp. 77–78).[12]

In an existentialist framework, Commander Flores represents a special case among the characters of *Tupac Amarú* and strikingly resembles General Cleómedes in *La peste viene de Melos*. He suffers a moral crisis in which he is torn between his patriotic duty and his sympathy for Tupac Amarú. However, since he has not made a total commitment one way or the other, he has not fully realized his essential being. This is reflected symbolically in a dialogue with the Inca in his cell:

Tupac Amarú. —¿Eres tú, sombra?

Flores.   —No, no soy...

Tupac Amarú. —¡Sí, eres una sombra!
    (*Lo interrumpe*)   [P. 69][13]

As a shadow being, Commander Flores is perhaps the most tragic figure of all in *Tupac Amarú*. He seems destined to exist meaninglessly under the sway of those who, for good or for evil, know who they are and why they live.

As victim of external forces, Commander Flores shares his fate with the protagonists of the short works entitled *Historias para ser contadas* ("Stories to be told"), which, like *Tupac Amarú*, appeared in 1957. Virtually *sui generis*, these works do without stage setting entirely, and four actors play all the roles. They skillfully combine pantomime, dialogue, and direct communication with the audience. In the prologue, recited in free verse, the actors introduce themselves as raconteurs of true stories from contemporary Buenos Aires. They invite anyone in the audience who has "una risa para ser reída o una lágrima para ser llorada," to tell them of it, and they will recite it "allá, en lejanas plazas,"[14] in a style reminiscent of the medieval *juglares*.

Historia de un flemón, una mujer y dos hombres ("Story of an abscess, a woman, and two men") presents the case of an impoverished street vendor who cannot afford medical treatment for his abscess. At the same time, his ailment keeps him from working, and, as a last resort, he sees a dentist, who, like everyone else, is indifferent to his pain and puts him through a long and expensive treatment that does him absolutely no good. The vendor's dilemma becomes tragicomic, as he has to run to his dental appointments, counting the seconds of work that he loses in the process. Since he stubbornly continues to work, the abscess is aggravated to the point that the vendor finally dies in a state of absolute destitution.

Historia de cómo nuestro amigo Panchito González se sintió responsable de la epidemia de peste en Africa del Sur ("Story of how our friend Panchito González felt responsible for the plague epidemic in South Africa") is like a footnote in explanation of its formidable title. Panchito González, like the street vendor, is unable to meet his minimum financial needs. He finds a solution in the opportunity to send canned rat meat disguised as food to the blacks of South Africa. As a reward for this profitable trick, the owners of his company, an Italian and an Englishman, raise his monthly salary to 5,000 pesos. At the same time, the city grants him the Gran Cruz de la Salud Pública in honor of his antirat campaign. When news of the bubonic plague in South Africa arrives, Panchito suffers a crisis of conscience, and, worse yet, his hypocritical employers fire him for being "muy poco humanitario."[15]

In *Historia del hombre que se convirtió en perro* ("Story of the man who became a dog"), the protagonist seeks employment desperately. He is in such dire straits that when he is offered the job of watchdog, he accepts merely to gain temporary respite. His continuing search leads to nothing but the same offer in another factory. However, since the salary is five pesos more per day, he accepts. As time passes, he becomes so accustomed to his role that he begins to question whether he is man or dog, and his speech is a garble of words and barking.

Obviously, there is more of the parable than of social realism in each of these works. In a symbolic way they explore the predicament of modern man in a society that has lost its human values. In this society money reigns supreme, and, to survive, man is forced to sacrifice his dignity even to the point of becoming a dog. The impact of each of these *historias* is heightened both by its brevity and by the lack of visual setting. Together these qualities sharpen the focus on the basic human conflict.

In the same volume with the above works, Dragún published *Historia de mi esquina* ("Story of my corner"). Although it differs very little from the others in theme and technique, it is longer and more complex, and its development is more realistic. As narrator-participant, Aldo, like all his friends, sees his dreams and happiness frustrated by economic need. Even his relationship with his girl-friend, Virginia, is destroyed by this problem. Following her mother's advice to marry a rich man, Virginia breaks with Aldo to go with her employer's son. However, when her brother, Gregorio, is arrested, her rich boyfriend rejects her, and in the end she goes back to Aldo.

While money is the single, most important problem in *Historia de mi esquina*, it is not the only one that the young people share. Their parents, rather than serve as examples, are miserable failures who merely stand in their children's way. Their only legacy is a harsh struggle for very limited goals. Both within and without the family, human relations are sterile, mechanical, and boring. This is reflected often in the dialogue:

> *Madre.* —¿Vas a salir?
>
> *Padre.* —Sí.
>
> *Madre.* —¿Otra vez?
>
> *Padre.* —Otra vez.
>
> *Madre.* —¿Volverás esta noche?
>
> *Padre.* —No sé. [P. 21][16]

It is in the factory where Gregorio and Aldo work that life is most completely mechanized. All the workers enter like marionettes to the beat of a military march and work to the rhythm of a waltz with exactly fifteen minutes for lunch. The factory is a microcosm of the world in which the young protagonists exist. Their freedom is destroyed by this environment, which wields absolute control over their lives. Aldo bears witness to this lack of freedom when he says to his father: "Yo nunca he decidido nada, viejo" (p. 50).[17]

While dehumanization in contemporary society is a universal problem, Dragún very clearly situates *Historia de mi esquina* in Buenos Aires. He does this through the use of local place names and through the use of language habits peculiar to the River Plate region, such as the use of the pronoun "vos." By insistently localizing the work, he places an unnecessary limitation on a universal theme, which tends to undermine audience identification with the characters if the audience is not specifically Argentine. This regionalism characterizes a number of his other works and, in general, weakens their appeal.

More successful than its regional qualities are the musical leitmotifs used to enhance dramatic elements in *Historia de mi esquina*. The most frequent and most suggestive is "Golondrinas de un solo verano, con ansias constantes de cielo lejano . . ."[18] A related technique is the creation of a choral effect to intensify Virginia's anguish:

Voz de Madre. —¡Cásate con un rico!

Voz de Padre. —De tus hijos ocúpate vos un poco más.

Voz de Gregorio. —Cásate con un rico...

Voz de Aldo. —Vos me querés Virginia...

Todos. —CÁSATE CON UN RICO. (*Cuatro veces se repiten 'in crescendo.'* Virginia *huye atormentada.*) [P. 23][19]

The predominantly financial troubles that beleaguer Virginia and Aldo give way in *Jardín del infierno* (1961, "Garden of Hell") to broader problems of human relations. The setting of *Jardín del infierno* is a poor neighborhood of Buenos Aires inhabited mainly by Neapolitan immigrants and people from the interior who have come to the city in quest of a better life. The action takes place from morning to evening and involves relatively few characters, producing a highly unified effect. Ricardo, only son of the Bernárdez family, is visiting home supposedly on a military leave. It is immediately evident that family relations are strained. Ricardo fights with his sister, René, who fights with the other sister, Lucy, and their mother complains of René's aloofness toward them all. Tension is heightened by the problem of perverse sexuality, first introduced through the rape of the Rosendos' daughter by unknown assailants. The problem reappears in an erotic scene that dramatizes the incestuous passions of Ricardo and Lucy. It is eventually learned that Ricardo was one of those who raped the Rosendos' daughter, and his crime becomes one of murder when she dies. Besides these crimes, it turns out that Ricardo is not on leave but that he has escaped from a military prison. At the end the police take him away in abject despair.

At first glance it would appear that *Jardín del infierno* provides little more than a naturalistic treatment of sex. On closer examination, however, it becomes evident that the problem of sex is only a visible symptom of something much deeper. Ricardo, for example, feels a bizarre attraction to trains. Every time he hears one he experiences a disconcerting reaction: "Cada vez que pasa un tren y veo la lucecita de atrás viene un fuego en la cintura y me dan ganas de correr" (p. 54).[20] This strange desire led to his military incarceration and continues to obsess him at home. In part, trains fascinate him because he does not understand them: "¿Dónde van los trenes, tana? ¿Dónde va la gente que viaja en tren?" (p. 64).[21]

The symbolic value of trains can best be understood against Ricardo's family background. In his home, fighting is the normal mode of human relations. His mother almost always refers disparagingly to Lucy as "mocosa," and when she tries to comfort Ricardo, he, himself, expresses a similar rejection: "¡Vos siempre me tuviste rabia...! ¡Dejá de manosearme, vieja!" (p. 79).[22] Ricardo's father does not care about him either, and only at the final moment does he attempt to communicate with him. Having experienced neither love nor real communication, Ricardo's life has become hollow and disoriented. He has developed no healthy means of release and fails to understand what life is all about. Consequently, when he hears or sees a train, his pent-up emotionality yearns for release. The train, like the force of his emotions, is powerful, but, unlike his emotions, the train has a path to follow and carries people to a destination. Ricardo yearns for a similar direction in his own life.

It is through sex that Ricardo acts out the psychological problems symbolized by trains. On the one hand, since he has never known love, sex is for him brutal and violent, manifested in rape. On the other hand, he desperately needs to find something more in sexual relations and finds purely physical sex repugnant. This is clearly evident in his answer to Renata concerning his experiences with other women: "Rabia, y ganas de llorar. Después corría. . . . Corría porque eran sucias y tenían olor" (p. 64).[23] With Renata herself, he seems to be on the verge of gaining the kind of relationship that he seeks. In this new-found sexuality Ricardo appears to have achieved the needed emotional outlet symbolized by trains: "A tu lado es la primera vez que me siento cansado. Sabes qué bueno es sentirse cansado?" (p. 69).[24] However, he is unable to develop this relationship further, because the police soon take him away.

Ricardo's incarceration, while legitimate, does not vindicate the system of justice in Argentine society. In fact, it gives rise to a note of social protest, suggesting that there is one kind of justice for the poor and another for the rich. The justice of the rich is exemplified in a similar case in which Ricardo's sister, René, is sexually molested by the son of a commissioner in whose home she is a servant. While the police are tenacious in bringing Ricardo to justice for rape, they do nothing to René's assailant because of his father's influence. Those who perpetrate this injustice are not, however, free from a sense of guilt. The police officer Enrique Martínez, for example, had arranged the job as a servant for René and feels guilty for having done nothing to protect her. He chose not to protect her, because it would have compromised his own position. In an obvious rationalization, he now tries to justify his cowardice by treating René and her family as though they were "pigs." If he can convince himself that they are, indeed, animals, his self-contempt will be alleviated.

Enrique Martínez's personal sense of guilt is paralleled on the collective level when the neighbors gather to stone the Bernárdez house. It is as though they were engaged in a primitive ritual of expiation, in which the Bernárdez family serves as the scapegoat of communal guilt. The theme of guilt is echoed by an offstage chorus whose chant begins with the moment of the Rosendo girl's death. In reality, the chorus is made up of neighbors who pray for the soul of the deceased, but the element of their prayer that is consistently heard emphasizes guilt: "Santa María madre de Dios, ruega por nosotros, pecadores" (p. 69).[25] At the same time, there is a change in the weather, and by the third act a storm is unleashed that seems to function as the *Dies Irae*. The weaving together of these elements with Ricardo's crime skillfully raises the issue of collective versus individual guilt and responsibility.

In 1962 Dragún returned to the genre of the *Historias para ser contadas* with *Los de la mesa diez* ("The couple at table ten"), which even carries the subtitle *Otra historia para ser contada*.[26] Like the others, it takes place in Buenos Aires, and, like *Historia de mi esquina*, it deals with young people who are trying to make a life for themselves under adverse conditions. José is a poor mechanic, and María is a recent graduate of the *colegio* from a well-to-do family. When they wish to get married, María's parents reject José as unacceptable, and the two find themselves without the financial resources to achieve their goal. Unable to marry, their growing desire to consummate their love sexually forces them to separate in order not to compromise their moral standards. However, after two months, they can no longer tolerate separation, and they reunite, determined to face life, no matter how difficult it may be.

The final resolve of José and María distinguishes *Los de la mesa diez* thematically from previous *Historias para ser contadas*. It is the first suggestion in this genre that the human spirit can, after all, successfully exert itself in the face of crushing forces of materialism. On the other hand, *Los de la mesa diez* is technically very similar to previous *historias*. As in *Historia de mi esquina*, there is no stage setting, and one character addresses the audience from time to time to provide necessary information. The language and place names come expressly from Buenos Aires. Phrases from songs are repeated in both works, infusing them with a poetic quality. In both works a chorus is also used to reflect anxiety. These similarities suggest that Dragún is developing the genre of the *Historias para ser contadas* into a definite form.

The following year, Dragún published *Milagro en el Mercado Viejo* ("Miracle in the Old Market"), in which a realistic stage setting is used. The play deals with a group of social outcasts who inhabit the Mercado by night. Having failed in conventional society, they form their own society in which poverty is the norm. One night, as they are celebrating the birthday of the "Judge," they are interrupted by José and María, a young couple in search of a retreat in which to make love. They receive the intruders with hostility and oblige them to tell of their love affair. José and María dramatize their story in a way that recalls the technique of the *Historias para ser contadas*. They are interrupted by the others who want to interpret the story their own way. When it is finally revealed that

María is pregnant and has stolen five thousand pesos from Mr. Fernández for an abortion, the tone changes. The people of the Mercado feel threatened that María may be found among them, especially since Mr. Fernández is the owner of the Mercado. They decide to betray her and arrange their own dramatization in order to discover and rehearse the best way of carrying out the betrayal. One of the characters nicknamed the "Actor" plays the role of Fernández, and another nicknamed "el Coya" serves as a policeman. However, they do not simply act but actually come to live their roles. The "Actor" is truly cruel, and "el Coya" is truly violent with his friends. When the latter flee, and the spell is broken, the actors regret their behavior, but, as the "Actor" says: "Sí, estoy arrepentido, pero si vuelvo a ser Fernández, ustedes volverán a crujir... y yo volveré a odiarlos" (p. 26).[27] So that this may not happen, "el Coya" takes the "Actor's" dinner jacket and pretends to strangle it. At that moment, the night watchman enters with the news that Mr. Fernández has, in fact, just died.

The conclusion is both forced and unconvincing. It solves nothing and fails to unify the work. However, it is only one of two basic structural weaknesses. The other is the shift in focus from the outcasts of the Mercado to José and María midway through the work. The two groups have little in common besides a relationship with Mr. Fernández, and that is too minor to bridge their differences. The only clearly defined theme is that every man has within him the capacity for evil.

In spite of its realistic stage setting, most of the formal aspects of this play recall those of the *Historias para ser contadas*. Ursula, like Aldo and the café waiter, speaks with the audience. Snatches of music from offstage provide a background to certain scenes, and when María gets to the most emotional part of her story, she breaks into song. Even more than these, however, the dramatizations within the play are done exactly as *Historias para ser contadas*.

In 1963, Dragún again dealt with the youth of Buenos Aires in *Y nos dijeron que éramos inmortales* (*And They Told Us We Were Immortal*). Jorge returns home from military service where he had developed a close friendship with Arón and Berto. The three had participated in a military action in which Jorge was superficially wounded, Berto was permanently disabled, and Arón was killed. Back home, Jorge soon returns to his old way of life and makes plans to marry his fiancée, Ada. Everything appears to be going well, but under the surface, Jorge is troubled by the fear that he is forgetting Arón and that the latter's death may have been in vain. A crisis is precipitated when Berto, who has been arrested for robbery, calls Jorge from the police station. When the call arrives, Jorge is celebrating Ada's birthday with his family, and they pressure him to ignore it. This, together with his concern over Arón's death, nearly destroys him emotionally. He goes into a monologue on his problems, but the only one who seems to understand is his brother Esteban, who by the end of the play is desperately trying to get through to him: "¡Gito! ¡Oíme! ¡La muerte existe y está allí, pero no es problema! ¡Nuestro único problema es cómo vivir! ¿Me oís? ¡Eso es lo que el Rengo espera que le digas! ¿Me oís, Gito, me oís?" (p. 116).[28]

Jorge's conflict has its immediate source in his family, but in a deeper sense its origins lie in society. His military experiences have convinced him that the life he had known at home is illusory. His mother had sheltered him excessively so that hardship of any kind would be unknown to him. On the one hand, this protected him from having to consider any of the fundamental questions of life, and, on the other, it produced an effeminate quality in him that was a major source of difficulty in the service. Years before, Jorge's mother had hung a poster on the wall with the motto: "Todo el mundo es este hogar," and, symbolically, Jorge now writes his own message on the wall: ". . . la puta madre que lo parió."[29]

Jorge discovers that it is not just his mother who wants him to fit quietly into the status quo. While nearly all members of his family defend things as they are, it can readily be seen that neither his parents, his brother, nor his sister and brother-in-law are really happy. Unhappiness is manifested especially through the use of alcohol in every scene as a means of escape. Berto represents another aspect of the social problem and recalls the case of Raúl in *Historia de mi esquina*. Both are promising athletes whose careers are destroyed by disabling injuries. The fortunes of both illustrate society's utilitarian attitude toward them. So long as they are able to entertain the public with their athletic feats, the public supports and stimulates them. However, that same public is totally indifferent when misfortune befalls its heroes and provides no useful alternative role for them. They are human merchandise, just like Acanto's daughter in *La peste viene de Melos*.

In *Y nos dijeron que éramos inmortales* Dragún uses song, dance, and poetry to highlight his theme. The title itself comes from a poem attributed to the deceased Arón. In it the play's basic thesis is stated: life, as society presents it to its youth, is false. As a solution, the poem discards traditional values and replaces them with the life of the individual as the ultimate value: "Ni Dios ni la muerte son problemas para mí. / Ni me curan el hígado ni me hacen reír. / El único milagro es la vida del hombre / porque está por hacer" (p. 76).[30] The emphasis on life "por hacer" echoes the existentialist position of the Inca Tupac Amarú, who takes it upon himself to forge his life on the basis of his own decisions. This idea of "becoming" is reflected symbolically in Laura's pregnancy and in the semifantastic figure of an old man who, as symbol of the world, sings an epilogue to the play: "¡Los viejos cuentos terminaron! / ¡Estoy a punto de parir!" (p. 116).[31]

Completely abandoning the fantastic element and the somber tone of *Y nos dijeron que éramos inmortales*, Dragún developed a similar theme more realistically in *Amoretta* (1964). In it, he again explores the relationship between mother and son, together with the theme of love as a vital necessity. Both are brought to light through the affair between Paco and Giuliana. Paco is a thirty-year-old adolescent, and Giuliana is a widow of about forty with a son, Rodolfo, half her age. Paco accidentally breaks Rodolfo's leg in a soccer game. Feeling somewhat guilty, Paco approaches Giuliana to offer his temporary help in her flower stall in the market. This offer provides the catalyst that eventually frees the repressed emotions of the two. In the process, the contrast in their personalities heightens dramatic tension and leads to humorous effects. Their initial roles of clown and aging widow are destroyed in a burst of kisses followed by a night in bed. When their actions are discovered, Rodolfo and Paco's mother, Asunción, react bitterly. Nevertheless, the potential tragedy comes to a happy end when Paco and Giuliana are reconciled amorously. Their rejection of outside influences is symbolized when they slam the door in the faces of their relatives.

The psychological study in Amoretta is formulated in rather obvious Freudian terms. Behind different façades, both Giuliana and Paco hide from their true sexuality. Both are also involved in an oedipal relationship that is resolved through their sexual intimacy. Giuliana rediscovers herself as a woman and accepts sexuality as a normal and integral part of her feminine nature. She is rejuvenated and freed from her neurosis. While Paco does not seem to have acquired the depth of insight that Giuliana has, he nevertheless appears to have experienced something unique that promises to modify his life in a similar way. Psychological realism is enhanced by the embittered reactions of Rodolfo and Asunción to the affair between Paco and Giuliana. The intensity of their resentment seems out of proportion to objective reality and shows that they feel deeply threatened by it, effectively dramatizing the symbiotic nature of the oedipal relationship.

The psychology in Amoretta differs in one major way from orthodox Freudianism. In the latter, psychological problems are the result of innate human characteristics, while in the play, as in nearly all of Dragún's plays, psychological problems grow out of aberrations in society. In Amoretta, worry about what the neighbors will say oppressively restricts human relationships. Paco and Giuliana have never been able to relate to each other naturally because social values do not permit such a relationship between a widow of her age and a man of his. Here, as in Y nos dijeron que éramos inmortales, Dragún suggests that the answer lies in placing individual need above social convention.

The dehumanizing effect of society on the individual leads to a far less happy conclusion in Heroica de Buenos Aires (1966, "Epic of Buenos Aires"). Unfortunately, when compared to Dragún's other works, Heroica de Buenos Aires represents a decline in artistic quality. Dramatic impact is diluted by its excessive length, and artistic suggestion is virtually eliminated by the leftist sociopolitical commitment.

Overburdened by peripheral elements, the play deals basically with the widow María and her children Carlos and Ada. María earns a barely adequate living selling varied items from her mobile "Super-Mercadito Doña María." To compensate for the limited horizons of her occupation, she dreams of greater success for her children and does everything in her power to assure it. Toward that end Carlos is a student of economics, and Ada is in the market for a rich husband. María's world is complicated, however, when she meets and falls in love with Adolfo, a simple laborer from the Selva de Montiel. Carlos participates in a student strike and disappears for a time. When he returns, he is considerably shrewder and soon establishes a comfortable life for himself working for "el Negro," a vendor who has become rich. At the same time, María's financial state deteriorates rapidly, and she ends up living among ragged outcasts like those of *Milagro en el Mercado Viejo*. In spite of her misery, she continues to feed on the hope of seeing her children financially secure. For this reason her disillusion is all the more striking when she sees her wish fulfilled. Ada, who had married "el Negro," accompanies Carlos in search of María. When they find her, it is evident that they have become the prototypes of the *nouveau riche*, and they treat her as an object rather than as their mother. María's only solution is to go back to the Selva de Montiel with Adolfo and repent of the influence she had exercised on her children.

The decline in María's fortunes is reflected in the two cycles into which *Heroica* is divided. The first is entitled "El calor" ("Heat"), and the second, "El frío" ("Cold"). Together, they represent the four seasons and symbolize María's evolution from hope to despair. The optimistic warmth of spring gradually becomes the cold of despair as she sees her materialistic aspirations realized and finds that they have destroyed rather than created happiness.

Two characters who remain aloof from this pendular development are Adolfo and "la tía Josefina." Both are by nature incapable of organizing their lives around materialistic value. Adolfo attempts it for a time while living with and at the expense of María, but he finds it unbearable. Self-sufficiency is far more important to him than material comfort, and the latter without the former leads only to shame. During this period, the Super-Mercadito Doña María is stationed near a cemetery, symbolic of the spiritual death that materialism represents for Adolfo.

Like Adolfo, "la tía Josefina" is also incapable of functioning as a materialist. She has the peculiar habit of spending the winter in the hospital. It is a symbolic gesture, because, as seen in María's case, winter represents materialistic dehumanization. For a time she seems to have found a permanent refuge in religion, becoming a member of the Fraternidad de los Hijos del Arrepentimiento. However, when "brother" Manuel dies, she discovers that she had become enamored of him rather than religion: "¿La fe...? Ay, mi vieja... cuando murió Manuel... el hermano Manuel... me di cuenta que mi fe era él" (p. 169).[32] Afterwards she discovers that religion, as such, is just as unbearable as materialism. This realization completes the indictment of bourgeois society. Both its materialistic values and its organized religion are found to dehumanize. The only remaining alternative is to replace them, as María and Adolfo do, with human relationships as the ultimate value.

While this work is thematically similar to most of Dragún's other works, there are a number of gratuitous elements that make it the least effective. For example, a group of soldiers functions as a caricature of the military—they are mere puppets of authority. When a rebellion breaks out, they do not know whether they are "anaranjados" or "violetas." Both factions are headed by generals Fernández, suggesting that it makes little difference anyway. While Dragún himself has cited a recent historical event to justify the episode, the stage events seem intended merely to satirize the government, thereby significantly limiting the work's appeal.[33]

To include the theme of class struggle and, at the same time, to caricature a certain type of student, Dragún introduces a classmate of Carlos. The son of a rich industrialist, he is one of the instigators of a student strike, but it turns out that his revolutionary fervor, and that of his companions, is nothing but the dilettantism of spoiled children.

At times even the basic theme in *Heroica* is stated in simplistic terms. There is a crude irony in Ada's statement to her disillusioned mother: ". . . todo lo que somos te lo debemos a vos" (p. 179).[34] María, in turn, expressly formulates the moral of the play: "¡Toda la vida soñé con esto! ¡Y ahora... son todo lo que yo soñé... todo lo que yo quise... pero son todo lo contrario! ¿Qué pasó, Adolfo?" (p. 182).[35] This insistence on a point that is clearly evident greatly diminishes the play's artistic suggestion.

Certain examples of sensationalism detract still further from the artistic quality of *Heroica de Buenos Aires*. In one erotic scene, a servant rips off Ada's blouse, and she remains onstage seminude for several moments. This episode can be compared with a similar one in *Jardín del infierno*, in which a young girl also appears in scant undergarments. However, in the latter play, the scene is in keeping with the general tone of the play and is an integral part of its thematic development. In *Heroica de Buenos Aires*, on the other hand, it would be difficult to justify the scene as in any way necessary to its theme. Equally unnecessary is the use of obscenities to shock and create humorous effects. These sensationalist techniques seem to have the sole purpose of gaining a certain kind of audience and entertaining it in a vulgar way.

The scene between Ada and the servant, while in itself artistically deficient, is part of a larger sequence that is of greater artistic interest. It is a flashback in which Carlos's classmate relives the events of the morning from the chronological perspective of the afternoon. The disruption of normal time is underscored by occasional dialogue between Carlos and his friend across the time barrier. It would have been better if Dragún had devoted more of his effort in

Heroica de Buenos Aires to this kind of experimentation instead of wasting it on vulgarity.

As though having reached the same conclusion himself, Dragún did, in fact, turn to greater experimentation with time and reality in the short play *El amasijo* (1968, "The hodgepodge"). Like many of his other works, this play basically resembles the *Historias para ser contadas* but is both technically and thematically more complex than the latter. The author's intent in *El amasijo* might best be summarized in his own words: "[*El amasijo*] presents a scenic game through which problems of time (mixture of past, present, and future in the same instant, without any change of scenery) are treated, and in addition it presents the idea that a man is: his past, his present, his future, and besides that, his truth and his lie."[36]

As the author's statement suggests, technique is at least as important as theme in *El amasijo*, and perhaps more so. Technical experimentation begins with the stage itself. While the last act of *Tupac Amarú* uses a two-part stage, *El amasijo* requires a three-part stage throughout. Setting is a compromise between the virtually barren stages of *Historias para ser contadas* and the realistic settings of *Tupac Amarú* and *Milagro en el Mercado Viejo*. Opposite ends of the stage in *El amasijo* realistically represent the bedrooms of José and María, and the sparsely furnished center serves as office, street, amusement park, and café, according to momentary need, in the fashion of the *Historias para ser contadas*. The bedrooms suggest the circumstances in which the characters experience their greatest loneliness and, by their location, the gap that must be bridged to achieve communication. The protean mid-stage represents the outside world in which José and María must function when they leave the refuge of their rooms. It is also the habitat of Ricardo, who acts as catalyst between them. He, like the characters in *Historias para ser contadas* assumes many roles during the play, while José and María retain a consistent identity.

Just as the stage distorts space, action distorts time. While there is a sketchy plot in the conventional sense, flashbacks and illusory projections into the future are the principal means through which the characters define themselves. Present reality covers a period of about a week, in which José and María meet casually, make another date, and develop illusions about how it might be between them. Through both the flashbacks and projections into the future, José and María, as well as Ricardo, reveal a conflict between their inner anxieties and their public image. Overt *machismo* and maidenly propriety are only façades behind which they hide their basic insecurities, as do the characters in *Amoretta*. Unlike the latter, however, José and María do not experience a clearly defined insight into and resolution of their problems. Instead, the constantly shifting planes of time and reality make it difficult to tell by the final scene whether José and María have at last come together or whether they are simply embarking on a new variation on the theme of their proposed encounter.

It is, however, clear that they both profoundly need to find each other and to find themselves so as to break the fetters of introversion that chain them to a routine of frustrating loneliness.

While José and María exist in Buenos Aires, there is nothing in *El amasijo* of the sociopolitical limitations that detract from *Heroica de Buenos Aires*. Their needs stem from the human condition rather than from the peculiarities of geography and history. In this respect as well as in that of technical experimentation, it is significant that Dragún feels that *El amasijo* is one of his best works.[37] With this evaluation he seems to recognize that his talents are better used when applied to themes of universal appeal and to technical innovation rather than to the narrower and more ephemeral area of sociopolitical protest, as in *Heroica de Buenos Aires*. In his opinion of *El amasijo*, Dragún also confirms his preference for the basic dramatic techniques of *Historias para ser contadas* and his interest in developing them further.

It is fortunate that with *El amasijo* Dragún is again exploring the avenues of technical innovation heralded by *Historias para ser contadas*, because it is in this area that he has contributed most to the Latin American theater. He has been able to achieve his dramatic intent without relying on elaborate visual effects, and, at the same time, he has managed to bring cinematic techniques, such as the flashback, to the stage without falling into the excesses to which a less mature dramatist might be victim. Above all, Dragún must be credited with creating virtually a new dramatic genre, represented by the *Historias para ser contadas*. Whether reinterpreting an episode from ancient Greece or examining the frustrations of his contemporaries, Dragún has set an example for other young Latin American dramatists in both the boldness of his innovations and in his command of the dramatic medium.[38]

NOTES

1. Frank Dauster, "Cinco años de teatro hispanoamericano," *Asomante* 15, no. 1 (1959): 60. My translation, as are all subsequent translations from texts in Spanish, unless otherwise indicated.

2. The editions to which references will be made are *La peste viene de Melos* (Buenos Aires: Editorial Ariadna, 1956); *Tupac Amarú* (Buenos Aires: Ediciones Losange, 1957); *Jardín del infierno, Revista de la Escuela de Arte Teatral*, no. 5 (1961), pp. 51–81; *Milagro en el Mercado Viejo* (Buenos Aires: Producciones Norte, 1963); *Y nos dijeron que éramos inmortales* (Buenos Aires: Ediciones Los Monteagudos, 1963); *Teatro: Historia de mi esquina; Historias para ser contadas* (Buenos Aires: Editorial Escorpio, 1965); *Amoretta* (Buenos Aires: Ediciones del Carro de Tespis, 1965); *Heroica de Buenos Aires* (Havana: Casa de las Américas, 1966); *El amasijo* (Buenos Aires: Catalayud Editor, 1968).

3. ". . . for a thing, however small, but that can be touched and can be grasped in the hand."

4. "One day you told me I was free. Then you taught me to defend my liberty. Now, at the minute of my death, I thank you, Pitias."

5. ". . . a small and profound land, with a round and soft bay like a woman's pregnant belly."

6. "It's no longer good for anything."

7. "I would prefer a clean fight."

8. "I had to decide. Many times I had to decide."

9. "No. Because I decided. And if in being able to choose something else I chose this, I have nothing to regret."

10. *Areche*. (*Softly*) What did you hope to gain? Power? I aspire to power! And you?

Tupac Amarú. I was more ambitious than you. I wanted them to believe in me, so that when I told them they were no longer slaves they would rush to the conquest of their land."

11. "I am the victor. But if you see me getting lost in the turmoil, stick me with your sword and remind me that I am the victor."

12. "I shouldn't have had you killed, Indian! You were the only one who kept me company—I shouldn't have had you killed! I should have taken you by the hand and wandered with you through the world."

13. *Tupac Amarú*. Is it you, shadow?

Flores. No, I'm not—

Tupac Amarú. (*Interrupting him*) Yes, you are a shadow!

14. ". . . a laugh to be laughed or a tear to be wept"; ". . . far off, in distant plazas."

15. ". . . not very humanitarian."

16. *Mother*. Are you going out?

Father. Yes.

Mother. Again?

Father. Again.

Mother. Are you going to come back tonight?

Father. I don't know.

17. "I have never decided anything, pop."

18. "Swallows of a single summer, with endless yearnings for a distant sky . . ." From the tango "Golondrinas" by Carlos Gardel.

19. *Mother's voice*. Marry a rich man!

Father's voice. You pay a little more attention to your kids.

Gregorio's voice. Marry a rich man—

Aldo's voice. You love me, Virginia—

In unison: MARRY A RICH MAN. (*Repeated four times 'in crescendo.'* Virginia flees tormented.)

20. "Every time a train passes and I see that little taillight, I get a burning in my stomach, and I feel like running."

21. "Where do the trains go, Tana? Where do the people go who travel on the train?"

22. "You've always had it in for me! Get your hands off me!"

23. "It would make me mad and make me want to cry. Afterwards I would run. . . . I would run because they were dirty and they smelled."

24. "At your side is the first time I have felt tired. Do you know how good it is to feel tired?"

25. "Holy Mary Mother of God, pray for us sinners."

26. Republished in 1965 in the *Teatro* collection mentioned above.

27. "Yes, I am sorry, but if I go back to being Fernández, you'll get crushed again—and I'll go back to hating you."

28. "Georgie, listen to me! Georgie! Death exists and is waiting, but it's not a problem. Our only problem is how to live. Do you hear me, Georgie? Do you hear me? That's what Limpie's waiting for you to tell him. Do you hear me, Georgie? Do you hear me?" (*And They Told Us We Were Immortal*, trans. Alden James Green, in *The Modern Stage in Latin America: Six Plays*, ed. George W. Woodyard [New York: E. P. Dutton & Co., 1971], p. 178). All further translations from *Y nos dijeron que éramos inmortales* come from this edition.

29. "This house is the whole world" (p. 132); ". . . the mother whore who dropped him" (p. 136).

30. "Neither God nor death are problems for me; / They neither cure my liver nor make me laugh. / The only miracle is the life of a man, / Because it has to be made" (p. 156).

31. "Old stories are finished: / I'm about to spawn" (p. 179).

32. "Faith? Ah, my dear, when Manuel died—'brother' Manuel—I realized that he was my faith."

33. Alvaro del Amo and Carlos Rodríguez Sanz, "Conversación con Osvaldo Dragún," *Primer Acto*, no. 77 (1966), p. 13.

34. ". . . everything we are we owe to you."

35. "All my life I have dreamed about this! And now, they are everything I dreamed of —everything I wanted—yet they are exactly the opposite! What happened, Adolfo?"

36. Osvaldo Dragún to Donald L. Schmidt, 9 May 1971, personal files.

37. Ibid.

38. This article has been expanded and rendered into English from my earlier "El teatro de Osvaldo Dragún," *Latin American Review 2*, no. 2 (Spring 1969): 3–20.

6. The Plays of Griselda Gambaro

Sandra Messinger Cypess

After a decade of work, Argentina's Griselda Gambaro has emerged as one of Latin America's more prominent dramatists. Her reputation is well established in her own country, and as her work has become more readily available, she has begun to gain recognition in the United States. This study will discuss her four major plays: *Las paredes* (1963, "The walls"), *El desatino* (1964, "The blunder"), *Los Siameses* (1965, "The Siamese twins"), and *El campo* (1967, *The Camp*).[1] The ideas for her dramatic works are often based on her short stories.[2] Dialogue, however, can be considered of secondary importance in the plays, since the essence of the work is communicated by means of gestures, movements, noises, and the use of inanimate objects that function with a dramatic vitality. This movement away from a purely verbal theater to one based on physical language reveals the influence of Artaudian theory.[3]

Although the physical environments of the plays are important and carefully described, Gambaro does not situate her dramatic world in any specific time or geographic location. Neither does she use language that would mark her characters as Argentines. With a vigor and brutality that often startle an audience, she depicts the individual cowed into a state of submission by social and political pressures that deprive him of dignity and self-determination. Her view of man transcends national boundaries, and her message has universal significance.

A recurring pattern of action is found in all the plays: an average man, thrust into an inexplicable, frightening situation, is confronted with adversaries who may be intimates or strangers. Always they turn out to be formidable opponents who victimize him to the point of complete destruction. An analysis of *Las paredes* reveals that it is the prototype of this pattern.

Las paredes is a stark play with one basic setting involving three characters identified by their generic titles—the Youth, the Custodian, the Official. The tone of the opening scene is much the same as Kafka's *The Trial*: a young man finds himself detained against his will for offenses unknown to him. We find him seated in a comfortable, almost luxurious room, puzzled by his confinement. He had been picked up after a day's outing in the countryside. The details of his detention, as with all incidents in the play, will be reinterpreted by his adversaries, the Custodian and the Official. The Youth is so manipulated by them that at the end he no longer can distinguish his own will from that of his captors. The transition of the Youth to this condition of almost mindless automaton is skillfully dramatized by Gambaro.

Her technique, based upon a repetition of events with variations, appears similar to Beckett's in *Waiting for Godot*. In *Godot*, "these variations merely serve to emphasize the essential sameness of the situation";[4] in *Las paredes*, however, each variation, each twist of interpretation of the situation propels the Youth further down the road to his ultimate degradation as a human being.

The mental transformation of the Youth is reflected in a parallel diminution of the physical surroundings. The initial well-appointed bedroom becomes progressively less comfortable, with less furnishings, and always smaller in space. The Youth's impression is not that he is being moved to different rooms, as is suggested at the end, but that somehow this same room grows frighteningly smaller.

While the control of his environment and psyche is reminiscent of George Orwell's *1984*, more subtle forms of punishment are inflicted on the Youth. His father's watch is taken from him, symbolizing his entrance into a world without time. Just as his room is stripped bare of appointments, so he, too, is dispossessed of his right to be called a *caballero* and is labelled instead a thief, an informer, a liar. The beating he receives at the hands of the Custodian also signifies the loss of his dignity and honor as a gentleman.

His self-confidence is further demeaned in the incident involving a statue that his captors have brought to him from the outside world. The statue is aesthetically displeasing to the Youth, but his landlady obligated him to keep it, and he did so out of fear of her. His inability to destroy the statue because of this fear is manipulated by his captors. The Official praises the statue and says the artistic quality of the work made the Youth keep it: "Es el arte, caballero. ¿Cómo no lo entiende usted? Por eso no se han atrevido a romperla, los huéspedes y usted mismo. . . . Usted no rompe la muñeca para asegurar la belleza de los mundos, el orden" (p. 27).[5] Then, to confuse the Youth, he abruptly reverses his opinion and demands the destruction of the figurine. His perplexed captive now defends the object as a work of art. The Official calls him a hypocrite for refusing to smash the ugly thing and coerces the Youth into saying he will break it. Now, despite the opportunity to perform the decisive act, fear and confusion paralyze him. The statue remains unbroken, a symbol of his inability to act of his own free will.

Although each encounter with his adversaries is a new frustration, the Youth accepts their degrading treatment, hoping that compliance will bring about his freedom. At first, his captors bolster his hopes of a quick discharge; then they make ambiguous references to his imminent death. Their mental teasing had been concretized earlier in the setting in which the curtain hides not an open window but a blank wall. After being continually teased about his death, he becomes desensitized to its possibility. In the final scene, when the Custodian confesses to the Youth that "a media noche, caerán las paredes sobre usted" (p. 40),[6] he rejects this admission of his impending death. That the walls had fallen on someone had been the first statement by the Custodian to explain the unusual screams heard at the onset of the play and that have recurred periodically. At first shocked by such violence, the Youth later mechanically repeats the explanation of the Official: "Gritan por vicio. Se lo conté al funcionario. No hay por qué inquietarse. El mismo me lo explicó. . . . Gritan porque se cansan, se aburren, pero no se mueren!" (p. 40).[7]

At the end of the play the conquest of his mind and body is complete. When the Custodian leaves him in the cell with the door to freedom opened at last, the Youth does not move to escape. He remains lying on his cot, as immobile as the statue clasped in his arms. "El joven mira hacia la puerta, luego, con obediente determinación, muy rígido, la muñeca entre los brazos, los ojos increíble y estupidamente abiertos, espera" (p. 43).[8] The Youth is waiting for his liberation, which can occur in two possible forms: either his release as he hopes, or his death. That the latter is the conclusion is supported by content as well as by the form of the first act. Its structure is circular in that it begins and ends with the anguished cries of unknown origin. There is also a sense of circularity in the progress of the Youth's knowledge, for despite his questions, he knows no more than when he was first detained. He is told at one point that he has been confined in order to verify that he is not Ruperto de Hentzau.[9] The absurdity of the explanation reveals that any excuse will serve his inquisitors. Just as the questioning of his identity seems pointless, so, too, does the possibility of his freedom appear an illusion. The screams are an indication of the fate others have met. The conclusion of *Las paredes*, then, appears to be directed toward the completion of the circle, or death for the individual.

The political significance of the play can be determined from the almost obvious symbolism. Both the Official and the Custodian wear uniforms suggesting their connection to a military or bureaucratic superstructure. The room where they incarcerate the Youth symbolizes a totalitarian state in which the individual is controlled by an omnipotent ruling class. This victimization is seen as inescapable, for no one exists in this world except those who are victims and those who wield power.

Las paredes also seems to present an exploration of a metaphysical question concerning the nature of being. The Youth can be seen to represent man caught at a point in time when he experiences a sense of freedom. This freedom cannot be considered absolute, since man has certain obligations and fears that control his free will. Yet even this limited sense of freedom proves to be false. At any moment we can be detained and our expectations thwarted by a hostile society as represented by the Official and the Custodian. We live hoping for freedom, yet we are ever threatened by death so that our ability to act independently becomes controlled by the fear of death. The question that remains is not whether the end will come, but when. The possibility of becoming paralyzed into inaction by the process of waiting is symbolized by the Youth's identification with the statue. The voice of protest against an existence necessarily limited by death is raised by the Custodian: "Pero, caballero, ¿la vida entera no es acaso un malentendido? ¿Llevamos la misma vida? Y entonces, ¿por qué el mismo final? ¿Es justo? ¿Cómo no perder la paciencia?" (p. 36).[10] The Custodian, not quite at the level of the Official, but superior to the Youth in terms of his knowledge of the universe, has the will to feel rebellious toward the equalizing effect of death, yet he is part of the powers that enforce it, another manifestation of the unavoidability of man's destiny.

The problem of man's victimization is recast in *El desatino*. The unidentified youth and his tormentors are replaced by a group of family and friends. The role of the victim is now less abstract, for the character has the specific name of Alfonso. His adversaries turn out to be his mother, doña Viola, his best friend Luis, and his wife Lily. Lily, who never appears on stage except in a dream sequence, has been interpreted as a symbol of his sexual obsession.[11] Since sexual proclivity in *El desatino* also seems to function as an expression of free will, Alfonso's creation of Lily also represents his desire to assert himself. Like the Youth of *Las paredes*, Alfonso becomes involved in an inexplicable predicament, the first of the blunders referred to in the title. He awakens one morning to find himself immobilized by a bulky iron object that has attached itself to his foot. This inanimate object functions as a concrete expression of Alfonso's dependency on others. Throughout the play Alfonso tries to extricate himself from the object, and he asks for help from his mother and his best friend. However, neither one attempts to free him from the obstacle that forces him to be dependent upon them. Their excuses for delaying their help and their lack of concern reveal the contradictory and inimical status of their relationship to Alfonso. The one person who attempts to free Alfonso is rejected because he is not a member of the intimate and favored circle of family and friends. The title, then, serves as a commentary on the confused, almost foolish relationships in the play.

Doña Viola and Luis are alike in that they are parasites, taking from others to sustain themselves. The mother figure—the nurturer—ironically deprives her own son of sustenance. She prefers to give Luis the food Alfonso needs. In the same manner, Luis takes food away from his own younger brother to satisfy himself. Food appears to represent more than physical nourishment; it symbolizes the love and companionship that enable a person to grow strong and independent. Just as Alfonso is deprived of food and not physically able to function because of the iron object, so, too, he is spiritually encumbered by his mother and best friend.

Alfonso's mother, preoccupied with her own needs, pays no attention to Alfonso's discomfort. Instead, she reproaches him for her own shortcomings: "Cuando te tuve, se me movió un disco de la columna. Así estoy ahora, por ti, completamente dura" (p. 14).[12] Indeed, she is *dura*, but in the figurative sense of being unkind and harsh. Her principal attitude toward her son is conditioned by her need to consume Alfonso's undivided attention and to dominate his will.

Her resentment of Lily leads her to ridicule his interest in this other woman. She uses the clothes Alfonso has bought for Lily, expressing her desire to usurp the identity of his wife. Despite her decaying eroticism, she flirts with Luis, and the two engage in an affair that pointedly excludes Alfonso.

Although his mother harms him in a passive way, Luis actively threatens Alfonso with physical injury. He brings a cigarette close to Alfonso's eyes, saying he will not burn him, but he does. He ties a scarf around Alfonso's neck saying, "Te abrigo, te abrigo" (p. 32);[13] despite such an endearing expression, he comes close to strangling his friend. Luis abuses him under the pretext that he is testing Alfonso's manhood. That Luis mocks Alfonso's masculinity is also evident in his attitude toward Lily and in his derogatory remarks about their marriage.

Lily's interest in Luis and her inattention to Alfonso contravene Alfonso's original need for her as an expression of his independence from his mother and Luis: "Qué felicidad nuestros primeros tiempos. . . . Nadie te conocía. Ni mamá ni Luis te conocían. . . . No tenía nada, salvo a mamá y los tachos de basura, y de pronto te tuve a ti. Nadie podía alcanzarte... Sí en los primeros tiempos nadie podía alcanzarte, pero ahora..." (pp. 80–81).[14] Thus, with the passage of time, Alfonso's desire for Lily and his efforts to assert himself have been frustrated by his own weakness of character, as symbolized by his inability to consummate his marriage.

Unlike the Youth of *Las paredes*, Alfonso is presented with someone who is willing to extricate him from his oppressive situation. This character, called simply *el muchacho* (the Boy), is described as a road-construction worker. The Boy neglects his job to give aid and comfort to Alfonso. The latter, however, rudely rejects the help of the intruder. His misplaced, *desatinado* ("foolish") sense of affiliation prevents him from seeking freedom from those who debase him and deprive him of his will. He not only identifies with his oppressors, but also he copies their arrogance and lack of compassion in dealing with the Boy. Completely victimized, Alfonso is unable to distinguish between his enemies and his benefactors. His inherent impotence leads him to propagate the very means of oppression used against himself. Thus, Alfonso not only permits his own destruction, but also he soon generates the conditions leading to the subversion of his would-be rescuer.

It would seem that the culminating moment of the play would be Alfonso's release from the obstacle. This had been Alfonso's aim and, more importantly, the goal toward which all the efforts of the Boy had been directed. Despite the attempts by Alfonso and his family to thwart him, the Boy does succeed in separating Alfonso from the iron block. Ironically, however, there is only separation and not liberation. As the imprisoning object falls away, "Alfonso lanza un alarido tremendo, se incorpora y vuelve a caer en la cama, como un trapo, los ojos abiertos" (p. 101).[15] Gambaro does not make explicit whether Alfonso is to be presumed dead. The critic of *Confirmado* of Buenos Aires believes Alfonso is dead,[16] while Tamara Holzapfel interprets the action to mean his regression to an infantile state.[17] What is apparent in either case is his uselessness and his inability to act independently. By becoming "como un trapo," Alfonso has lost his humanity and therefore the possibility of acting like the older brother, the friend of the Boy's dream. When the Boy realizes that his dream has been aborted before it was able to bloom, his disappointment overwhelms his good nature. There is a transformation in the Boy, as evidenced in the violence of his confrontation with Luis's younger brother: "(El niño . . . *comienza a sacar las estacas de los tiestos y se las pone bajo el brazo. El muchacho lo ve, le grita ferozmente.*) ¡Deja las estacas, puerco! ¡Deja las estacas!" (p. 104).[18] His exaggerated antagonism toward the little boy is motivated by his grief over the loss of Alfonso and the failure of his search for friendship. The ending of *El desatino* suggests, then, that the cycle might begin again, with one more compassionate soul being converted to the service of oppression.

The play's statement concerning the victimization of the individual represents one of the possible readings of its thematic message. Holzapfel has offered another interpretation, seeing the play as "an allegory about contemporary Argentine or Latin American society in which the middle class male (Alfonso) is fettered by his own self-indulgent sexual fantasies, by a matriarchally dominated family and by a calloused and shallow society. The efforts of the working class, although well-meant, are arrogantly scorned by and ultimately wasted on the degenerate middle class."[19] Writing the prologue to the play, Roberto Villanueva aptly considers still another dimension of *El desatino*, its commentary on the absurdity of the human condition: "Out of all this misplaced logic and out of that tension toward the limits of the absurd in which the words, gestures, reactions, motivations, the very dreams of the characters are arranged, out of all that exasperation of the quotidian, the normal, comes forth a kind of demonstration by means of the absurd. The ridiculous and the tragic spring forth together" (p. 8).

Gambaro's study of the victimization of man, which first explored a situation among strangers and then proceeded to the family circle, now focuses on a twosome in *Los Siameses*. The play develops as a series of encounters in which Lorenzo, apparently motivated by envy, causes the destruction of Ignacio. This relationship recalls the Cain-and-Abel motif, yet the two main characters are tied together not by blood but by situation—like the pair in *Waiting for Godot*. Although Lorenzo and Ignacio are the couple referred to in the title, their fraternal relationship seems to be a myth exploited by Lorenzo, or, if true, a fact not willingly accepted by Ignacio.

It is Lorenzo who first alludes to their having been born together and to their identical nature: "Pero ¿quién es capaz de distinguir algo entre los dos? Yo no puedo. Somos iguales. Esa es nuestra desgracia. Somos tan iguales que nuestras acciones se confunden" (p. 15).[20] Many critics have accepted at face value Lorenzo's statements, yet more careful attention to the text reveals that Lorenzo is consistently unreliable. For example, although Lorenzo says they look alike (p. 15), the stage directions make explicit that Ignacio "no se parece nada a Lorenzo" (p. 18).[21] Furthermore, the entire play is a refutation that "nuestras acciones se confunden."[22] Ignacio, with his "sonrisa bondadosa e ingenua" (p. 21),[23] is the more compassionate, docile character. He is interested in women and hopes to be able to marry the girl of his choice. Lorenzo, on the contrary, is cunning, envious, and treacherous. Unlike Ignacio, Lorenzo is said to be impotent. His sexual impotence is symbolic of his overall inability to give of himself. His physical weakness acts as a metaphor for his lack of moral strength.

It is in an attempt to reflect their condition as Siamese twins that Lorenzo forces Ignacio to perform with him a walking exercise: "Los dos empiezan a caminar por la pieza. Se pegan costado contra costado y ejecutan el mismo paso, la pierna derecha de Lorenzo pegada a la pierna izquierda de Ignacio" (p. 21).[24] This gesture of walking in unison parodies a togetherness that does not exist internally. Rather, Lorenzo and Ignacio are brothers only in the sense of two mortals bound together in the human condition. Their lack of similarity, coupled with their inability to live harmoniously together or to exist successfully apart, suggests that they are also incomplete parts of a whole. Their relationship therefore implies two vital complementary aspects of man—one cunning and aggressive, the other trusting and receptive. Gambaro has confirmed this interpretation that they are not literally Siamese twins; her own explanation of their brotherhood is that "Ignacio always believed that Lorenzo was his brother—his brother in the sense of being his fellow man, and Lorenzo is going to learn finally that each fellow man is our brother. He only made use of the fiction of a nonexistent blood relationship whenever it suited him."[25]

From the moment we meet Lorenzo on stage he is engaged in his most characteristic behavior—creating destructive situations in which to torment Ignacio. Six of the seven scenes show how Lorenzo successfully contrives to have Ignacio receive bloody beatings at the hands of a stranger, then by the police, whom he gladly helps, and finally by the father of the girl Ignacio had hoped to marry. The brutal physical punishment succeeds in changing Ignacio so that he is less trusting and more wary. Nevertheless, he never accuses Lorenzo outright of the latter's role in his misfortune. He acknowledges only his doubt: "No sé si no me hiciste nada" (p. 62).[26] Part of our sympathy for Ignacio is based on this resilient faith in his fellow man, despite the many provocations and despite, too, Lorenzo's admission of his envy: "Me gusta . . . la forma en que ríes. Por eso te hago perradas para que rías lo menos posible. Cada vez... que ríes, me quitas algo, lo que no es mío" (p. 52).[27] The laugh that Lorenzo covets is symbolic of Ignacio's vitality, his ability to communicate with others. Thus, although Lorenzo calls Ignacio the deficient, incomplete member of the pair, his inherent, Cain-like feeling is that Ignacio is the favored one.

Lorenzo's machinations in ridding himself of Ignacio are predicated on the erroneous belief that without Ignacio he will somehow be more whole, more independent. With Ignacio's death, however, Lorenzo does not find satisfaction or freedom. Rather, Ignacio's destruction ironically results in Lorenzo's own victimization. He learns too late that his well-being was tied to Ignacio's, that their strongest bond was not their physical but their psychological interdependence. Gambaro depicts this realization not through words but by means of Lorenzo's final actions. Alone on an empty stage, Lorenzo appears to have assumed at last the identity of Ignacio—ironically, the dead Ignacio: "(*Se queda inmóvil, un silencio. Tímida, desoladamente.*) Ignacio, Ignacio... (*Se dobla en una pose semejante a la de* Ignacio *en el carrito, la cabeza sobre las rodillas. Un gran silencio.*)" (p. 86).[28]

The impact of the final scene is strengthened by its power to recall the final moments of Beckett's *Waiting for Godot.* Just as there is ironic inaction after Estragon's famous "allons y," Lorenzo's "Me voy, ahora sí, me voy" (p. 86) leads him nowhere.[29] As Holzapfel has aptly expressed it, "The stigma of Cain destines Lorenzo to total isolation."[30]

The emptiness of the stage in the final moments of the work contrasts with earlier scenes in which the stage was crowded with objects. An imposing pile of old newspapers seems to represent man's ties with the past, as did the watch in *Las paredes.* Here is man's recorded past, Gambaro seems to imply, useless as a means of instruction for the improvement of mankind. This idea is not left unexpressed verbally, for the newspapers are used to bring in a reference to the audience's world of verifiable reality. An article on the assassination of President John F. Kennedy causes Lorenzo to feel threatened by unexpected death. The fear and horror provoked by Kennedy's murder, however, does nothing to change Lorenzo's subsequent part in the death of Ignacio.

In addition to the newspapers, there is also a pile of bread on the patio. Ignacio bought the bread from the bakery so he could meet with his sweetheart Inés, the baker's daughter. Lorenzo, too, has added to the pile of bread, proof of his having been to the bakery also. This decaying food, stale, unused, seems to objectify Ignacio's frustrated love for Inés as well as the useless outcome of his own life.

The violence contained in the theme finds concrete expression in the many examples of physical punishment presented throughout the play. Ignacio, as the chief victim, receives most of the blows. The only time he appears to fight back occurs when his dead body resists being shoved into the little cart that is to transport him for burial. Ironically, there is now "una lucha obstinada, de contenida violencia" (p. 79),[31] between Ignacio and the policemen who are trying to get rid of him. Further macabre irony follows when Lorenzo is hit with force by the shovel with which he is to dig Ignacio's grave. Lorenzo continues to show his inherent lack of compassion toward others when, despite his own pain, he gives vent to his bad nature by hitting the two old men and the young boy who are his accessories in the burial of Ignacio.

Although *Los Siameses* concentrates on the interactions of two men, it is not Lorenzo alone who victimizes Ignacio. That he has accomplices in his brutality broadens Gambaro's theme to include once again society's role in the exploitation of man. Thus, the two policemen, who so willingly accept Lorenzo's falsification of evidence against Ignacio, represent the state's role. The play contains a cynical commentary on justice, too, as Ignacio tells Lorenzo that he was beaten by the police not on the basis of his guilt, but because "no les caí simpático" (p. 50).[32] The willingness of the two old men to help bury Ignacio points out how the complicity of other men is achieved by working on their self-interests. It is important to note that the two old men are frustrated in satisfying their desires. Despite compliance with the authorities, their simple wishes are sacrificed to the will of those more powerful than they.

The tragic outcome of the pair in *Los Siameses* depicts the result of victimization on the involved individuals. There is tragedy in the unnecessary sacrifice of human life represented by Ignacio's death. Yet the greatest loss, at least in this play, is shown to be suffered by the victimizer, who lingers in a state of isolated agony.

In the three preceding plays, the spectator is given the task of transposing the situations of the characters to the events of our contemporary society. In *El campo*, Gambaro approaches more openly the particular details of life in the twentieth century. The ambiguous title acts as the password to this world: *el campo* can be interpreted to refer to the countryside, or to a military camp, or to a place of detention. It is in connection with the latter usage that Gambaro recalls the twentieth-century political convulsions of Nazi Germany and Vietnam. However, no references to a specific locale or time are indicated within the text.

The central character, Martin, unlike his prototype in *Las paredes*, freely enters the camp on assignment as a bookkeeper. He is directed in his duties by Franco, who is dressed in a Gestapo uniform and armed with a whip. Franco's outfit, the prison garb of the third main character, Emma, and the presence of guards and prisoners all suggest that the camp is a prison. Yet Franco claims to see children, farm peasants, and hunters to support the illusion of the first, more harmless meaning of *campo*.

The equivocal title is indicative of Gambaro's technique throughout the play. Irony and counterpoint are manipulated to create an atmosphere of confusion and terror in which Martin and the audience are made to mistrust, then fear, whatever is seen, heard, and done.

The dichotomy of this *campo* is presented immediately by the noises Martin hears: the shouts of children playing are juxtaposed with the sounds of harsh commands and with groans coming from the distance. These are recurring noises, disrupting the deceptive tranquility of the environment. Although Martin never sees the carefree children or the singing farmworkers or the happy hunters, he does smell burning flesh, and he soon becomes both a witness to and a recipient of the strange tortures and degradations inflicted upon the inmates of this camp.

When Franco first appears, his Gestapo uniform seems incongruous, since his demeanor and actions contradict his attire: "Su aspecto no es para nada amenazador, es un hombre joven, de rostro casi bondadoso" (p. 8).[33] This incongruity is dispelled with the passage of time, and Franco's behavior soon conforms to his uniform. Although at first his points of disagreement with Martin are trivial, his requests gradually come to be orders dictating all aspects of Martin's behavior. He also reveals a fundamental lack of respect for Martin in very simple yet annoying behavior—by mishandling Martin's overcoat, by taking off his own boots and placing his bare feet on the desk so they are in Martin's face. Such conflicts seem more absurd than life threatening, yet they serve to put Martin in a position as adversary to Franco when the real contest begins with the entrance of Emma.

The figure of Emma is also full of contradictions. Her visual appearance—shaven head, bare feet, prison garb, wounded hand—does not conform to her gestures or words. As Gambaro makes explicit in her stage directions, "Sus gestos no concuerdan para nada con su aspecto. Son los gestos, actitudes, de una mujer que luciera un vestido de fiesta. La voz es mundana hasta el amaneramiento, salvo oportunidades en las que la voz se desnuda y corresponde angustiosa, desoladamente, a su aspecto" (p. 28).[34] Martin is confused by the disparity between her story and her appearance and does not know how to react. Her wounds and prison markings, however, arouse his sympathy so that he finally becomes involved in her predicament. Martin's feelings of pity and his expression of tenderness mark both his humanity and his inevitable victimization by the same forces that worked upon Emma.

Franco directs Emma's behavior as he tried to do with Martin. The two play at being genteel friends, acting in "un tono de sociabilidad amanerada" (p. 38).[35] At times, each drops the tone of forced friendliness so that we see their true relationship of tormentor and victim. Franco refuses to let Emma scratch herself, although she is evidently suffering from some annoying itch. He also plagues her with questions about the wound on her hand. He denies or affirms the existence of the wound as evidence of his power to manipulate the conditions of reality in their world. This manipulation is graphically demonstrated when Franco, by merely striking the ground with his whip, causes Emma to react as if she had been physically hit. Her conditioned response implies the tortures she has suffered in the past.

The nature of the punishment meted out by those in power is not left to the audience's imagination. The concert scene that ends act I is at once a grotesque mockery of a piano recital and an exhibition of physical and emotional punishment. Prisoners and SS Troops comprise the hostile audience; they function as perpetrators of sadistic orders, mechanically acting on command. Just as all of Emma's efforts to play are frustrated, Martin experiences parallel feelings as he is constrained to behave according to the dictates of the SS Troops. They force him to sit, to stand, to move his head like a puppet in response to their demands. At the end, his reactions conform with their will without the need for their physical interference; he exhibits the same kind of conditioned reflexes as did Emma in the whipping scene.

The antagonists act out of a sense of almost solicitous cruelty. When Emma begins to scratch herself furiously, Franco simulates concern by applying a lotion, which only causes her to itch in greater agony. The prisoners mock her uncontrollable actions by scratching each other. At the same time, Martin becomes the victim of the troops, who scratch his face until blood appears. Gambaro strikes a further note of irony when she directs that this cruel mistreatment be executed "casi tiernamente, sin violencia" (p. 59).[36]

Each aspect of the concert, as in other experiences recorded in the play, exhibits a disparity between expectation and result: the piano tuner fixes the piano but it does not play; Franco's lotion does not bring relief but further pain; the soldiers' tender attitude toward Martin results in his molestation. The outcome of each action is unpredictable yet always brings with it stress or damage to the individual. Such reversals of actions are a means to break down the individual's confidence in his own judgment and destroy his sense of independence.

The beginning scenes of act II continue the technique of unexpected reversals. Despite the punishment they suffered at the concert, Martin and Emma reappear, apparently free of their oppressors. When Franco does enter the scene, it is to bring the unexpected news that Martin is at liberty to leave the camp and to take Emma with him.

After having been unnecessarily bullied and beaten, Martin reacts with bewilderment to the news of his release, but, nevertheless, he does leave with Emma through the proffered door to freedom. There is a marked transformation in him as he returns home. Externally, we see that he lacks his belongings—overcoat, gloves, and scarf—losses symbolic of the layers of dignity and integrity that were stripped from him in his passage through the camp. Existentially, he is no longer at ease in his newly liberated situation. His uneasiness is justified when an intruder appears at his home. Emma identifies the man "con cara de cerdo feliz" (p. 95)[37] as one of Franco's subordinates. He is soon joined by three other men, who bring with them equipment of menacing significance: hypo-dermic needles and a branding iron.

The ensuing scene dispels the short-lived notion that Martin and Emma had escaped from their tormentors. This second lease on freedom is as illusory for them as the open door was for the Youth of *Las Paredes*. In an atmosphere of mounting terror, Martin is solicitously menaced with questions about his iden-tity (¿judío? ¿comunista?), then about his health (¿Está inmunizado?). His answers are irrelevant, his protests and resistance powerless to avert the con-sequences. Martin, resembling "un animal a punto de ser cazado" (p. 100),[38] is subdued and given an injection that destroys his will to protest. The branding iron is next, but the curtain falls before we see it applied directly to Martin.

Martin, like the other protagonist-victims before him, winds up both literally and figuratively against the wall, cornered into a situation from which there is no escape. He has been divested of his ability to act independently and rendered helpless in the face of powerful forces over which he has no control.

El campo provides an effective warning of the dangers and the repercussions of any form of oppression—political, social, or artistic. Focusing on Emma as the "mutilated and degraded artist," Holzapfel has interpreted the play as "an allegory about the pressures exerted by political dictatorships on the arts."[39] With Martin's circumstances as the springboard, the social significance of the play asserts itself as a commentary on the gratuitous obstacles that the im-personal bureaucracies of our institutions invent to molest us. The actions of Franco and his subordinates sharpen the political thrust of the play to show how the individual is deprived of his freedom in order to conform to the oppres-sive will of the state.

Gambaro's recurrent exploration of the victimization of man gives thematic unity to her theater. She presents a hostile environment in which both charac-ters and spectators feel threatened and tormented not only by others but also by the very objects and physical space that comprise their milieu. Her ability to utilize space, sounds, objects, gestures, and actions for dramatic effect reveals how well she has put into practice the theories of Antonin Artaud.

For all its somberness of theme, her dramatic world nevertheless does con-tain humor. The comic elements, however, do not lighten the mood but in-stead emphasize the ultimate tragedy of the individual's condition. The humor arises from her use of language as well as from specific situations and always seems to have a thematic meaning. The comic distortions of familiar sayings by the Official in *Las paredes* reflect his freedom to manipulate not only language but also the lives of other men. Some pertinent examples: "Mañana vendré, espéreme sentado" (p. 29), "Pero, ¿por qué esa prisa? Vita longa, res breve" (p. 23).[40]

Humor incarnated in characters seems to be exemplified, at first, in the pair of policemen in *Los Siameses*. Laughter is stimulated by *el sonriente* always smiling and *el gangoso* always gagging on his words—until their sinister intentions become apparent. Their alteration reveals that the forces of oppression can take many forms. Similarly, Franco's excessive annoyance at Martin's habit of chewing gum seems funny until it is seen as a presage of Franco's far more violent attempts to control Martin's behavior.

The discrepancies between gestures and dialogue that characterize so many members of Gambaro's dramatic world bring her humor within the realm of the grotesque.[41] For, while we may laugh momentarily at the incongruities presented, the unexpected reversals of action and the confusing behavior function to undermine the individual's sense of integrity and well-being and lead to his subsequent victimization. The disparate elements, like the physical imagery, serve to define Gambaro's vision of man's existence as being essentially absurd. Though her protagonist-victims may suffer from a sense of alienation in an incomprehensible universe, her dramatic world is significant for the spectator on many levels—sensorily, emotionally, and intellectually.

NOTES

1. *Las paredes*, copy of original manuscript, personal files; *El desatino* (Buenos Aires: Centro de Experimentación Audiovisual del Instituto Torcuato di Tella, 1965); *Los Siameses* (Buenos Aires: Insurrexit, 1967); *El campo* (Buenos Aires: Insurrexit, 1967). Subsequent quotations from the plays will refer to these respective editions. Translations from the Spanish text are my own unless otherwise indicated.

2. "Teatro," *Confirmado*, 9 September 1965, p. 43.

3. See Sandra M. Cypess, "Physical Imagery in the Plays of Griselda Gambaro," *Modern Drama*, in press.

4. Martin Esslin, *Theatre of the Absurd*, rev. ed. (Garden City, N.Y.: Doubleday Anchor Books, 1969), p. 31.

5. "It is art, sir. In what way don't you understand it? That's why no one has dared to break it, neither the lodgers nor you yourself. You don't break the doll in order to assert the concept of beauty and order in the world."

6. ". . . at midnight, the walls will fall on top of you."

7. "They scream out of habit. I told the official about it. There's no reason to become worried. He himself explained it to me. They scream because they get tired, they get bored, but they don't die!"

8. "The young man looks toward the door; then with submissive determination, very rigid, holding the doll in his arms, his blank eyes incredibly open, he waits expectantly."

9. Ruperto de Hentzau is a character from *The Prisoner of Zenda* by Anthony Hope. The allusion is comically absurd, since Hentzau is called the most evil of men, a description the Youth does not seem to fit at all.

10. "But, sir, is it not that all of life is perhaps a misunderstanding? Do we lead the

same lives? But then, why the same end? Is it fair? How is it possible not to lose one's patience?"

11. Tamara Holzapfel, "Griselda Gambaro's Theatre of the Absurd," *Latin American Theatre Review* 4, no. 1 (Fall 1970): 6.

12. "When I had you, I slipped a disc. Here I am now, because of you, completely stiff."

13. "I'm wrapping you up, I'm wrapping you up."

14. "How happy we were at the beginning. . . . Nobody knew you. Neither Mother nor Luis knew you. . . . I didn't have anything except Mother and the garbage cans, but suddenly I had you. Nobody could reach you. Yes, at first, nobody could reach you, but now—"

15. "Alfonso lets out a tremendous scream, he sits up in bed, then falls back again, like a rag, with his eyes wide open."

16. "Teatro," p. 43.

17. Holzapfel, "Griselda Gambaro's Theatre of the Absurd," p. 7.

18. "(*The* Child . . . *begins to take the cuttings from the pots and puts them under his arm. The* Boy *sees him, screams at him fiercely.*) Leave the cuttings, you pig, leave the cuttings!",

19. Holzapfel, "Griselda Gambaro's Theatre of the Absurd," p. 7.

20. "But, who could tell us apart? I cannot. We are the same. That is our misfortune. We are so much the same that our actions are misattributed."

21. ". . . does not look like Lorenzo at all."

22. ". . . our actions are misattributed."

23. ". . . kind and candid smile."

24. "The two start walking around the room. They line up side by side and execute the same step, the right foot of Lorenzo lined up with the left foot of Ignacio."

25. Griselda Gambaro to Sandra M. Cypess, 20 August 1972, personal files.

26. "I don't know whether you did anything to me or not."

27. "I like . . . the way you laugh. That's why I do mean things to you, so that you laugh as little as possible. Each time you laugh, you take away something from me, that part of me which is not mine."

28. "(*He stays motionless, a silence. Timidly, disconsolately.*) Ignacio, Ignacio—(*He bends over in a pose similar to that of* Ignacio *in the little cart, his head on his knees. A profound silence.*)"

29. "I'm going, now I'm really going away."

30. Holzapfel, "Griselda Gambaro's Theatre of the Absurd," p. 9.

31. ". . . an obstinate fight of contained violence."

32. "I wasn't appealing to them."

33. "There seems to be nothing threatening about his demeanor. He is a young man, and his face is almost kind" (*The Camp*, in *Voices of Change in the Spanish American Theater: An Anthology*, ed. and trans. William I. Oliver [Austin: University of Texas Press, 1971], p. 51).

34. "Her gestures in no way agree with her appearance. They are the gestures and attitudes of a lady dressed in a party gown. She speaks in a sophisticated and worldly manner. Only upon occasion does her real voice break through, expressing the anguish and desperation of her appearance" (ibid., p. 62).

35. ". . . a tone of mannered and high society" (ibid., p. 68).

36. ". . . almost tenderly and without violence" (ibid., p. 80).

37. ". . . with the face of a contented hog."

38. ". . . an animal about to be caught" (*The Camp*, trans. Oliver, p. 103).

39. Holzapfel, "Griselda Gambaro's Theatre of the Absurd," p. 11

40. "Tomorrow I'll come, wait for me seated. But, why that rush? Life is long, things are short."

41. See Wilhelm Kayser, *The Grotesque in Art and Literature* (New York: McGraw-Hill Paperbacks, 1963), pp. 118–119, for his discussion about the connections between the comic and the grotesque.

7. The Theater of Carlos Gorostiza

Merlin H. Forster

The inclusion of Carlos Gorostiza (Buenos Aires, 1920–) in a volume dedicated to the theater in Latin America as an expression of revolt may seem open to question. Gorostiza is conventional in theme and technique, and when compared to younger and more controversial figures, such as Jorge Díaz, Griselda Gambaro, or José Triana, he certainly does not appear as revolutionary. Nonetheless, several of Gorostiza's plays are landmarks in the early development of contemporary Argentine drama, and it is appropriate to accord him an important place among the initiators of the contemporary theater in Latin America.

Gorostiza's first involvement in the theater came at an early age with his activities as a puppeteer, and he organized in the 1940s "Los Títeres de la Estrella Grande." During the same period he wrote two works for children's puppet theater: *La clave encantada* (1943, "The enchanted key") and *Nuevos títeres de la clave encantada* (1949, "New puppets of the enchanted key"). Gorostiza directed his own successful first play in 1949 and since then has served as director for a number of other plays. He was in charge of "El Grupo del Sur," which performed at the Teatro San Telmo in Buenos Aires during the early 1960s. Shortly thereafter he directed the theatrical group "Los Caobos" in Caracas, Venezuela, and in 1970–1971 he was responsible for several productions at the Teatro Sullivan in Mexico City. Gorostiza has also distinguished himself for his *mise en scène* of a number of plays, and since 1962 he has been active in the production of television scripts. During the academic year 1965–1966, Gorostiza taught at Indiana State University (Terre Haute), lectured on Spanish American drama in a number of other universities in the United States, and directed some of his own work in English as well. At the present time, Gorostiza teaches in the Escuela Nacional de Arte Dramático in Buenos Aires and runs a private school for actors.

Gorostiza's most important contribution, however, has been as a playwright, and he has written and produced twelve plays. The first of these is *El puente* (1949, "The bridge"),[1] which at the time of its appearance became the most important box-office success of the independent theater movement in Buenos Aires. *El puente* is a somber and moving social drama in which the characters are sharply divided between well-to-do people in the comfortable setting of a luxurious Buenos Aires apartment and others whose more humble lives are depicted in the street outside the apartment building. The central conflict of the play is produced by the delayed arrival of an industrial engineer (from the well-to-do) and his assistant (from a laboring family) who have been working on a bridge outside the city. The two have been killed in an accident at the construction site, and as the play ends the bodies are mistakenly returned to the wrong houses. It is apparent that the two worlds have been bridged by the tragedy; neither the engineer's wife nor the mother and sister of the assistant will be able to continue life in the same way, but at the same time there is nothing left to do but accept the blow with sorrow.

Gorostiza followed this first success with a rapid series of six other plays, written between 1950 and 1955, in which he combined elements of fantasy with elements of the real world.[2] Perhaps the best of this series of plays is *El reloj de Baltasar* (1955, "Baltasar's watch").[3] Baltasar is unable to grow old and, consequently, has difficulty in appreciating time and its consequences. He is cured of this malady as the play progresses, and his changed perspective precipitates a reevaluation of time and life on the part of the other characters in the play.

Gorostiza's most substantial production has come since 1955. The first of five major plays is *El pan de la locura* (1958, "Bread of insanity"),[4] in which a dingy lower-class bakery in Buenos Aires becomes the scene for an intense examination of conscience. There is a possibility that moldy flour was used in making a batch of bread and that this bread has caused illness among those who may have eaten it. This turns out not to be the case, but, nonetheless, the possibility causes each of the characters to look at himself sharply and to decide in his own way whether an established relationship should be jeopardized by revealing the matter to the authorities. This play was successful at the box office, as *El puente* had been almost ten years before.

Gorostiza's last four plays appeared in rather close succession. *Vivir aquí* (1964, "Living here")[5] is set in a once-elegant manorial house in the Belgrano section of Buenos Aires. The family has fallen on bad times, and the remaining members have rented the front part of the house and are now living in the servant's quarters (which are exposed to the audience's view). They talk of selling the house and moving into an apartment, but there are reasons for wanting to remain. Each of the characters again must come to grips with his own reality and must decide whether to continue living within an ugly but nonetheless established world or to seize uncertain opportunities for better fortune elsewhere. *Los prójimos* (1966, "Neighbors")[6] is, according to the author himself, based on a real-life situation in which a girl in New York City was killed in full sight of a number of witnesses. Again, the scene is set in a Buenos Aires apartment building that looks out over a quiet street. As in the real situation, a woman is killed in full sight of the characters in the play and of other occupants of the building. Obviously, the central conflict of the play is focused on the reluctance to take responsibility for something that happens outside one's own immediate world, and each character explores this cowardice in himself and in those about him. *¿A qué jugamos?* (1968, "What shall we play?")[7] takes place in a middle-class apartment in Buenos Aires. Five people (one married couple, a single friend, and a younger unmarried couple) find out more and more about each other in a strange game invented to while away an evening spent together. They agree to imagine that the end of the world is but minutes away and to reveal their innermost reactions to that oncoming calamity. At first the reactions are very superficial, but as the play progresses they become more and more profound and violent. As the alarm clock sounds, signifying the agreed time for the end of the world, the characters of the play have come to blows and have revealed passions and biases that can never be hidden again.

Gorostiza's most recent play, *El lugar* (1970, "The place"),[8] is an attempt at theater of the absurd. The action is set in a single room that is completely empty of furniture or objects. A succession of characters enter, each to mark off a part of the available space with identical suitcases, until the room is filled to overflowing. Conflicts of increasing intensity result in the death or withdrawal of the occupants of the room, and finally only one, the pugnacious and uncomprehending Man, is left in complete isolation.

In spite of his substantial contributions as playwright, director, and stage designer, Carlos Gorostiza has been little studied, particularly outside Argentina. His plays have been reviewed, and he is mentioned in passing in the various manuals on Spanish American drama,[9] but a detailed and synthetic study of Gorostiza's plays is certainly in order at this point.

Two fundamental conflicts, or problems, appear throughout Gorostiza's plays, providing direction and motive force. First, human relationships, especially those within the family, are extremely difficult and often produce bitterness and a sense of isolation rather than harmony and love. Second, the circumstances of existence drive each of Gorostiza's principal characters toward an increased awareness of himself and a need to take action based on that awareness.

Gorostiza suggests that superficial relationships between people can be fairly cordial, but a more profound involvement becomes taxing and uncertain. For example, the boys in the street scenes of *El puente* and the bakery workers in *El pan de la locura* display at first an easy camaraderie with each other, and, without revealing themselves completely, they depend on the conventional relationships of people thrown together by the circumstances of school or employment. As the plays progress, however, the connections between characters become less easy, and the sense of crisis in the plays is accompanied by a corresponding development of abrasive complexity. Even in the plays without so conventional a beginning, this same movement is visible. In *¿A qué jugamos?*, for example, a liaison triangle is revealed by the stress of the developing situation, and in *El lugar* the tenuous arrangements set at the beginning of the play corrode to such a degree that several characters are murdered and their bodies thrown out of the closed room.

In the development of this conflict, Gorostiza uses repeatedly the emotional and often conventional ties produced by marriage or by an established family. Husbands and wives appear to have an acceptable relationship, but beneath the surface it is often one of abrasive recrimination. Parents control their children beyond the point of responsibility, and the in-law connections produced by marriage often create emotions of resentment on the part of the younger people or isolation on the part of the older. Gorostiza uses marriage or the family in all his plays—almost always to express the increasingly problematic nature of the interrelationship between characters.

Second, Gorostiza drives his principal characters, each within his own possibilities, toward a crucial choice. Very often the circumstances of the play lead toward an increased awareness that is then the basis for such a choice, but in one play (*El lugar*) the central character makes a series of choices irrationally and under the stress of extreme emotion.

At times the choices made by the characters yield positive results. For example, in *El reloj de Baltasar*, Andrés and Julia are brought to the point where they can continue their lives with new meaning and depth. Several of the characters in *El pan de la locura* are also pushed by an examination of conscience to new awareness and even new relationships:

Juana. (*Pausa*) —¿Eso quiere decir, entonces, que nosotros...

Antonio.   —Primero tendremos que salir de esto. Usted y yo, sí; pero cada uno por su cuenta, hasta que cada uno se convenza de que es capaz de aguantar y seguir adelante: de ser libre. (*Tiempo*) Después...

Juana. (*Como si* —¿Después?
lo esperara
desde hace
mucho tiempo)

Antonio.   —Me imagino que los que son capaces de encontrarse se encuentran, algún día.[10]

The family in *Vivir aquí* is finally reconciled to the continuation of their current lives with positive and negative features:

Padre de Elsa. (*Se atreve*)   —¿No... no cambiarás de idea?

Elsa. (*Firme*)   —No, papá. Ahora conozco mi realidad... y no voy a escaparle. Está aquí. Y tengo que enfrentarla aquí.

Padre de Elsa. (*Con cuidado*)—¿Con... Marcelo?

Elsa. *(Tiempo.*   —Algo empezó a entender, creo. Y no tiene en
Recuerda al padre de Pablo.) el mundo a nadie más que a mí.

Padre de Elsa.   —No va a ser una vida muy linda.

Elsa.   —Quién sabe. No lo fue hasta ahora. Pero
                          desde ahora será una vida distinta: una vida
                          clara, real.[11]

On the other hand, the crucial choices taken lead more often to negative results. In *El puente*, for example, both the opposing groups of characters are
forced to accept the bitter results of sudden death and are joined together in
their grief. In *Los prójimos* each character must accept, both individually and
collectively, the burdens of his cowardice. In *¿A qué jugamos?* the veneer of
gentility is stripped away, and each character views those about him with a new
ferocity and clarity:

Leonor. *(No lo deja*   —¡Y me ocupé! ¡Me acosté con Pasco! ¿No es
hablar. Lo enfrenta.)   cierto, Pasco, que al fin me acosté con vos?
                          ¡Era como una deuda que tenía con él, después
                          de tanto tiempo! ¡Y ahora la deuda está paga!
                          ¡Y la deuda que tenía con vos también está paga,
                          ahora! ¡Y la deuda conmigo! ¡Todas las deudas
                          están pagas, ahora, entendés? *(Fede se abalanza*
                          sobre Leonor. Pasco *se interpone tomándolo de*
                          un brazo.)

Pasco.   —No la vas a tocar.

Cacho. *(Al mismo tiempo)*—¡No, Fede!

Fede.   —Dejame, ¿querés?

Pasco. *(Forcejeando*   —Te digo que no...
con Fede)*

Fede.   —¡Hijo de puta! *(Y le da un golpe)*[12]

In general, the structure of Gorostiza's plays is conventional. With the exception of *El reloj de Baltasar*, which has three acts, all the major plays are in
two acts, and there is a general linear development of time. The focus of attention and conflict is often imagined or is something that takes place offstage (the
deaths of the engineer and his assistant in *El puente*, the possible food poisoning in *El pan de la locura*, the girl who is being killed on the street in *Los
prójimos*, and the imagined end of the world in *¿A qué jugamos?*). Several plays,
however, have interesting structural devices. In *El puente*, for example, the
playwright sets up a parallel interlocking structure in order to underscore

the events that take place on the street and inside the apartment. There are two "movimientos" in each act, and the action of the play shifts back and forth from outside to inside through the use of repeated sounds, events, or speeches that create an overlaying temporal effect. *Vivir aquí* has several scenes that depend on simultaneous conversations with the characters standing in different parts of the house. This device results in additional complexity of dialogue and characterization, as well as an intensification of the present circumstance of the family. In *¿A qué jugamos?* the playwright makes use of extended projections of home movies, together with simultaneous conversations. These devices heighten suspense and conflict between various characters and express both extension and overlaying of time.

In general, Gorostiza does not structure his plays around a protagonist struggling against monumental difficulties and supported by secondary or tertiary figures but prefers groupings of people in ordinary situations (a soccer game, a quiet evening at home, a day's work, the occupying of a new apartment, etc.). The characters are usually shaken out of this routine by some unusual event (the arrival of a stranger, something that happens on the street, the revelation of an unexpected connection between people), and the stronger characters are driven to the point of decision. At times, the choices made by the principal characters lead to significant development. For example, in *¿A qué jugamos?* the characters can never return to the state of mind that they had before their imaginary game began, and in *El reloj de Baltasar* attitudes are irrevocably affected by the visit of the stranger. However, the characters are often shaken only to remain the same. In *Los prójimos*, for example, there is little indication that a fundamental change has occurred in the attitudes of those who have witnessed the crime, and in *El lugar* Mario proceeds virtually unchanged through the series of violent encounters in which he is a major participant.

Gorostiza is not particularly showy in his use of lighting, sound effects, or staging, but, nonetheless, they have an important function in his plays. The use of bell sounds in *El puente* to mark passage of time and shifts of conflict, the use of film, music, and lighting in *¿A qué jugamos?*, and the use of music and certain key sound effects in *El lugar* are examples of expert manipulation of these devices. In addition, note should be taken of the complex realistic settings for *El pan de la locura* (a lower-class bakery) and *Vivir aquí* (the various parts of the down-at-the-heel manorial house). At the opposite end of the spectrum, the barren setting for *El lugar* is notable, as is the playwright's use of a number of identical large suitcases that are carried by the successive characters who come onstage, then used to partition off the increasingly small space given to each person.

Gorostiza's style and language varies from one play to another but is always in keeping with the situation. In the essentially realistic settings and conflicts of a number of plays, the style is consciously simple and the language direct.

In *El puente* and *El pan de la locura*, the speeches are delivered in colloquial Argentine Spanish, which is consistent with the characters being developed. However, in some of the less realistic settings the language is obviously less local. In *El lugar*, for example, the interchange between characters is almost entirely in the formal, and in only one case does the characteristic Argentine familiar form of address become apparent. This is an effective linguistic device to portray insistently the lack of intimacy and communication, but at the same time it forces a kind of neutral language with very little local flavor.

In the preceding sections, the essential elements of Gorostiza's dramatic work have been examined, and themes, structures, and techniques that transcend the limits of any one play have been considered. What remains is an evaluation of his theater, first in terms of individual plays and then as an entire production.

El puente is one of Gorostiza's most important plays, both for its notable box-office success and as the beginning of the naturalistic-realistic portrayals that are most typical of Gorostiza. Technically and structurally the play is interesting, though by no means extremely experimental or complex. The handling of internal versus external characters and the building up of suspense are particularly noteworthy. Gorostiza very soon took a different direction ("*El puente* had turned out to be 'too easy' for my 28 years, and I wanted to look for new horizons"[13]), but *El puente* remains as one of his most notable achievements.

The next five plays are not available for this study, but as indicated earlier, the playwright himself does not view them as acceptable and finished works. Nonetheless, they represent collectively an attempt to move away from the realism of *El puente*. *El reloj de Baltasar* is the clearest expression of this departure in its use of fantasy, which is reminiscent of Casona and Nalé Roxlo. Nonetheless, fantasy is connected to the real-life necessity for decisions that allow a full and meaningful existence, and in this sense at least the play is successful.

El pan de la locura is a return to the realistic settings of Argentine life. This piece has a less intricate structure than *El puente*, but the strong theme and the grouping of believable personalities around a central conflict are very persuasive. The representation of character is careful, and development is evident in some of the principal figures. This play is an excellent and straightforward examination of individual conscience in a real-life setting.

Vivir aquí follows the line begun by *El puente* and *El pan de la locura*. The setting is realistic, and the characters fit easily within it. There are some technical complexities, but in general the play is moved along by the problems faced in the family; each individual must grapple in his own terms with the somber realities of his existence. This play is less compelling than the two previous plays in the same style.

Los prójimos is dependent in large part on the force of the external event that moves the action along. Each of the witnesses probes himself and his reactions as he watches what goes on, but there is little sense of change in any of the principal figures. The situation permits the internal-external representation that Gorostiza has used in other plays, and the dialogues are fitted carefully to the characters who speak them. The play is very successful in depicting a strange quality of passive-active nightmare.

¿A qué jugamos? departs somewhat from the realism of most of the preceding plays and deals with the dimensions of an invented game on the end of the world. The characters are convincingly represented, and time flashbacks are effectively used as are visual and auditory effects. This play is a progressive revelation of conflicts and biases and expresses very well a sense of movement beyond a point of no return.

El lugar is an attempt to express the absurdity of life in a crowded and repetitious world and has some interesting staging and technical effects. However, the situation seems overly contrived and the characters move toward a resolution that is visible almost from the beginning. The play too closely follows previous patterns from the theater of the absurd and does not have the strength and persuasion of some of the other plays.

Taken together, Gorostiza's works quite obviously demonstrate skill, sensitivity, and wide readings. He is at his best in those plays that have a strong realistic basis and whose conflicts and characters explore the problems of the real world. Gorostiza's incursions into fantasy and the absurd are skillful but overly derivative.

Carlos Gorostiza merits an important place in the history of recent Spanish American drama, both as a playwright and as a director and stage designer. He has some failures, but his best three or four plays are substantial contributions to the dramatic expression of a Spanish American reality.

NOTES

1. *El puente* had its premier performance on May 4, 1949, in the Teatro La Máscara in Buenos Aires. It was published the same year (Buenos Aires: El Junco, 1949), and a second edition appeared as no. 8 of the "Publicación Teatral Periódica" (Buenos Aires: Losange, 1954). More recently, it was published together with *El pan de la locura* (Buenos Aires: Talía, 1963) and with *Los prójimos* and *El pan de la locura* (Buenos Aires: Sudamericana, 1966).

2. Four of these plays were produced but not published (*El fabricante de piolín*, 1950; *Marta Ferrari*, 1954; *El último perro*, 1954; *El juicio*, 1954), and one appeared in a short edition (*El caso del hombre de la valija negra*, 1951) not available in library collections in the United States. Gorostiza himself discounts the importance of these plays: "You should consider them as those unpublished works that every playwright keeps in his desk drawer. I had the misfortune, as soon as my works were finished and known about in

theatrical circles, to see them rushed into production and presentation. I protected myself against this a posteriori by preventing their publication" (Carlos Gorostiza to Merlin H. Forster, 30 August 1972, personal files. This and all subsequent translations are my own).

3. *El reloj de Baltasar* was first performed August 25, 1955, in the Teatro Grand Splendid in Buenos Aires and was published as no. 24 of the "Publicación Teatral Periódica" (Buenos Aires: Losange, 1955).

4. *El pan de la locura* was first performed July 18, 1958, in the Teatro Cervantes of Buenos Aires and was published the same year (Buenos Aires: Talía, 1958). It has appeared more recently along with other Gorostiza plays (see note 1).

5. *Vivir aquí* was first performed September 11, 1964, in the Teatro San Telmo of Buenos Aires and was published the same year (Buenos Aires: Talía, 1964).

6. *Los prójimos* was first performed June 3, 1966, in the Centro de Artes y Ciencias of Buenos Aires and was published the same year with two other plays (see note 1).

7. *¿A qué jugamos?* was first performed September 12, 1968, in the Teatro Ateneo of Buenos Aires and was published the following year (Buenos Aires: Sudamericana, 1969).

8. *El lugar* was first performed September 16, 1970, in the Teatro Liceo of Buenos Aires and was recently published (Buenos Aires: Sudamericana, 1972).

9. See, for example, Agustín del Saz Sánchez, *Teatro hispanoamericano*, 2 vols. (Barcelona: Editorial Vergara, 1963–1964), II, 228; Carlos Solórzano, *El teatro latinoamericano en el siglo XX* (Mexico City: Editorial Pormaca, 1964), pp. 144–146; Frank N. Dauster, *Historia del teatro hispanoamericano: Siglos XIX y XX* (Mexico City: Ediciones de Andrea, 1966), pp. 75–76; Willis Knapp Jones, *Behind Spanish American Footlights* (Austin: University of Texas Press, 1966), pp. 159–160; George W. Woodyard, "The Search for Identity: A Comparative Study in Contemporary Latin American Drama" (Ph.D. dissertation, University of Illinois, 1966), pp. 50–51, 185–202, 246–247; Pedro Orgambide and Roberto Yahni, *Enciclopedia de la literatura argentina* (Buenos Aires: Sudamericana, 1970), pp. 293–294; John E. Lyon, "The Argentine Theatre and the Problem of National Identity: A Critical Survey," *Latin American Theatre Review* 5, no. 2 (Spring 1972): 12–13.

10. *Juana*. (*Pause*) Does that mean, then, that we—

Antonio. We'll have to get out of all of this first. You and I, right, but everybody is on his own, until he can convince himself that he is capable of controlling himself and continuing on: of being free. (*Pause*) After that—

Juana. (*As if she had been expecting it for a long time*) After that?

Antonio. I imagine that those who can get together will get together, someday.

[*El pan de la locura* (Buenos Aires: Sudamericana, 1966), p. 218]

11. *Elsa's Father*. (*Tentatively*) You won't change your mind?

Elsa. (*Firmly*) No, father. Now I'm aware of my reality, and I'm not going to run away from it. It's here, and I have to face it here.

Elsa's Father. (*Carefully*) With Marcelo?

Elsa. (*Pause. She remembers Pablo's father.*) He has begun to understand a few things, I think. And he has no one else in the world except me.

Elsa's Father. It's not going to be a very beautiful life.

Elsa. Who knows. It hasn't been all that beautiful up until now. But from now on it will be a different life: a life that is clear and real.

[*Vivir aquí* (Buenos Aires: Talía, 1964), p. 73]

12. *Leonor.* (*Does not let him speak. Faces him.*) And I did keep myself busy! I went to bed with Pasco! Isn't it true, Pasco, that I finally went to bed with you? It was like a debt that I had with him, after such a long time! And now the debt is paid! And the debt that I had with you is paid, now! And the debt with myself! All the debts are paid now, do you understand? (Fede *throws himself on* Leonor. Pasco *steps between them, taking him by one arm.*)

    Pasco. You're not going to touch her.

    Cacho. (*At the same time*) No, Fede!

    Fede. Let me alone, do you mind?

    Pasco. (*Struggling with Fede*) No, I tell you—

    Fede. You son of a bitch! (*And he hits him*)
               [¿*A qué jugamos?* (Buenos Aires: Sudamericana, 1969), p. 117]
   13. "*El puente* me había resultado 'demasiado fácil' para mis 28 años, y quise asomarme a otros panoramas" (Gorostiza to Forster, 30 August 1972.)

8. The Theater of

Luis Alberto Heiremans: 1928–1964

Margaret Sayers Peden

Luis Alberto Heiremans: young, handsome, admired, talented, economically independent. One would have said this Chilean author and playwright was blessed by the gods. But as life so often vies with theater for drama, all this seeming good fortune was cancelled by an untimely death. Born in 1928, he died of cancer on October 25, 1964, in his home in Santiago.

Heiremans, a member of the Generation of 1950,[1] played a major role in revitalizing the theater of Chile. His contribution was unique. Working as translator, student and teacher of theater, actor, and playwright, he gathered his knowledge from the widest possible spectrum, fusing all aspects into a single experience. He was truly a man of theater.

Heiremans traveled extensively, studying both formally and independently in the United States and on the Continent. He was an actor in England—most unusual for a Latin American in the 1950s. He was the recipient of a Rockefeller Foundation grant in 1963, which allowed him to study and lecture in the United States; it was during the term of the Rockefeller scholarship that Heiremans, who had received a medical degree, discovered the signs of the cancer that caused his death the following year. After completing his commitments in the United States, Heiremans returned to Santiago, where he continued working feverishly on translations and television programs for as long as he was able. A novel, *Puerta de salida* ("This way out") was published during this period. Plans were also effected for the establishment of the Fundación Luis Alberto Heiremans, which would reward and encourage the talents of young writers. This foundation assured that Heiremans's influence in the theater would continue after his death.[2]

The situation of Chilean theater in this century is similar to the pattern of theater throughout Latin America. After a flurry of activity in the early part of the century, led by figures like Antonio Acevedo Hernández, Armando Moock, and Germán Luco Cruchaga, the cinema had stolen what little audience had been established to date. The 1930s were the low point of theatrical activity: quality was low; commercial theater was stultified. It was generally true throughout Latin America that the establishment of experimental independent theaters during the forties revived public interest in the legitimate stage, a stage enormously improved through adaptations and translations of the plays of European innovators. Specifically, in Chile, it was with the founding in 1941 of the Teatro Experimental de la Universidad de Chile (TEUCH) that a real "national" theater began to evolve. This group later merged with the Departamento del Teatro Nacional to become the Instituto del Teatro de la Universidad de Chile (ITUCH). The men responsible for the founding of TEUCH are referred to as the Generation of '41, a landmark in Chilean theater. Other groups followed the example and guiding influence of TEUCH, and the group with which Heiremans was most closely affiliated, the Teatro de Ensayo de la Universidad Católica (TEUC—not to be confused with TEUCH), was formed in 1943: they performed his *Jaula en el árbol* ("Cage in the treetops") in 1957, *Es de contarlo y no creerlo* ("Who could believe it?") in 1959, *Versos de ciego*, ("Songs of a blind man") in 1961, and *El tony chico* ("The littlest clown"), posthumously, in 1964.

As is so often the case with Latin American dramatists, Heiremans did not study to be a playwright. His initial professional direction, perhaps encouraged by his family, was toward medicine. But throughout the course of his medical studies he was constantly drawn toward writing and the theater, and in the early fifties he became a member of a little-theater group. This practical experience, derived from his interest in acting, undoubtedly served him well when he began later to write. In addition to plays, Heiremans also wrote short stories: *Cuentos y canciones de la mamá* ("Mama's stories and songs"), *Los demás* ("The others"), *Los niños extraños* ("Strange children"), and the posthumous *Los mejores cuentos de Luis Alberto Heiremans* ("The best stories of Luis Alberto Heiremans"). His *Seres de un día* ("Passing ships") can also be classified as short stories, or perhaps as four novellas. *Puerta de salida*, the novel published shortly before his death, received especially favorable reviews. But, for the purposes of this study, it is primarily as a playwright that we are interested in Heiremans.

Several impressions emerge after reading Heiremans's plays. Perhaps the most striking is the fact that very few of his characters achieve their goals; seldom does an individual find what he is seeking, although occasionally one is led to assume that fulfillment may lie ahead—just offstage. The seeking itself is perhaps the single most outstanding feature of his work. If applied to Heiremans's own life, one might deduce that it was spent in such a search, a search for fulfillment, for immortality. What the failure of such fulfillment can mean is poignantly stated by Landa in *El tony chico*, Heiremans's last play: "¡Me voy sin haber dejado nada!"[3]

A second interesting feature is the marked contrast between the two worlds Heiremans portrays in his plays. *Moscas sobre el mármol* ("Flies upon the marble"), as well as some of his early plays and narratives, depicts the life of the privileged; this is a very different world from that of the poor in such plays as *Sigue la estrella* ("Follow the star"), *El abanderado* ("The man with the white kerchief"), and *El tony chico*.

Even within these two very different worlds, belonging to the superior social class does not assure stability or success. If possible, Heiremans's upper-class characters are more despairing, more riddled with angst than those of more humble origins. The prostitutes, the criminals, the vagabonds, the abandoned and neglected of the world of his trilogy (*Versos de ciego*, *El aban-derado*, and *El tony chico*) at least seem to be in contact with the basic realities of life. They are more sympathetic, more worthy of our compassion than others in Heiremans's fiction; their suffering seems more real to us. Perhaps it is simply that it is more difficult to sympathize with problems of wealth when compared to problems of basic survival.

Another contrast in Heiremans's work is the one drawn between religion and superstition. Two of his most successful plays, *El abanderado* and *Sigue la es-trella*, are based on Christian symbolism, quite beautifully effected. In contrast, his first two dramas, *Noche de equinoccio* ("Night of the equinox") and *La hora robada* ("Stolen hour"), rely heavily on spiritism for their effect. And, in *Moscas sobre el mármol*, a vital structural part of the play is dependent upon the super-stitious fear of a servant. The protagonist of this play, Julián, is an agnostic with an existential view of the pointlessness of existence. This concept is diametrical-ly opposed to the simple religiosity of the faith that leads the characters in *Sigue la estrella* to abandon what little they have to follow the star that appears in the heavens.

A third contrast is exhibited in the dramatic portraits of two types of mother love: the smothering love of Amalia in *Moscas sobre el mármol* (a type that also appears in *Puerta de salida*) as opposed to the complete denial of motherhood displayed in *El abanderado*.

Moscas sobre el mármol is a play with an extremely despairing world vision. The basic metaphor of the work is that of a planet of marble uglied and befouled by insignificant flies—human beings: "Mira este mundo, mira esta tierra, mira este planeta, mira esta cosa toda hecha de mármol por quién sabe quién... Y esas moscas crean sus propias relaciones, tejen su destino y tratan de ordenar la confusión . . . . Y no hay nada más, nada sino una esfera de mármol que pudo ser hermosa plagada de moscas que la ensucian."[4]

This evaluation is expressed by Julián, a character whose background and situation are not unlike Heiremans's own. Inevitably one questions to what degree the characters are extensions of Heiremans's own personality, especially when one considers the overall frustration and unhappiness experienced by his char-acters.

The situation of *Moscas* is based upon two triangles. The more important is that involving Julián, his wife Teresa, and his mother Amalia. The mother is a classic Freudian-Wylie-type devourer. Afraid of growing old and losing her beauty, she has, for survival, fastened parasitically onto her son's affection. She actively and aggressively competes with Teresa for the role of wife-lover in every aspect except the physical. The second triangle is comprised of Julián, Teresa, and Julián's friend Ernesto. Julián, aware of the true but unconsummated love between his wife and his friend, has devised a plan by which his friend will die. The plan hinges on a house-party *chasse* in which everyone will hunt a *fantasma*, a family ghost. Julián asks Ernesto to play the part of the *fantasma*. He then primes the superstitious servant Segundo to shoot the *fantasma* he fears. Things do not proceed as planned. Ernesto, frustrated by Teresa's refusal to desert Julián, leaves. Julián, embittered, knowing he has Teresa but not her love, decides to kill the *fantasma* once and for all: "Esa cosa ya muerta que hay que matar de una vez por todas... ¿Y por qué no yo? ¿Por qué no el propio fantasma?"[5] Julián drapes himself in the gauze that was to be worn by Ernesto and is killed by Segundo. And, at last, Amalia has total possession of her son: ". . . No, no vengas... Ahora es mío... Es mío mi niño, nada más que mío, nada más que mío..."[6]

What a striking contrast between this mother and the totally uncaring mother of *El abanderado*! El Abanderado is a criminal, given his nickname because the white kerchief he wears flutters in the air like a banner as he gallops by in the distance. His mother is la Pepa de Oro, madam of a house of prostitution where el Abanderado grew up. He remembers that as a child he was hidden away at night in the attic, but he watched what was going on below through a hole in the floor. While very young he ran away and embarked on a life of robbery and violence as a romantic highwayman. Finally, his longing for maternal love drew him back once more to the brothel, where he was betrayed by a friend and apprehended by the constabulary. (As the play begins he has been sentenced and is being transported to prison: this trip takes him once more to the place where he was apprehended.) Lack of mother love destroys el Abanderado just as too much mother love destroys Julián in *Moscas sobre el mármol*.

When a career is ended, one always speculates about the direction the author's work might have taken. Heiremans experimented widely, searching for his own particular style. As noted, he moved between two extremes for subject matter, from the sophisticated to the folkloric, and his treatment ranged from the realistic to the symbolic-poetic. In the existing criticism of his plays, it is the poetic that is most often cited as being typical. Heiremans was interested in North American musical comedy, and it was he who introduced this genre to Chilean audiences. His *Esta señorita Trini* ("Senorita Trini"), with its colorful 1912 costumes, was such a smash hit that it completely disrupted Teatro de Ensayo's timetable of other productions.[7] If his translations are any indication— and we assume that interest and admiration dictated his selections—he was greatly interested in French playwrights: Henri Ghéon, Georges Bernanos, Barillet and Grédy, and Anouilh. More important, we have Heiremans's own comments about his philosophy of theater: "Our theater, having already mastered realism, must follow the path of stylization of reality—never, however, disembodying reality to the point of being abstract. All characters are real, but real characters carry within them a symbol, an internal fruit, as it were, fruit that illuminates and radiates, fruit whose light must envelop and bathe the entire work."[8]

But perhaps most important of all, we have the testimony of Heiremans's last three plays, which indicate that his more mature judgment was leading to expression through the vehicle of the poetic and folkloric. This trilogy, rightly considered as his best work, also demonstrates a shift of philosophical stance away from the earlier existentialist despair of *Moscas sobre el mármol*. While not optimistic, certainly, each of these plays does exhibit an aspect of the reward of faith—of belief in *something*. In the last of the three, *El tony chico*, Landa dies—unnecessarily, absurdly—but he leaves something positive behind: his protegé, the *tony chico*. In *El abanderado*, Cornelia's faith and love is a most positive element, and in *Versos de ciego*, faith in the star's promise is the conceptual basis of the play. Each of these plays merits a more detailed observation, for they are not only Heiremans's best, but also the best indication of the direction of his writing had his career not been so unfortunately interrupted.

Versos de ciego, the first of three works that Heiremans himself conceived of as a trilogy, evolved from two earlier pieces, *Los güenos versos* ("The bestest poems")—an *auto sacramental* about the funeral of an infant[9]—and *Sigue la estrella*. *Versos de ciego* is about a troupe of itinerant musicians who decide to follow a star and about the people they encounter on their pilgrimage. Although it received bad reviews in Chile, this play was enthusiastically acclaimed in Spain, where it was performed along with Isidora Aguirre's *La pérgola de las flores* ("The flower pergola") and Sergio Vodanovíc's *Deja que los perros ladren* ("Let the dogs bark").[10]

The *ciego* ("blind man") of the title, always present either as spectator or actor, acts as narrator much in the manner of the Stage Manager in *Our Town*. His opening song tells what is to come:

> Denme tiempo pa'cantarla
> pa'que pue pueda relatarla,
> esta historia de un camino
> y de aquellos sin destino
> que supieron encarnarla.[11]

Three musicians, Melitón, Sebastián, and Buenaventura, trying to earn a few pesos at a local fair, have come to the end of their resources. They see a blazing star in the heavens, and although it is leading toward the south, rather than the north where they had hoped to find warmer days, they decide to follow it. In this decision and in all the others that follow, the following leitmotif determines their choices:

Melitón.   —Algo hay que perder.

Buenaventura. —¿Para qué?

Melitón.   —Para ganar algo.[12]

Ultimately the travelers are joined by Juana Buey, Oliverio Pastor, Perico Burro, and a girl. Those who do not join the musicians are neither as pure, as simple, nor as good: a seeress, Ana—and her manager Fanor—a businessman, Perico Burro's superstitious grandmother, and Laura Candela and her gaggle of prostitutes. At the end of the play the faithful voyagers still have found nothing concretely rewarding, although the indications are that some have found love in the process of following. They have pledged to continue, and the *ciego* ends, as he began, with a song:

> Quedan unos cuantos versos
> Pa'contar qu'ellos siguieron
> Cuando allá arriba la vieron
> Aclarando el cielo adverso
> Por un viento tan disperso.
>
> Y por el camino van
> Como antes buscarán
> Y es posible que buscando
> Por el mundo caminando
> Algun día encontrarán.[13]

The experiment in form and symbolism expressed in *Versos de ciego* is less successful than the beautifully simple *Sigue la estrella* from which it evolved. The Christian symbolism of the earlier play is only obfuscated by additional interludes like those of the funeral cortege and Laura Candela. What is beautiful about *Sigue la estrella* is its utter simplicity. In this play there are seven characters (as opposed to thirty-two and assorted chorus in the expanded version): Juana (Buey), Angélica, Perico (Burro), and Oliverio (Pastor). In a very natural way, each of the latter four joins the trio of musicians on their peregrination. Their song, too, is simple and effective:

> En tierra de Judá
> está el Guiador,
> me han dicho con amor
> y esa es la verdá.
>
> En tierra de Judá,
> allá en el Belén,
> podrás decir amén
> a toda esta maldá.

En tierra de Judá
lo iremos a buscar;
lo habremos de encontrar
con esta gran piedá.[14]

In this version the leitmotif—*algo hay que perder*—is given greater emphasis; each of the seven comprising the procession is convinced of this necessity: you lose something to gain something. The symbolism of the original trek after the star of Bethlehem is very effectively duplicated by Heiremans. The first musician, the leader, carries a set of drums topped by cymbals he insists are gold, handed down to him from his father. When Juana joins them, she is carrying a basket intended for a picnic for her master's children. The basket contains a curative resinous gum from a native tree—the children always hurt themselves, and the *goma* is a primitive first-aid device. "Ah," says the third musician, "Eso es mirra." The frankincense is provided by the second musician as a gift to Angélica: it is a powder removed from the seeds of flowers, he explains, that emits a sweet perfume when burned. So, with the gold, frankincense, and myrrh, an angel, a shepherd, a burro, and an ox, the end of the play reveals to us that the three musicians, previously called Hombre I, II, and III, are named Melchior, Gaspar, and Baltasar. The play ends as the star stops over a stable and as the pilgrims are approaching the stable with gifts in their hands and in their hearts.

This quiet, fragile play is clearly the most optimistic of Heiremans's work. Fulfillment for these characters seemingly lies immediately ahead. Artistically, too, it is one of his most felicitous and most successful plays.

El abanderado, the play that most critics consider to be Heireman's best, springs from the same inspiration as *Versos de ciego* and *Sigue la estrella*. It is, says Domingo Piga, "the search for a superior Christian ideal, working always with poetic, realistic, and folkloric elements."[15] Piga sees a clear parallel to the trial of Jesus in this play. And Julio Durán Cerda is among others who have noted the Christian symbology of *El abanderado*.

The Passion of Christ . . . is objectified through the calvary el Abanderado suffers. . . . In the pagan image are conserved all the biblical elements of the Passion: thus, for example, el Abanderado's mother, the madam of a house of prostitution, corresponds to the Virgin Mary; the constables who harass Christ are the carabineers, or "fuzz," charged with the transport of the prisoner; the police chiefs are Pilates and Caiaphas; the old friend who betrays the bandit is Judas; a country girl secretly in love with the hero is Magdalene; and the ominous searching of the prisoners' clothing is the involvement of the prelate; the crucifixion, the placing of the handcuffs, etc. Neither is metaphysical theology lacking, the Christian message of purity and redemption contained in the chalice and the host, symbolized by a crystal punchbowl and in "a thought, all clear and white, like a piece of a star."[16]

We must acknowledge that this symbolism is indeed present in *El abandera-do* and that Heiremans must have structured his play with a very clear aware-ness of the parallel in mind. But to focus all one's attention on the play's sym-bolism is to overlook one very important element, the motivations of the protagonist. We agree that el Abanderado suffers a *calvario*. He has led the life of a highwayman, and now society demands redress for his wrongs. But what motivated him? What led him to crime? This question is central to the play. El Abanderado is a classic incarnation of one of sociopsychology's favorite types: the unloved child. He is captured only because he is drawn to his mother's house, although he himself cannot vocalize his attraction:

Torrealba. —Fue aquí donde lo agarraron ¿no es así?

Abanderado. —No sé por qué vine. Me entraron ganas de repente.

Torrealba. —(*Con un gesto*) ¿De volverla a ver?

Abanderado. —(*Se encoge de hombros*) No sé.[17]

El Abanderado speaks repeatedly throughout the play of his solitude. This aloneness, he recalls, began on the day that he accompanied his mother shopping and she saw a beautiful cut-glass punch bowl in the window. To la Pepa de Oro, the punch bowl represented a beauty she had never attained. But to el Abanderado it will always represent loss, the day his mother deserted him:

Pepa de Oro. —¿De qué estás hablando?

Abanderado. —De esa tarde en esa calle, cuando usted la descubrió en la vitrina...

Pepa de Oro. —No entiendo nada.

Abanderado. —Y de repente me soltó la mano... Y me dejó solo. Sí. Y yo sentí un ruido, un ruido como el de esa bala que me anda buscando.

Pepa de Oro. —No entiendo nada. No quiero saber más.

Abanderado. —Y volvimos. Usted con la ponchera entre los brazos y yo atrás, sólo... Me dijo que subiera al entretecho, que esa noche iban a celebrar, que no bajara, que no bajara nunca más...[18]

The only love el Abanderado knows is depicted in his very moving scene with Cornelia, a highly romantic country girl. They meet once, by the river where she is washing clothes. To her, he represents freedom and unfulfilled wishes as she sees him galloping in the distance. They do not speak of their love, but it is pledged with a white kerchief she has embroidered for him, which he exchanges for the one he is wearing—in the manner of a courtly token—after their only meeting. But Fate decrees that this love, too, is forbidden to el Abanderado. He will always represent something ineffable to Cornelia, but reality presents her with a more realistic mate: the sympathetic soldier assigned to guard el Abanderado as he is transported to prison. Cornelia and el Abanderado realize what they have lost:

> *Cornelia.* —Me gustaba saber que alguien podía galopar en la tarde, libre
> como una bandera con ese pañuelo... Ojalá haya sido[perdi-
> do] para el lado del río.
>
> *Torrealba.* —¿Para qué?
>
> *Cornelia.* —Para que siga, y llegue al mar.

(*Ya muy lejano se escucha un pitazo del tren. Ambos lo contemplan. Las luces disminuyen lentamente. Telón.*)[19]

El tony chico, the last play of the trilogy, is in concept more similar to *El abanderado* than to *Versos de ciego*. Life ends for the protagonist, Landa, as it does for el Abanderado, but, like him, Landa leaves something positive behind —a testament of love. This may be Heiremans's final message: life is short, death is inevitable, and the love we leave behind is the greatest contribution we can offer to the world.

The setting of *El tony chico* is the world of the circus (the circus and the madhouse, incidentally, are among the most frequent world metaphors in contemporary fiction, for reasons that need no comment). Landa is an outsider, a failure in his own milieu, who wanders into the circus during his long, unfruitful quest for his "angels," a quest that has become his only aim in life. We are soon aware that it is no ordinary circus he has stumbled into:

> *Sonia.* —Este circo es redondo como el mundo, con todos adentro atrapados
> como moscas en el engrudo. El que cae aquí adentro ya no sale.[20]

All the members of the circus troupe are *fracasados*, failures in some aspect of their lives. The Emperatriz (the owner) lives with memories of her dead husband, Doménico—memories that may have been embroidered with the passage of time. The ringmaster, el Capitán, treats both his wife Rucia and his lover Sonia cruelly, finding no happiness in them or in the other women he pursues. The two women live in suspicion of each other and of the Capitán. There is also a young boy, Juanucho, who does menial chores around the circus and who is miserable and unloved. It is the encounter between Landa and Juanucho that evolves into the positive statement of the play. Landa is signed on as the *tony* ("clown"). He and Juanucho develop an act that becomes the star attraction of the circus. The boy finds a father, and the man, a son. This momentary happiness is interrupted when Landa is the accidental victim of a bullet fired by Rucia and intended for her rival Sonia. Landa dies fearing that he has not instructed Juanucho in the quest for the angels; he fears he has left nothing behind, but actually he has bequeathed his quest along with his love. As the final curtain closes, the boy is experiencing a vision of white-coiffed angels; he too will follow them.

In her overall consideration of Heiremans's work, Cajiao Salas suggests the following principal themes: love, death, solitude, existential anguish, and *búsqueda* ("the quest"). There is no argument here. However, these five might be simplified to three more principal themes: quest, love, and loss. Love is the central motif here, and quest and loss return to and evolve from love. For example, in *El abanderado* and *El tony chico*, loss is the result of the quest for love. In *Versos de ciego* and *Sigue la estrella*, something more positive results from the quest—always remembering the leitmotif: *hay que perder algo*. In *Moscas sobre el mármol*, loss is the predominant effect of the quest for love. In *Es de contarlo y no creerlo*, loss seems to predominate—witness the failure of the angels to redeem the protagonist. In *La jaula en el árbol*, loss is experienced by some, love by others; the *paloma*, at least, soars free—but is lost to one who loves him. These three themes, constantly interwoven in differing patterns, form the real texture of Heiremans's work.

Symbolism, too, is a very conscious and important element in Heiremans's writing. Cajiao Salas devotes a great deal of attention to symbolism in her study, dividing the symbols into universal and personal categories: the star, the cage, the circus, the brothel, water symbols, and Christian symbols. There is little that can be added to the complete and exhaustive list of her study, with the possible exception of the train. Often the train represents the ineffable—freedom and adventure—and the lonely whistle of the distant train elicits great feelings of sadness and loss.

In terms of style, the obvious influence of French dramatists like Lenormand and Anouilh has already been mentioned. Cajiao Salas points out Heiremans's stated admiration for Brecht and comments: "The influence of Brecht and of the concept of epic theater is perhaps the most easily recognizable influence in Heiremans's mature writing."[21] This similarity to Brecht is there, but superficially. It is apparent in Heiremans's incorporation of music and verse for dramatic effect in plays treating major human and social questions. The single most important element in his work, however, was his desire to infuse poetry into theater. Not verse, but poetry. It is here that we can see his greatest allegiance to a European theatrical figure, to a man whose name has not been mentioned in connection with Heiremans, Antonin Artaud.

Cajiao Salas herself emphasizes the Artaudesque quality of Heiremans's theater without specifically mentioning the source of these theories: "When we speak of the poetic language of theater, we are not referring to versification, nor to simple spoken speech that underlines the text, but to theatrical language as such: *spoken words, gestures, screams, tears, ornament, color, light, music, dance, costume, set, emotion, intrigue, sentiments, etc.*"[22] Although the effect is very different, we are speaking of the same concept: total theater.

Other similarities—not influences—that come to mind are the poetic-folkloric plays of the Mexican Miguel Lira and the more recent success of plays like Carlos Solórzano's *Las manos de Dios*. Heiremans's theater, though, has a specific flavor; it is uniquely Heiremans. Through the poetry and the folklore, one perceives the educated and sophisticated man—the seeker. Luis Alberto Heiremans is the Chilean Quixote; his quest, "the impossible dream."

NOTES

1. The "Generation of '50" is a term designated by Enrique Lafourcade, a Chilean critic and author.

2. I am indebted to Professor Teresa Cajiao Salas's study, *Temas y símbolos en la obra de Luis Alberto Heiremans* (Santiago: Fundación Luis Alberto Heiremans 1970), for much of the general information contained in this article.

3. "I go, leaving nothing behind!" (*El tony chico, Mapocho*, no. 16 [Autumn 1968], p. 177. This and all subsequent translations are my own.)

4. "Look at this world, look at this earth, this planet, look at this thing of marble created by who knows whom. And those flies create their own relationships, weave their own destinies, and attempt to establish order from chaos. And that is all, there is nothing more, nothing but a marble sphere that might be beautiful but is plagued with filthy flies" (*Moscas sobre el mármol* [Santiago: Editorial de Nuevo Extremo, 1958], pp. 52–53).

5. "The thing—really already dead—must be killed once and for all. Why not I? Why not the phantom himself?" (ibid., p. 86).

6. "No, don't come near. He's mine now. He's my baby, only mine, no one's but mine" (ibid., p. 89).

7. Willis Knapp Jones, *Behind Spanish American Footlights* (Austin: University of Texas Press, 1966), p. 239.

8. *Teatro chileno actual* (Santiago: Editorial Zig Zag, 1966), p. 227.

9. Jones, *Behind Spanish American Footlights*, p. 239.

10. Ibid.

11. Give me a chance to sing it,
   sing it, and tell you of it,
   this story of a highway, and
   those who had no future, who
   found a way to make it come true.
                    [*Versos de ciego* (Santiago: Imprenta Mueller, 1962), p. 7]

12. *Melitón.* Something has to be lost.

Buenaventura. Why?

Melitón. So something may be gained. [Ibid., p. 25]

13. There are a few more lines
To tell you that they continued
When they saw, way up high,
The threatening sky begin to clear,
Swept clean by the scattering wind.

And down the highway they go,
As before, they are still seeking,
And it is possible that in their search—
Traveling the whole world over—
They will some day find. [Ibid., p. 80]

14. In the land of Judah
there is a Leader,
they have told me, with love,
and I know it to be true.

In the land of Judah,
there in Bethlehem,
you can say amen,
to all the evil 'round.

In the land of Judah,
we shall go to seek;
and we will surely find,
with all the love we have.

[Sigue la estrella, in *Teatro chileno actual*, pp. 229–230]

15. Domingo Piga T. and Orlando Rodríguez B., *Teatro chileno del siglo veinte* (Santiago: Publicaciones Escuela de Teatro, 1964), p. 107.

16. Julio Durán Cerda, "Actuales tendencias del teatro chileno," *Inter-American Review of Bibliography* 13, no. 2 (April–June 1963): 173.

17. *Torrealba.* This is where they got you, isn't it?

Abanderado. I don't know why I came. I just wanted to, all of a sudden.

Torrealba. (*With a gesture*) To see her again?

Abanderado. (*Shrugs his shoulders*) I don't know.

[*El abanderado*, in *Teatro chileno contemporáneo*, ed. Julio Durán Cerda
(Mexico City: Aguilar, 1970), p. 248]

18. *Pepa de Oro.* What are you talking about?

Abanderado. About that afternoon in the street when you first saw it in the shop window.

Pepa de Oro. I don't know what you're talking about.

Abanderado. Suddenly, you let go my hand—and left me standing there alone. That's right. And I heard a noise, a noise that sounded like the bullet that's always looking for me.

Pepa de Oro. I don't understand. I don't want to know anymore.

Abanderado. We came home. You carrying your punch bowl, and me behind you, alone. You told me to go upstairs, that you were going to celebrate that night, not to come down, not ever to come down. [Ibid., p. 262]

19. *Cornelia*. I'd like to think that someone was still galloping at eveningtime, with that kerchief around his neck, free as—I wish it'd been [lost] down by the river.

Torrealba. Why?

Cornelia. So it would drift down to the sea.
(Very far away, a train whistle. They listen. The lights slowly dim. Curtain.)
[Ibid., p. 296]

20. *Sonia*. This circus is as round as the world, with everyone inside trapped like flies in molasses. He who drops in here never leaves. [*El tony chico*, p. 131]

21. Cajiao Salas, *Temas y símbolos*, p. 133.

22. Ibid., p. 135. My italics.

9. Luisa Josefina Hernández:

The Labyrinth of Form

John K. Knowles

Luisa Josefina Hernández began writing for the theater at the close of World War II. Her early drama was realistic in form and relied heavily for character development upon psychological analysis, which was then capturing the interest of Mexican authors. In time, however, new needs and perceptions required of her new forms of expression. In the ensuing years, she experimented successfully with farce, comedy, tragicomedy, and the theater of commitment. This individual development coincides closely with the evolution of Mexican drama generally, from psychological realism to theater of cruelty and impact drama. So it is that, at one and the same time, she is both a microcosm of Mexican drama of the last twenty-odd years and her own unique personality expressed in dramatic form.

Luisa Josefina Hernández was born in 1928 in Mexico City. Her father, a pervasive influence in her life, was a supreme court judge directly concerned with justice and education among the dispossessed. Her mother, like her father, came from the province of Chiapas and attempted to bring up her daughter within the framework of traditional values. Her mother's insistence on these values has continually produced tensions between the two. The influence of this upbringing, and the resentment it produced, are mirrored in *Los huéspedes reales* (1958, "The royal guests"),[1] a work that examines many of the assumptions underlying traditional upbringing.

Luisa Josefina Hernández enrolled in the Facultad de Leyes at the Universidad Nacional Autónoma de México and was a brilliant student. Nevertheless, she changed her major to languages, for which she had a sustaining interest. This change led to a degree in English letters and theater and formed the basis of her broad knowledge of English and American literature, from which she has drawn inspiration.

In the years immediately following graduation, Hernández wrote various works, some for television, some for theater, almost all of which are in a highly realistic fashion and dealing with middle-class problems. Two plays in particular serve to indicate the eventual evolution of her style that leads to *Los frutos caídos* (1956, "The fallen fruit")[2] and *Los huéspedes reales*, generally considered to be her most important works. Her first work, *Agonía* (1951, "Agony"),[3] is of interest mainly for the way Hernández endeavors to handle structurally the traditional pattern of climactic form. Her orchestration of characters leading to the necessary climax indicates her awareness of dramatic necessity, but the result is pedestrian and rudimentary. The seams marking exits and entrances are arbitrary and visible. The speeches are an awkward combination of personally felt anguish of the characters and an awareness of passing on certain information about those characters to the audience, so that the expository portion of the work is quite weak. But, in common with her two masterpieces, *Agonía* shows the author's ability to build an exceedingly tight climax. At that point in the drama, characters, language, and stagecraft mesh in such a fashion that the main character, a divorced mother dying of cancer, is isolated in a most convincing way from those who love her but are unable to reach her. The suffering of the combined family, united in sorrow and divided in tranquility, reaches us most effectively.

Botica Modelo (1953, "The corner pharmacy"),[4] curiously a prize winner when produced, is a dramatic failure, providing, as it does, a demonstration of the difficulty of averting the mixing of dramatic ideas. The disappointment centers on the magnitude of keeping figures realistic when they are placed within a context that can render them symbolic and one-dimensional in a moment. The work, like its predecessor, begins on a realistic level. The characters and their problems are introduced within the setting of a typical small town store, a combination of pharmacy and beauty shop. Hernández gives close attention to such details as dress, language, and place. The exposition also clearly delineates the characters' abject indifference to each other.

However, Hernández fails to develop the latent fury embedded beneath the characters' banal conversation. Instead, the theme of social inequity, which eventually becomes a major thematic concern in later plays, overpowers the original realistic design. Now, the dramatist is drawn to the town's shimmering veneer of calmness, which is unable to hide the insidious power struggle over the town's rather shabby wealth and dubious future. Nor can the author conceal the fact that she chooses sides in the town's struggle; what starts as a conventional piece of realism suddenly is melodrama.

The most successful of these early plays is a farce, *Los duendes*, (1960, "The elves").[5] Dedicated to her small daughter, this work again investigates the breakdown in human relationships, notwithstanding the great deal of joviality that marks it. We accept the most implausible resolution to the most complicated problems without question. Indeed, the fun is so appealing that the theme refuses to emerge until contemplation requires us to ascertain the real problems and reconsider the ease with which we accept the implausible. Two facts then invade our sense of well-being. The problems of the characters are disquieting. A grandmother is detested, the grandchildren are abandoned by their parents, the granddaughter is jilted and falls in love unwisely on the rebound, and the grandson's wife, an exceedingly ugly woman, seems incapable of accepting her husband's love. Cases of generation gaps and distrust abound.

The second fact is that this incompatibility is resolved happily at the close of the piece, but since the means are not those of the real world, the solutions are not viable. Rather, the recourse available to Hernández to reconcile the disparate personalities is magic and blind love, neither of which is a reasonable solution in the normal world. The acceptance of these two facts permits us to arrive at the conclusion that Hernández was writing a work dealing with the theme established in *Botica Modelo* and *Agonía*. Additionally, the surface mirth heightens our despair rather than assuaging it when we do eventually feel the full impact of all the drama's pessimistic implications.

In 1955, Hernández finished her early masterpiece, *Los frutos caídos*. This work benefits from the earlier exercises, for none of the prior deficiencies appear. Hernández weaves theme and character into a whole and orchestrates the separate parts together toward a climax that is altogether a fitting conclusion to the sparse exposition. The predominant theme remains basically the same as that of her prior efforts: in spite of the characters' desire to overcome their isolation one from another, the unhappy destiny suggested at the beginning of the work is met. Half-truths are the watchword. Each individual feeds on the other's needs and weaknesses. Finally, they are led to understand that their lives cannot be changed although they find their present existence intolerable. Their despair is unalleviated when the work closes; clearly, Hernández wished to indicate her view that middle-class life in Mexico was empty and futile. The audience comprehends that view.

Los frutos caídos is the culmination not only of the thematic concerns established in this initial stage in Hernández's development but also of her final mastering of this dramatic form. The work also shows the strong influence that her drama professor, Rodolfo Usigli, had in Hernández's initial phase. In particular, Usigli's drama shows remarkable care given to structure and balance. Not surprisingly, these same dramatic elements were the main concern in his dramatic composition classes. In addition, his students remember the great stress he gave to following the model established by the Russian realists, particularly Chekov.[6] Furthermore, Usigli, in his capacity as her thesis director, required that the thesis, *Los frutos caídos*, be accompanied by a lengthy exegesis of the work demonstrating that it followed the tenets of dramatic realism.

Freudian psychology is the second major influence that forged Hernández's point of view in her early works. Her interest in it tends to manifest itself in prototypal behavior based upon complexes. *Los huéspedes reales* considers the consequences of an Electra complex in contemporary dress. It also underscores her frank admiration for Eugene O'Neill's *Mourning Becomes Electra*. Her *La hija del rey* (1965, "The king's daughter"),[7] a little-known but extremely complicated monologue, is the dramatization of an idea reflected in this quote from the author: "I wanted to see the behavior, the dissimulation of a weak woman in the situation of Electra."[8] It is not a pleasant thing to watch—Hernández is very severe in her treatment of the character, a trait that will occupy our attention shortly—but the psychological overlapping of the character, based on feigned humility, fear, and self-conscious justification, is extremely effective.

The concept of sublimation supplies the key to her two farces, *Los duendes* and *Arpas blancas, conejos dorados* (1963, "White harps, golden rabbits").[9] *Los duendes*, for example, is almost unintelligible—which is not to say chaotic or nonsensical, for the instincts, if left to follow the intricacies of the farce, do "understand" what is happening—unless one begins to "read" the *behavior* of the people rather than their superficial identities. In this way the grandmother is a small child playing as a witch, the granddaughter is the mother, the sister-in-law is the ugly duckling on one level (a witch on another), and love is the all-conquering agent, reconciling the apparently disparate parts into one beautiful unit.

Even a work as apparently clear as *Los frutos caídos* requires an audience conditioned to accept general Freudian theories of human motivation and frustration in order to appreciate fully the painful revelation of character through conflict. Freud, Usigli, her character, and her position as a woman in Mexico—these are the principal circumstances that conditioned Hernández's early works. As previously indicated, nearly all should be considered exercises in blending form, character, and language. Hernández considers the bulk of these early efforts, such as *El ambiente jurídico* (1950, "Law's lie"),[10] *Agonía, Los sordomudos* (1954, "The deaf-mutes"),[11] and *Botico modelo* as inferior works, necessary for developing her skill but, in retrospect, capable of producing in her feelings of discomfort, or even distaste.

These works do, nevertheless, afford an insight into one of Hernández's key characteristics as a dramatist, that of her relationship with the characters she has created. As a rule, she places her characters in extreme conditions in order to evoke strong action or revelation from them. *Agonía*, as an example, illustrates the kind of pressure that she applies to her characters. A divorced woman in her early forties has been very ill. She returns to her home, to a father with whom she has not spoken in five years, to a daughter who has adored her from afar, and to a husband who still loves her. She comes into the middle of all this—to die. She has to return, but she foresees that her return will agitate an already unstable situation. She will suffer, but her innate honesty compels her on, so that in her last moment of life she has no tranquility. Hers is an ugly, demeaning death.

Another early work is the taut *El ambiente jurídico*. It depicts a young woman who has never been able to condone the innocence and naïveté that betrayed her and caused the alienation between her first love and herself. Dispassionately, she begins a series of illicit affairs with various men. Her intelligence never ignores, overlooks, nor forgives. When one of her lovers proposes marriage, she desperately wants to accept; yet her guilt drives the man away. Alone, on the edge of a breakdown, she grasps for the only order that is able to save her—an intellectual one. We see her reciting Roman laws one by one: "La primera trata de la Organización judicial, la segunda del Procedimiento, la tercera sobre la Ejecución de juicios contra deudores insolventes, la cuarta . . ."[12] She has a kind of order, but one that is emotionally sterile.

These works indicate a pattern that Hernández repeats: the psyche is stripped, brought to the hall of truth, and is branded. No realistic drama works without these moments. But Hernández takes this dramatic movement and carries it to the outer edge by being particularly unsparing of her own characters. Hernández is, it seems, basically a person filled with moral anger. Her ire is especially aroused when it deals with the human propensity for protective cover when that cover becomes a license and justification for deceit or just plain weakness. When her characters demonstrate those traits, or are simply naïve, she is uncompromisingly rough on them. As she makes them work back toward the essence of their being—its limits, it energies, its general nature—they are made to feel that each day, each parting, each encounter is but a remembrance of things to come. This knowledge is searing and personal; it is also unavoidable, and we share it with them.

The tragedy *Los huéspedes reales* is a case in point. The dramatic problem is the converse of *La hija del rey*: a daughter who grows in strength during the play, an Electra who perverts the normal family relationships by challenging a powerful, jealous mother and nearly seducing an ineffectual, emotionally impotent father. The figure who supplies us with the sample of extremely harsh character treatment is the father, Ernesto. He is a good man in many ways, but strangely unworldly and innocent. A kind of blindness toward potential deviate behavior in members of his family prevents him from exorcising dangerous traits when they initially appear. Although he has governed his life according to the best of intentions, he almost accepts his daughter's incestuous love. He has desired nothing of life other than to grow old gracefully and with dignity, but his wife has ensnared him and rendered him impotent. When he finally realizes the repercussions of the general deviate behavior and his complicity resulting from this blindness, it is too late. Suicide is the only solution available to him in order to obviate the women's deleterious dominance.

This process of working toward awareness is instrumental if the tragedy is to work. Nevertheless, the feeling remains that the illusion of life in the play is just that, while the real strength rests with the author. Thus, it is she who places Ernesto in this most adverse of situations, and it is her will that he should suffer this way. To classify this kind of character treatment as harsh could be a matter of personal taste, but other examples of similar character development exist, suggesting a rather consistent attitude toward her dramatic figures.

A comparison of two curiously similar works, Carballido's *Rosalba y los Llaveros* (1950, "Rosalba and the Llavero family") and Hernández's own *Los frutos caídos*, further illuminates Hernández's quest for honesty through pain in her characters. Both deal with young women from the city who return to the provinces, with the attending shock between life styles and the automatic expectations of the opposing worlds. To depict such a clash of assumptions is one of the particular energies of drama, for the character can be revealed most precisely.

In *Rosalba y los Llaveros*, Carballido delights in the archaic behavior of the provincial family. A fine example occurs when Rosalba's uncle constantly changes the subject each time she openly discusses sex. Carballido also appreciates the potential humor in theory attempting to capture reality, the oversimplified answer to all problems. Thus, Rosalba's repetitive recourse to Freudian psychology, particularly about inhibitions and sex, works well for us, the audience, when we realize that it is an inflexible yardstick in a constantly changing world.

We need not be reminded that inflexible patterns can be humorless. Hernández, for one, sees nothing funny in the destruction of an individual because society establishes an unyielding, oversimplified attitude. Thus, in *Los frutos caídos* there is nothing humorous in the fact that Celia, a twenty-six–year–old mother of two who sincerely seeks to work her way out of spiritual bondage, is called a "puta" because, and only because, she is a divorcee. Nor is drunkenness appealing or funny when it becomes the automatic answer to conflict or the justification for violence. Fernando, Celia's uncle in *Los frutos caídos*, exemplifies Hernández's dramatization of these two destructive powers, and, in the context of the play, they aid in establishing the particularly grim mood that pervades the work.

Nevertheless, Hernández's ruthlessly frank treatment of her characters is not simply a question of mood or of the harm done one of the characters by another. Nor is it attributable solely to exigencies of form. It goes deeper than that, for a comedy can embarrass or destroy, and a tragedy can dignify and instruct.

The cause of this harshness is the dramatic perspective of the author. In *Rosalba y los Llaveros* and *Los frutos caídos*, both the lead characters, Rosalba and Celia, are exposed and vulnerable at the end of their respective works. In *Rosalba y los Llaveros*, Rosalba has brought the family to the point of accepting their son and illegitimate granddaughter. She has also fallen in love with the son, but, in the process, her compulsive manipulation of people and ideas alienates him from her.

If the work were to run true to the spirit of comic convention, Rosalba would be punished; no reconciliation would be made, and her loneliness would be fitting for the abuse she created through her words. But Carballido will not allow this basically well intentioned young lady to suffer permanent alienation or rejection. A reconciliation is achieved after she is made aware of the potential loss that would be hers. This type of denouement also allows Carballido to bring about a larger reconciliation between the two life styles and suggests his conviction or hope that a harmonized adjustment between city and province can be achieved. Such a harmony would reject the wholly antiquated patterns of the province along with the superficial, facile theorizing of the city slicker. Carballido's unwillingness to punish his characters beyond tolerable limits may have cost the drama some of its "message," but the gentleness with which he unfailingly treats his characters is appreciated by a grateful audience, which is spared some intense discomfort.

Los frutos caídos places its lead character, Celia, in a situation not altogether dissimilar from Rosalba's. As a product of the city, educated, belonging to an increasingly mobile middle class, it is not surprising to learn that she is twice married, once divorced, and experiencing some doubts about her second marriage. The reason for her trip to the provincial town also represents something new in Mexico—a woman with the power to dispose of property, to obtain and use the power of attorney. Her life style, her needs, and the new legal power clash violently with the colonial mentality still holding rigid sway in the provinces. Her uncle, Fernando, who apparently represents the decaying provincial order, receives full force the blow that this new "order" configures. Hernández sees this clash between two inherently opposing forces as irreconcilable. Logic, therefore, is satisfied when the denouement resolves none of the conflicts—frustration, inadequacies, and anger continue to seethe under the bland faces of this bourgeois group.

The general pessimism that marks this denouement is carried over to character treatment. Celia is made to reject her potential lover, to refuse to sell the estate, and, finally, to accept the fact that though she may change the superficial aspects of her life, she is locked into a pattern over which she has no control. She will be an outsider, living on the margin of dignity, for the rest of her life. She knows it and is embittered.

However, the dramatist's strength of character, the tendency to denude her dramatic personages, is not felt here. Celia's treatment is dramatically and realistically consistent. She suffers, but we feel the suffering to be fair, since she is greatly responsible for much that has happened to her.

It is rather with the figure of Dora, the teenage girl who lives with Celia's aunt, that Hernández seems to press her pursuit too far. Her point—the inescapability of living within a corrupt form—is made with Celia. But Hernández has Celia expand and extend her awareness of her entrapment to the frivolous and innocent Dora and makes her a party to her own disillusionment. This conscious destruction of Dora's innocence seems stronger than need be and appears to underline the dramatist's urgent need to express the truth in the severest of terms.

As mentioned previously, most of Hernández's early works were in the realistic vein. The forms and tones permitted her to express her dramatic needs and spirit and should be considered as a serious effort to understand her world. Yet some critics have denigrated the writings of Hernández, along with those of Carballido, Magaña, and others as being merely academic. *Costumbristas*, they are called—local colorists who fail to penetrate surface reality. Carlos Solórzano, for one, feels that the playwrights of the movement that grew out of *A Streetcar Named Desire*—the initial play that Hernández and the others used as a model—committed a serious error in judgment when they thought they had understood and captured the essence of Mexico by copying its external face: "Alongside the *costumbrista* tendency, which attempts to capture the drama of Mexico in the most superficial and external formal sense, there is another that has the achieved goal of handling this same reality in a transcendental way. . . . This tendency (*vanguardismo*) has created a theater that is a true face [of Mexico] and not some superficial form of the popular soul."[13]

But it is impossible to wish away the fine works written in this style that have demonstrated viable dramatic truths. If one rightly understands the nature of dramatic realism, he has to accept that the dramatist must portray some environment with as high a degree of accuracy as possible. That is the nature of realism. But, realism in the hands of talented artists does not stop there. Rather, the atmosphere—the environment portrayed—becomes the backdrop against which the characters reveal themselves. Further, it often becomes an important adjunct of our understanding of the motivation of the characters. Anyone who misinterprets this point will surely fail to appreciate the movement of the work, of the character in conflict. In effect, the problem seems to be not so much a matter of willingness to understand what the author is doing as an inability to be patient with a less theatrical, less flashy drama than the *vanguardista*.

The common denominator joining this realistic stage and Hernández's later nonrealistic drama is the presence of her anger. Its subjective form in the early drama seems to originate in some of the personal circumstances of the dramatist. This view is strengthened by the relatively high correlation between her life and her main characters, as well as the general nature of her plots, the location of her work, and her own viewpoint as gleaned from a careful reading of her works. However, as Hernández's work matures, there seems to be less desire to personalize the dramatic conflict in her works—the dramas become less hers and more Mexico's. This new direction was anticipated in the earlier drama *Botica Modelo*; now she attacks the problem directly by aiming her anger at a society in which political, social, and economic power is held by the few but justified in the flowery rhetoric of the PRI or the church. The gap between ideological clichés and the living reality of many dispossessed souls is unbreachable as things stand and unbearable to Hernández's sensitivities and morality. She attempts to explode all the social and political myths that have accumulated since the Revolution in protest dramas. Because she directs her attention at all of society rather than the smallest unit of it (the individual), and since the forms and methods employed to involve the audience are now much different, Hernández's anger seems more objective, but no less felt.

In addition to this broadening scope of the dramatist's concern, Hernández also learned the limits of realism and found it wanting for her new dramatic needs. As a result, in the 1950s and early 1960s, she moved on to new forms and new content with apparent ease. Of the forms that most attracted her, the theater of commitment was dominant. The major works in this form are three: *La paz ficticia* (1960, "The fictitious peace"),[14] *La historia de un anillo* (1961, "The story of a ring"),[15] and *La fiesta del mulato* (1966, "The mulatto's festival").[16] All were written under commission for school groups, as was her first tragicomedy, *Popol Vuh* (1966, "Popol Vuh").[17]

Hernández's great strength is her ability to handle structure. These non-realistic pieces give free reign to this strength, with the result that the stage becomes in part the message. Astute use of space, light, music, and dramatic juxtaposition gives these works great vitality and symbolic quality. These dramas of commitment are, in addition, compelling, thought provoking, and sharply critical, slashing at the political and religious establishment. Her ire has not abated.

The plot of *La paz ficticia* is straightforward. In the 1880s, the Yaqui tribe loses its land after a hard-fought, unequal war with federal and state troops. The cause of the war is the desire by state officials to obtain the land so that they can in turn sell it to foreign interests for the purpose of developing the mining industry. Once the Yaquis lose the land, they are unmercifully mistreated. There are many indignities, but perhaps the worst is that families are separated, with individual members dispersed throughout the republic. As a result, peace is achieved, but its nature is so abhorrent that Hernández considers it to be a false one that must be destroyed.

Hernández builds a case against the Díaz regime that purchased its power by selling out to foreign investors. The emotional impact on the audience is weighed through its sense of loss by the sheer number of humans destroyed for this power. The dramatist hopes that the anger and frustration piqued by this symbolic struggle between good and evil, in which evil dominates, will turn the audience's attention toward preventing the return of any analogous attitude, including well-intentioned but ultimately dangerous periods of "law and order."

This appeal to the audience's sense of patriotism and justice also gives thrust to *La historia de un anillo*. With slight modifications, this latter play is based on an event that had occurred in an isolated mountain town, the account of which appeared in a Mexico City paper. The mayor and the priest supported each other in their wish to keep constitutional reforms, and, indeed, the knowledge of the very existence of the constitution, from the town. Their desire resulted in the termination of the teaching contract of a young lady who had been attempting to instruct the children in the constitutional basis for individual rights. The mayor replaced the teacher with his mistress, whom he instructed to teach only sewing and cooking.

The ring, to which the title refers, is an inexpensive one that the mayor had bought at a local *feria* and had given to his mistress. When she loses it at school, she blames it on the humble Indian caretaker, a poor woman of meager material wealth but great dignity, who is jailed and made to sign a false confession. The townspeople can no longer accept the mayor's behavior; they become a mob, set fire to his home and the jail, and threaten him bodily. The mayor acts in character and summons the federal troops, who massacre the local population.

Hernández tells this story in such a way that the melodramatic qualities inherent in it are tempered. Adroit dramatic juxtaposition of the characters, short, rapid-fire scenes, and music composed especially for the work provide emotional qualities that give it depth. Again, as in *La paz ficticia*, the portrayal of underdogs who fight with valor emerges from the play and strengthens the impact on the audience. The dignity of the townspeople is summed up in the final lines of the song ending the work, which reflects their willingness to enter into a deathly confrontation with the town's conservative forces: "Mejor morir honrados / que vivir engañados. / No se puede evitar, / estamos obligados."[18]

La fiesta del mulato shares with the other two dramas the desire to examine certain incidents of Mexican history that can be made to reveal insights into basic Mexican traits and mentalities. In it we see the symbolic appreciation of the inherent disparity that was the social subsoil of Mexico. This disparity was due to the three racial types and the different mentalities produced by the existing socioeconomic-political system during the viceroyalty—the creole, a "holding" element, the Indians and other have-nots, like the slaves, and those who move in the shadows between the two extremes, here represented by the figure of the mulatto. The historic incident that permits Hernández to demonstrate the manner in which all these mutually exclusive elements become forged into the unifying concept of a new independent Mexico is related in a diary of a friar who was in Guanajuato during a trial of a mulatto charged with embezzlement of mining funds. During the trial scenes especially, Hernández adroitly brings out all the assumptions underlying each opposing element. By the close of the drama, we are privileged to witness a willingness on the part of all to give up their own private visions and yield to a larger, all-embracing one— Mexico and its renewing force, justice for all.

The myriad facets of Hernández's theater that we have seen—her anger, her sense of structure, the influence of her own life—have a unifying intellectual framework that was established remarkably early in the dramatist's career. The first serious play Hernández saw was *A Streetcar Named Desire*, a work whose premise still has meaning for understanding Hernández's own theater. Elia Kazan, the play's original director, states the premise in the following quote: "Blanche is a social type, an emblem of a dying order . . . her problem has to do with her tradition . . . which worked in the nineteenth century. It made a woman feel important, with her own special worth. It also made a woman at that time one with her society. But today, it does not work . . . it makes Blanche feel alone, outside of her society. Blanche is an outdated creature, approaching extinction."[19]

The clue we seek comes from the idea of an individual moving toward extinction as a result of having been formed by a social structure that has become archaic, thereby rendering the person himself archaic. Hernández is concerned that in the dynamics between society and the individual, certain forms will outlast their "usefulness," become self-perpetuating, and produce maimed humans. When a form becomes useless, it must be discarded and a new one must be constructed. Society must be renewed to be relevant, and often revolution is the answer.[20] In her realistic period, this conceptualization of the tension between form and content focuses on the individual. The form—traditional patterns between the sexes, use of power, concept of the self—crushes and thwarts any individual whose conduct deviates from the traditional norms. The classical study is *Los frutos caídos*, whose title suggests precisely the sense of futility of the individuals. The tree keeps producing the same rotting fruit, season after season. Furthermore, the seeds nurtured upon the putrid fruit will grow into similar trees. The unending cycle prophesies a doomed, stifling future for Mexico, the awareness of which is the most devastating impact of the work on the spectator.

Thus, Celia, once divorced, twice a mother, eventually surrenders to her fate as a woman in a society that prevents her expression, but it is a yielding with none of the grace of harmonized reconciliation that often accompanies a new grasp upon reality. Indeed, so bitter is she about a lifeless pattern that she must follow the rest of her days that she attacks the new generation (the seeds of the future) in the person of Dora, destroying her innocence and enervating her energies by making her aware that her wants, no matter how humble, will never be satisfied.

Form as prison also offers a key to *Los huéspedes reales*, since the tragedy turns on a traditional pattern, that which assumes the right of the parents to select a husband for the daughter, and, of course, the daughter's acceptance of that parental privilege.

Hernández's nonrealistic theater also challenges the primacy of form over content in Mexico. From *La paz ficticia* through *La historia de un anillo* to

La fiesta del mulato, Hernández repeatedly demonstrates the bankruptcy of *la mano dura*, *caciquismo*, and the Establishment. Even though the characters are not psychologically developed, there is great audience identification with the values they represent. When arbitrary power is unleashed and the audience sees the destruction carried out in the name of progress, we feel with the author that form selectively and consistently destroys the individual.

With the exception of *Quetzalcoatl* (1968),[21] an unproduced drama addressing itself to yet another important moment of transition in Mexican history, Hernández has of late dedicated herself to the novel and to teaching. She appears now to be returning to the theater, however, and there is every reason to expect that this sensitive and highly intelligent dramatist will offer us new and rewarding works.

NOTES

1. In *Teatro mexicano del siglo XX*, Letras mexicanas 98 (Mexico City: Fondo de Cultura Económica, 1970), IV, 84–138.

2. In *Teatro mexicano del siglo XX*, Letras mexicanas 27 (Mexico City: Fondo de Cultura Económica, 1970), III, 403–478.

3. In *América*, no. 65 (April–May 1951), pp. 95–110.

4. In serial form in *El Nacional* (Mexico City), 1953.

5. In *La Palabra y el Hombre*, no. 14 (April–June 1960), pp. 153–204.

6. From unpublished interviews of Hernández, Carballido, and Magaña with John K. Knowles, Mexico City, July 1970.

7. In *Cuarta antología de obras en un acto*, colección de teatro mexicano (Mexico City: Editorial Peregrina, 1965), pp. 7–15.

8. Luisa Josefina Hernández, from an interview with John K. Knowles, 13 February 1966. My translation.

9. In *La Palabra y el Hombre*, no. 28 (October–December 1963), pp. 634–691.

10. In *América*, no. 64 (December 1950), pp. 209–224.

11. In *América*, no. 69 (March 1954), pp. 95–110.

12. "The first treats the judicial organization, the second, that of proceedings, the third, the handling of cases against indigent debtors, the fourth . . ." (In *América*, no. 64, p. 224, my translation).

13. Carlos Solórzano, *Teatro latinoamericano en el siglo XX* (Mexico City: Editorial Pormaca, 1964), pp. 211–212. My translation.

14. In *México en la Cultura*, 28 August 1960, pp. 3, 10, and 4 September 1960, p. 5.

15. In *La Palabra y el Hombre*, no. 20 (October–December 1961), pp. 693–723.

16. In manuscript form only, 1966. Original retained by Hernández in her home in Mexico City. English translation by William I. Oliver appeared in his *Voices of Change in the Spanish American Theater* (Austin: University of Texas Press, 1971), pp. 219–255.

17. In *La Palabra y el Hombre*, no. 40 (October–December 1966), pp. 699–734.

18. "It's better to die with honor / than live with deceit. / It is ordained, / we are obliged thus to act" (in *México en la Cultura*, 4 September 1960, p. 5).

19. Francis D. Donahue, *The Dramatic World of Tennessee Williams* (New York: Frederick Ungar, 1964), p. 32.

20. It is this concern over archaic form that ties Hernández to the mainstream of Mexican cultural history, for there has been developing over the years a general concept about the nature of man and society in Mexico. Octavio Paz's *El laberinto de la soledad* (Mexico City: Fondo de Cultura Económica, 1950) seems to be the originator of the concept that states that the Mexican is a lover of form, a mechanism that somehow seems to destroy both the object and the lover. Form hides, masks, and protects. To break form is to open oneself. To open oneself is to increase the potential of being penetrated, of being taken advantage of—assumed signs of weakness. In the personal realm, the compulsive need to prove one's "closedness" gives rise to expressions like "soy tu padre" and attitudes like *machismo*, passiveness in women, and an abhorrence toward homosexuality.

Paz sees this love of form as the heritage of years of foreign forms imposed over the Mexican spirit, stifling expression and communication. In *El laberinto de la soledad*, Paz traces the evolution from the pre-Columbian era to the present and claims that even the Revolution has been unable to give rise to true, natural forms for the Mexican population. Hernández shares Paz's concept of form as preventing authentic expression, as her theater of commitment so obviously represents.

21. In *Cuadernos de lectura popular*, La honda del espíritu, no. 172 (Mexico City, 1968).

10. The Theater of René Marqués:

In Search of Identity and Form

Tamara Holzapfel

In 1938 the Ateneo de Puerto Rico made the first serious attempt to bring before the public a program of dramas by native playwrights. This event marks the beginning of a literary and cultural activity of the Puerto Rican theater that remains vital to the present. René Marqués (b. 1919) is among the four or five men who have made outstanding contributions to this movement. He has distinguished himself in all areas of the theater. His name is initially associated with Areyto, the dramatic society Emilio S. Belaval founded in 1940. A newcomer to the theater, Marqués (who had previously completed his studies of agronomy and spent a year in Madrid studying literature at the Universidad Central) started by establishing a provincial branch of Areyto in Arecibo, his hometown, and by writing articles in favor of a national theater. In 1947 he founded the society Pro-Arte, also in Arecibo, and in 1948 he tried his hand at playwriting, producing a short piece entitled *El hombre y sus sueños* ("The man and his dreams"). The following year a grant from the Rockefeller Foundation made it possible for him to study drama at Columbia University. On returning to Puerto Rico, he organized the group Teatro Nuestro (1950) and became cofounder of the Teatro Experimental del Ateneo (1951), of which he was later named director. His total commitment to the theater has on occasion prompted him to take on the roles of producer, stage designer, and actor.

Since his first playwriting effort, Marqués has composed fourteen dramas, many of which have enjoyed stage success in Puerto Rico and abroad.[1] Their content generally attests to his genuine concern for the destiny of his country within the national and universal circumstance. He explores with fervor the Nationalist phenomenon and the moral and psychological consequences brought about by Puerto Rico's affiliation with the United States. The wider context of his plays is man's existential isolation and time as a philosophical problem. Although these ideas are shared by contemporary man, they are presented with insight and passion. Form is of primary interest, and the variety of molds into which he casts his ideas reveals the author to be a ceaseless experimenter, one who always strives for technical versatility and perfection.

Marqués's literary talents go beyond the drama to include the novel, short story, and essay. He seems, however, to prefer the drama to the other genres for psychological and sociological reasons. In his own definition, the literature of his generation is a "synchronized" expression of the deep psychological realities of the Puerto Rican.[2] What better testing ground for his nationalistic concerns than the theater, where an author's views are scrutinized and where success and failure are tangible factors?

El hombre y sus sueños,[3] René Marqués's first play and his only one-act play, is essentially an exercise in playwriting but represents an important experiment anticipating later stages in the development of his craftsmanship. Marqués sets out to allegorize and parody Unamuno's ideas about man's longing for an existence after death. He follows the Spanish author in debating the three ways by which man hopes to perpetuate his individuality—through an offspring, through religion, and through his works. However, in dealing with this theme Marqués avoids the tone dictated by an overly egotistical sensibility, completely rejecting the notion that immortality can be attained through procreation or religious faith. The play's subtitle, "An intranscendental sketch for a transcendental drama,"[4] is an apt description of its meaning. Irony takes the place of the Unamunian paradox.

El hombre is a rational drama, rationally constructed. The initial visit by the three Amigos (politician, poet, and philosopher) to the bedside of the dying man, el Hombre, is counterbalanced at the end by the appearance of the Sombras representing the three types of immortality. In the manner of a religious allegory, they arrive to claim el Hombre's soul the moment he dies. The winner is the Sombra Azul who symbolizes man's works. Between these conceptual levels of the play—the debate of the friends about what makes a man great and the final dispute over his soul by the shadows—a drama of lust, envy, greed, and superstition is acted out by the remaining characters, el Hijo, la Mujer, la Enfermera, la Criada, and el Sacerdote.[5] It is a drama of the irrational side of human nature.

The directions for the stage design reflect the essential symmetry and symbolism of the play. The bed elevated on a platform against the semicircle of columns is located stage center. Since the action revolves around a great man, this picture with its regal color scheme of red (carpet) and white (columns and bed) also suggests a monument. The black background lends the scene a sense of timelessness. Colors (red, black, and blue) are also used to distinguish the Sombras.

Light and sound effects are important throughout the play to convey emotions and changes in the fate of el Hombre. A yellow light on his face turns blue at the end when the Sombra Azul triumphs over the other contenders for his soul. Similarly, the sad tolling of the funereal bell becomes a triumphal ringing of many bells at the same moment. In addition, the death knell alternates with the ominous howling of a dog, and when el Hombre dies, the laughter of la Mujer erupts into an infernal confusion of noises. The crescendo of the auditory effects at this point suggests a final manifestation of the "sound and fury" of the dying man's world.

El hombre reflects the existential position that "life's but a shadow . . . full of sound and fury," but which, despite the chaos, can have meaning if the individual devotes his energy to improving his circumstance in the world. The destiny of man lies in his own hands. His work, the Sombra Azul, is the monument that will survive his ephemeral existence.

When he wrote *El hombre y sus sueños*, Marqués was obviously attracted by the then already outdated expressionistic mode. Subsequently, the author's experiences at Columbia University oriented him toward the new realism in vogue at that time on the American stage. Arthur Miller suggests that "the force or pressure that makes for Realism, that even requires it, is the magnetic force of the family relationship."[6] All three of the next group of Marqués's plays, *Palm Sunday* (1949), *El sol y los MacDonald* (1950, "The sun and the Mac-Donalds"), and *La carreta* (1952, *The Cart*), are centered around the family, but the intent is to dramatize the personal as well as the social conflicts of the characters, a synthesis achieved by Eugene O'Neill and Arthur Miller, among others.

Palm Sunday, Marqués's first nationalistic drama, is based on a historic event, the Palm Sunday massacre of 1937. The protagonist Alberto is a victim of the designs of his own father who orders the massacre. This work will not be discussed at length because it was originally written in English as an exercise at Columbia University and remains unpublished at the time of this writing.

El sol y los MacDonald deals with a decadent southern (United States) family whose members are enmeshed in a tradition of incest and white supremacy and in a fear of foreigners. Only Ramiro García, the last MacDonald produced by the female side of the family, is able to break out of this seemingly predetermined situation. Structurally and technically, *El sol* is the most innovative of this group of plays. Although all action transpires in the MacDonalds' living room, the author is able to suggest through sound and light effects the different levels of inner and outer reality. The drama is divided into three acts, each one opening with a long monologue of the "stream-of-consciousness" variety: in acts I and III by Gustavo MacDonald, and in act II by Ramiro García. The protagonists are uncle and nephew. A striking similarity of character is established in the first two acts on the interior and exterior planes of action. Gustavo is an O'Neillian double personality in so far as he also represents a choric character, one who comments on the action of the others.

In addition to the initial interior monologue, there is, in all three acts, a second introspective passage involving the same character, and in act II retrospective action represents Ramiro's mental effort to reconstruct his family's past. At the climactic moment, a red spotlight symbolizes the incestual love he has for his mother. Hoofbeat rhythms and a blue spotlight are the sensorial effects associated with the past. At the end of the last mental picture a car horn suddenly interrupts the hoofbeats to bring the action back to the present. In the final scene, a blue light illuminates Gustavo leaning against a tree (family tree). His monologue together with the image onstage inform us that he is inescapably bound to the past and doomed to live in a twilight zone of inaction. The moonlight used in all three acts has a similar effect with regard to the entire MacDonald clan. There is no "sun" except that of the title, which refers to the ancient Greek myth about incest.[7]

During the retrospective scene Ramiro reconstructs the family tree, evoking three sets of ancestors who represent the roots, the trunk, and the branches. Through this analysis of the past he discovers that incest is not a hereditary trait but brought about by the authoritarian and despotic nature of the MacDonald men, who committed incest and murder to insure the continuity of the family name. Ramiro is freed from the oppressive past, not because his last name is Spanish (his father degenerates with the MacDonalds), but because of his striving for personal independence and the insight he gains through introspection.

The best moments of El sol foreshadow Marqués's later achievements in playwriting. But in spite of its potentially powerful theme, poetic suggestiveness, and innovative techniques, the play fails. The author does not move convincingly in the southern milieu. What he knows about tradition and family life in the South is too obviously second hand, learned from a William Faulkner or a Tennessee Williams.

In La carreta the members of a Puerto Rican peasant family are victimized by an outside force. Lured by the promise of a better life, they abandon their ancestral land for a sorrowful existence, first in the La Perla slum of San Juan, and later in the Bronx. More than a simple presentation of a Puerto Rican "slice of life," this play is a parable about modern Puerto Rico, built around the concepts of la tierra, la madre, and la máquina. A closer look at the three estampas ("images") that make up the play reveals that the first has at its center the land, the second focuses on doña Gabriela's maternal role, and the third discloses the fatality of the country of the machine—the United States.

Significantly, the male protagonist Luis is an orphan raised since infancy by doña Gabriela. Everybody knows this, including Luis, but the truth is never brought out into the open. The consequence of this repression is a deep-seated guilt complex that destroys in him the noblest of human emotions. Incapable of love, Luis is obsessed with the mystery of the machine. In an attempt to discover its secret he is destroyed by the mechanical monster. His death is clearly suicidal and symbolizes, ironically, a "return to the womb."

A parallel can be drawn between Luis's predicament and that of his countrymen who are orphans in their own land because of domination by the United States. If they truly loved their country, they would work or fight for independence. Instead, they yearn for material progress promised them by North America and willingly submit to colonialism. For this reason, Puerto Ricans suffer from a guilt complex and are easily driven to suicide.[8]

With *La carreta*, Marqués is holding up a mirror for his people to see themselves as they really are. He warns them not to follow Luis in his search for the "tesoro escondido por Juan Bobo en la barriga de la caldera de acero,"[9] but to take up the struggle for national independence. Puerto Rico is essentially an agricultural country; the glory of the Puerto Rican lies in his recognition of this condition and in his assenting to it.

The structure of *La carreta* is circular. The cart of the title provides not only the original means of transportation for the family from the country to the city, but it also remains a major motif throughout the play in the form of a replica carved by Miguel. It stands as a reminder of the ultimate return of the family to their barrio in the mountains. The movement of going and returning is also supported by the idea of an imminent departure in all three acts: from the land, from San Juan, from New York back to the land.

Marqués avails himself of many technical devices to create atmosphere and poetry onstage. In the first *estampa*, set in the country, the mood, a nostalgia for the past combined with humor, is due to the presence of don Chago and the antics of Chaguito. Also, each character is associated with an animal or object that has a poetic-symbolic meaning: doña Gabriela's saint (love for tradition), Chaguito's rooster (love for country life), don Chago's cave (love for the land), Juanita's nightingale (love for the peon Miguel) and, finally, Luis's ominous cart. Its approach, indicated by the creaking of wheels, casts a shadow of uncertainty and fear over the family. This tension at the end of act I anticipates the increasingly angry tone of acts II and III.

Offstage sound effects are always disturbing and become more frequent as the play progresses. The roar of an angry sea and loud jukebox music accompany the series of misfortunes that befall the family in the La Perla district. Nature, at least, seems to be sympathetic to the family's plight, while the strident music produced by the machine contrasts sharply with the desperate situation. In New York, life is made unbearable by constant noises from the motors of elevated trains and cement drills. The threat of violence inherent in a racist society is suggested in action behind the scenes (running, shouting, shooting), in which a Negro is pursued and killed by the police.

The final calamity, Luis's death, however, is a liberation. His cowardliness and false faith were responsible for the splintering of the family and for his mother's and sister's untenable existence in New York. Now, the women who had borne all the misfortunes courageously are able to return to the land where Chaguito and Miguel await them. The work thus ends on a positive note, exhorting the people of Puerto Rico not to forsake their traditional way of life.

Although this play is clearly nationalistic and written entirely in dialect, it transcends the limitations of pure regionalism and social preachment, for the author places man above idea and presents his characters and their problems with love and indignation. Successful characterization combined with skillful technical devices make *La carreta* a dramatic success. Marqués's material is this time close at hand, in the conflict precipitated by the United States' domination of Puerto Rican families and of the mind of individuals.

Juan Bobo y la Dama de Occidente (1954, "Juan the Fool and the Lady of the West") is not a drama but a pantomime for a ballet. It stands as a kind of interlude between *La carreta* and Marqués's next play and attests to his general interest in the theater arts as well as to his ability to visualize scenic movement and outward expression not transmitted by language. Gesture and pantomime occupy an important intermediate position between perception and illusion and are inherent elements in the art of acting.

Thematically, *Juan Bobo* represents a logical link between *La carreta* and the plays that follow. It satirizes the "tontería occidentalista," a craze started by Jaime Benítez (then rector of the University of Puerto Rico) to "westernize" the country. Marqués, who fully identifies himself and Puerto Rico with the western tradition, ridicules this false occidentalism, which is nothing more than "a politico-cultural game of Jaime [Benítez] intended to destroy the identity of the Puerto Rican."[10]

Juan Bobo is endowed by Marqués with what the author considers to be national traits: "candor, ingenuity, childish enthusiasm, curiosity."[11] He is a positive representation, not the clumsy fool of the folk tradition alluded to in *La carreta*. Marqués's Juan Bobo can redeem himself when he recognizes his own cultural values as being those of the western tradition not perverted for purposes of political propaganda.

Even more than *La carreta* and *Juan Bobo*, Marqués's next play, *La muerte no entrará en palacio* (1957, "Death shall not enter the palace"), was written to awaken the political conscience of Puerto Ricans who had succumbed to passivity and conformism during the years 1948–1952, also known as the Era of Silence. This period, interrupted by the brief and unsuccessful Nationalist uprising of October 1950 and ultimately culminating in Puerto Rico's becoming a protectorate of the United States, as well as other events leading up to and forming part of this crucial moment in the island's history, are the background of Marqués's most overtly political drama.

At least three important characters in the work can readily be identified with historical personalities: don Rodrigo fits the role of the Nationalist leader of the thirties, Albizu Campos, who was convicted for his part in the revolt of 1950 and pardoned in 1952; don José, the governor in the play, bears a striking resemblance to the governor-dictator Muñoz Marín; Casandra, who attempts to kill her father (the governor) at the signing of the agreement of the protectorate, evokes Lolita Lebrón and her pistol shots fired on the same occasion in the Congress of the United States in 1952.

Disappointed and deeply grieved by the extension of colonialism under the guise of the protectorate, Marqués seeks in his play an explanation of this secular tragedy, all the while maintaining his conviction that truth of conduct can be defined and that redemption is possible thrugh love and sacrifice. Although labeled a tragedy by the author, *La muerte*, like most attempts in this genre by twentieth-century dramatists, falls short of this highest of universal categories. In its presentation of a specific historical circumstance that contains elements of political irony and social satire, it comes close to what one might call a tragic ordering of life.

Marqués does not attach any stylistic implications to the term "tragedy." The play is executed in two long acts, each one subdivided into two scenes. The traditional unities are discarded. As in some of his earlier works, he gives elaborate stage directions, specifying the use of music, offstage voices (individual and choral), and a great variety of sounds and lighting to suggest various levels of reality. Material objects, such as the peasants' stone and the ceiba tree, are employed to concentrate symbolic values. The play opens and closes with a similar scene depicting Casandra's statue against the ruins of the palace. These scenes, presided over by Teresias in his choric role, with their references to Time and the Moral Order, are intended to set the tragic atmosphere. The remaining action is carried out, in part, within the outward convention of realism and, in part, on the level of poetic suggestiveness.

Another important aspect of this drama is Marqués's recurrence to the allegoric means already used in his first play. The triumvirate of philosopher, poet, and politician, considering the attributes of a great man in *El hombre y sus sueños*, appears here in the persons of the original revolutionaries who had followed don Rodrigo (the great man) in his struggle for national independence. In accordance with their allegoric function, the three men are also representative of time. The philosopher, the father of don José's youthful military aide Alberto, is associated with the past. Appropriately, he is already dead but appears as a memory of a man who had instilled the love of truth in his son. Teresias fulfills the role of the poet-visionary who is able to foresee the future of the palace and the fate of its inhabitants. The Governor lives only for the present, wholly absorbed by his personal ambitions. He does not come off as a tragic hero, and Marqués probably did not have this in mind when he created the character. Teresias's remark, "Tu mundo y mi mundo no podrán jamás sincronizarse,"[12] clearly shows what we are led to suspect all along: don José is a demagogue in disguise, more a villain than a hero.

Nonetheless, the author takes great pains to avoid drawing a stereotyped image of a corrupt politician. Don José makes a benevolent impression and stands out as a giant among the officials surrounding him. Because of his active idealism in his youth, he has won for himself the devotion of an admirable woman and noble-hearted friends. His only flaw, but an unforgiveable one in a man aspiring to greatness, is the lack of courage. This weakness of character symbolized by his dependence on his wife and on alcohol makes him a traitor to the ideals of his youth and to the people. Unable to comprehend the workings of destiny and urged by his need for protection, he leads his nation into becoming a protectorate of a foreign power. Despite all warnings to the contrary, don José insists on signing the treaty and thereby inflicts irreparable damage on himself and those he loves. His daughter becomes the instrument of justice, killing her lover, her father, and herself. The destruction of the palace is final.

There is a tragic resonance at the conclusion of the play when the chorus chants triumphantly, "Amor, amor. Dolor y miseria. ¡Amor!"[13] This combination of words is used to convey the fusion of grief and joy mandatory in the final moments of true tragedy. Casandra's transformation at this point into a hieratic statue is an effective device to produce a last moment of concrete poetry onstage. This scene is also reminiscent of *El hombre y sus sueños*, in which the visual impact onstage evokes a monument symbolizing man's attainment of immortality through positive social action. It seems obvious that the author has concealed behind Casandra's sacrifice a militant hope, which, however, is a purpose beyond tragedy.[14]

Poetic drama is the ultimate attainment of contemporary playwrights who combine effectively inner movement with poetic suggestiveness through visual and auditory techniques. If a complete synthesis is not achieved, the result is, at best, psychological drama with poetic overtones. Marqués's most successful plays, *Los soles truncos* (1958, *The Fanlights*) and *Un niño azul para esa sombra* (1958, "A blue boy for that shadow"), to which he fails to attach a subtitle, are fine examples of naturally poetic drama.

In *Los soles truncos*, Marqués treats more obliquely and with greater economy of means a theme already explored in one of his earlier plays, *El sol y los MacDonald*: the crushing effect of a guilty past on the members of a family. The play's only characters are three sisters who have been living for nearly half a century in self-imposed isolation in a decaying San Juan mansion doomed to total disappearance in the wake of modern urban renewal. All the action transpires in the living room on the day of Hortensia's death, which is previous to the opening scene. Time had come to a standstill in the household of the three spinsters, but now the necessity of a funeral precipitates on the surviving sisters a confrontation with the present. Both Emilia's often repeated gesture of shading her eyes against the sun coming through the window and the threatening sounds from the outside (the voice of the street barker and the knocking at the door of the auctioneers) underscore how unbearable this moment is.

Emilia's conversation with an imaginary gentleman at the beginning of act I reveals not only her mental instability but also her obsessive attachment to the past. Portrayed as the most sympathetic of the sisters, with her poetic sensitivity and physical frailty (she is lame like the protagonist in *The Glass Menagerie*, whom she also resembles in other ways), Emilia seems, at first, to be an innocent victim of time. However, later in the play it will be made evident that she shares in the guilt of her family.

Three retrospective scenes (two in act I, one in act II) disclose the reasons for the sisters' voluntary retreat from the world as well as the sources of their guilt. In their youth, all three had fallen in love with the same man, a Spanish officer. When the beautiful Hortensia became engaged to him, the spiteful Inés destroyed her illusion of happiness by informing her of her fiancé's love affair with another woman, who was, in addition, socially inferior to them. The marriage was called off, and Hortensia ordered the house permanently closed to the outside.

The real evil underlying their unfulfilled lives, however, can be traced back to the family's attachment to everything foreign. This is symbolized by the sisters' infatuation with the same man, a Spaniard, and is further supported by the parents' European origin. They had grown prosperous on Puerto Rican soil without having learned to love the land. Hortensia, by virtue of her Nordic beauty, is her racist father's favorite child, one of several allusions to an oedipal relationship existing between them. As in *El sol y los MacDonald*, the author uncovers the guilt in a past of racism, only now he inverts the Southerners' fear of foreigners to love of everything foreign to suit the Puerto Rican scene. His intent is no longer to explore social attitudes leading to personal aberrations (incest) but to find an explanation for Puerto Rico's cultural and political dilemma.

Both acts of *Los soles truncos* are structured around the highly symbolic rites of marriage and death. In act I, after a brief exposition of the sisters' present circumstance of extreme isolation and poverty, the main action is laid in the past, initiated by Emilia's conversation with an imaginary visitor. This transitional scene sets the unreal tone maintained throughout the play and leads effectively to the next two scenes showing Hortensia at earlier stages in life. She first appears as a nineteen-year-old making preparations for her wedding with the officer, and later she appears at the age of thirty mourning her mother's death, brought on, symbolically, by the War of Independence.

The unreal atmosphere created in act I by placing the action in the past and enhanced by special staging techniques is intensified in act II by the grotesque activities of the sisters preparing Hortensia's body for burial. The occasion has finally arrived for her to wear her unused bridal dress. A kind of climax of the grotesque is achieved as the limping Emilia descends the stairs to the melody of the wedding march, carrying before her the gown bought in Paris so many years ago. The music grows increasingly louder until it reaches deafening proportions.

Following this scene, the flashback to the father's death, when Hortensia was twenty-five, can almost be perceived as a return to a more "real" situation. This inversion in the perspective of the first act, making the activities of the present seem "unreal," is not only highly dramatic but also underscores the fundamental confrontation of inner and outer reality.

A state of unrelieved anguish, created by the passing of time, is the dominant mood of the play and is especially heightened in the final scene as the present threatens to break into the house in the form of the violent knocking at the door. The only way open for the sisters is self-destruction, which, according to Marqués, is a manifestation of the guilt complex inherent in a colonial nation.[15] The ending is intended to be cathartic. Unable to face present reality, the sisters set the house on fire and let the flames engulf them.

Some of the special staging devices used in this play have already been mentioned. Many more could be enumerated, among them the noises that mark the shifting from one temporal level to another, lighting, and the color symbolism of the glass panes in the three "truncated suns" of the doors. In the effective employment of these as well as all other staging techniques of this drama, Marqués continues to display a skill already fully developed in his earlier works. What is new in *Los soles truncos* and contributes to making it one of the highest expressions of his art is the author's approach to reduction and integration. This he achieves spectacularly, especially in the final act, when grotesque images are placed on a stage dimly lit by candles and oil lamps, a fitting prelude to the final holocaust.

Equally successful as a drama of inner movement is *Un niño azul para esa sombra*. This work has a child protagonist, Michelín, who is caught and ultimately destroyed in a family conflict, the result of Puerto Rico's sociopolitical circumstance. The child's father, a revolutionary idealist, participated in the Nationalist uprising of 1950, for which he was condemned to eight years of imprisonment. His mother, a banker's daughter spoiled by wealth, compromises herself during her husband's prolonged absence with the new social order of the protectorate. The falseness of her position is revealed by her love affair with a North American, who later abandons her to marry a girl from California. When the father finally comes home, he finds the political climate on the island unbearable and leaves the country.

Whereas Mercedes, Michelín's mother, represents a departure from the traditional matriarchal pattern to the type found in Anglo-Saxon societies, Cecilia, the boy's only companion and mother substitute, is a warmhearted Puerto Rican woman deeply rooted in the past of her country. Her traditional and motherly role is enhanced by her singing of folksongs, a child's funeral song (also serving as a foreshadowing device), and a lullaby. From her the extremely sensitive Michelín learns about the revolutionary idealism of his French great-grandfather and how it was passed on to the sons of the subsequent generations. The impressionable boy thus forms in his mind an image of an ideal father, who, however, is but a weak intellectual: "He is at best a weak, if not docile intellectual whom direct action leads to destruction."[16]

The child's retreat into a world of fantasy is beautifully presented in act I, which opens on his birthday, two years after his father's departure for New York. Instead of playing with Andrés, a boy his own age, Michelín prefers to engage Cecilia in a game designated by him as "playing the past." In a scene illuminated with a blue light and accompanied by music, they act out the poisoning of a large tree that formerly had shaded the patio. The mother pours poison on its roots in order to make room for more guests at her garden parties. Her action is symbolic of the destruction of traditional values, but in the child's mind it represents his father's fate suffered at the hands of Mercedes. Michelín observes the murder of the tree as he hangs on a trellis in the garden. This image, suggesting a "crucified victim,"[17] is a brilliant foreshadowing device for the ending of the play.

Emotionally exhausted from the game, Michelín falls into a deep sleep. His father appears to him in a dream sequence as the idealist who, in a different country, continues to fight for a just cause. The dialogue between Michelín and his father is profoundly moving because it reveals the child's need for parental affection and guidance to cope with life's problems. The father's explanation of the demands of courageous living is basic to the meaning of the play and, at the same time, is a succinct statement defining Marqués's position on the national as well as the universal responsibilities of man: "Y es preciso vivir en el presente. Aunque el presente sea la más dolorosa realidad. No, no hay escape posible. Es horrible, lo sé. Pero la realidad, no importa cuán dolorosa, hay que encararla."[18]

Act II takes place two years earlier when the father is released from prison. It includes the exposition (the mother's infidelity, the father's homecoming and departure), two retrospective scenes (one produced offstage by auditory means evoking the sentencing of the father eight years earlier, one showing him in prison), and the development of the boy into a little patriot. Children's voices heard behind the scenes engage in a debate about the homeland, with Michelín emerging as its only defender. Later, prompted by his father's departure, he decides to "assassinate" the replica of the Statue of Liberty to be dedicated in San Juan. The ceremony and the resulting uproar over the desecration of the statue are conveyed through voices, music, and other sounds heard offstage.

The action in act III is a direct continuation of that in act I. Michelín is awakened from his dreams by his mother's voice. Mercedes, having just found out about the return to Puerto Rico of her former lover, now married, is living a moment of personal crisis and in desperate need of her son's affection. In an effort to draw him closer to her, she reveals to him that his father has died anonymously in New York. This destruction of his ideal world drives the child to a final, solitary reenactment of the killing of the tree—only, this time, he poisons himself and dies "colgado en el enrejado como un pequeño Cristo,"[19] as off-stage the children invited to his birthday party sing, in English, the birthday song.

The child's suffering is the unifying emotion of the play. In several scenes of act II, in which Michelín does not enter into the action, his personal involvement is kept concretely before the eyes of the audience. He comes running onto the stage after a ball that has rolled from the terrace into the living room. This outwardly inconsequential interruption of a childish game causes him to overhear his mother's secret telephone conversation concerning her former lover. The child's grief at this discovery is expressed by a slamming of doors (offstage) and Cecilia's running to his side. In another scene, part of his body is seen flattened against the wall trying to conceal himself from his parents' view as he listens in on their last confrontation with one another. His father's announcement that he intends to leave the country comes as a shock to the boy, who is caught helpless and is reduced to mute anguish in his position of clandestine listener. This mental torment is concentrated in the image of the crucified child in acts I and III, which, from a temporal perspective, continue the action of act II.

Un niño azul, while treating a theme similar to the one Marqués dramatized in *La muerte no entrará en palacio*, achieves greater poignancy through its dreamlike texture as the child protagonist moves in a twilight zone of fantasy, suffused by his personal anguish. In this emphasis on mood and inner movement rather than ideological rhetoric lies the true value of the play.

Although the next group of Marqués's dramas, *La casa sin reloj* (1960, "The house without a clock"), *Carnaval afuera, carnaval adentro* (1960, "Carnival outside, carnival inside") and *El apartamiento* (1963, "The apartment"), offer certain features and techniques that a first, superficial reading might lead one to interpret as "absurd" in the sense now current in contemporary theater, we must be careful in drawing such conclusions from works that, on closer inspection, are parables of present-day Puerto Rican or Latin American reality. It seems that the designation by the author of *La casa sin reloj* (the first of this group of plays to appear in print) as an "antipoetic comedy in two absurd acts and a reasonable ending"[20] has also contributed to the application by critics of this ready-made label to the three plays. In an attempt to clarify his position vis-à-vis the theater of the absurd, the author is adamant that his philosophical position hardly coincides with that of the absurdists:

. . . because the absurd in the life of contemporary man need not be dramatized—of no importance is what those say who pretend to be snobs through such unnatural and dehumanized symbols as chairs, trash cans, and rhinoceros. As if the absurd were something outside the very human everyday reality of man. No! The most absurd thing in contemporary life is that man lives the absurd simply and routinely, in common and repeated circumstances, without even being aware of it. In other words, in life as it is now, the absurd slips into our daily routine without improbable monstrosities, nor distortions of apparent reality, nor situations of unusual spectacularity. It is not apparent but existential reality that man nowadays has distorted to the point of the absurd.[21]

Marqués seems to imply in this statement that the more absurd the events on stage, the more natural distorted reality will appear, thus making it easy for us not to worry about the pressing problems of life.

La casa sin reloj dramatizes absurd or unauthentic living in the character of Micaela, the thirty-seven–year–old mistress of the house that has no clock. The denial of the reality of measured time, however, is presented not only as an individual loss of consciousness but also applies to Puerto Rico as a whole. Through two telephone conversations, one at the very beginning of the play and one in act II, we find out that the clocks elsewhere on the island are not functioning properly.

Reality enters the house through the back door in the person of José, a Nationalist fleeing from the police. His presence in act I serves to reveal the ambiguity of Micaela's character. Behind a mask of a simple housewife who performs her duties routinely is hidden an unfeeling, monstrous personality. She stands as a warning against acceptance of the commonplace and conformity.

Act II presents the "taming of the monster," as José (in the meantime identified as her husband's brother) confronts Micaela with the total meaninglessness of her life. He succeeds in awakening in her a desire to know love and suffering and, through a kind of self-hypnosis that culminates in a swoon, she is enabled to experience these basic human emotions. Significantly, her incipient feeling of love for José coincides with her hearing the chiming of a clock.

The rest of the drama is devoted to destroying what is left of the absurd in Micaela's life. While José remains unafraid and confident of his love, Micaela fears that, if he is taken away by the police, her tender emotion will also disappear. Her lack of faith prompts her to shoot José, a desperate attempt on her part to perpetuate love through guilt. In choosing to kill her lover, Micaela falls back on the words José had spoken earlier, explaining to her the relationship between love, guilt, time, and redemption: "¿Cómo puede redimirse el hombre si no hay en él conciencia de culpa? ¿Y qué es la redención si no una lucha a muerte contra el tiempo? Amor es la clave."[22] José is a Christ figure, killed by the person he came to redeem.

La casa sin reloj, in contrast to Marqués's previous works, has a minimum of special staging effects. They consist primarily of sounds produced by knocking at the door, radio, telephone, car horn, and the firing of a pistol. The play adheres strictly to the traditional unities. There is no time lapse between the two acts; the place is the drab interior of the house, reflecting the mediocrity of the lives of its inhabitants; the sparse action is subordinated to dialogue and revolves entirely around Micaela's unmasking and conversion. *La casa* is the author's first attempt to write comedy. Hilarity alternates with sinister humor. As the play progresses, it takes on an increasingly serious tone. It ends earnestly and rationally when the protagonist, confronted by the emptiness of her existence, decides to act. This ending dispels the feeling that life is absurd and futile.

Like *Un niño azul para esa sombra*, Marqués's *Carnaval afuera, carnaval adentro* deals with the theme of innocence sacrificed on the cross of two cultures. This new drama, however, is a farce, "a carnivalesque play in three steps and several beats of the drum,"[23] and as such exposes the absurdity of Puerto Rican sociopolitical reality. The author avails himself of all the expressive means of the theater (special lighting, music, noises, dance, pantomime, acrobatics, masks, disguises, rhythmic, onomatopoeic, and expressionistic speeches, allegorical figures, and double roles) to exorcise the evil spirits from the island.

The drama opens with an auditory scene suggesting the carnival celebrations in the streets of San Juan. This setting allows Marqués to use masks and disguises and also supplies him with a literary framework for his play. All the characters are allegorical. Mack (who does not appear on stage) is the United States affiliated establishment. A cannibal, he requires human flesh for his sustenance. Rosita is his victim. The daughter of *nouveaux riches*, María and Guillermito (alias Mary and Willy), Rosita is still innocent and in love with Angel, an artist symbolizing a guardian angel of national ideals. In act I Rosita's father closes a deal, in which he is double-crossed, with Mack's attorney selling his daughter to be devoured by the monster. In the next act, a group of visitors arrive to celebrate the transaction. All are capitalists or accomplices of the system: la Condesa, a Cuban millionairess and her entourage consisting of a North American friend George, her nephew Rasputo, and a Latin American diplomat, Pito Jilguera. Their conversation centers around the profitable idea of selling the island. The "good guys" are, besides Angel and Rosita, Tía Matilde, who is a symbol for life, and doña Rosita, the grandmother, a kindly and idealized representation of traditional Puerto Rican womanhood. These two appear briefly when the curtain first rises to announce the beginning of the play. Befitting her symbolic role, Tía Matilde brandishes a whip, the kind used by a lion tamer in a circus. She is the person in charge while the other characters merely do her bidding. Tía Matilde leaves for the mountains (representing the stronghold of tradition) and returns only at the end of act II to direct the farce to be acted out "para bien nuestro."[24]

During a mock inquisition presided over by Willy, the docile Puerto Rican, and la Condesa, Angel is condemned to torture and death. The jury is made up of la Condesa's followers, whose roles have been somewhat modified. George is now a Puritan pilgrim, Rasputo a bishop, and Pito Jilguera the president of a Latin American republic. The scene is a mordant satire on an immoral judicial system disguised as democratic process of law. Angel, however, is saved by Tía Matilde, who has him replaced on the rack by Rosita. When he realizes that his love has been put to death, he wants to die with her. Tía Matilde reprimands Angel for acting like a stupid Romeo and reminds him of his duty: "Hay una isla que defender, hay un mundo que salvar, el tuyo."[25]

The allegory, as well as the message of the play, are intentionally transparent. By the time Marqués wrote *Carnaval*, he knew his former plays, although applauded by large crowds, had not produced a change in the attitude of his Puerto Rican public. He appraises the effect on the people of Puerto Rican literature dealing with the national problem: ". . . paradoxically, an aggressive, ethically oriented literature, conceived to combat passivity and conformity, is absorbed by the social body into its peculiar colonial psychology and not only makes it perfectly innocuous but also converts it into one more instrument of the psychological mechanism of docility."[26]

Justifiably disappointed, the author now poses the Puerto Rican question in a straightforward manner. Additionally, he avails himself of Brechtian distancing techniques to inform his audience that the purpose of the play is dead serious. At the end, Angel steps out of his role in the farce to let the spectators know that he is aware of their insincerity and their demand for cheap entertainment: "¡La farsa ha terminado! Para ustedes, ahí afuera, sigue el carnaval. ¡Siempre el carnaval de afuera!"[27] Tía Matilde then incites the actors to take part in the carnival, like the audience, as "farsantes e hipócritas."[28] The play ends with a grotesque dance. Taking off their masks, the actors salute the public with their faces distorted by silent laughter. Theater and life join hands as the spectators walk out to participate in the "carnival outside." The feeling of absurdity gives way to a feeling of necessity, a militant need to change the existing order.

With *El apartamiento*, called a "confinement in two acts,"[29] Marqués shows that although he has fully assimilated the techniques of the theater of the absurd, he rejects its claim that man is condemned to an existence of futility and purposelessness. Elpidio and Carola, with their faces and hands painted a deathly white, are reduced to total isolation in their apartment and are reminiscent of Beckettian clowns playing their "last game" in a claustrophobic interior. In a sparsely furnished room without windows and doors to the outside, the old couple is engaged in activities designed to suggest the problem of modern man's aspirations to a meaningful life in a world dominated by science and technology and their corollaries of efficiency and specialization. Elpidio is unsuccessfully trying to fit together the pieces of a puzzle that represents, significantly, a human figure. Carola is measuring, in decreasing numbers, a ribbon that has the symbolic blue color of idealism. The reason for the diminishing return of their work is a television program, the only one they can receive, intended to instruct them in their respective skills.

The dramatic tension in act I of the play depends on the atmosphere of suspense and expectancy produced by the ringing of the doorbell, by the subsequent discovery of several packages deposited at their door, and by the appearance of two visitors, Lucío and Terra, youthful versions of Elpidio and Carola. However, they represent not only the past but also art (music and poetry), as well as the spirit of enlightenment and the genius of the land, which are also suggested by their respective names. These are the values that can save the old couple from a gray existence, with the fountain of inspiration gone dry, but throughout the first act they remain aloof and afraid of their visitors.

A sense of anguish and uncertainty combined with expectancy also pervades act II, as additional characters appear and threaten or astonish the couple with their presence. Cuprila and Landrila are the inspectors of the system. Upon discovering Lucío and Terra, they kill them. They are not, however, prepared to deal with Tlo, the Ibero-American Indian who erupts onstage with a blood-curdling war cry. They merely tie his hands, giving Elpidio his obsidian knife. But the old man does not kill him. Instead, Carola cuts his fetters, and Tlo disappears from the stage. The Indian representing the primitive man of Ibero-America with his original creative powers intact is the symbol of the continent's ultimate possibility of liberation.

The play ends as it began, with the ringing of the doorbell and a reiteration of the initial sense of expectancy as the couple decides to open the door, not knowing whether it is death or liberation waiting for them on the other side. Clearly, what matters here is that the characters are on the threshold of a new awareness, ready to break out of the *apartamiento*.[30] If man will listen to his inner voice, he can reach the painful but fruitful awareness of the full reality of being.

In *El apartamiento*, Marqués uses symmetrical movements and groups his characters (except for the Indian) in symmetrical pairs in the manner of the convention of the theater of the absurd. He achieves, like Beckett in *Endgame*, a kind of monodrama in which everything takes place on the inside of man. We have the inseparable couple in an enclosed space: the visitors represent their suppressed creative urge, the inspectors their complacency toward conformity, and, finally, the Indian is the manifestation of their consciousness. Although the play conveys an almost overwhelming sense of anguish through isolation, its overall mood is not one of negation and futility. By suggesting a way out, Marqués has once again written an antiabsurd drama.

In 1868, during the reign of Isabella II of Spain, the first Puerto Rican rebellion against the mother country took place in Lares, hence the designation of this important historic moment as "El grito de Lares." Following the liberation ideals of the Puerto Rican patriot, Ramón Emeterio Betances, Manuel Rojas, a landowner of Venezuelan origin, led about four hundred men—landowners and slaves—on the night of September 23 in an uprising against the Spanish authorities. They triumphed at Lares, proclaiming the emancipation of slaves and declaring Puerto Rico a republic. However, the next morning the rebellious forces were defeated at San Sebastián del Pepino, where the Spaniards, tipped off by a spy, took them by surprise. Reprisals against all those associated with the revolutionary movement followed. Its leader, Manuel Rojas, was exiled to Venezuela. His sister-in-law, Mariana Bracetti de Rojas, who embroidered the rebel flag, was put in jail.

The circumstances surrounding this historic episode are the subject of *Mariana o el alba* (1965, "Mariana or the dawn"), written in anticipation of its hundredth anniversary. The drama is a realistic presentation of the preparations on the eve of the uprising, the victory at Lares, and the aftermath. Its heroine is the matron who embroidered the flag. Except for the short final act, which is set in the prison where Mariana's child is stillborn on the eve of her release, all the action transpires in the living room of Mariana's solidly elegant estate.

The action revolves around the heroine. In act I, we see her first in her role as wife and mistress of the household, and later we observe her as the hostess entertaining friends and Spanish foes. She emerges as an idealized personality, one who is delicately feminine and motherly, yet one who is determined, if necessary, to sacrifice herself and her loved ones for liberty and justice.

In act II, Mariana receives the news of the victory and the defeat through messengers. She rejoices at the triumph and remains calm and courageous during the critical moments. Even when she is taken prisoner, her attitude is dignified and serene. She is conscious of having fulfilled her duty: "He cumplido con Dios y con la Patria."[31] Her child, who represents the hope of the future, is born dead in the final act. Although Mariana's faith is not broken by this personal tragedy, the stillborn baby serves as an ill omen, foretelling Puerto Rico's colonial status. The new dawn of Puerto Rican national independence was never given a chance.

Elaborate staging instructions describing the architecture, furnishings, costumes, regional customs, and speech habits precede each act of the play. The author's endeavor to recreate the flavor of a bygone era is evident on every page. His effort to commemorate the past as well as to inspire present-day Puerto Ricans with a patriotic message is eminently successful.

René Marqués owes his inspiration for his most recent plays, *Sacrificio en el Monte Moriah* (1968, "Sacrifice on Mount Moriah") and *David y Jonatán* and *Tito y Berenice* (1969), to a casual comment by his oldest son concerning Kierkegaard's use of the biblical story of the sacrifice of Isaac to present his concept of dread. As the preliminary note to *Sacrificio* suggests, the author researched the topic extensively, consulting the original account in the Bible, secondary sources, and books on ancient history. In the process he obtained not only the information pertinent to his dramatization of the Isaac and Abraham story but also the material for *David y Jonatán* and *Tito y Berenice*. The author presents the latter as twin dramas, that is, as individual plays that should be staged together. In the published version, they share the subtitle and the epigraph from Ecclesiastes that "there is nothing new under the sun." This motto would be equally appropriate for *Sacrificio*, for Marqués projects in all three plays the human as well as the cultural and sociopolitical conflicts of the ancient world on the present.

Sacrificio deviates significantly from the biblical story of Abraham as a man of faith. Marqués undoubtedly follows one of Kierkegaard's speculations that the patriarch's "life was not blameless."[32] In fact, the Abrahán of the play is an idolater who, in the name of Jehovah, enslaves the people of Canaan to Egypt, prostitutes his wife for favors from neighboring princes, and is prepared to sacrifice his only son. In the sacrificial scene he becomes transformed into a beast, reminiscent again of an Abraham envisioned by the Danish philosopher: "He was unrecognizable to Isaac, his eyes were wild, his venerable locks had risen like the locks of furies over his head. He seized Isaac by the throat, he drew his knife, he said: 'Thou didst believe it was for God's sake I would do this, thou art mistaken, I am an idolater, this desire has again awakened in my soul, I want to murder thee.'"[33] In the play Abrahán is not Isaac's carnal father. Since he was impotent, Sara arranged a pregnancy in order to fulfill Jehovah's promise to her husband.

Sara, presented as a strong-willed and motherly woman, is capable of counteracting Abrahán's wrongs. She prevents him from sacrificing her son by disguising herself as an angel. Outwardly, however, she obeys him and even acts unjustly toward Agar and Ismael in order to keep up appearances. It is only after Isaac leaves home that she acts in accordance with her feelings and kills Abrahán.

The trauma experienced on Mount Moriah has made Isaac sensitive to what is right and wrong. Aware of his parents' false values, he leaves them as soon as he comes of age. This generational conflict reflects on the recent problems associated with the contemporary youth rebellion. Marqués's parable castigates specifically those Puerto Ricans who, practicing the idolatry of the United States, are disposed to sacrifice their sons to the Vietnam War.

From a technical standpoint, *Sacrificio* is an attempt to adapt certain techniques of the cinema to the stage. At the opening of the play, a momentary plastic effect is created by a kind of ballet of knives and daggers, without human hands being visible, evoking the decorative imagery that accompanies the credits at the beginning of a film. The author, who imagined himself directing the play as he wrote it, envisions an essentially bare stage for the fourteen scenes (designated as "cinematographic"), which will flow without interruption. The duration of the play should equal that of an average-length film. Time and place move easily forward and backward, distant and near. Lighting is of special importance in the staging of this drama, since it serves, in addition to regular use, as a camera to produce close-ups of faces and of the sacrificial knife.

Other technical elements include the focusing of a red spotlight on the audience as a distancing device, the sound of thunder, and offstage voices of a prophet, a chorus, and other individuals. The amplified voices of Hombre I and Hombre II provide the framework for the play and function as a device to project the action of the past on the present moment. In reply to the first man's question of what he has seen in the night, the sentry answers at the beginning of the play: "He visto venir, esperanzado..., la mañana" (p. 57). However, at the end his message is one of dread: "He visto venir con horror..., *el mañana*" (p. 141).[34]

David y Jonatán and *Tito y Berenice*, relatively short pieces of ten scenes each, share the common theme alluded to in the subtitle "Two dramas of love, power, and indifference."[35] The subject and the time are different in each play. The author demands, however, that they be staged (and published) together in order to fulfill the requisite stated in the motto. The temptation of power has and always will turn love into hate or indifference.

David y Jonatán, based on the bibliohistorical account of the first kings of Israel, focuses on the love (incestual, homosexual, and heterosexual) of David and Saúl's children, Jonatán and Mikol. Through the priest Samuel, who is presented as a self-appointed spokesman of God, David is forced into a struggle for power and, in the end, betrays his friendship, causing Saúl's and Jonatán's deaths.

Tito y Berenice takes place at the beginning of the Christian era and deals with the love affair between the Roman general, later emperor, Titus Flavius Vespasianus and the daughter of Herodus Agrippa, king of Judea. Tito comes to Jerusalem as a conqueror. He falls in love with Berenice and marries her. But although he loves her deeply, he obeys the call of Rome, repudiating his marriage to become emperor. After many years of separation, Tito decides to make good his promise to return to the Judean princess. He obtains permission from the Roman Senate to bring her back as his wife, but it is too late because Berenice has grown old. Tito learns the bitter lesson that time does not wait.

For his twin dramas, Marqués retains the cinematographic technique used in *Sacrificio* to produce fluid movement with only the briefest blackouts between scenes. He discards the chorus and offstage voices but keeps and adds other staging devices to suit his purpose: music, dance, a movable throne for Saúl, visual and auditory effects for the destruction of Pompeii, a divided stage for simultaneous scenes in Judea and Rome, and the distancing technique of Tito's address to the Roman Senate directed to the audience. As in *Sacrificio*, time and place change from scene to scene, completely subordinated to the action of the play.

Marqués's latest group of plays confirms once again our claim that the author is an untiring and successful experimenter with dramatic form. The subject matter, although borrowed from bibliohistorical sources, is treated freely and imaginatively in all three plays and reveals his preference for topics he explored in his previous works: the question of human dignity and integrity in a colonial nation; the existential position that man must face his own situation without counting on help from God or other men; and, finally, the problem of time. Since man lives in the present, it is imperative that he act now; postponement can only mean discouragement and defeat. The presence of these themes in Marqués's most recent dramas shows conclusively the existence of an organic and progressive unity of thought in his dramatic production.

NOTES

1. Up-to-date information on the staging and publication history of Marqués's plays is given in the introduction to his play *Sacrificio en el Monte Moriah* (Río Piedras, P.R.: Editorial Antillana, 1969), pp. 12–18.

2. *Ensayos: 1953–1966* (Río Piedras, P.R.: Editorial Antillana, 1966), p. 76.

3. The plays will be discussed in chronological order; the dates correspond to the time of the writing, not the publication of the work.

4. This and all subsequent translations in the text and in the notes are mine.

5. The Son, the Wife, the Nurse, the Servant, and the Priest.

6. Arthur Miller, "The Family in Modern Drama," in *Modern Drama*, ed. Travis Bogard and William I. Oliver (New York: Oxford University Press, 1965), p. 122.

7. "The sun kills his father, who is night. . . . Then he marries his mother, dawn, and continues his fatal course inexorably until death" (*El sol y los MacDonald*, in *Asomante* 8, no. 1 [1957]: 75).

8. "Puerto Rico is the Catholic country with the highest incidence of suicide in the world. . . . Perhaps the psychological root is to be found in the intensification during the last ten years of the guilt complex inherent in a colonial people" (*Ensayos*, p. 91).

9. ". . . treasure hidden by Juan Bobo in the belly of the iron boiler" (*La carreta* [Río Piedras, P.R.: Editorial Cultural, 1963], p. 91).

10. *Juan Bobo y la Dama de Occidente* (Río Piedras, P.R.: Editorial Antillana, 1971), p. 9.

11. *Ensayos*, p. 39.

12. "Your world and mine can never be synchronized" (*La muerte no entrará en palacio*, in *El teatro hispanoamericano contemporáneo*, ed. Carlos Solórzano, 2 vols. [Mexico City: Fondo de Cultura Económica, 1964], I, 371).

13. "Love, love. Sorrow and suffering. Love!" (ibid., p. 417).

14. D. L. Shaw has written on the aspects of tragedy in "René Marqués' *La muerte no entrará en palacio*: An analysis," *Latin American Theatre Review* 2, no. 1 (Fall 1968): 31–38.

15. *Ensayos*, p. 91.

16. Ibid., p. 156.

17. *Un niño azul para esa sombra* (Río Piedras, P.R.: Editorial Cultural, 1970), p. 26.

18. "It is necessary to live in the present. Though the present may be the most painful reality. No, escape is not possible. It is terrible, I know. But reality, no matter how painful, must be faced" (ibid., p. 36).

19. ". . . hanging in the trellis like a little Christ" (ibid., p. 118).

20. *La casa sin reloj* (Jalapa, Mexico: Universidad Veracruzana, 1962).

21. Quoted by María Victoria Morales, "La actividad teatral en Puerto Rico," *Horizontes* 5, no. 10 (1962): 97.

22. "How can man redeem himself if he does not have a sense of guilt? What is redemption if not a fight unto the death against time? Love is the key" (*La casa sin reloj*, p. 106).

23. *Carnaval afuera, carnaval adentro* (Río Piedras, P.R.: Editorial Antillana, 1971).

24. "For our own good" (ibid., p. 79).

25. "An island must be defended, a world must be saved, your own world" (ibid., p. 126).

26. *Ensayos*, p. 194.

27. "The farce is over! For you out there the carnival goes on. Your same old carnival!" (*Carnaval afuera, carnaval adentro*, p. 128).

28. "Farce actors and hypocrites" (ibid., p. 130).

29. *El apartamiento* (Barcelona: Ediciones Rumbo, 1966).

30. The first meaning of *apartamiento* is "separation."

31. "I have fulfilled my duty to God and country" (*Mariana o el alba* [Río Piedras, P.R.: Editorial Antillana, 1968], p. 208).

32. Søren Kierkegaard, *Fear and Trembling* and *The Sickness Unto Death*, trans. Walter Lowrie (Garden City, N.Y.: Doubleday and Co., 1941), p. 11.

33. Ibid.

34. "I have seen the coming, with hope, of the morning"; "I have seen the coming, with horror, of the morrow" (*Sacrificio en el Monte Moriah* [Río Piedras, P.R.: Editorial Antillana, 1969]).

35. *David y Jonatán* and *Tito y Berenice* (Río Piedras, P.R.: Editorial Antillana, 1970).

11. The Game of Chance:

The Theater of José Triana

Frank N. Dauster

José Triana, born in 1932, is one of a brilliant group of young dramatists who made the Cuban theater of the 1960s one of the most vital in the Spanish-speaking world. He is preoccupied with the irrational and the incoherent in human behavior patterns and with the violence that he sees as a fundamental part of Cuban psychology; like most of his generation, he is absorbed in the need to ferret out the meaning of the realities underlying his society. He finds his characters in urban society and particularly in its substructures—the world of vagabonds, beggars, and political bosses.

Triana's attitude toward the theater has been made clear in a series of interviews.

> It is not my purpose to write political pamphlets but to look, to dig, to dig into ourselves, into our defects, the sense of evil, of cruelty. That decomposition which we lived and which made possible, opened a window, opened a door, opened a road for our own improvement.
>
> I am interested in digging into myself and everyone else, to give the measure of what we are.[1]
>
> . . . I am interested above all else in man, man as he shows himself, man as he is produced every day, always in search of living situations. I look at man in his critical attitudes, in a key position, in the moment of possible transformations or possible cataclysms.[2]

This may be interpreted as meaning that he regards his theater as essentially tragic, if tragedy is the presentation of a human being at a crucial moment of his existence, at the moment of critical choice. He is remote from conventional realism; Triana has called his own style "poetic realism": "I seek always a synthesis of reality, basing myself on the data of the imagination, of memory."[3] His purpose, he states, is the "intention to catch reality and raise it to a poetic level."[4]

Triana's works, nevertheless, are rooted in a critical sense of Cuban reality, and his characters represent sectors of that reality. He is preoccupied with the precariousness of man, especially Cuban man. His central theme has been seen as a universe whose social relationships "are controlled by a general law of lack of foresight and structural disorder, which only reflects openly a cosmos whose culmination is beyond the individual."[5] Triana's obsession with the irrational and the incoherent is related to the theater of the absurd, but has, as Julio Miranda points out, a different purpose: "The fact is that the absurd has not been utilized in Cuba as an instrument of metaphysical investigation, with reactionary results à la Ionesco and Beckett, in which the nothingness winds up filling the stage, with its oppressive negativity, but rather as an effort at a sociopolitical search for a judgement of an antihuman order of things, absurdly sanctioned by law and custom and penetrated, as such, absurdly, by the new theater."[6]

El mayor general hablará de teogonía ("The Major General will speak of theogony") and *El incidente cotidiano* ("The daily incident"), both in one act, were written in 1957 while Triana was living in Spain. *El incidente* has never been performed or published, and Triana dismisses it as a sort of minor amusement. In the same article, he says of *El mayor general* that it was written "remembering situations that I had lived, here, in my country, but full of a somewhat mocking intellectualism."[7] First performed in 1960, the play's action takes place in 1929, in an unspecified city. The characters are Petronila, her husband Higinio, and her sister Elisiria. Such names are not specifically Cuban and are more common in Latin American families of lower-class or rural background; they often indicate gullibility or naïve traditionalism.

As the play opens, Petronila and Elisiria renew an old argument about having taken refuge many years before in what appears to be a boardinghouse owned by the Major General, whom Petronila has now invited to a small party in honor of her twenty-seventh wedding anniversary. She defends the General against the attacks of Elisiria; his paternalism is contrasted with his ill temper, Petronila's gratitude with Elisiria's constant references to "that damned old man." Petronila speaks yearningly of her "daughter," still-born twenty-five years earlier because of a fall—the disaster that drove them to refuge in the General's house. Soon, Higinio returns from his office, and the three are united in a mutually painful entanglement of fear and guilt, each blaming himself for the accident. There are contradictions; Petronila blames herself, but both Elisiria and Higinio state flatly that they attempted to kill her.

This is a household, if it can be called such, obsessed by guilt. Elisiria chews eternally on her own entrails; she considers the family's stay in the General's house a punishment and longs for a vaguely Edenic time before they took up residence with the General. Petronila salves her conscience by keeping her daughter's "cuerpecito disecado" in an urn as a "reliquia de amor,"[8] and Higinio is harassed by guilt and frustration as he and Elisiria finally confess the love that provoked the ancient attempted murder. Although the Major General is absent except for an occasional burst of song and an ambiguous bellow that his guests are doomed, he entirely dominates the minds of the other characters. Two entirely different versions of him emerge: Elisiria creates an ill-tempered, tyrannical, and unstable judge who may go mad and kill them all, while Petronila portrays a benevolent old gentleman who delights in telling absurd tales.

Higinio sides with Elisiria, and they plot to kill the Major General, contemplating with delectation the choice between poison and an oversized knife. There are no plans beyond the murder itself, but Elisiria says, "Hay que empezar de nuevo sin él."[9] The hesitant invitation has become a revenge murder that will both wipe out the General, who is obscurely involved in their guilt, and wash the conspirators, who now include Petronila, of their sins.

But the plot dissolves when the Major General finally appears. He is benevolent and only mildly admonitory, although their pleas for his help produce a guffaw that swells unbearably. The conspirators stammer helplessly until the General suddenly hurls the urn to the floor. As the work ends, the promised discourse on theogony becomes the whining of a tired and disillusioned man: "¿Hablar? ¿Hablar, para qué? Ya no queda nada. Todos en el fondo se sentían satisfechos. (*Comienza a subir las escaleras*) ¿Hablar del origen, de los dioses? Como si uno fuera un payaso. ¿Hablar de conceptos? ¿Y de proyectos cósmicos? Que atrevimiento... Ofrezco mi hospitalidad y todavía se permiten... seguiré mi labor. ¿Qué hora es? ¿Las nueve? Tengo hambre. (*Mirando a los tres personajes*) Y vendrán otros y vendrán otros... (*Suspira*) Algún día."[10] The identity of the Major General is hardly a secret. The play is larded with religious allusions: everyone, including the General, refers to his sermonizing; the common knowledge of the family's shame is called by Petronila "the deluge"; she admits that in moments of connubial activity she calls Higinio "The Apostle." There is an ironic allusion to religious practices in the grisly reference to the urn as a "relic," and the Flood is clearly alluded to by Elisiria when she says, "Cualquier día se volverá loco y nos matará a todos... Como dicen que pasó hace ya bastante tiempo."[11] But the parallels run far deeper. Petronila's preparations for the party bear an obvious resemblance to the Mass; the wine, *bocaditos*, and *entremeses* are a parody of the Communion. The distant bell, followed by Petronila's noisy, squalling parody of the communicants' joy at the Epiphany and Elisiria's savage delight at the prospect of the murder ("Su sangre nos servirá de alimento. Seremos santificados después."[12]), bitterly mocks the whole notion of Christ's sacrifice.

The play is, in one dimension, a parody of the Mass, and Petronila fulfills a loose function as reluctant priestess, aided by her two murderous acolytes. It is, of course, a Black Mass in that its purpose is the death of the god rather than the celebration of his mystery. But theirs is a useless rebellion, for at the final showing of the god, when the Major General grumblingly enunciates his platitudes, all three collapse to their knees. It is not enough, however, to see the play as an ingenious if overdone parody of the Christian myth. There is a curious reversal between Christ-General and Judas-Higinio; the former has betrayed his apostle—recall the words of Petronila—to the multitude, and the betrayal, the telling of the guilty secret to Higinio's coworkers, took place "en la bodega de los Olivos."[13] But this General is neither vicious nor evil; he desires no one's death. He is merely tired, bored and a bit supercilious. Human existence depends on his hospitality, and he would prefer not to bother.

Triana's attack is directed not at God but at his worshippers, who are stupid, weak, and vacillating. Their imprisonment is entirely imaginary. They have but to exercise their will and they are free. But these supine worshippers would be helpless within freedom; if, by some extraordinary accident, they were to destroy the Major General, they would inevitably find or fabricate another.[14] It matters not at all that he never speaks of theogony, that the revelation of the meaning of God never takes place. Life without the General's house in which to dwell, without his boots to clean, would be intolerable for them. Obviously, the play has been influenced by the absurd. The banal conversation is a legacy of Ionesco and Beckett; this General is a Godot who has finally appeared with nothing whatsoever to say, while his audience is too unintelligent to perceive his nullity.

El mayor general was not well received by Cuban critics, although none of them appeared to note the elaborate sacramental overtones. Virgilio Piñera dismissed it in cavalier fashion as unimportant,[15] and Natividad González Freire objected to the monotonous repetition of situation.[16] There is certainly too much inconsequential repetition and lengthy discourse; occasional side comments, as though to the audience, add nothing, and the use of dance in Higinio's and Elisiria's confession scene is an inexperienced effort at theatricality. Curiously, González Freire liked the development of character, which is almost nonexistent. *El mayor general* suffers from serious weaknesses, but they are the weaknesses of youth. There are also strengths: the ironic conception of a divine genealogy owing exclusively to man's unwillingness to go it alone is an exercise in mythmaking that leads directly to the later plays.

Medea en el espejo ("Medea in the mirror") was written in 1959 and premiered in 1960. The Medea theme is set in an urban tenement; Triana follows Euripides closely, the chief difference being that he discloses Julián's treachery gradually, while in Euripides it is established at the beginning. Medea becomes María, Jason is Julián, and the children's attendant becomes la señorita Amparo. Medea's nurse becomes Erundina, who has a much-expanded role, and Creon is metamorphosed into Perico Piedra Fina. María is a mulatto; Julián, her blond, white-skinned lover, is an unsavory individual who plans to marry the daughter of the local political boss for his own advantage. Like Jason, he is willing to shift the blame for María's unhappiness to her. Although less important dramatically than Jason, he is equally self-serving. His profession is unclear, but he is certainly of the underworld; morally, he is of the same stuff as Jason, of whom H. D. F. Kitto has said, "In him it is impossible to find anything that is not mean."[17]

The inspiration for *Medea en el espejo* was probably Virgilio Piñera's *Electra Garrigó*, written in 1941 and staged in 1948, 1958, 1960, and 1961.[18] Piñera transports a classical theme to modern Cuba, and although he is more overtly social than Triana, his approach is quite similar. In both cases the play barely skirts the picturesque. Erundina is straight from Cuban folklore; she is the old Negress, part servant, part family, speaking a catalogue of proverbs spiced with reminiscences of African cults. Perico Piedra Fina, Triana's Creon, is sheer parody, and the minor characters become a gallery of urban motley.

This effort to find some meaning in social substructures fascinates Cuban dramatists; Carlos Felipe and José Brene have dealt extensively with it, even to writing works based on Alejandro Yarini, a notorious pimp of the early twentieth century. Both have tried to confer upon him mythic stature. Obviously, all three dramatists are attempting to discover something of lasting meaning underlying a sordid and insignificant social reality. Rine Leal has said that *Medea en el espejo* "showed its author lowering the dignity of the buskin to the humbleness of the slipper, transforming the Hellenic myth into tenement gossip, discovering in our folk characters the existence of a different and unexpected reality."[19]

Curiously, it is in María that Triana has remained closest to Euripides. She is a woman all fire, unthinking and uncontrolled; only her love for Julián matters. Her murder of Perico and his daughter, her butchery of her children, are of no import to her. Like Medea, she is uncontrolled and totally destructive in her passion. However, she has two highly individual characteristics: her idiosyncratic use of language, and her obsession with mirrors. During much of the play, her actions oscillate between calculation and uncontrolled anger; in the last scene of act I she appears to be hallucinating, and by scene 3 of act III she has lost control entirely. She unsuccessfully struggles against her own humiliation and defeat in a lengthy soliloquy, hears mysterious voices, and is finally led to her bloody decision by a vision.

It is clear that at this point María is sunk in madness, but her earlier passionate behavior is less clear. As the curtain rises on the play, María muses on the rumor that the absent Julián plans to abandon her. She comments to herself, "Julián, Julián, Julián. Mi destino eres tú... Representaré. Me pondré a la altura de las circunstancias."[20] Her later actions may mean that she does indeed put on a performance, feigning, like Hamlet, as part of a plan for revenge. This erratic behavior is reflected in her language, which swings violently from rhetorical grandiloquence to common speech, a technique almost certainly inspired by *Electra Garrigó*. These contrasting modes of language may be intended to underline María's tragic potential by demonstrating that her passions and motivations are on the level of Medea, although her normal functioning is not.[21] Calvert Casey has pointed out the value of popular speech in this context: "Against the falsely cultured dialogue with which Medea and Erundina open the first act, suddenly he counterposes the uncontrolled and frank manner of speaking which characterizes us. By this contrast, the author reveals the dramatic value of popular speech, when he makes the actors pass from an uncomfortable attitude to supreme comfort."[22] However, this soon becomes exaggerated and the dramatic effect attenuated.

María herself comments ironically on her own speech while speaking with Erundina, who expresses herself in a street idiom contrasting sharply with María's grandiloquence. She says, "Hablamos idiomas distintos."[23] Almost literally true, it has another line of significance. Erundina is incapable of comprehending the depth of María's passion; they function vitally on different levels. María is no Medea, and Medea en el espejo is a highly uneven play, but María fits the configuration of the tragic rhythm to a nearly schematic extent.[24] Her purpose, clearly enough, is the recapture of Julián, and her passion, the terrible moment when all rational control is lost and she resolves to murder her children as she has murdered Perico and his daughter. She is an uneven, erratic, and, ultimately, truncated function of the tragic rhythm in that there is no perception, no final revelation of the significance of her actions. Her final scream that she is God may be her descent into madness or Triana's declaration of her total individuality, but, in either case, it is hardly a perception of any cosmic meaning. Whatever María may be, she is not the complete tragic figure who perceives through her suffering the significance of her existence.

María's obsession with mirrors is also a constant; in moments of emotional stress she peers into them, hoping to find her true face, her real meaning. But the mirror is an analogue of her being, all surface with no depth, and she must go ever further, until she finds her true mirror, her final affirmation, in the knife. But all this is only partially successful; the ironic contrast between commotion and pomposity led Triana to create whole sections that are too close to the Greek, followed by others lacking in dramatic interest. The parody is sometimes self-defeating, a parody of itself. This exaggeration is especially obvious in the final scenes. María's climactic struggle is weakened by the apparatus of delirium and drums. Triana was trapped into attempting to recreate Medea's great scene of moral suffering, and the result is simply overdone. The same is true of the chorus; their repetitive chanting appears to be an effort at the effect of strophe and antistrophe. Although these obsessive responses sometimes help create a climate of unyielding tension, more often they are reduced to hollow rote, as though Triana had not thought out their role carefully.

In Medea en el espejo, José Triana attempted to subvert the established order of crassness, mediocrity, and vulgarity; he tried to invest the ordinary with extraordinary meaning. It would be exceedingly simplistic to say that he has in fact attempted to create a Cuban Medea, but he has certainly tried to show that Medea was a being of flesh and blood and that twentieth century beings of flesh and blood are capable of tragic passion. His creatures are Cuban in their speech, in their social setting, and in the violent burlesque of their reactions. He has sometimes faltered, but at the core of Medea en el espejo we find the same concerns that would be startlingly formulated in *La muerte del Ñeque* ("The death of the Ñeque") and *La noche de los asesinos (The Criminals)*.

In 1962 *La casa ardiendo* ("The burning house") and *El Parque de la Fraternidad* ("Brotherhood Park") were staged to a generally negative critical reaction. The former is a monodrama of a prostitute's dreams and frustrations. It, like *El incidente cotidiano* and *La visita del Angel* ("The angel's visit") in 1963, has never been published and is totally unavailable. Triana has the—for him—happy faculty of causing unsuccessful plays to vanish entirely. *El Parque de la Fraternidad* takes place in the plaza of that name; the characters are la Negra, el Viejo, and el Muchacho. La Negra is seemingly based on a well-known character; she wears a ludicrous outfit and mumbles in Lucumí, the language of the Yoruba. El Viejo also recalls a popular character, mixing gentleman with vagabond. The action of this one-act work is almost negligible; the characters alternately insult and ignore each other. The whole burden of the play appears to be their mutual lack of communication. Whether it is entirely legitimate to regard la Negra as representative of the oppressed Negro, el Viejo as a sample of a rundown and no longer functioning bourgeois intelligentsia, and el Muchacho as representative of the undisciplined and hopeless youth of pre-Revolutionary days, is questionable. There are indications, including the ironic location of the action, that such is the purpose. Another obvious symbolic level exists, so obvious as to be almost destructive of its purpose. La Negra mumbles "Santísima" interspersed with Lucumí; el Viejo is immersed in a volume in which he professes to find the truth. They both babble incoherently; he makes strange gestures vaguely reminiscent of a blessing, while she quite specifically crosses herself. El Viejo babbles of "the beginning" and "the seventh day"; as the play ends, he becomes increasingly incoherent, and as he prepares to sleep, he echoes the words of Christ: "Mamá, papá, ¿por qué me han abandonado?"[25]

Whatever Triana may have had in mind in terms of social awareness and class interaction, he was also overtly attacking the Christian myth. Not only does he criticize the bankruptcy of impractical and ineffective religious ideas, but also he directly parodies the Trinity. The play rejects the incoherence of modern social structures while simultaneously rejecting the incoherence of a religious structure that neither addresses itself to social ills nor cares to do so. Facing the alternative of nihilism, Triana finds affirmation in la Negra's last speech, which is a statement of a dogged but foggy belief in life. Further, the author is too intrusive for the play to be successful; the strings are too visible, the religious symbolism and Beckettian negation too loaded.

Triana took the first real step since *Medea en el espejo* with *La muerte del Ñeque*, first performed in 1963. It takes place in the same murky world of violence and crime, but here they are more clearly defined. Hilario García is a forty-five–year–old mulatto who has achieved, through chicanery and violence, a position of power in the corrupt police administration. His mistress is Blanca Estela, white, and a former prostitute, whom he won at gambling. The triangle is completed by Juvencio, a young white man and son of a victim of Hilario; Juvencio plots both the seduction of Blanca Estela and Hilario's murder. Pablo, Hilario's son by his dead wife, is white; he has an ambiguous attitude toward both Blanca Estela and the mulatto Berta, a childhood friend who loves him. The cast is completed by Cachita, the old black servant, and three ruffians, Pepe, Juan el Cojo, and Nico, who both comment on the action in the fashion of a chorus and take an integral part in some developments.

The action is relatively simple. In act I we are given the antecedents: Pablo's rejection, as yet unmotivated, of Berta; Juvencio's plot and, as the act ends, his seduction of Blanca Estela. Act II presents the downfall of Hilario, *el Ñeque*; the expected promotion, which will mean greater wealth and power, has not come. Instead, he is in virtual disgrace. His enemies prepare their plot, and Blanca Estela taunts Pablo, accusing him of being sexually jealous of his father. Hilario finally appears personally in act III. He is brutal, almost animal in his behavior. He breaks with Blanca Estela and with Pablo; finally, alone, he is surrounded and killed by the three conspirators.

Although the anecdote is simple, Triana creates tension by revealing a bit at a time. In any case, he is concerned with matters other than the simple story. He has made use of ritual forms to raise to another level this tale of the downfall of a doomed house. Hilario is as bluff and uncomprehending, as fated to violent death, as any Mycenean chieftain. His *hubris* is his total faith in his own strength and in the fortune that has favored him. There is even a *peripeteia* as the expected rise to greater power is suddenly and inexplicably thwarted. The dance of the three murderers about their victim is the *sparagmos*, the ritual tearing-apart of the divine king. But there is no *anagnorisis*, no perception in this truncated tragic movement. Hilario dies as uncomprehending as he lived. The closest he manages is this maimed vision: "Mierda. Hoy me he dado cuenta, he visto claro... Todo es mentira. Algo que se nos va entre los dedos."[26] There is no true tragic vision because there is no tragic meaning. Richard Sewall has said, "The modern tragic problem is not what values or loyalties to choose, but the bankruptcy of all values and loyalties."[27] This is precisely the situation at the climax of *La muerte del Ñeque*; for whatever reasons, all values have been subverted and the loyalty of Blanca and Pablo thwarted. Hilario falls, abandoned by fate as blindly and inexplicably as he had been favored, and the violence of his life takes its toll. This is not the tragedy of a man upon whom the gods exact revenge but the tragedy of a man who falls because it chances to be so, because of what Kitto calls "one of the most purely tragic situations: the Flaw in the Universe."[28] Hilario is a flawed being, but his flaws have no relationship to his rise or his fall. Pure chance rules; it has given him wealth, power, and women, and now it will abandon him.

Nor is Hilario in any sense a truly tragic figure within the play. He appears only toward the end, and this shift from the external figures to the focus of the work weakens both the figure of Hilario and the play as a whole. Nor is there any true *agon* between Hilario and Juvencio; the confrontation is with his son Pablo, for Juvencio is not the real cause of Hilario's downfall. He, too, is a toy of chance.

The air of evil about this doomed family infects them all, even to Pablo and Cachita, who are hardly villainous. Pablo rejects Berta because he is totally focused on aiding his father, but he is needlessly cruel to her. In act II another reason begins to emerge, as Blanca Estela deliberately provokes him with caresses and references to his father's sexual prowess. But Pablo's hesitant overture is rejected with laughter. Pablo is horrified, but he has obviously been sexually stimulated by her. This incident both clarifies his attitude toward Berta and prepares his abandonment of Hilario. Blanca is pure sensuality, attracted to Hilario and now to Juvencio by their sheer maleness. Juvencio, in turn, uses her both sexually and as an instrument of revenge.

This complex fabric of hate, lust, revenge, and pride is held together by the three murderers, Nico, Juan el Cojo, and Pepe. In addition to their active intervention as characters, they are the Fates, forever in the background awaiting the moment of death. Simultaneously, they are the chorus, commenting on activities onstage and off. Not coincidentally, Juan is black, Nico is white, and Pepe is a mulatto; they are the Cuban world. But they have still a further function: they are, above all, the mythos of evil. They set the stage, and, during much of the action, their activity sustains the tension and makes viable the tone of terror and menace that grows steadily. As the play opens, they are shooting dice, establishing a sense of random evil. The play's first words are Pepe's: "Mátalo. Mátalo. Tiene que morir."[29] Triana's use of game is again effective at the close of act I. Juvencio and Blanca Estela engage in an erotic scene as the three murderers watch. The lovers withdraw to culminate the act, and the three engage in an imaginary game of billiards whose rapid rhythmic action and highly suggestive vocabulary heighten the erotic symbolism of the game's instruments.

Nico. —Suave.

Pepe. —Por acá.

Nico. —Suave.

Pepe. —Afinca, dale duro.

Juan. —No lo pienses.

Pepe. —En el centro, en el centro.

Juan. —Un golpe y nada más.

Pepe. —Métela.

Nico. —Suave.

Pepe. —Rápido.

Juan. —Carambola.[30]
(En un grito)

Act II also ends on this note of sardonic game as the three dance grotesquely, burlesquing a children's game, and the murder in which the last act culminates takes place in a tone horrifyingly like this deformed game. The scene begins with offstage shouts.

Juan. —¿Dónde estás, Hilario?
(Violento)

Pepe. —Hay que actuar rápido.

Nico. —Un solo golpe.

Juan. —Venimos en nombre de los muertos.

Nico. —Coge tú por allí.

Juan. —Agárralo.

(Los tres personajes entran, agarran violentamente a Hilario. *Luego hacen una rueda.* Hilario *lucha por salir de la rueda. Los tres personajes lo arrastran hasta la escalera y allí lo matan.)*

Nico. —No lo sueltes.

Pepe. —Ahí mismo.

Nico. —Dale duro.

Juan. —Mátalo.

Pepe. —Mátalo.

Juan. —No te demores.

Nico. —Mátalo.

Juan. —Llévatelo en la golilla.

Pepe. —Tiene que morir.

(Se oye un quejido espantoso y luego un grito)

Hilario. —Blanca Estela.[31]

There is a pause, and the sounds of *clave*, *maraca*, and *bongo* are heard in a violent rhythm as the three murderers advance smilingly, singing their denial of any complicity. In one sense, they are indeed innocent; they have been, on this level, the instruments of blind chance. Hilario had risen and now, abandoned by fortune, Hilario must fall.

This scene repeats the tone and many of the words of the earlier game scenes, as the ring formed about the victim is an evil vision of the game already parodied at the end of act II. The word *juego* recurs constantly and menacingly. In Pablo's first confrontation with Blanca Estela, she rejects his almost casual but cruel overtures as she rejects his plea that she avoid Juvencio. But Pablo, an ambiguous figure who alternates between sensitivity and cold cruelty, is unwilling to let the matter die thus.

> (*En tono de sarcasmo*) Cálmese, señora, no se agite. (*En tono hiriente*) Pronto hablaremos, tú y yo, frente a frente. Entonces... veremos. Ese es el juego.[32]

Characters repeatedly refer to their own actions and words as *juego*, and, as we have seen, specific games are used as metaphorical versions of the sexual act and the murder. Blanca Estela almost literally plays with Pablo and he with Berta. Even Cachita, seemingly devoted to Hilario and Pablo, is playing a game; she feigns indignant anguish when Pablo confesses his inability or unwillingness to marry Berta but shortly unmasks herself in an abrupt denunciation of Hilario. Even Hilario's nickname is used in a children's game. This insistence on game playing is not arbitrary or capricious; it underlines Triana's vision of this doomed house and of all human existence. The Murderers-Chorus-Fates are addicted to games of chance because in their character of fates they are chance incarnate. We are all toys of the gods, children playing some monstrous random game.

Triana's latest play is *La noche de los asesinos*, written in 1964 and first produced in 1966 at the Sixth Havana Festival of Latin American theater. It has since been performed with critical acclaim in a number of European and American nations. The play takes place in a "sótano o el último cuarto-desván. Una mesa, tres sillas, alfombras raídas, cortinas sucias con grandes parches de telas floreadas, floreros, una campanilla, un cuchillo y algunos objetos ya en desuso, arrinconados, junto a la escoba y el plumero."[33] In this shabby setting, three characters play out a series of intricately shifting relationships. Cuca, Beba, and Lalo are two sisters and a brother, of undetermined age. They appear to be in late adolescence, although Cuca at one point refers to Lalo as being thirty years old, and Beba states that she is twenty. This may be true; it may equally well be a projection toward the future. Given the characters' actions, it is more reasonable to assume that they are in late adolescence, an assumption shared by critics who specifically refer to them as such. Triana says, ". . . son adultos y sin embargo conservan cierta gracia adolescente, aunque un tanto marchita."[34] This ambiguity does not detract from the play's effect and, as we shall see, adds a dimension. The play begins on a note of shock.

Lalo.	—Cierra esa puerta. (*Golpeándose el pecho. Exaltado, con los ojos muy abiertos*.) Un asesino. Un asesino. (*Cae de rodillas*)
Cuca. (A Beba)	—¿Y eso?
Beba. (*Indiferente. Observando a Lalo*.)	—La representación ha empezado.
Cuca.	—¿Otra vez?
Beba. (*Molesta*)	—Mira que tú eres... ¡Como si esto fuera algo nuevo![35]

In these few seconds of dialogue, Triana establishes the tone for the shifting fabric of the whole work. The audience is jolted by a supposed murder, further shocked by the news that this is all "representación," and finally dislocated entirely by the information that it is neither new or unusual. The climactic horror is revealed five lines later, when Lalo says that the victims of the pretended murder are the parents. Cuca is reluctant but finally convinced to play when Beba enters the game. The game itself is a savage parody of the parents' world, as the three adolescents engage in a spirited and horrifying discussion of the various ills of their parents and the supposed guests.

Lalo.	—¿Y usted, Pantaleón? Hacía tiempo que no lo veía. ¿Estaba perdido?
Beba. (*Acosando a los personajes imaginarios*)	—¿Cómo anda de la orina? A mi me dijeron los otros días...
Cuca. (*Acosando a los personajes imaginarios*)	—¿Funciona bien su vejiga?
Beba. (*Asombrada*)	—¿Cómo? ¿Todavía no se ha operado el esfínter?
Cuca. (*Escandalizada*)	—Oh, pero, ¿es así? ¿Y la hernia?
Lalo. (*Con una sonrisa hipócrita*)	—Usted, Margarita, se ve de lo mejor. ¿Le sigue creciendo el fibroma?[36]

This incantatory recital of the adult world's narcissistic infatuation with the decaying body is followed by a reversion to the roles of the parents as they play out a violent family argument before the guests.

But this strange game becomes increasingly serious, until it is more than a game. Within his role as father, Lalo taunts Cuca-Mother: "Nunca te decides a fondo. Quieres y no quieres. Eres y no eres. ¿Crees que siendo así ya basta? Siempre hay que jugársela."[37] It is increasingly clear that Lalo speaks both as father and as himself. For the others, this may be some sort of monstrous purgation, but for Lalo it is literally a deadly game. Soon they revert to their real selves; the purpose of the game is now focused. Lalo rejects his parents and all they represent in a mediocre and insensitive world.

> ¿Qué importa esta casa, qué importan estos muebles si nosotros no somos nada, si nosotros simplemente vamos y venimos por ella y entre ellos igual que un cenicero, un florero o un cuchillo flotante? (*A Cuca*) ¿Eres tú acaso un florero? ¿Te gustaría descubrir un día que eres realmente eso? ¿O qué como eso te han estado tratando buena parte de tu vida? ¿Soy yo acaso un cuchillo? Y tú, Beba, ¿te conformas con ser un cenicero? No, no. Eso es estúpido. (*Con ritmo mecánico*) Ponte aquí. Ponte allá. Haz esto. Haz lo otro. Haz lo de más allá. (*En otro tono*) Yo quiero mi vida: estos días, estas horas, estos minutos... Quiero andar y hacer cosas que deseo o siento. Sin embargo, tengo las manos atadas. Tengo los pies atados. Tengo los ojos vendados. Esta casa es mi mundo. Y esta casa se pone vieja, sucia y huele mal. Mamá y Papá son los culpables. Me da pena, pero es así. Y lo más terrible es que ellos no se detienen un minuto a pensar si las cosas no debieran ser de otro modo. Ni tú tampoco. Y Beba mucho menos... Si Beba juega, es porque no puede hacer otra cosa.[38]

This is Lalo's absolute rebellion. Cuca, in contrast, defends her parents and accepts their world; her participation is reluctant, while Beba oscillates between the two attitudes, unable to resolve her hatred of the parents' pedestrian world, their rancors and pettiness, and the alternatives offered by Cuca and Lalo: total acceptance or total rebellion.

But the rebellion becomes more serious still. Lalo seizes two knives and prepares to repeat still another stage of what is rapidly taking the shape of a premonitory ritual. Beba's feverish acceptance indicates that this holds for her some sort of purgation. Now we perceive Lalo's choice of the knife among the domestic objects with which he has compared the three; he is indeed a knife in his own mind. They slip again into roles: Beba as a neighbor recounts the horror of the murder, the pools of blood, and the smell of death. Even Cuca takes part, acting out a newsboy crying of the "forty stabs" and the "terrible slaughter." As background, Lalo steadily files the knife.

There is yet another sudden shift as they recapitulate the life that has led to this gruesome extreme. Beba as the father and Cuca as the mother are cruelly uncomprehending toward an adolescent Lalo; a child Beba is unjustly punished. But the tension is too much for Beba; she cannot withstand the stress and pleads for the game to end. This leads to a complex counterpoint in which Beba, outside the game, is consoled by Cuca, in the role of the mother, as Lalo alternates violently between himself and the father role, in both of which he is murderously angry at Beba. And yet another abrupt change: Lalo as the mother is bitter because she has been trapped into marriage by pregnancy; Cuca as the mother is only too willing to have the unwanted Lalo leave home. And abruptly the game ends. Lalo thrusts the knife into the table. This is for him not a game but a rehearsal. As the sisters softly chant their battle cry, symbolically reduced to the "La sala no es la sala. La sala es la cocina," which conveys their whole rebellion against the fixed order of things, Lalo rehearses the steps of the murder, Cuca cleans the knife, and the three chat quietly as the first act ends.

Cuca. (A Beba) —¿Cómo te sientes?

Beba. (A Cuca) —Regular.

Cuca. (A Beba) —Cuesta un poco de trabajo.

Beba. (A Cuca) —Lo malo es que uno se acostumbra.

Cuca. (A Beba) —Pero, algún día...

Beba. (A Cuca) —Es como todo.

Lalo. —Abre esa puerta. (Se golpea el pecho. Exaltado. Con los ojos muy abiertos.) Un asesino. Un asesino. (Cae de rodillas)

Cuca. (A Beba) —¿Y eso?

Beba. —La primera parte ha terminado.

(Apagón)[39]

We are again trapped in the world of make-believe, once more uncertain whether this is a gruesome game invented by bored and angry children or some sort of bloody dress rehearsal. A series of patterns has been established. The parents are uniformly evil; the mother is vulgar and crude, the father crass and materialistic. Lalo is murderously violent and derives sadistic joy from the game rehearsal, while Cuca becomes increasingly involved and Beba distressed to the point of physical illness. In act II, much of this is reversed. In another quasi-real, quasi-fantastic situation, Beba and Cuca continue the game. The parents are dead, and the police have been called. As the two girls prepare a cover story, the murderous Lalo is almost incapable of functioning. His efforts to leave—

remorse? emotional collapse? or more playacting?—are halted by Cuca, who has now replaced him as the avenging angel.

The bulk of act II consists of the police investigation. The girls are the investigators, casual, slangy, and crude. Abruptly, we are in the police station, where Cuca dictates her report. The entire scene is depersonalized, cold, and Lalo refuses to sign the confession. He admits his guilt but cannot take the crime coldly, as do the police. The immediacy, the impact, the real nature of the crime are erased by the legalistic, terminological world of the police. The heart of the trial scene is a determined questioning by Cuca in which the defiant Lalo is reduced to an almost hypnotized state and, ultimately, to a delirious collapse.

Despite the intensity of these scenes, which tempt the audience to forget that it is, after all, a double illusion, Triana does not lose sight of his goal. As Cuca-Mother appears as a witness for the prosecution, we begin to see the other side of the coin. Vicious this mother may be, but behind her viciousness lie the pathetic wants of a human being, the discomfort and resentment of an unwanted pregnancy, the rejection by a son so insistent on his own freedom of action that he took no heed of another's freedom, the distress of approaching age and the loss of her husband's love, and disgust with his mediocrity. But the father, too, has his moment; his infidelities, his search for a more interesting life beyond the walls of his house, are the result of constant nagging. He, too, is resentful; she has complained and whined until all love has evaporated. As Lalo-Father and Cuca-Mother shriek their rancor, Beba-Lalo dances wildly about the stage shouting the revolutionary chant: "Hay que quitar las alfombras. Vengan abajo las cortinas. La sala no es la sala. La sala es la cocina. El cuarto no es el cuarto. El cuarto es el inodoro."[40]

Abruptly, the play-within-a-play has ended. The girls calmly discuss the game.

Beba. (*Tono normal*)　　　—¿Cómo te sientes?

Cuca. (*Tono normal*)　　　—Más segura.

Beba.　　　　　　　　　　—¿Estás satisfecha?

Cuca.　　　　　　　　　　—Sí.

Beba.　　　　　　　　　　—¿De veras?

Cuca.　　　　　　　　　　—De veras.

Beba.　　　　　　　　　　—¿Estás dispuesta, otra vez?

Cuca.　　　　　　　　　　—Eso no se pregunta.

Beba.　　　　　　　　　　—Llegaremos a hacerlo un día...

Cuca. (*Interrumpiendo*)　—Sin que nada falle.

Beba. —¿No te sorprendió que pudiera?

Cuca. —Uno siempre se sorprende.

Cuca and Beba have come through the ordeal hardened; only Lalo is shaken.

Lalo. (*Entre sollozos*) —Ay, hermanas mías, si el amor
pudiera... Sólo el amor... Porque a
pesar de todo yo los quiero.

But the girls laugh sardonically. Their moment has come.

Cuca. (A Beba. —Míralo.
Entre risas burlonas.)
(A Lalo) —Así quería verte.

Beba. (*Seria de nuevo*) —Está bien. Ahora me toca a mí.[41]

The game has ended, but it will, inevitably, begin again.

In this shifting sequence of plays-within-a-play, Triana has created an enormously complex exposition of the tensions within a family. In the madhouse that is this home, they are all guilty: the petty father and mother, the unreasoning and uncompromising children. Obviously, this is not simply a presentation of the unpleasantries of a single family but a dramatic metaphor of a decaying institution, a great blasphemy against the foundations of social life. The children are, in Triana's words, "figuras de un museo en ruinas."[42] The Colombian critic Carlos José Reyes, perhaps spurred by the time of the play, described as somewhere in the 1950s, has called the work a reconstruction of society, as though it were a display of the tawdriness of the bourgeois family.[43] Such an interpretation is simplistic. This is no social drama in the usual political sense but rather in the sense that it presents in almost unique fashion the terrible conflict of generations that is literally shaking the roots of society in our world. This is not agitprop but a desolated vision of the relationships between generations, of the anguish and oppression of adolescence, of the dismay of growing old. Like María of *Medea en el espejo*, Lalo, Cuca, and Beba are seeking their own faces, their own meaning. They feel alone, unjustified, different. The obsessive chant of "La sala es la cocina" and Lalo's seemingly irrational insistence on shifting furniture are symbols of their need to make their own world, without prefabricated regulations. They are basically negative; moving the old ways around will solve nothing, and the destruction of family authority and ties without a replacement is simply nihilistic. The symbolic murder of authority leads only to chaos.

But *La noche de los asesinos* is far from a domestic drama. Triana is once more engaged in his construction of myths, and again it is a myth of pure unreason, of violent irrationality. The "game" of murder is clearly a ritual ceremony, even to the incantatory chanting and the sacramental placing of objects. Further, it is a ritual that has been performed before and will be performed again. But this ritual is no substitute, no replacement, for a rite from which all substance has been removed, to be replaced by a hollow symbolism. This rite is a dress rehearsal, a preparation, a cleansing and training. It is a ritual before the fact, rather than after, and, as such, it is far grimmer than might at first appear.

Triana shows in *La noche de los asesinos* the same preoccupation with formalized structure within which fantasy functions. As Cuca says, "En esta casa todo está en juego. Ayúdame a dar los últimos toques."[44] Although she is speaking of the final rearrangement of furniture that so obsesses them, they are also about to give the final touches to the game and to the preparation for murder. In her role as policeman, she says, "No me irás a decir que todo ha sido un juego."[45] But, of course, it *has* been a game, a game that will ineluctably lead to fact, as Triana constructs ever wider circles that re-create the past and prefigure the future. And, again, as the prosecutor, Cuca says, "¿Qué tipo de juego tenían en la casa? (*Pausa*) ¿No había en él algo... enfermizo? (*Pausa*) Responda: ¿No era un juego monstruoso?"[46] And a monstrous game is exactly what it is, carried out by three potential murderers, just as the same ritual preparation was performed through games by the murderers of Hilario.

There are some obvious similarities with Jean Genet. In addition to the playing with the illusion of multiple realities and the changing of roles, there is the eschatology of adult conversation and the shifting of sex with changing roles. The assumption by inferiors of the role of an absent superior is a clear parallel with *The Maids* and much more of Genet's work, as is the lapsing from ritual role to stage reality. But despite these and other more specific similarities, *La noche de los asesinos* is far from an adaptation of *The Maids*. Triana has incorporated other elements: the easy shifting of the multiple characters, possibly as an influence of Dragún's *Historias para ser contadas*, and the change from a subcriminal group to adolescents, with the consequent shift of orientation. Triana, too, has created a revolt of the slaves, but his slaves are no longer adult criminal slaves rebelling against adult criminal masters. They are youth who rebel against an establishment that has created rules that the slaves cannot accept. It is no accident that these adolescents take on an age they do not possess, for they are all people who would reject a corrupt and meaningless world.

There is a further dimension of difference, for Genet's ritual in *The Maids* is a hollow ritual, a substitute, as Martin Esslin has made clear.

The revolt of the maids against their masters is not a social gesture, a revolutionary action; it is tinged with nostalgia and longing, like the revolt of the fallen angel Satan against the world of light from which he is forever banished. That is why this revolt finds its expression not in protest but in ritual. Each of the maids in turn acts the part of the lady, expressing her longing to *be* the lady, and each in turn takes it upon herself to act the other maid, progressing from adoration and servility to abuse and violence—the discharge of all the hatred and envy of the outcast who sees himself as a rejected lover. This ritual, as Sartre points out, is a kind of Black Mass— the wish to murder the loved and envied object congealed and forever repeated as a ceremonial, stereotyped action. Such a ritual is frustration become flesh—an action that will never be performed in the real world is repeated over and over as a mere game. And not even this ritual ever reaches its natural climax. The lady always returns before that. As Sartre sees it, this failure is, as it were, subconsciously built into the ritual. The game is played in such a way that the time wasted on the preliminaries is always too long for the climax ever to be reached.[47]

Triana's ritual is far longer and more complex than that of Claire and Solange, but there is a more important substantive difference. The maids sublimate their hatreds in a hollow rite because they wish to *be* the objects of the love-hate; Cuca, Beba, and Lalo use the ritual framework to act out their hatred of an establishment that they most desperately want *not* to be. And theirs is no hollow rite; there is every reason to believe that, far from a frozen fantasy, replacing the desired action, their ritual is a preparation, a purgation of all the emotions and attitudes that might inhibit its actualization.

José Triana is certainly not a social critic in any orthodox sense. In his obsessive presentation of the mythos of violence and the irrational in Cuban life, there is no overt treatment of social, economic, or political problems. He is, rather, profoundly critical of the stagnancy that led to the need for revolt, of the blind religiosity, political corruption, and family decay that prevailed: "Our normal life, until almost the other day, was the past social structure in which we have lived and moved. It is just that we judge that social structure, and it is legitimate to expect that we will live within the new structure which is being created, that is, live within it with the same naturalness with which one has a beer, that is, so that we may reflect it with identical naturalness, without false diagrams or learned lessons."[48] This is obviously no partisan political line but the search for a life that will do away not only with the rantings of Petronila and the rest but also with their *need* to rant, which will not tolerate the savage reign of deadly games, which will be purified of the need for bloody ritual. It is perhaps not entirely by chance that Triana appears not to have produced any original plays since *La noche de los asesinos*. After the purifying holocaust, the way is still uncharted.

NOTES

1. "El teatro actual," *Casa de las Américas*, January–April 1964, p. 104. This and all subsequent translations from the Spanish are my own.

2. Ibid., p. 100.

3. "El nuevo teatro cubano," *La Gaceta de Cuba*, 3 June 1963, p. 7.

4. "El teatro actual," p. 100.

5. Rine Leal, "El teatro en un acto en Cuba," *Revista Unión*, nos. 5 and 6 (January–April 1963), p. 68.

6. "El nuevo teatro cubano," *La Estafeta Literaria*, 25 February 1967, p. 34.

7. "El teatro actual," p. 100.

8. ". . . dessicated little body"; ". . . relic of love" (*El Parque de la Fraternidad* [Havana: Ediciones Unión, 1962], p. 73).

9. "We must start again without him" (ibid., p. 77).

10. "Talk? Talk, what for? There's nothing left any more. Inside, everybody felt satisfied. (*He begins to climb the stairs*) Talk about the origin, about the gods? As if I were a clown. Talk about concepts? And about cosmic projects? What daring—I offer my hospitality and they still allow themselves. I will continue my labors. What time is it? Nine? I am hungry. (*Looking at the three characters*) And there will come others and others. (*Sighs*) Some day" (ibid., p. 89).

11. "One of these days he'll go crazy and kill us all—just like they say happened a long time ago" (ibid., p. 70).

12. "His blood will serve us as food. We will be sanctified afterward" (ibid., p. 76).

13. ". . . in the Olivos's winecellar" (ibid., p. 77).

14. This argument has been presented in a brief but penetrating essay by Calvert Casey, which he was kind enough to send me without any indication of place of publication. It was only through Casey's cooperation that I was able to secure much of the material upon which the present study depends. Several years later, unable to resolve the conflict of two irreconcilable ideals, Calvert Casey died by his own hand, leaving a debt that I can no longer repay. *Vale.*

15. "El teatro actual," p. 97.

16. Natividad González Freire, in a review in *Verde olivo*, 12 November 1960, reprinted in *La Gaceta de Cuba*, 3 June 1963, p. 8.

17. H. D. F. Kitto, *Greek Tragedy* (Garden City, N.Y.: Doubleday Anchor Books, 1954), p. 198.

18. It is conceivable that Triana's source may have been Kitto, whose conception of *Medea* as a "bitter domestic strife in a setting of ordinary social life—children, nurses, curious neighbors, old men gossiping around the spring" (ibid., p. 208), is strikingly close to Triana's vision.

19. Rine Leal, "El nuevo rostro del teatro cubano," *La Gaceta de Cuba*, 3 June 1963, p. 12.

20. "Julian, Julian, Julian. You are my destiny. I will perform. I will rise to the height of the circumstances" (*El Parque de la Fraternidad*, p. 13).

21. This is hardly new, but it bears repeating that such a function of language can be both effective and misunderstood. I still recall with dismay an instructor who disqualified Maxwell Anderson's *Winterset* from serious consideration on the grounds that slum dwellers don't speak that way.

22. Calvert Casey, "Teatro/61," *Casa de las Américas*, January 1962, p. 104.

23. "We speak different languages" (*El Parque de la Fraternidad*, p. 13).

24. In this, as throughout, references to the tragic rhythm are based on Francis Fergusson's *The Idea of a Theater* (Garden City, N.Y.: Doubleday Anchor Books, 1953).

25. "Mother, father, why have you abandoned me?" (*El Parque de la Fraternidad*, p. 108).

26. "Shit. Now I've caught on, I have seen clearly. It is all a lie. Something that slips away between our fingers" (*La muerte del Ñeque* [Havana: Ediciones R, 1964], p. 107).

27. Richard Sewall, *The Vision of Tragedy* (New Haven: Yale University Press, 1959), p. 108.
28. Kitto, *Greek Tragedy*, p. 10.
29. "Kill him. Kill him. He's got to die" (*La muerte del Ñeque*, p. 17).
30. *Nico.* Smooth.

> *Pepe.* Over here.
>
> *Nico.* Smooth.
>
> *Pepe.* Go on, go to it.
>
> *Juan.* No way.
>
> *Pepe.* In the center, in the center.
>
> *Juan.* One bang and no more.
>
> *Pepe.* Shove it in.
>
> *Nico.* Smooth.
>
> *Pepe.* Quick.
>
> *Juan.* (*In a shout*) Eight ball! [Ibid.]

31. *Juan.* (*Violently*) Where are you, Hilario?

> *Pepe.* We've got to move fast.
>
> *Nico.* Just one smash.
>
> *Juan.* We come in the name of the dead.
>
> *Nico.* You go through there.
>
> *Juan.* Grab him.
>
> (*The three characters enter; they seize* Hilario *violently. Then, they form a ring.* Hilario *struggles to escape from the ring. The three characters drag him to the stairs, and there they kill him.*)
>
> *Nico.* Don't turn him loose.
>
> *Pepe.* Right there.
>
> *Nico.* Get him good.
>
> *Juan.* Kill him.
>
> *Pepe.* Kill him.
>
> *Juan.* Don't waste time.
>
> *Nico.* Kill him.
>
> *Juan.* Wear that around your neck.

Pepe. He's got to die.

(A horrible moan is heard and then a cry)

Hilario. Blanca Estela. [Ibid., pp. 58–59]
32. *(In a sarcastic tone)* Calm yourself, madam. Don't get excited. *(In a cutting tone)* Soon we'll talk, you and I, face to face. Then, we will see. That is the game.
[Ibid., p. 51]
33. ". . . cellar or the back attic. A table, three chairs, frayed rugs, dirty curtains with big floral-patterned patches, vases, a small bell, a knife, and some objects no longer used, in a corner, by the broom and the feather duster" *(La noche de los asesinos* [Havana: Casa de las Américas, 1965], p. 1).
34. ". . . they are adults and nevertheless they retain a certain adolescent grace, although a bit faded" (ibid.).
35. *Lalo.* Close that door. *(Beating his chest. Excited, with his eyes wide open.)* A murderer. A murderer. *(Falls to his knees)*

Cuca. *(To* Beba) What's all that?

Beba. *(Indifferent. Observing* Lalo.) The performance has begun.

Cuca. Again?

Beba. *(Annoyed)* But you are. As if it were something new! [Ibid., p. 3]
36. *Lalo.* . . . And you, Pantaleón? I haven't seen you for a long time. Where have you been?

Beba. *(Badgering the imaginary characters)* How is your specimen? They told me the other day—

Cuca. *(Badgering the imaginary characters)* Is your bladder working all right?

Beba. *(Astonished)* What? You haven't had your sphincter operated on yet?

Cuca. *(Scandalized)* Really? What about the hernia?

Lalo. *(With a hypocritical smile)* Margarita, you look marvelous. Is your tumor still growing? [Ibid., p. 14]
37. "You never make up your mind. You want and you don't want. You are and you aren't. Do you think that's enough? You've always got to risk the whole thing" (ibid., p. 37).
38. "What does this house matter, what does this furniture matter if we are nothing, if we simply come and go like a floating ashtray, a vase, or knife? *(To* Cuca) Are you a vase? Would you like to find out one day that that's what you really are? Or that they've been treating you that way for most of your life? Am I a knife? And you, Beba, are you satisfied with being an ashtray? No, no. That's stupid. *(With a mechanical rhythm)* Go here. Go there. Do this. Do that. Do the other. *(In a different tone)* I want my life; these days, these hours, these minutes—I want to do what I feel like doing. And yet my hands are tied. My feet are tied. My eyes are blindfolded. This house is my world. And this house is getting old, it's dirty and it smells. Mama and Papa are guilty. I'm sorry, but that's how it is. And the worst of all is that they never stop for a minute to think whether things shouldn't be different. Neither do you. And much less Beba—if Beba plays, it's because she can't help it" (ibid., pp. 21–22).
39. *Cuca.* *(To* Beba) How do you feel?

Beba. (*To* Cuca) Okay.

Cuca. (*To* Beba) It takes a lot out of you.

Beba. (*To* Cuca) The worst part is that you get used to it.

Cuca. (*To* Beba) But, some day—

Beba. (*To* Cuca) It's like everything else.

Lalo. Open that door. (*He beats his chest. Excited. With his eyes wide open.*) A murderer. A murderer. (*Falls to his knees*)

Cuca (*To* Beba) What's all that?

Beba. The first part is over.

(*Lights out*)   [Ibid., pp. 51–52]
    40. "We have to take up the rugs. Down with the curtains. The parlor isn't the parlor. The parlor is the kitchen. The room isn't the room. The room is the bathroom" (ibid., p. 108).
    41. *Beba*. (*Normal tone*) How do you feel?

Cuca. (*Normal tone*) Surer.

Beba. Are you satisfied?

Cuca. Yes.

Beba. Really?

Cuca. Really.

Beba. Are you ready again?

Cuca. You don't have to ask that.

Beba. We'll do it some day—

Cuca. (*Interrupting*) And nothing will go wrong.

Beba. Weren't you surprised that it worked?

Cuca. It's always a surprise.

. . . .

Lalo. (*Sobbing*) Oh my sisters, if love could—if only love—because, in spite of everything, I love them.

. . . .

Cuca. (*To* Beba. *Laughing mockingly*.) Look at him. (*To* Lalo) That's how I wanted to see you.

Beba. (*Serious again*.) All right. Now it's my turn.   [Ibid., p. 109]
    42. ". . . figures in a museum in ruins" (ibid., p. 1).
    43. Carlos José Reyes, quoted in Natividad González Freire, "El VI Festival de teatro latinoamericano," *Casa de las Américas*, March–April 1967, p. 119.

44. "In this house everything is involved. Help me give the final touches" (*La noche de los asesinos*, p. 60).

45. "You're not going to tell me it's all been a game" (ibid., p. 67).

46. "What kind of game did you play in the house? (*Pause*) Wasn't there something unhealthy about it? (*Pause*) Answer: wasn't it a monstrous game?" (ibid., p. 85).

47. Martin Esslin, *The Theatre of the Absurd* (Garden City, N.Y.: Doubleday Anchor Books, 1961), p. 148.

48. "El teatro actual," p. 106.

12. The Theater of Egon Wolff

Margaret Sayers Peden

Egon Wolff, born in Chile in 1926 of German parents, is one of Latin America's best playwrights. Originally a career chemical engineer, Wolff began writing plays in 1957. To date he has ten published or produced plays plus "six or seven finished, or half-finished, works lying around here maturing—dying?"[1] The unique and peculiar flavor of Wolff's writing is perhaps due to the duality inherent in his heritage. Where his Latinity might lead him toward the subjective, the mystic, and the magic, which are most obvious in *Los invasores* ("The invaders") and *Flores de papel* (*Paper Flowers*), his Teutonism may provide him with the logic and the sense of order and thoroughness so apparent in all his work. Wolff himself is aware of an ambivalence in his philosophy of theater: "Neither am I naturally and entirely that [moving closer to the philosophies of Genet, Beckett, and, to some degree, Pinter] because my German blood entices me, leads me towards the spheres of reason and pure logic. So that's where I am now: struggling to free myself from my blood, and, at the same time, tempted by it."[2] That Wolff is a Chilean may also explain some of the complexity in his writing. In spite of the fact that North Americans think of Latin American countries as being basically Spanish in heritage (hence, volatile in passion) and dictator- or militarist-oriented, a strong tradition of democratic order underlies the domestic and governmental life of Chile, and this order may be reflected in some of Wolff's depictions of Chilean reality.

Domingo Piga has commented on the possible twofold influence of Wolff's Germanic heritage and his interest in science to explain his analytical propensities: "It is difficult to say whether his Germanic heritage or his scientific inclinations gave him that profound, conscientious, quiet, grave personality."[3] But then one may suggest that the Germanic heritage and the interest in the scientific are not contradictory, but rather that the interest in the scientific is *inherent* in the Germanic heritage. Piga is correct when he says: "This silent, modest, and tenacious man learned a great deal from what he saw, and what he discovered, in his performed works."[4] Wolff's theater, always competent, has progressed steadily in quality to the point that his is currently one of the most original, penetrating, and important voices in Latin American theater.

In the past, Latin America has not produced a convincing body of psychological plays. The good, basically realistic play, based on the investigation of individual—and by extension, societal—problems and insight into motivations, is similarly far from frequent. (This is not to imply that realism does not exist in Latin American theater. It abounds! But most "realistic" plays tend toward the didactic and propagandistic on the one hand and costumbristic, slice-of-life re-creations of distinct national realities on the other.) If we consider, for questions of terms, that psychological theater originates after Freud, then the Argentine Samuel Eichelbaum was among the first psychological dramatists. His plays, especially his well-known *La mala sed* ("Bad blood"), are flawed by overly melodramatic passions and deformed by an unconvincing reliance on determin-ist-oriented motivations and resolutions. The Mexican Xavier Villaurrutia also touched on psychological theater. Most of his three-act plays, however, are slick comedies of manners that do not maintain the level of excellence of his early one-acts. The exception is *Invitación a la muerte* ("Invitation to death"), and its most impressive quality is not so much the motivations of the protagonist as the mood of broodingly morbid curiosity and fascination with death that pervades the play. The Argentine Conrado Nalé Roxlo's *La cola de la sirena* ("The mermaid's tail") is a very deft and amusing examination of the psychology of not wanting something once it is attained, but none of Nalé's subsequent plays lives up to the promise of that one, and in some way each is a recapitula-tion of it. Until recently, Rodolfo Usigli has been the most convincing and suc-cessful playwright in the vein of psychological realism. Looking back over these years, which produced so little of excellence in a line of theater that was thriving in other cultures, one might propose that the Latin temperament is not particu-larly receptive to the kind of analytical thinking that results in psychological in-vestigation and that perhaps Usigli's avowed admiration for George Bernard Shaw has had an Anglicizing or de-Latinizing effect on his writing. If there is any substance to this possibility, then Wolff's debt to his Teutonic heritage may in-deed contribute to his excellence in this area of contemporary theater.[5]

Gabriela Mora has said that Wolff, "a profound observer of the psychologi-cal," creates characters that are dramatically very convincing and that these characters represent Chilean types.[6] Indeed, Wolff does draw most convincing characters, but the second part of Mora's statement suggests a kind of *costum-brismo* of which Wolff is not guilty. Of the six plays in this study, the first three—*Mansión de lechuzas* (1966, "Owl mansion"), *Discípulos del miedo* (1957, "Disciples of fear"), and *Niñamadre* (1960, "Childmother")—are less "trans-ferable" than Wolff's more recent plays. This is not because they are costum-bristic, however, but because they contain a certain cultural incompatibility. In general, the basic problems of these plays have been confronted by earlier generations in the United States. For example, the acquisitive mother figure in *Discípulos del miedo* who destroys the lives of her husband and children in her steadfast determination to become a member of the owner class is more perti-nent to periods in our history when the middle class was less affluent. That kind of drive undoubtedly still exists in the United States, but it is no longer one of the predominant characteristics of the middle-class mother. Similarly, the problem basic to *Niñamadre*, the extreme subservience of female to male, is less applicable to the liberated woman of English-speaking cultures than to this continuing problem in Chile. Wolff comments: "It [*Niñamadre*] has a distinctly Latin American flavor. It is an excessively Latin American problem—that of brutal patriarchy—and the subjection of the woman to the whim and will of the man is a Moorish-Christian, patriarchal-biblical heritage from which we have been unable to free ourselves. Above all in the lower classes. The middle- and upper-class woman has already begun the emancipating crusade."[7]

Mansión de lechuzas is an elegantly symmetrical play.[8] Wolff's first play, it won an honorable mention in the yearly competition sponsored by the theater of the University of Chile. The theme of the play is the breakdown of old cultural values and the related omnipresent problem of generational conflict. The human problem is reflected in the physical setting. A home that once stood in splendid isolation amidst formal grounds is presently in a state of decay, its gardens replaced by new housing developments. This encroachment is symbolic of the menace that Marta feels the outside world poses to the two sons she has striven to protect from it. The truth is, of course, that she has not so much protected her sons as suffocated them, and inevitably they must escape this suffocation and move into the real world—or die. The strength of the play lies in the evocation of atmosphere. One experiences vividly the Gothic presence of the past: there is a mossy dank odor of imminent decay throughout the piece. The flaw in *Mansión de lechuzas* is that the effect produced is greater than the problem of the play merits. The problem is not as "high" as the emotions. Ideas are more important here than people, and, as a result, realism suffers.

Discípulos del miedo, too, is dominated by a mother figure, but in this case the mother is not striving to protect her sons and her life from change. It is she who is the spur to change. Matilde, in *Discípulos*, is the reality that Marta, in *Mansión*, wishes to escape. Marta is an extremely unsympathetic character, but she is unforgettable. She is close to being the heroic mother we have known in the past—holding her family together against adversity, "making something" of herself and her children. Matilde's flaw, as revealed by the play, is that she wants these things for herself. In a tense scene at the end of the play, Matilde, her dreams shattered, the money that was to buy a factory lost, stands ignoring her dying husband and pleading children:

Sara. (En la escala)	—¡Mamá! ¡Mamá! ¡Mamá! ¡Ven! Papá está muy mal. ¡Dice que quiere verte! ¡Apúrate!
	(Desaparece. Jorge la sigue apresuradamente. Matilde se queda sola. Está de pie, con las manos empuñadas.)
Matilde.	—Todo... Todo perdido.

(*Asoma* Jorge *en la escala, baja*)

Jorge. (*Con emoción grave*)   —Mi papá se muere, mamá. Te está
esperando... (*Descuelga su sombrero de
la percha*) Voy a buscar a Ricardo. (*Sale*)

(Matilde *queda sola. Después de un rato cae el telón.*)[9]

An epilogue following this scene contains one of the most perceptive moments in Wolff's theater. Ricardo, the son whom Matilde has valued least and who, ironically, is the only one of her three children who will care for her now that she has need, brings her a gift:

Matilde. —¿Qué me traes ahí, Ricardo?

Ricardo. —Cosas de comer. ¿Dónde está la Ester?

Matilde. —Haciendo la comida. Y este arbolito, ¿lo traes para mí?

Ricardo. —Sí, mamá.

(Ricardo *va a la cocina.* Matilde *se para y bota el arbolito.*)

(*Entra* Ricardo *al sentir el ruido*)

Matilde. —Se me cayó sin querer, hijo. . . .[10]

In this single action we see the blind and bitter frustration of a woman whose goals have been thwarted. Matilde wants radios and rugs and new furniture and fancy curtains. Instead, she has been offered a plant for Easter. When Ricardo tells her they will never have the things she wants and turns away from her, Matilde's last words are, "Tengo miedo, tengo miedo." There are very few moments in theater where the "disciples of fear" resulting from social and financial insecurity are so graphically illustrated. In a few lines we are presented with the definition of an emerging class.

Niñamadre, the first Chilean play ever to be staged at the Yale Drama School, was originally entitled *El osito teté amarillo* ("The yellow teddy bear"). When Rafael Benavente Pinochet, who was on a fellowship at Yale, was offered the opportunity to stage a Latin American work, he found that this play had the qualities he was looking for: "The work shows us the Santiago of Cueto Street, a Santiago that has something of the provincial, and for that reason, perhaps, it seemed to me more valid as an expression of Chilean ambience. Its characters belong to the middle class, in varying degrees, it is true, but with all the power that constituting the really meaningful segment of a country signifies. If the problems it exposes are Chilean, they are expressed in such a form that, dramatically speaking, they have a universal context. In addition, it is evident that as a dramatist Egon occupies a clear critical position, and—what in my

opinion makes him more worthwhile—without propaganda. . . . And it is evident that this position makes of Egon a dramatist of clearly universal values."[11]
Niñamadre was produced in 1961 as *A Touch of Blue* and was published in Spanish in 1966.

The *niñamadre* of the play is a prostitute, slightly worn but basically good. Her one desire is to have the child she is carrying. The conflicting emotions evoked by this desire torture her lover. To admit his love for her, even to himself, would indicate a flaw in his manhood. It takes a crippling accident and the intervention of a wise neighbor woman for him to achieve the necessary maturity to accept the love of the *niñamadre*. There is an interesting subplot in this play involving the shifting lines of tension among a quartet of types: a hearty German immigrant, a prissy, slightly "uppity" sign painter who once had artistic aspirations, and two women, one sweet and weak, the other bossy and strong. The resolution of the play effects a certain peace among all these disparate characters, because each has experienced some psychological growth and change. Again, it is Wolff's interest in the interaction of human relationships that is most apparent in the play.

Los invasores (1962) is perhaps Wolff's most important play. This is not because it is necessarily his best, but because it marks a definite dramatic maturity that is apparent in this work and in others to follow, *El signo de Caín* (1971, "The mark of Cain") and *Flores de papel* (1971). *Los invasores* is Wolff's most widely disseminated and discussed play. Juan Guerrero Zamora, in his *Historia del teatro contemporáneo*, considers that it is one of the supreme examples of the coming-of-age of Spanish American theater. "Here we find an unparalleled exponent of hallucinatory treatment of social semantics. . . . This logical treatment of what we see as illogical, characteristic of Kafka, is the best quality of the drama of Egon Wolff, and with it he opens the neoconventional possibilities . . . of the Chilean theater."[12] This "illogical logic" is characteristic of two of Wolff's plays, *Los invasores* and, to a certain degree, *Flores de papel*. After the publication of the former play, Frank Dauster commented: "This is not the former realism; Wolff has evolved towards a dramatic philosophy in which apparent realism serves to underline the surreal elements."[13] This quality—the irrational realism—is due to the masterful concept behind *Los invasores*. Obviously intended as a warning to an indifferent bourgeoisie, Wolff conceived of a mode of expression that would have a more profound dramatic impact than that possible through traditional realism. The home of an affluent bourgeois family, the Meyers, is "invaded" by several characters from the lower class; their family safety is threatened and their property destroyed. Physical threat is paralleled by psychological menace. China, the principal invading figure, is as effective in invading Meyer's emotional security as he is in intruding into his physical property. Complete and total destruction is unavoidable. The play seems to have nothing further to say. Then, there is a break in the line of action;

Meyer awakens from a nightmare. The audience reaction is—relief? chagrin? But that momentary release from tension is interrupted by the most dramatic moment of the play. A window pane is broken, and an intruding hand appears at the lock. The sequence that took place within Meyer's dream will be reenacted. Reality is all the more shattering following the illusion of release.

Los invasores is a circular play. After a short preamble—which Leon Lyday has interestingly suggested is also within the dream-reality[14]—the action of the play takes place within a dream, which will be repeated as reality. The spectator can only realize the absolute appropriateness of the increasingly surrealistic behavior *after* he is aware that this is the growing distortion of a dream. This carefully constructed distortion is the strongest feature of the play.

Some of the characters are partial stereotypes. The Meyers represent well-known bourgeois values. The son is a caricature of the self-serving liberal who knows nothing about real revolution, although it is true that he adapts to their situation more readily than other members of his family. The daughter, Marcela, is the most extreme of the family group, arrogant and totally intransigent. The most interesting characters are the invaders. China, especially, has a fascinating complexity. In view of the political events that have been taking place in Chile since the election of a Marxist president in 1970, *Los invasores* has proved to be a prophetic and particularly insightful work of art.

El signo de Caín shares the physical realism of Wolff's earlier plays but displays the maturity of the second phase of his career initiated by *Los invasores*. It is a four-character play focusing on the psychological relationships among the personages of the drama. The protagonist Portus is from a middle- or upper-class family. He has apparently willingly chosen to divorce himself from his prominent position and is living in poverty with an uneducated lower-class woman, Charito, who has a son by another man. The boy is never present, but Charito's concern for him is a strong factor in her behavior. The rhythm of the simple but mutually agreeable life of Portus and Charito is interrupted by the visit of an old friend, Joaquín Icaza. Joaquín and his wife Leonor, for subtle and complex reasons, will completely disrupt the delicate and pleasant balance of the Portus-Charito relationship.

The sign of Cain of the title refers to a brash, youthful philosophy, flamboyantly proclaimed by Portus and Joaquín, the emblem of liberated spirits and intellectual freedom.

Joaquín. —(*Le toma un brazo, íntimamente*) ¿Qué es Harry Haller? ¿La
        vida bella? ¿El ser trascendental? ¿El espíritu liberado?
        ¿El signo de Caín?

Portus. —¿No has olvidado, eh?

Joaquín. —¿Cómo iba a olvidar? (*Declama*) "Hay hombres que llevan en la frente el signo de Caín. La señal que los demás interpretan y temen como signo del mal, pero que en verdad no es más que la seña de una clara mente analítica, de un espíritu inquietante, de hombres sin miedo."[15]

On the strength of their old relationship—Portus was always the leader—Joaquín has come to "reclaim" Portus, to "free" him from Charito, and to reinstate him into the only world worthy of him, a world into which, of course, he cannot take Charito. Portus resents this insult to Charito. He in turn strikes out against Joaquín. All four characters become enmeshed in a web of invidious games of attack and counterattack that destroy all past relationships. Portus implies before Leonor that Joaquín had been involved in a homosexual love affair in his youth. By offering opportunities to Charito's son that Portus cannot provide and of which he does not approve, Leonor attempts to woo Charito away from Portus, to repay him for being more important to Joaquín than she. Charito is led to feel resentment against Portus. Portus sees his peace destroyed. Portus accuses Joaquín of cowardice, of having spoiled the potential purity and beauty of life by marrying Leonor for her money and her position.

We learn in a final and powerful climactic scene between Leonor and Portus that Portus, too, is a coward. Although he had claimed to have withdrawn from the crassness of a bourgeois, materialistic society for idealistic causes, we learn that he fled from his former life because of a failure in an experiment for which he was responsible, a failure he blamed on an innocent man. Honor stands dishonored. Portus and Leonor, for contradictory reasons—because each is strong, but also because each needs the one he loves—strip themselves of all pretense before each other. Portus offers Leonor the information about his dishonor in exchange for regaining the peace he had known with Charito. But Leonor shocks Portus with the truth:

Portus. —¡Vuelva! ¡Vaya donde su Joaco, y dígale que su amigo es un desgraciado, lo que quiera! No me importa. ¡Déjeme sólo con mi mujer!

Leonor. —El lo sabe.

(Portus *la mira perplejo*)

Joaco lo sabe todo. La primera vez que vinimos aquí, aún subiendo por esa escala, me venía recordando que no fuera a decir nada... "Ahora, necesita todo nuestro apoyo," me venía diciendo. "Todos podemos caer alguna vez."[16]

The play has an open ending. One wonders whether now there is any possibility of peace for any of the four. Not even truth, once the open sesame to the beautiful challenge of life, has any efficacy. Each one has been brought low, each guilty to some degree of the sin of lack of faith, though some are more guilty than others. The mark Jehovah left on the brow of Cain for murdering his brother, the mark Portus once exalted with fierce braggadocio, has been revealed for the curse it is. Man must not smite down his brother, even in the name of "una clara mente analítica, un espíritu inquietante, un hombre sin miedo."[17] Man *does* live by fear.

Fear, possibly, is the key word in a study of Wolff's theater. It is vital, certainly, to a consideration of *Flores de papel*, which is Wolff's most recent play and his most carefully controlled. All the tension and action emerge through its two characters—a difficult technical feat. Realism, lack of logic, symbolism, and insight are all skillfully handled. It is interesting that during the editing of the English-language version of *Flores de papel*, various interpretations of the "meaning" of the play were communicated to me. One reader suggested that it was a parable of the subjugation of female to male. This interpretation recalls Wolff's comments about *Niñamadre*, that the brutal domination of female by male is a problem Latin Americans have not yet been able to shake. Another reader offered the thesis that *Flores de papel* demonstrated the pathology of the born victim. Abnormal psychology has ample and abundant proof that there are aberrant personalities who seek subjugation, just as there are those capable only of destruction. Still another reading—one that seems almost inevitable if one has previously read *Los invasores*—reveals that *Flores de papel* is a continuation, an intensification in degree, and a diminution in scope of the earlier play; Eva and el Merluza are symbols of their respective classes, and, once again, a complacent bourgeoisie is invaded by an intruder who shows no mercy because he has never known mercy.

What happens in *Flores de papel* is extremely simple at first view. What is not simple is *why* Eva allows the things that lead to her destruction to happen, and what, precisely, is el Merluza's motivation in bringing Eva down, rather than attempting, himself, to rise.

A middle-class woman, Eva—a widow, as one assumes from revelations during the play—allows a vagrant, el Merluza, to carry home her groceries. She allows him to enter to deposit the bundles. She attempts to pay him for his services. He requests, instead, a cup of tea. From the moment of that first capitulation, there is no retreat for Eva. El Merluza stays for a meal. He stays for the night. He moves in. But change in their routine reality is not as simple as that. They are from two radically differing worlds. This disparity demands adjustment, which in this case is accomplished not by compromise but by mandate. El Merluza, neurotic, possessed by weird energies that not even he seems to understand, proceeds to establish the kind of order he has known upon the middle-class, affected "decor" of Eva's apartment. Little by little el Merluza tears, rips, overturns, and destroys every semblance of the superficial reality we recognize as middle class. In like manner, he criticizes, confuses, torments, and destroys Eva. He furnishes the physical milieu with rudely hammered-together chairs and torn upholstery, and everywhere he hangs streamers and bouquets of the ubiquitous paper flowers of the title. In the final scene of the play we see two contrasting but similarly dehumanized beings. While el Merluza has been speaking with maniacal frenzy, "Eva trata de hablar, pero no puede. Desiste."[18] As in other plays, Wolff graphically illustrates the human situation through symbolic action: "[El Merluza] pone una de las grandes flores de papel en el escote de Eva, que le cubre toda la cara."[19] Eva has been completely obliterated as a human being. As the two leave to take up a life together in the dumps "on the other side of the river," Wolff's last words are issued not through the characters but rather through the stage directions: "Salen. En la habitación reina ahora el desorden total. Nada está como era. Sólo queda en ella la nueva belleza. Las toscas, enormes, casi deformes flores de papel. Telón."[20]

In a previous study of *Mansión de lechuzas, Los invasores,* and *Flores de papel,* I commented on three preoccupations in these plays: the need of the human animal to be loved, the destruction of the old (status quo) by the new, and Wolff's continuing exploration of our social reality and of the absurdity and lack of logic in what happens to human beings within this reality. I suggested that Wolff agrees with Beckett, Ionesco, and Pinter that our world is absurd and that we may already have lost the option of choice in the betterment of the human condition. I would expand these opinions, which I still hold to be true, to say that Wolff's overall preoccupation, as we see it in his work to date, can be stated in the simple theme of man's inhumaneness to man. His plays are an oblique plea—and a warning—for dignified and rational consideration for our fellow human beings. This is true whether the problem is sexist—as in *Niña-madre* and, possibly, *Flores de papel*—or social—as in *Flores de papel* and *Los invasores.* Two plays at least touch on indignities perpetrated within the family circle, where, supposedly, love should be most evident—*Mansión de lechuzas* and *Discípulos del miedo. El signo de Caín* demonstrates the cruelty and pain inflicted under the name of truth—pain that could be avoided were kindness and love the dominant motivating forces of man.

Wolff's plays present a roster of carefully and penetratingly drawn characters: Toletole, the appealing waif of *Los invasores*; the psychopathic el Merluza; Meyer, the bulwark of bourgeois stupidity; Matilde, steam-rolling her way over an entire family in her crushing climb up the social and economic ladder. Each of these characters is in some way deprived, crippled. Yet it is often difficult to discern the finely drawn line between victim and victimization. This acute perception of human reality is a result of Wolff's painful acquaintance with the human being. We are all cripples, all victims, and all victimizers. The world is illogical. Rational man is surrounded by chaos and destruction. The old is constantly changing—as it must—but it is moving, seemingly, toward a vacuum where love and dignity and beneficence cannot exist.

The eternal upheaval of man's surroundings varies from the painful to the unbearable, from one's personal pain to suffering beyond our comprehension. We know the frowns of people in a crowded street, and we try to know cataclysms like Vietnam and Bangladesh, though we are stupefied in the contemplation. In a less dramatic and less violent way, both Egon Wolff and Chile are caught up in the eternal crisis of change.[21] In response to an inquiry regarding his recent work, Wolff writes: "Once everything is again calm . . . there will be time to look at life as a spectator and to see it as history. Today we are too much the protagonists to be able to stop and think."[22] We await Wolff's return to the role of "spectator" of life. The Latin American theater has need of such voices.

NOTES

1. Egon Wolff to Margaret S. Peden, 15 January 1969, personal files. This and all subsequent translations are my own.

2. Ibid.

3. Domingo Piga T. and Orlando Rodríguez B., *Teatro chileno del siglo veinte* (Santiago, Chile: Publicaciones Escuela de Teatro, 1964), pp. 103–104.

4. Ibid., p. 104.

5. There are contemporary playwrights (one thinks of Emilio Carballido), whose interest in normal and abnormal psychology is readily apparent. In the best of these plays, however, "magical realism" is more the mode than the traditional psychological realism I referred to here.

6. Gabriela Mora, "Notas sobre el teatro chileno actual," *Revista Interamericana de Bibliografía* 18, no. 4 (October–December 1968): 419.

7. Egon Wolff to Margaret S. Peden, 10 October 1969, personal files.

8. Margaret S. Peden, in a paper read at the Kentucky Foreign Language Conference, Spring 1969, and later published as "Three Plays of Egon Wolff," *Latin American Theatre Review* 3, no. 1 (Fall 1969): 29–35.

9. *Sara*. (*On the stairs*) Mama! Mama! Mama! Come quickly! Papa's very sick. He says he wants to see you. Hurry!

(*Disappears.* Jorge *hastily follows her.* Matilde *is alone. She is standing, her fists clenched.*)

Matilde. Gone. All gone.

(Jorge *appears on the stairway, descends.*)

Jorge. (*Grave, emotional*) My father is dying, mama. He's waiting for you. (*He takes his hat from the hatrack*) I'm going for Ricardo. (*Exits*)

(Matilde *is alone. After a moment, the curtain falls.*)

[*El signo de Caín* and *Discípulos del miedo* (Santiago, Chile: Editores Ediciones Valores Literarios, 1971), p. 159]
10. *Matilde*. What have you brought me, Ricardo?

Ricardo. Just some things to eat. Where's Ester?

Matilde. Preparing dinner. And that plant, did you bring it for me?

Ricardo. Yes, mama.

(Ricardo *exits to kitchen*. Matilde *stops and kicks over the plant*.)

(Ricardo *enters when he hears the noise*.)

Matilde. I dropped it, son... I couldn't help it.   [Ibid., pp. 111–112]
11. *Niñamadre* (Santiago: Instituto Chileno-Norteamericano de Cultura, 1966), p. 6.
12. Juan Guerrero Zamora, *Historia del teatro contemporáneo* (Barcelona: J. Flors, 1967), pp. 557–559.
13. Frank Dauster, *Historia del teatro hispanoamericano: Siglos XIX y XX* (Mexico City: Ediciones de Andrea, 1966), p. 91. Gabriela Mora, in "Notas sobre el teatro chileno actual," has commented on the minor similarities between *Los invasores* and Max Frisch's *Biedermann und die Brandstifter* but concludes: "There are undeniable similarities; but, in our opinion, the work of the Chilean carries out, in a more direct and effective fashion than the Swiss writer, the fearful extermination of a conciliatory and deceitful bourgeoisie" (p. 420).
14. Leon Lyday, "Egon Wolff's *Los invasores*: A Play Within a Dream," *Latin American Theatre Review* 6, no. 1 (Fall 1972):19–26.
15. *Joaquín*. (*Takes his arm, confidentially*) What is Harry Haller? The beautiful life? The transcendental being? The liberated spirit? The mark of Cain?

Portus. You haven't forgotten, eh?

Joaquín. How could I forget? (*Declaims*) "There are men who bear the mark of Cain on their foreheads. The sign that others interpret and fear as the sign of evil, but which in truth is only the sign of a clear analytical mind, of an unquiet spirit, of men without fear."
                                                       [*El signo de Caín*, p. 31]
16. *Portus*. Get out of here! Go back to your Joaco and tell him his friend is a bum, whatever you want! I don't care. Just leave me and my woman alone!

Leonor. He knows all about it.

(Portus *looks at her, perplexed*.)

Joaco knows everything. The first time we came here, while we were still coming up those stairs, he kept reminding me not to say anything. "He needs all the help we can give him now," he told me. "Anyone can make one mistake."   [Ibid., p. 90]
17. ". . . a clear analytical mind, an unquiet spirit, a man without fear" (ibid., p. 32).
18. "Eva tries to speak, but she is not able. She gives up" (*Flores de papel, Tres obras de teatro* [Havana: Casa de las Américas, 1970], pp. 243–244).
19. "[El Merluza] places one of the enormous paper flowers in the neck of Eva's dress. It completely covers her face" (ibid., p. 245).
20. "They exit. Total chaos reigns now in the room. Nothing is as it was before. There is only the new beauty. The crude, enormous, almost-deformed paper flowers. Curtain" (ibid., p. 245).

21. This sentence was written following the peaceful "revolution" of the democratic election of Salvador Allende but before the unfortunate events of 1973.

22. Egon Wolff to Margaret S. Peden, 9 January 1972, personal files.

Part Two

Brazilian Dramatists

13. The Theater of Jorge Andrade

Richard A. Mazzara

Para se escrever sôbre um meio, é necessário senti-lo, até no sangue, e não poder viver nêle. Assim como, para escrever sôbre um ser humano, é necessário compreendê-lo, a ponto de amá-lo... e não poder fazer nada por êle às vêzes, nem suportá-lo.[1]

These words of Jorge Andrade have been repeated by his critics in evaluations of his work and most appropriately, for indeed he has lived and felt the subjects of his plays either directly, or by hearsay, study, and meditation; but in general he has written about them most objectively. Following Arthur Miller's advice—also repeated in several articles and introductions in Portuguese on Jorge Andrade's plays—and the inspiration of other world dramatists, he has recorded discrepancies between the concrete ability and aspirations of people whom he has observed since childhood. What follows is another introduction to Jorge Andrade's work, with analyses of his best-known plays.[2]

In 1951, during a performance of the Teatro Brasileiro de Comédia, Jorge Andrade felt a sudden vocation for the theater, first as an actor, but soon as a dramatist. He was to be the sensitive historian and understanding judge of a fast-disappearing society. He has become in every sense the first completely successful modern Brazilian playwright, doing for São Paulo what the novelists and dramatists of the northeast, and Erico Veríssimo in the south (whose attitudes and techniques are at times very close to those of Jorge Andrade), have been accomplishing for their regions, for Brazil, and for the world since the 1930s. That São Paulo should find its literary spokesman in the drama rather than the novel is probably due in part to the more active, extroverted, and particularly industrial-urban climate of the state and also to the nature of the theater, whose flowering often indicates the peak of a civilization, and which has begun, sporadically, to flower in Brazil only since the 1940s.

O Telescópio (1951, "The telescope," later revised)[3] is a one-act play in two scenes, with one basic set, whose action takes place within the space of a few hours. It shows the disintegration of a fazendeiro's family, in part because of incompatibility between city life, depicted as a corrupting force toward which some of the children gravitate, and the traditional family life of a fazenda ("plantation"). On the one hand, the children seem to be pitted against the parents and their contemporaries, and on the other they are pitted against each other, somewhat prematurely, for inheritance of the land. The parents are aging and tired yet still able to work hard to support the family. The handwriting is on the wall, however, and the crisis of *A Moratória* ("The moratorium") is approaching. Rita hopes that her children will awaken to responsibility and uphold tradition. More severe and realistic, Francisco has lost hope in his heirs, taking refuge in the study of astronomy and, through his telescope, visiting other worlds. The stars satisfy him intellectually and spiritually, and he loves to share his poetry with his wife and guests.

The children are contemptuous of this aspect of their father's life as of everything that their parents represent. Attitudes are crystallized in a masterful scene in which, in the living room, the heirs squabble over cards, revealing their rivalries, but also their animosities toward their elders, while on the veranda the latter escape into the past and to the stars. This counterpoint in space and time, literal and figurative, is dramatized by occasional exchanges in the otherwise separate dialogues of older and younger generations. For the time being the conflicts seem irreconcilable. Yet the tragic inevitability that the young will triumph over the old, regrettable though this may be, is symbolized in the destruction of the telescope by the older son as he returns home drunkenly, heedlessly.

A Moratória[4] (1954) is a play in three acts with two sets, and it demonstrates greater maturity. The subject is essentially a continuation of that of *O Telescópio*, both chronologically and thematically, but reflects considerable development of the author as a person and artist. Here, the slow, painful, and somehow inconclusive passage from one era to another is emphasized more sharply. Simultaneous use of two sets, one the *fazenda* in 1929, the other a city apartment in 1932, necessitates superior technical skills and literary sophistication for full realization and appreciation.

The play opens on the first level, that of the present (1932). The *fazendeiros* live in the city, eking out their existence as best they can, primarily on what the daughter, Lucília, earns as a seamstress. Her servitude and acceptance of harsh reality is symbolized concretely by the presence of a sewing machine whose whirring punctuates shifts from past to present. Joaquim exits, appearing soon thereafter on the second level (1929), in different attire but speaking of the need for rain for the coffee crop, which was the subject of the last remarks on level one. He converses further with Helena, his wife, on the falling price of coffee, on a sale that he has made on credit, and on a loan that he needs but refuses to ask of a wealthy relative. Helena exits, then Joaquim shouts to awaken his son Marcelo for a serious talk. Back in the present, Marcelo is still sleeping as Helena returns from church.

Physical and thematic liaisons thus bind the two levels very tightly and with marked, though varied, rhythm. The counterpoint becomes most pronounced as Helena finally begins to engage the charming Marcelo in semiserious conversation on level two (later continued on one and two), while on level one Joaquim and Lucília discuss Olímpio, now his lawyer and her former fiancé. Marcelo is to go to the city to invite Elvira to visit Helena. He will also recall Lucília who, against Joaquim's wishes, is with her aunt while taking a course in dress-making (social bias) and keeping company with Olímpio (political bias). Joaquim asks Lucília what progress Olímpio has made in obtaining the moratorium (on which Joaquim's hopes rest), and when they plan to marry. The obstacles to this marriage raised by Joaquim in the past and, as his attitudes change partially, those raised by Lucília in their present circumstances form another constant. A complementary exposition having been given on both levels, a crisis must similarly be developed on each at the close of act I.

On level one, Joaquim reads of the moratorium on debts of the economic crisis, and he and his daughter rejoice. The tragic situation in the past and the joy of the present are pitted one against the other simultaneously, leaving the spectator with mixed emotions, but only temporarily, for his hindsight causes him to anticipate tragedy in the future. Each line is at first developed in contrast with the other, the one in a minor key, the other in major-minor keys, in crescendo, to the end of act II. There, both come together in a single tragic climax: the *fazenda* is lost a first and a second time. The denouement is in diminuendo on both levels. For Lucília, there may be some hope with Olímpio, while all that seems to remain for the others is to pretend that they are back on the plantation.

Employing carefully selected situations, emotions, and language, which appear simple and natural without "naturalistic" triviality, the author solves the age-old problems of classical tragedy with Flaubertian precision. The entire, balanced action turns on the past and its influence on the present through the use of graphic reminiscences, which join the two times and places for the author and spectator, whereas the characters must rely on memory alone. With both the past (1929) and the fictional present (1932), we in the actual present have additional perspective historically and dramatically. Transitions from hope to despair on one level, underscored ironically or fatalistically on the other, grip the audience emotionally but also with the objectivity of art.

A *Moratória* has been greatly appreciated, if only by a relatively enlightened public within the limited circles of Brazilian theatergoers. Although influenced by Nelson Rodrigues's *Vestido de Noiva* ("Bridal gown") and Arthur Miller's *Death of a Salesman*, in A *Moratória* (as in the revised *Telescópio*) Jorge Andrade avoided the sensational and maintained authenticity both with his material and with his own deep though restrained feelings. Perhaps the subject was too pessimistically treated for São Paulo audiences, too local for others; perhaps the author was insufficiently objective for some sophisticates, insufficiently sentimental for still others; certainly the theme and artistry were too subtle for most. At any rate, with A *Moratória* Jorge Andrade began to acquire considerable reputation, albeit that of a somewhat too "intellectual" and "difficult" author.

This opinion was strengthened by *Pedreira das Almas*[5] (written in 1956–1957, later revised), which is less directly authentic and more ambitious artistically. In it, Jorge Andrade is inspired by the history of his *mineiro* forebears, epic heroes for *paulistas*, and his form and style are tragic. Experimentation with ancient tragedy and adaptation to Brazilian subjects had already been practiced in Pernambuco by Hermilo Borba Filho and Ariano Suassuna, whose works were perhaps known to Jorge Andrade. However, the heroic origins of the *fazendeiros* of São Paulo (and of his own family) had long interested the playwright. In historical and fictional time (1842), the subject of *Pedreira das Almas* precedes that of his first plays (1920s and 1930s), and the treatment given it is logically archaic. The author turned to the ancients more explicitly than in *A Moratória*, and, because of some similarity in theme, one is specifically reminded of *Antigone*. The action of the play, in two acts and four scenes or tableaux, takes place over a period of some two weeks, in one setting, and is very tightly knit. In the end, Pedreira das Almas is all but deserted, and the few persons remaining try to dissuade Mariana from staying. She has, however, taken over her mother's (Urbana's) role because of her promise to stay and her feelings of guilt at her mother's death and so that Urbana's sacrifice shall not be in vain. Gabriel, Mariana's fiancé, must lead the people to São Paulo for similar reasons, although the adventure has no meaning for him without Mariana. Urbana has been noble and generous to the living in her death and has at the same time gained control over them to serve the dead. Thus, the ancestors pave the way for succeeding generations, and their sacrifices deserve respect and commemoration.

Having thus vindicated through its ancestors a society whose demise he had begun to record, Jorge Andrade now turned to another class of that society, the tenant farmers. *A Vereda da Salvação*[6] ("Way of salvation"; written in 1957, produced in 1964) has as its point of departure a true incident in Catulé, Malacacheta, Minas Gerais, the details and analyses of which the playwright studied most carefully. During the long period of revision, Jorge Andrade reconsidered the events, the theatrical and public criticism of his work, but chiefly his intimate knowledge of the lower class of his own *fazenda* and later meditations on the human condition. In *O Telescópio* and *A Moratória* the family is all-important, and in *Pedreira das Almas* the group is stressed, but *Vereda* emphasizes the collective. The masses are prone to accept religious demagoguery to escape their misery, perhaps to encounter a greater disaster in the end. More than ever, the new *Vereda da Salvação* is neither *mineiro* nor *paulista*, but Brazilian and universal. In fact, it has enjoyed long successful runs in Poland, where it was produced in the translation of the great Ziembinsky. Its success may be attributed to political overtones, but the author concentrates on philosophical and aesthetic purity rather than on any propagandistic thesis. Fanaticism has often been treated in Brazilian literature, yet seldom prior to

Vereda da Salvação with Andrade's insistence on collective action, for better as well as worse, and seldom with his powerful voice of protest and poetry. The individual may face reality squarely and save himself in the midst of general disintegration. The family may derive a certain valid inspiration from its forebears, and the group may thus find new frontiers to conquer. Without sound guidance, however, one may easily lose one's way. This is the thematic progression from the realistic *A Moratória* to the epic *Pedreira* to the more classic spirit and form of tragedy of *A Vereda da Salvação*. A new Passion play, *Vereda* does not repeat a myth but creates one by distillation of recent sociopsychological data whose tradition, too, is both recognizable and novel. The horror of the deeds of real-life figures is tempered by verisimilitude and decorum, according to which Jorge Andrade's creatures become touching, sympathetic, tragic.

In its definitive version, *Vereda* is compressed into two acts having greater impact and unity of action within a single though diversified setting and brief period of time. All action is confined to the narrow world of the tenant farmers on a *fazenda* and is presented from their point of view, in language that is stylized for the audience's comprehension but derived from their speech. They are largely an anonymous mass, in their world as well as on the outside, and the limitation of time prevents delineation of all but the principal characters upon which the whole structure depends. Far more than environmental determinants, it is the human factors that matter, thematically and formally. Joaquim, assuming spiritual leadership during the patriarch's absence, vents his many frustrations on Manoel, who is the temporal leader, Manoel's mistress Artuliana, and the others. His weaknesses, however, become strengths in the eyes of the tenants. Artuliana opposes him, but her unborn child is destroyed by her own mother's denunciation and the action of their neighbors under his command. Manoel's authority undermined now in every way, he, too, accepts Joaquim's weakness as a sign of grace or divinity. Joaquim begins to acquire stature in his own eyes and in ours, for, despite the repeated infanticides and mounting hysteria of act II (reminiscent of Arthur Miller's *The Crucible*), he does in a sense purify his people and himself (which is not the case of the witch hunters in *The Crucible*).

The second half of the play is clearly dominated by Joaquim, then, who delivers his people from evil and bondage. Dolor, Joaquim's mother and the only character created entirely by Jorge Andrade, is the other principal of act II. She has opposed her son in order to protect him on rational, practical bases, but gradually she realizes that he has passed the bounds of reason. She now defends him on irrational but equally practical grounds in a new context. She is undeniably a *mater dolorosa*; perhaps she deserves the title of *Maria das Purezas* conferred by her son. Although evil technically resides in her as the unwed mother of many and in Joaquim as her only surviving (and unconsciously incestuous) son, have they not been purified by much suffering? Does their sole joy not stem from Joaquim's desire to die a new Christ on a cross that all have borne during their whole lives? And is their sole hope not that of ascending into Heaven with him? After the public confessions and assumption of biblical names by Joaquim's congregation, one is prone to believe, but with Dolor's ambivalence. To underscore this, the author eliminated the third act of his earlier version, lengthening the first two in order to have the end of the play coincide on one level of understanding, with the ascension or effort literally to fly to Heaven.

Dolor's reproach to Ana for abandoning the circle of tenant farmers and for having called in the *fazendeiro* and the police, representatives of all that is rational and yet unjust, emphasizes in a masterful scene the bankrupt society that can bring physical but not spiritual defeat to its masses. The massacre of the tenants by the police, who remain offstage, is simultaneous with their attempted flight. One might suspect that Joaquim would fail to ascend with his people— as he did at the close of act II in the earlier version of the work—but this failure is prevented by death. On another level of understanding, then, an evil cause may have a good effect. Like Dias Gomes in *O Pagador de Promessas* (*Payment as Pledged*) and other plays, Jorge Andrade has found the perfect tragic conclusion with its characteristic note of triumph in defeat.

Despite many similarities in theme between *A Moratória* and *A Escada* ("The staircase"), the latter is sufficiently different in subject, form, and attitudes to warrant considerable discussion.[7] The two works deal basically with the same class, the ex-*fazendeiros* who, although usually upper-middle class in their natural habitat in the country, seem to belong more to the aristocracy in the city. The crucial distinction is concern with still valid socioeconomic traditions versus sterile preoccupation with the trappings of this society.

A Moratória treats both aspects of this class, but *A Escada* deals only with the second. And while Jorge Andrade understands the former thoroughly, he is physically removed from the latter and quite uninvolved. This, as well as the subject, makes for a simpler objectivity and a certain superficiality, accentuated by a more panoramic form and relatively large numbers of characters. The setting, while always the same, is a simultaneous one, with the stairway, central figures, and family relationships uniting the four apartments and their occupants. It seems appropriate to compare *A Moratória* to Erico Veríssimo's *O Tempo e o Vento* ("Time and the wind"), for example, in which counterpoint in time is more significant than in space, and *A Escada* to *Caminhos Cruzados* ("Crossroads"), in which many characters and places are emphasized. The latter are tours de force, while the former are more subtle and penetrating. Conflicts in attitudes, both between the plays and in *A Escada*, are crystallized in a figure familiar also to readers of Veríssimo, that of the writer-son-of-the-family who is, of course, the author's mouthpiece. His emotions remain mixed, however, and he cannot break completely with tradition, as does the granddaughter who marries the mulatto in *A Escada*.

Chief points of criticism are centered in the old couple, Amélia and Antenor, and their oldest son, Francisco. The old people's prejudices might have tragic significance were they not so ludicrous in their unconscious exaggeration (especially Antenor's) and so pathetic in their automatous repetition (especially Amélia's). They are senile, as is everything that they represent. Their clinging to glories and possessions of the past is both irritating and touching, but becomes intolerable when their son begins to take it all seriously. This side of Francisco is developed only to provide the climax of the crisis in act III but is corrected soon enough to keep the play uncontroversial. What is useless and harmful in the past is and should remain irrevocably past.

This is not to say that the modern types are without their faults, many of them reminiscent of defects of character found in *O Telescópio* and *A Moratória*. There is the granddaughter whose engagement has been broken by the grandparents' interference, and who, like Lucília, works furiously at her knitting to earn a living but also to punish her family. Sons are likely to be too charming and carefree. There are loving, dedicated wives and mothers but intolerant, weak husbands and fathers. While the old people bring out the worst in their children during rotating visits to the four apartments, they serve also to excuse them. They are both the cause and the victims of all their faults. They can no longer help their children but must be helped by them. As roles are gradually reversed, painful, violent crises are inevitable until the new idea is accepted by all, and Amélia and Antenor are sent to a home. It is the only solution possible and a welcome one, even to the old people. Yet it is a familiar one also, and sad, because everyone must eventually repeat the process.

Os Ossos do Barão[8] clearly deals with the solution of some contemporary socioeconomic problems, albeit on an individual level. The growth of São Paulo depends on the alliance of the old aristocracy with the vigorous descendants of immigrants. The former have created Brazilian history, and their traditions are important. But the latter's new blood and money are needed to preserve and continue them. As usual, especially since *Pedreira das Almas*, Jorge Andrade presents two seemingly irreconcilable points of view and attempts to find a satisfactory compromise. The complement of characters is accordingly well balanced on both sides: Miguel, Verônica, and Izabel (with the old aunts and uncle as a pendant) are the aristocrats; Egisto, Bianca, and Martino are the immigrant family, augmented by Izabel and little Egisto, who is the result and assurance of the sometimes precarious compromise. Here, however, instead of tragic means the author has used those of classical comedy and of Molière. Necessarily, for the plot is a slim one, the author has employed considerable variety in his comedy, including transparent scenes of *dépit amoureux* and serious *comédie larmoyante*.

Although there is satire and sentimentality, the subject is essentially a delicate one, and extremes of caricature and inverisimilitude are avoided. Face is saved for aristocrats obsessed with genealogies in the audience through the obviously humorous pedantry of those in the play, who, though encouraged by Egisto, are counterbalanced by Tia Ismália from among their ranks. While his machinations are plebian in the extreme, Egisto's basic honesty and thoroughly honorable intentions make him a sympathetic character. Modern young people cannot be expected to fall in love on their parents' request. Yet Izabel and Martino do want to break down their respective walls "of the dead" and "of machinery," for which the author permits them a decent period of rebellion (onstage) and accommodation (offstage). He then presents them in act III about to christen their first son and complete the synthesis physically and symbolically, which is the honorable and practical solution to the problem.

Products of the classical method used by Jorge Andrade to create characters, those of *Os Ossos do Barão* are types, comic in this case and so even less individualized than other creations of his. Chief among the characters of this play are Miguel and Egisto. The former is the representative *par excellence* of the four-hundred-year-old aristocracy of São Paulo, his full ancestry containing the essence of the sixteen families that came over on the Brazilian counterpart of the *Mayflower*. Egisto, on the other hand, is the epitome of the Italian immigrant who has struck it rich in São Paulo and influenced the state and city in every cultural detail. (Witness the flavor of the Portuguese heard in São Paulo, a pidgin form of which is used with the age-old comic effect of dialect by Egisto and Bianca throughout the play.) Unlikely though their fellowship may seem at first glance, the economic factor—the old need to *redorer le blason*—makes their association inevitable for the aristocrat, while the psychological factor, the need to be assimilated, drives the immigrant. Practical as he is, Jorge Andrade, through Egisto, has a financial arrangement precede family ties. However, Egisto has not only bought, but also in every way earned, the right to have his bones repose one day with those of his former master, the Baron, through hard work, shrewdness, and, above all, good will. He sincerely wishes to restore what the aristocrats have allowed to slip through their fingers. As has been pointed out, winning over the aristocrat is a delicate operation. Characteristic of Jorge Andrade's realistic women, Miguel's opportunistic wife and emancipated daughter, as well as the earthy Bianca and practical Ismália, assist Egisto in forming a new nobility to guide the great destiny of São Paulo. Thus, *Os Ossos do Barão* is another in the episodes dealing with the history of São Paulo *fazendeiros* so dear to Jorge Andrade.

Although completed by 1963, *Senhora na Bôca do Lixo* ("Lady in the trash") was staged and published only in 1968.[9] In this play Jorge Andrade continues to trace the sociological history of São Paulo. Noêmia is the aristocratic woman, unable and unwilling to adapt to reduced economic status, who is often found in other works by Andrade. Her escape into the glorious past is made possible by a refined form of smuggling; like so many Brazilians of her class, she is disdainful of her culture and must travel in search of the elegance she craves. Noêmia is supported by more affluent aristocrats, or *nouveaux riches*, who purchase the luxury items that she imports as "objects of personal use." Indeed, wealthy Brazilians are well organized to perpetuate their way of life at the expense of the government and the democracy. This is the *lixo* ("trash" or "garbage") in the midst of which Noêmia, in a semiconscious way, finds herself. The lower classes, generally little represented in Andrade's plays, are presented in dramatic contrast to Noêmia, whose attitude and actions contribute to their particular form of *lixo*.

Caught between the two social extremes are Camila, Noêmia's daughter, and Hélio, the police officer in charge of contraband and Camila's coworker and boyfriend. The latter is a member of the *petit fonctionnaire* class, incarnating its morality, desirable but intransigent. Camila, the typical aristocratic girl found in many Andrade plays, has been obliged to face economic reality and earn her family's living; she has joined Hélio's class willingly but cannot entirely reject her mother and background. For these two, Noêmia's situation, with all its ramifications, is or becomes a personalized, painful moral issue.

At the outset, Camila and Noêmia are found in a setting and situation reminiscent of the *drame bourgeois*, with comic overtones in the figures of Noêmia's friends and, later, the "French Decorator," Simon. Problems, exposed or foreshadowed in references to Noêmia's activities and to Camila's job and boyfriend, are first dramatized by the appearance of another of Camila's coworkers, Carmem. She is an interesting blend of frank *soubrette* and modern working girl. After Simon's explanation to Noêmia of the organization of upper-class smugglers, there is further drama with the entrance of Hélio to seize the contraband and arrest Noêmia, who suspects that he is Camila's boyfriend. At the end of act I Hélio is nearly comic, for he does not know that Noêmia is the mother of the proper girl who has never allowed him to escort her home. His devotion both to principle and to Camila, coupled with frustration on all sides, will make him almost a Cornelian hero.

Acts II and III are filled with contrasts of all sorts: what the police headquarters are now and what the building still represents to Noêmia; the latter's predicament and that of the poor wretches at the mercy of their conditions; sociopolitical favoritism in the case of *a senhora* and injustice in punishing the lower classes; and Noêmia's escapism and incomprehension, together with her deliberate snobbery and efforts at blackmail. Above all, the idealism of Hélio and Camila comes into conflict with the harsh realities of society, politics, and love. This, then, is the more conventional type of counterpoint used in *Senhora na Bôca do Lixo*.

Act II deals with the discoveries on the part of the chief characters, brought about partially by Garcia, the somewhat cynical believer in compromise. Hélio has arrested Noêmia and, although he was unaware of her identity, would arrest her again. Camila needs proof that Hélio has not used her, and, in turn, offers proof that she has not used him by denouncing her mother, much as Corneille's heroine (for whom her mother named her) denounced Rome to prove her love.

Act III provides a tragic-triumphant solution for a tragic dilemma. Like Rodrigue or Horace, Hélio wants to believe that love can be reconciled to duty; but, again like her classical counterpart, Camila renounces devotion to futile principles in favor of love and continues her efforts to find a practicable way of life. She persuades Hélio to follow her and the shaken but unregenerate Noêmia. It is not the most satisfactory solution, but to admit defeat in one direction and seek victory in another is modern, realistic, and not entirely tragic. If these comparisons may be extended to Cornelian drama—although the setting here is contemporary, and there is a mixture of the comic and the serious—the basic concept is not unlike Corneille's on tragedy (or tragicomedy). While the world about us wallows in garbage, the best that we can do is to avoid contamination and strive to be pure.[10]

This moral lesson applies more or less equally to *Rasto Atrás*, which advances in accomplishment the increasingly important theater of Jorge Andrade. This play is based on the author's most personal experiences and is more frankly autobiographical than any work of his to date.[11] Artistically, it is a synthesis of his previous works, incorporating as they do influences from world theater, but it is nevertheless most original and a landmark in the Brazilian theater.

The action of *Rasto Atrás* extends from 1922 (the year of Jorge Andrade's birth) to 1965, and the author-protagonist is shown at ages five, fifteen, twenty-three, and forty-three. The play represents the final stage in a series of emotional struggles on the part of the author, in general from work to work, but specifically with respect to *Rasto Atrás*, dating from 1957. His effort has been to make a sentimental journey back in time in order to resolve conflicts with himself and between himself and his father. The journey in *Rasto Atrás* is made both spatially and temporally; the graphic element—props are mainly suggested with various audio-visual effects—complements the flashback, which, in addition to providing background, depicts the mental probings of the author. Thus, the title has several meanings, literal and symbolic, crystallized in Vicente's father's explanation of backtracking in hunting, except that, in *Rasto Atrás*, the process leads to an encounter between hunter and hunted. The deeper meanings, social and psychological, are further exemplified in the author's choice of an epigraph from the writings of Eça de Queiroz and in the dedication to his father. More than ever, theme and structure are one, epitomizing the counterpoint in space and time so typical of Jorge Andrade and of modern literature.

Essential information on Vicente as a famous dramatist is given in scenes between him and his wife. His problems are not only individual but also general, for they are those of all Brazilian intellectuals since 1964—problems caused by inflation and the political situation. Vicente speaks, for example, of a theatrical failure (Andrade's *Vereda da Salvação*, an international success), of the need to support his family by teaching (admittedly one of Andrade's most rewarding human experiences), of a number of his plays awaiting an impresario, and of television, with its frequent prostitution of art (he alludes particularly to an adaptation of *Os Ossos do Barão*, which was rejected by Andrade). Other autobiographical details of the artist Vicente-Jorge have been (and will continue to be) reworked from version to version, not the least of which pertains to the typical attitude of the Brazilian male toward art as an effeminate occupation. This, of course, is the chief basis of the hostility between Vicente-Jorge and his father. Only after many years of searching, when the dramatist has justified his existence by success, can he be reconciled with himself and others; for, to be fully justified, he requires the approval of the father whose name he rejected (Jorge Andrade's paternal surname is Franco).

In order to prepare his audience for the final tragic-triumphant encounter between father and son in the most concise dramatic fashion, Andrade presents a series of flashbacks showing the two at several decisive moments in their lives, sometimes simultaneously. These free associations are made possible through the memories of the protagonist and his father. The five-year-old boy's imagination and sensitivity already come into conflict with João José's consuming love of hunting. At fifteen, the adolescent's budding interest in art is understood only by an aunt, and he attempts to leave home for São Paulo. At twenty-three, after a terrible scene with his father, Vicente breaks his engagement to his childhood sweetheart, following which he finally departs for the big city. The points of similarity between Vicente's life and Jorge's are numerous.

There are several differences, however, due in part to the process of artistic selection and transformation. Vicente's aunts, the chief characters of an earlier version in which he did not appear, were not Jorge Andrade's aunts, but neighbors, friends of his grandmother. Vicente's grandmother, Mariana, figures prominently in *Rasto Atrás* as the strong matriarch that the author's grandmother in fact was; she is to be found in his earlier plays, too. The three friends become her daughters in this work, and their father in the earlier version, reminiscent of Joaquim in *A Moratória*, is now Vicente's father.

Not only characters but also situations are transformed from real life and other plays, yet there is always evidence of Jorge Andrade's desire to study and clarify his "people" and society. His first works focused on the coffee crisis in São Paulo in 1929, making only the vaguest references to events leading up to it. Subsequent plays similarly treated immediate problems. *Rasto Atrás* gives antecedents and consequences with greater precision, always in language appropriate to character and intent. The psychological, particularly personal, aspects of the play far outweigh its documentary value; nonetheless, this latter value is an important one in the Andrade canon.

The recently published collection, *Marta, a Arvore e o Relógio*, is a very interesting one from several points of view.[12] Not only does it contain two new plays, which will form the basis of most of the remainder of this study, but also it presents Jorge Andrade's major works in an historicofictional chronology to create his full cycle of São Paulo, rather than according to the chronology of writing. Thus, the newest play, As Confrarias ("The confraternities"), is the first in the collection, and O Sumidouro ("The underground river"), long in progress and the second newest, is the last play in the series. The other eight plays are inserted between these two in more or less fictional order and not in the order in which they were written or as they have been studied here. In addition to having internal unifying devices, some of which have been noted, the works are unified externally by means of a prefatory poem by the author and an impressionistic photograph preceding each play along with an epigraph taken from Carlos Drummond de Andrade's "O Fazendeiro do Ar" ("Rancher in the air").

The title, comprised of symbols that recur throughout the series of plays, much as in Erico Veríssimo's trilogy O Tempo e o Vento, is itself most significant. The central figure in As Confrarias, Marta, or her namesakes and reincarnations, is alluded to or makes brief appearances in several plays and represents the realistic woman who is the backbone of the nation, to judge by the works of Andrade, Veríssimo, and others in Brazilian as in world literature generally. In the same play, Martiniano—another of Jorge Andrade's reappearing characters—introduces the clock that will symbolize the passage or stoppage of time, among other things, in "subsequent" plays. The tree appears for the first time also in As Confrarias. It will represent much in the other works, suggesting paulista genealogy and especially the strength of tradition, which may be a refuge but whose force may strangle those who cannot or will not break with it.

His latest plays fulfill Jorge Andrade not only as an artist but also as an individual and member of his society, past and present. Tendencies of his earlier work are continued and draw him closer to his compatriots and fellow artists. The historical approach, perhaps for reasons of security and, without doubt, more for reasons of sharper analogy than of greater objectivity, is typical of many Brazilian playwrights. One thinks, for example, of Dias Gomes and Borba Filho.[13] The creation of historicolegendary figures and use of baroque-expressionistic devices, such as the play-within-the-play, trompe-l'oeil, and various metamorphoses, are as characteristic of world literature today as similar techniques discussed above.[14]

As Confrarias comprises four basic units, with numerous flashbacks, whose staging recalls the medieval simultaneous approach but is accomplished by modern techniques. Each unit consists of a confrontation between Marta and one of four religious confraternities, during which the lives of Marta and her family are gradually revealed by means of dialogue, narrative, and past action. At the same time, panoramic views are unfolded of the cruel history of Minas Gerais at the end of the eighteenth century, including the rebellion of the

Inconfidência, and Brazilian racial and class struggles that obtain to the present. As in *Pedreira das Almas*, the theme resembles that of *Antigone*, except that Urbana wishes to bury her son while Marta, in fact, does not. Seemingly unnatural, Marta seeks to avenge the execution of her husband, also left unburied, as well as of José, by parading the latter's decomposing corpse before the different strata of society represented by the confraternities. Included in her vengeance is the desire to expose the corruption of this society and to reform it, which is the author's intent with respect to contemporary society in this as in other plays. It has become increasingly clear to Jorge Andrade and his audience that the dead must help bury the dead, and this conclusion must initiate and inform the entire cycle, which is dedicated to the living and to future generations.

For several reasons it is significant that the second most important character in *As Confrarias* is an actor, Marta's son José, who is alive in the flashbacks. Contrary to the wishes of his mother, whose background is somewhat mysterious and for whom the land represents security, but with the approval of his father, who loves the land passionately, José sets out to make his way in the world. He has become an actor when his father's death and hard times cause Marta to join him and his mistress. By this time the mother has changed and finds that the son is not fulfilling himself or justifying his existence adequately. She makes him her instrument to arouse the downtrodden masses, but as an actor he must stir himself by playing either Beaumarchais's Figaro or Almeida Garrett's Cato. Yet these roles are too intellectual for the people, as Marta repeatedly informs José and as the playwright informs us. As Diderot would have it, the perception of roles by actor and spectator must be reversed. This is not only the *paradoxe du comédien* ("paradox of the actor") but also of every artist and free man in more than one sense. The artist is easily a pariah, a "mulatto" in the context of *As Confrarias*, belonging to no group yet identifying with and torn between both "black" and "white." When he dies, he can be buried only in unconsecrated and therefore free ground.

More explicitly biographical than *As Confrarias* and not so obviously similar to it in structure, *O Sumidouro* appears most closely to resemble *Rasto Atrás* in both these respects. Yet this last play in the series joins (and even precedes) the first as much as it does the next to the last, as has already been indicated. The principal characters of *As Confrarias* have many points of contact with the dramatist Vicente-Jorge thematically, and the work's diverse structural elements and literary qualities bring it very close to *O Sumidouro* as well as to other works in the cycle.

O Sumidouro is in two parts, and, although the literal scene is always Vicente's study in the present, the time and scene shift between present and past with the aid of the narrator's imagination and modern staging techniques. Unlike *Rasto Atrás*, however, the past is an epic one, re-created by Vicente and related by him to his professional and personal life chiefly through his interpretations of Fernão Dias and his sons, the famous *bandeirantes* and emerald hunters of São Paulo, and other historic personages of the seventeenth century. The objectivization of the modern epic theater causes the character, in this case Fernão Dias, to reflect not only his supposed understanding of his life but also an awareness of posterity's understanding of his role in history, much as modern novelistic devices complement the traditional view of the omniscient author, the better to free the reader in time and space. Here, the conventions of the epic play and novel are somewhat reversed, but the effect is the same, to make them superior to the linear historical work by providing more than one perspective. The difference is clear in *O Sumidouro* when, for example, figures of the court of Portugal are conjured up by Vicente and confronted by him and Fernão Dias, but only these two are aware of the confrontation.

Like Fernão Dias, Vicente-Jorge has a compulsion to search, to fulfill himself, to attain glory, except that his compulsion extends to discovering completely what he is, why, and for whom. He forces this comprehensive existential view on Fernão Dias as he re-creates the character, writes his play, and learns more about himself through the process, teaching his audience all the while. Vicente-Jorge must continually seek the truth in the past, in others, and in himself, realizing that, without many perspectives on the truth, he will betray the wife who "has taught him to bury the dead" (as Fernão Dias has betrayed his), and he will "hang" his son on the "tree" (as his own father almost "hanged" him, and as Fernão Dias literally hanged João José, his Mameluke bastard whose truth was a partial one but at least as valid as that of his father). Further, the artist will enslave himself and his audiences if he does not discover and provide all the truth possible in the most complete art possible. One need not sink in *O Sumidouro*, but, by plumbing the depths of the river, replenished and refreshed, one can succeed in swimming it.

NOTES

Very substantial portions of this essay have appeared as two articles: "The Theatre of Jorge Andrade," *Latin American Theatre Review* 1, no. 1 (Fall 1967): 3–18; and "Jorge Andrade's Newest Plays," *Latin American Theatre Review* 2, no. 1 (Fall 1968): 49–52. Other portions have been used in a paper, "The Most Recent Theatre of Jorge Andrade," read in the Luso-Brazilian section of the Pacific Northwest Conference on Foreign Languages, 20 April 1974, and to appear in the Proceedings of the PNCFL. Much of the research and writing were subsidized by a National Defense Education Act grant, Franklin and Marshall College, the American Philosophical Society, the Organization of American States, the Social Science Research Council, and Oakland University.

1. "In order to write about a milieu, one must feel it in one's blood and be unable to live in it. Just as to write about a human being it is necessary to understand him, to the point

of loving him—and be unable to do anything for him, or even put up with him" (my translation).

2. In Portuguese one may profitably consult, among others, Sábato Magaldi, *Panorama do Teatro Brasileiro* (São Paulo: Difusão Européia do Livro, 1962), pp. 212–219; and Delmiro Gonçalves, "Drama do Café Encontrou seu Autor," *Visão*, 19 June 1964, pp. 20–23.

Three unpublished or unproduced plays by Jorge Andrade exist on which there is little or no information: *O Faqueiro de Prata* (1954, "The silver cutler," later revised as *As Colunas do Templo*, "The columns of the temple"); *Os Vínculos* (1960, "The bonds"), written in collaboration with Clô Prado, apparently a bid for "commercial" success; and *O Incêndio* (1962, "The fire"), another plea for social and political justice, based on a true incident in Paraná.

3. *Pedreira das Almas* ("Quarry of souls") and *O Telescópio* (Rio de Janeiro: Agir, 1960), introduction by Paulo Mendonça.

4. *A Moratória* (Rio de Janeiro: Agir, 1959), introduction by Décio de Almeida Prado. See also the latter's *Apresentação do Teatro Brasileiro Moderno: Crítica Teatral, 1947–1955* (São Paulo: Livraria Martins Editôra, 1956), pp. 143–151.

5. See note 3.

6. *A Vereda da Salvação* (São Paulo: Editôra Brasiliense, 1965), preface by Antônio Cândido, introduction by Sábato Magaldi.

7. *A Escada* and *Os Ossos do Barão* ("The bones of the baron") (São Paulo: Editôra Brasiliense, 1964), introductions by Décio de Almeida Prado and Sábato Magaldi.

8. See note 7.

9. *Senhora na Bôca do Lixo: Peça em três atos* (Rio de Janeiro: Civilização Brasileira, 1968).

10. In his recent collection of plays, old and new, entitled *Marta, a Arvore e o Relógio* ("Martha, the tree, and the clock") (São Paulo: Editôra Perspectiva, 1970), Jorge Andrade has provided the play with a more purely tragic ending, much in the manner of Tennessee Williams. Camila and Hélio are engulfed in Noêmia's and Garcia's cynicism and escapism. Camila is overwhelmed by the situation, while Hélio will attempt a new life, free of corruption but without Camila. He thus becomes a stronger hero. Although not necessarily weaker, Camila is now still more in line with other stoical heroines of Jorge Andrade, who devote themselves to tradition and family rather than to passion, or certainly to higher causes. The author's new solution is more characteristic of his pessimistic vein as historian of a decadent society; yet the Cornelian overtones with regard to Hélio are far from abandoned.

An interesting touch in this version is the clear reference at the end (p. 336) to the events that occur at the conclusion of *A Vereda da Salvação*. This reentry, so to speak, analogous to the use of reappearing characters and similar unifying devices in Balzac and many other authors, serves here to justify in a broader social as well as personal context Hélio's revulsion with society and his determination to start afresh.

As a collection of new plays, as well, *Marta, a Arvore e o Relógio* will receive further treatment below. The volume also includes a number of useful studies by various critics.

11. *Rasto Atrás: Peça em 2 partes* ("Backtracking: Play in two parts") (São Paulo: Editôra Brasiliense, 1967), preface by Delmiro Gonçalves. This play took first place in the 1966 National Theater Service Prize Contest in Brazil. See Sábato Magaldi, "A Procura de Rasto Atrás," *Comentário*, First Quarter, 1968, pp. 42–50.

12. See note 10.

13. See Richard A. Mazzara, "Alfredo Dias Gomes, Social Commentator and Artist," *Latin American Theatre Review* 2, no. 2 (Spring 1969): 41–59; and "Hermilo Borba Filho's

A *Donzela Joana* and the Brazilianization of Joan of Arc," Ball State University *Forum* 11 (Autumn 1970): 27–32.

14. In addition to the articles cited in note 13, see Richard A. Mazzara, "The Hope of God's Kingdom on Earth in Seventeenth-Century French Tragedy," Ball State University *Forum* 7 (Autumn 1966): 23–26.

14. The Theater of Alfredo Dias Gomes

Leon F. Lyday

"Essayer of many types, master of most" is the statement that perhaps best characterizes the Brazilian playwright Alfredo Dias Gomes to date. Essential to this description, and thus worthy of repetition, is the qualifier "to date," for his is clearly a theater in progress, a theater that continues to evolve. Nonetheless, he must even now be ranked along with Jorge Andrade as Brazil's foremost contemporary dramatists.[1]

Born in Bahia in 1922, Dias Gomes soon revealed literary vocation and by the early fifties had written and published several novels and had written ten plays: *Pé-de-Cabra* ("The crowbar"); *Amanhã Será Outro Dia* ("Tomorrow's another day"); *Sulamita* (later retitled *Doutor Ninguém*, "Doctor Nobody"); *Zeca Diabo* ("Joe Devil"); *Um Pobre Gênio* ("An unfortunate genius"); *João Cambão* ("John Cambão"); *Os Cinco Fugitivos do Juizo Final* ("The five fugitives from the Day of Judgment"); *Sinhazinha* ("Missy"); *Eu Acuso o Céu* ("I accuse heaven"); and *O Homem Que Não Era Seu* ("The man who wasn't his own master").[2]

The first of these works, *Pé-de-Cabra*, was summarily prohibited by the censors and freed only after many cuts in the text. Flávio Rangel cites as the principal reason for this censorship the fact that "the play dealt with the reactions of a group of workers on strike, and the general opinion of the impresarios of the period was that 'blacks must be servants' (the point or allegation which brought about the strike), and that the public 'would not accept a working-class hero'" (I, 122). The impresario who staged *Sulamita* had the color of its protagonist changed from black to white in an act of self-censorship, and the play's title, as mentioned above, was changed to *Doutor Ninguém* at that time (I, 122). Two hallmarks of Dias Gomes's theater, his concern for treating aspects of Brazilian reality and his consequent difficulties with censorship and theater impresarios, thus are to be found very early in his career.

Refusing to conform to tastes and topical limitations imposed on the theater in Brazil through much of the 1950s, Dias Gomes turned to radio and television for his livelihood. However, as other playwrights, among them Jorge Andrade and Gianfrancesco Guarnieri, began to experience some success in staging works that realistically portrayed Brazilian society, his interest in the stage was rekindled, and he began to write for it once again.

The first fruit of this new phase of Dias Gomes's literary career was *O Pagador de Promessas* (*Payment as Pledged*), and its unparalleled success at home and abroad vaulted him to national prominence as a playwright. First performed in 1960, *O Pagador* has been translated into at least a half-dozen languages and presented in many different countries. The play has also been the recipient of numerous national prizes, and the film version was awarded the Gold Palm at the 1962 Cannes Festival.

In three acts, *O Pagador* takes place on the series of steps leading to a church and spans a period of about twelve hours. Its plot concerns the quest of a simple farmer, Zé-do-Burro, to comply with the promise he has made to a saint. The central theme is the uphill struggle of the individual for true personal freedom in a capitalist society or, as the playwright himself has stated, "the myth of capitalist liberty" (I, 9). This theme, a recurring one in Dias Gomes's theater, is closely related to two others: the problem of communication, in the existentialist sense, and that of intolerance, particularly religious intolerance, in modern society.

The play has many strengths and few weaknesses. Principal among the latter is the fact that the key minor characters are not consistently well drawn and that the motivations for their actions, especially those of Zé's wife, are at times questionable. Rosa, however, can herself be considered a kind of *pagadora de promessas* in that, by being unfaithful to Zé, she is guilty of breaking a promise and ultimately must suffer the consequences. This broken promise, which exemplifies well her physical and moral weakness, is in counterpoint to Zé's constancy and strength, and the contrast heightens the conflict in the play.

Ironically, the play's strongest point also relates to characterization, for the two major figures, Zé-do-Burro and Padre Olavo, the local parish priest, are quite skillfully depicted. Zé, although a poor, ignorant farmer, is a tragic hero in many respects. His struggle to keep his pledge is a valiant one, and his almost irrational stubbornness could be considered a tragic flaw. Even his death, which comes in a struggle with police who are attempting to remove him from the church steps, is the unpremeditated demise of the hero rather than the conscious sacrifice of the martyr. The willful priest, every bit as intransigent as Zé, stands as the play's principal antagonist, and although Dias Gomes describes him as the symbol of universal rather than merely religious intolerance, the priest's attitude and actions constitute a rather caustic commentary on the fanaticism sometimes found in representatives of the church (I, 9–10).

The carefully elaborated plot of *O Pagador* is basically in the mold of classical tragedy, both in its observance of the so-called traditional unities and in its denouement.[3] Yet another strength of the play is the adroitness with which the dramatist parallels the "Afro-Catholic syncretism"[4] that characterizes the religious views of Zé and several other characters with a similar syncretism in setting and symbol. The play takes place on the steps of a church, but on the day set aside to honor Iansan, the *candomblé* counterpart of the Catholic Santa Bárbara. Symbolically, Zé is shown to be something of a Christ figure, but the huge clap of thunder that resounds at his death could come from the Christian God or, as Richard Mazzara suggests, from Iansan herself.[5]

O Pagador, then, with compelling plot, carefully elaborated structure, and a protagonist who is almost certainly the most memorable character of all Brazilian drama, deservedly ranks as one of the best plays of that country's theatrical tradition.

The tragic mold involving an individual protagonist, used in *O Pagador* and one of his later plays, is handled by Dias Gomes with great success. Not quite so successful is his *A Invasão* ("The invasion"), first staged in 1962. This play, while retaining certain elements of tragedy, differs radically from *O Pagador* in that its protagonist is collective rather than individual, and also because there is no true climax but rather an ending that, through the *tranche de vie* technique used in the work, remains open.

A Invasão provides an account of the lives of about a dozen peasants over a span of some six months. The setting for the play is a large, unfinished building in Rio; the time, 1960. The action begins as a number of peasant families from the Northeast invade and occupy this building during the night. They do so because the shacks in which they had been living since arriving in Rio were destroyed, and the government, despite various assurances, has done nothing to help provide new quarters.

The plot centers around the lives of three of the invading families, and something of the hopes, fears, and frustrations of almost every member of these three families is revealed during the course of the play. Through his plot, Dias Gomes depicts vividly the plight of the urban poor in Brazil, and, indeed, in many parts of the world. Early in the play, there is a highly pathetic scene in which a baby dies of hunger and the mother seems almost relieved that the infant will not have to suffer through life. Equally gripping is the moment near the end when the fourteen-year-old daughter in one of the families emerges in garish dress and lips red with lipstick, for it is clear that she, obviously having decided to follow her older sister into prostitution, symbolizes what the author views as the unchanging, basically circular, pattern of the lives of these people. Antonio Buero Vallejo treats the same idea in his *Historia de una escalera*, and Dias Gomes, like Buero, provides just enough hope for change to permit an open ending. The over-all effect, nonetheless, is quite pessimistic.

In addition to describing the life of the downtrodden, *A Invasão* criticizes the government for its lack of concern for these members of society. Those individuals with political or legal power who attempt to take advantage of the poor are also attacked. In terms of dramatic technique, this play reveals a marked improvement over *O Pagador* in characterization and character motivation of the minor figures. Here, however, all the characters are in a sense minor, whereas in the earlier play there are two major figures whose strength seems to rob life from all the others. *A Invasão* is also enhanced by several scenes of high emotion, but generally it suffers from an excessive emphasis on thesis, an affliction common to most examples of *littérature engagée*.

In 1962, when *A Invasão* was first presented, Dias Gomes's third major play also reached the stage. Entitled *A Revolução dos Beatos* ("The revolution of the devout") and set in the town of Juàzeiro, Ceará, in 1920, the piece is an attack on political intrigue and, like *O Pagador*, on religious fanaticism. However, these two works differ radically in tone, for *A Revolução* is generally light, with a substantial amount of humor and satire throughout.

As the point of departure for his plot, the playwright chooses the figure of Padre Cícero, the famed priest who created a political and religious theocracy in Ceará. Dias Gomes presents him not as a hero, however, but as an old man in his dotage—sick, pathologically disturbed, and completely dominated by an unscrupulous local politician. Early in the play, both the townspeople and pilgrims from all over Brazil continue to flock to Padre Cícero's house in hopes of having their prayers answered. But, through a strange series of events, an ox belonging to the Padre also comes to be considered a saint and soon virtually replaces his owner in the esteem of the masses. Aware that the ox, who is drawn from the "bumba meu boi" tradition, threatens his power over the populace, the politician decides to have it killed and calls in troops to help. A veritable, though small-scale, religious war erupts between these troops and the ox's followers, with the government forces emerging victorious.

The ox, about to be executed, is found dead, and the politician manages to convince the people that its death was an act of God. Ironically, the ox was secretly slain by the man who first proclaimed it a miracle worker when he discovered that the "miracles" were mere coincidence. The town, rid of one false prophet, is placed back in the hands of the other.

As a work of art, *A Revolução dos Beatos* does not measure up to *O Pagador*; it lacks the tightly knit plot, the carefully drawn protagonists, and the moments of high emotion that characterize the latter piece. Nonetheless, in terms of the evolution of Dias Gomes's theater, *A Revolução* is a highly significant work, for it is here that one of his real fortes, his satiric bent, first comes to the fore. His concern for expressionistic dramatic technique also becomes evident for the first time in this play. `

The satirical humor in *A Revolução* is directed at the two targets mentioned earlier: religious fanaticism and political intrigue. The first of these was, of course, prominent in *O Pagador* and the second in *A Invasão*, and one or both—now treated seriously, now satirically—will stand in bold relief in almost all of Dias Gomes's subsequent plays.

In *A Revolução* the caricatural presentation of Padre Cícero, who was worshipped by the common people of Brazil, as a weak and obsessed old man, and of the politician as an "Antichrist," clearly ridicules the religious and political institutions as represented by these two individuals. With a somewhat softer stroke, Dias Gomes also twits the common people for both the zeal and the naïveté with which they adopt and adore "sacred cows," be they animal or human. Additional light parody is seen with the selling, in the play, of the ox's excrements as medicinal aids, a version of the fetishism so prominent as the butt of religious satire,[6] and with the scene, verging on black humor, in which a dying, bedridden man miraculously stands and begins walking toward Padre Cícero's house, only to topple over dead after several steps.

As mentioned above, *A Revolução* is the play in which Dias Gomes first departs from stark realism toward expressionistic techniques, and it is chiefly through the presentation of the ox that this is achieved. The very human machinations of this beast are delightful and provide the play with most of the life it holds. Equally alluring, and a high point in these first major plays, is the parallelistic scene late in the drama in which a woman tries to ward off the advances of the politician while simultaneously (through split staging) the "saintly" ox diabolically fends off a man who is seeking to get into the house to aid the lady in distress.

Dias Gomes's fourth major play, *Odorico, o Bem Amado* (1962, "Odoric, the beloved"), is termed by its author a "socio-politico-pathological farce."[7] Subtitled *Uma Obra de Govêrno* ("A work about government") and presented in eight scenes, the work is set in a small town on an island off the Bahian coast, and the time of action is 1960.

The plot centers on the political and personal fortunes and misfortunes of Odorico, a small-time demagogue who, largely because of his campaign pledge to build a cemetery for his town, is elected its mayor. Once in office, he complies with his promise to construct a cemetery, even though in doing so he finds it necessary to use funds designated for schools and for vital physical improvements for the town. He justifies this expenditure by contending that, as a dedicated public servant, he cannot allow the immediate wants and needs of his people to override their future needs, and since the future for all of them is the cemetery he must act accordingly.

When the cemetery is completed, Odorico ponders offering a prize to the first person to be buried there, but, after some reflection, he decrees that the cemetery will be dedicated with the first interment and that the town will both pay the cost of this funeral and erect a plaque commemorating the pioneering spirit of the person involved. As time goes by and no one in the town dies, however, Odorico's political fortunes begin to wane, and he is forced into desperate yet unsuccessful measures to come up with a corpse: a dying man is brought in, but he recovers; a killer is brought in, but he reforms; and a woman is murdered, but her parents insist that her body be shipped home for burial.

The local paper attacks Odorico's policies, and even his staunchest supporters, a gaggle of frustrated townswomen, begin to abandon him when they learn of the measures he has employed to try to obtain a cadaver. In a final attempt to regain the sympathy of his former supporters and discredit his opponents, Odorico stages an attack on his own life, attempting to shoot himself in the foot. Ironically, he is off target and actually kills himself. Thus, he appropriately comes to be his cemetery's first inhabitant.

The farcical tone of the play, though evident from the plot outline, finds its mainspring in the dialogue. Much of the humor is black, relating to death and the cemetery, but there is some sexually and politically oriented humor as well. Typical of the black humor is the statement by Odorico alluded to earlier: "Bom governante, minha gente, é aquêle que governa com os olhos no futuro. E o futuro de todos nós é o campo santo."[8] And when Dudu, a local townswoman, is murdered, supposedly because she is an adulteress, Odorico declares a holiday. One disgruntled citizen reacts by commenting: "A Banda e tôda a população da cidade. Até o comércio fechou. Odorico decretou feriado municipal. E se fôsse verdade o que dizem por aí, seria o único feriado no mundo que comemora um adultério."[9]

Later, in a demonstration, a chorus of participants chants its support for Odorico's efforts to have the murdered woman buried in the local cemetery:

Coro.   —Dudu no cemitério! Dudu no cemitério!

Cotinha. —Viva o Cemitério Municipal!

Todos.   —Vivaaaaa!

Odorico. —E o Direito, é a Liberdade, é a Civilização cristã que está em jôgo. Ou enterramos Dudu, ou nos enterramos.[10]

In another humorous passage, the local editor describes the town as a "cidade atrasada, onde não há crimes, desastres, roubos, onde nem mesmo as mulheres corneiam os maridos."[11] There is also the story, recounted by a local fisherman, of the man who saw a mermaid and asked if by chance she had a sister built the opposite way.

A number of the themes and concerns found in Dias Gomes's other major plays are also present in Odorico, o Bem Amado, but here they are generally treated with such a light touch as to be innocuous. Just as in O Pagador and later in O Berço do Herói ("The cradle of the hero"), reference is made to the subordination of the individual to collective society. When, at one point, a follower of Odorico comments, "A inauguração do cemitério é uma grande vitória, ainda que tenha custado a vida de um dos nossos,"[12] the latter responds, "As obras que vencem o tempo são sempre construídas com lágrimas e sangue."[13] In O Berço do Herói Cabo Jorge's uncle says virtually the same thing when he comments that his nephew's death will insure the town a new highway and that "ninguém constrói uma estrada sem sacrificar muitas vidas. E a paga do progresso."[14]

Odorico's wife is depicted as sexually frustrated and somewhat alienated from her husband, as is Zé's wife in *O Pagador*. In *Odorico, o Bem Amado* this frustration, like the conflict between the individual and society, is of only minimal consequence, however. Similarly, the priest in *Odorico, o Bem Amado* is seen as a reasonable and prudent man—"Compreende, quando dois podêres se digladiam, O Executivo e o Judiciário, é prudente que a Igreja não tome partido"[15]— and, as such, he differs radically from the priests depicted in *O Pagador* and later in *O Berço do Herói* and *O Santo Inquérito* ("The holy inquiry").

The manner in which *Odorico, o Bem Amado* is presented is basically realistic; the only inkling of expressionistic technique comes at the very end when the members of Odorico's funeral cortege, all inebriated, break into song and dance in the samba tradition to accompanying music. This touch provides the plot with a momentary aura of folklore or myth but does not suffice to elevate it from realism to a more poetic plane.

Odorico, o Bem Amado provides obvious satire on politicians, political campaigns, and on the small-town mentality, but this satire is rendered generally inoffensive by the farcical tone that pervades the work. The humorous treatment of death falls within a lengthy Iberian tradition, just as the farcical elements reflect a trend that has been prevalent in Brazilian theater since Martins Pena. The play, in sum, is a praiseworthy farce with well-turned dialogue and situation. Within the scope of Dias Gomes's theater, nonetheless, it lacks both the depth of *O Pagador* and of his later *O Santo Inquérito* and *Dr. Getúlio, Sua Vida e Sua Glória* ("Dr. Getulio, his life and his glory"), as well as the impact of *O Berço do Herói*, his fifth major dramatic work.

It is in *O Berço do Herói* that the satiric humor and the expressionistic techniques introduced in *A Revolução dos Beatos* and *Odorico, o Bem Amado* find their fruition. Published in 1965, but still awaiting its initial performance, the work concerns itself chiefly with the problem of true individual liberty in a capitalist society, much as does *O Pagador*. Various critics, in fact, have stated that *O Berço* is a very pessimistic answer to the questions concerning individual freedom and liberty that are raised in *O Pagador*.

In terms of story line, *O Berço* resembles rather closely Ibsen's *An Enemy of the People* and Dürrenmatt's *The Visit*; the central conflict is drawn between a man set on living the truth and a town whose economic well-being depends on a compromise in principle on the part of this individual. While Henrik Ibsen's work is essentially quite serious in tone, however, and Friedrich Dürrenmatt's is characterized by an engaging, almost surrealistic, levity, Dias Gomes's piece is heavily satirical, though at times it borders on farce. This satire, in getting at the problem of individual freedom, falls mainly on the church, or rather on its representatives, and on the military, and it is doubtless the attack on the latter that has preserved *O Berço* as a reluctant virgin, unsullied by the boards and bright lights of the stage.[16]

The play is set in a small town whose thriving economy is based almost exclusively on the commercialism attendant upon the perpetuation of the memory
of one of its native sons, whose alleged act of valor just before his purported
death in combat in World War II made him a national hero and his hometown a
national shrine. The plot revolves around the dilemma faced by the town fathers
and by the Brazilian army when the man, Cabo Jorge by name, innocently
appears one day and reveals that he had deserted after having been wounded
slightly and had spent the past ten years hiding in Italy.

Cabo Jorge, viewing his status as a dead military hero with understandable
disbelief, at first finds great humor in the situation and remarks accordingly:
"Ah, mas é muito dura a profissão de herói. Se eu tivesse morrido, era fácil.
Ou se tivesse sido herói por acaso, sem querer, como muitos. Mas sou um herói
por convicção. Um herói de carreira. Por isso tenho de ser herói vinte e quatro
horas por dia. E cansativo."[17] However, when he realizes that he may be in
some danger for his safety, Jorge's thoughts on the absurdity of personal heroism
in the atomic age and his own rights as an individual in society become more
serious. At one point he states: "Claro que não vou ao ponto de achar que meu
procedimento mereça uma estátua. Mas será que sou tão repulsivo assim? Só
porque num momento lá da minha vida achei que era um homem livre e podia
usar a minha liberdade como bem entendesse. Então, pra que o homem é livre,
senão pra isso, pra escolher o seu caminho?"[18]

In An Enemy of the People the citizenry decides that the economic well-being
of its town is more important than the rights of an individual, even though this
well-being is based on a lie (mineral springs that are, in fact, polluted). Likewise, in O Berço the town fathers decide that the myth of Jorge's heroism must
be preserved, even though it means ridding itself of him. And, since the army,
which sets Jorge up as an example for all its troops, refuses to allow him to be
jailed or exiled for fear that the truth might eventually get out—"A honra do
Exército não pode ficar dependendo da sorte de um homem"[19]—the only
solution is to have him killed. The madam of the local brothel has him poisoned,
appropriately in return for permission to open a second house of prostitution.
Thus, the preservation of the town's economy, made possible by an act of prostitution on the part of the town fathers, is masterfully symbolized at play's end by
the inauguration of the new brothel.

Evident in O Berço, and for the first time to a significant extent in Dias
Gomes's works, are several of those technical innovations that have come to define the contemporary theater. Prominent among these are multiple staging and
the incorporation of elements of mixed media, such as film segments and sound
recordings, all of which are used to lend added resonance to the satirical tone of
the play. At several points throughout O Berço a chorus, reminiscent of classical tragedy, is employed to comment ironically on the plot and on the general
concept of heroism, and, midway through the play, a kind of farcical ballet is

interpolated that, like the comic interlude in *noh* theater, functions to parody the main plot.

As in Zé-do-Burro in *O Pagador*, Cabo Jorge is something of a Christ figure. Both men experience one phase of the Calvary—Zé the journey with the cross and Jorge the trial—and both are alluded to as being Christlike. This parallel is but one of a number existing between the two plays. The similarity between them is such, in fact, that they seem to comprise a dramatic experiment in which the same set of basic ingredients is poured into two distinct molds—one tragic and the other burlesque. What emerges is a figure and its distorted mirror image.[20]

The major aesthetic flaw in *O Berço* is probably the predominance of thesis over other aspects of the work. This weakness is minimized, nonetheless, by the effective satirical edge prevailing throughout. In summary, the play must be ranked as one of Dias Gomes's outstanding achievements; moreover, it is perhaps the best satire to be found in the contemporary Brazilian theater.

O Berço do Herói, which was to have premiered in July of 1966, was banned and, as mentioned earlier, has not yet been staged. Dias Gomes's sixth major play, *O Santo Inquérito*, received more favorable comment, however, and was first presented in Rio in September of 1966. This play, based on the life of Branca Dias, is one of two by the dramatist dealing with a historical personage (the other, as we shall presently see, treats Getúlio Vargas) and is the only one of his works whose setting is in the rather distant past: 1750, in the state of Paraíba.

The plot of *O Santo Inquérito* centers on the circumstances leading to the conviction and sentencing of Branca, a young woman burned at the stake by the Holy Inquisition about the middle of the eighteenth century. The major concerns or themes, just as in *O Pagador*, are individual freedom within a tightly structured societal force (here, the church), communication, and religious fanaticism. Strong evidence, nonetheless, supports George Woodyard's postulation that the Inquisition is employed primarily as a metaphor to describe military and political repression in present-day Brazil.[21]

The principal characters are Branca Dias and a Jesuit priest named Padre Bernardo. Branca, whose life is filled with love for all God's kingdom, even for the lowly ant, is presented as a pure and guileless young woman whose sense of decency and honor will not allow her to lie or to help herself at the expense of others. Padre Bernardo, on the other hand, is depicted as a weak individual who offers to help Branca understand and follow the dictates of the Church. He is soon overcome by physical desire for her, however, and attempts to expiate his feeling of guilt by having her tried and condemned by the Inquisition. He appears to believe that, by so doing, he will, in effect, be punishing himself.

O Santo Inquérito is staged in a highly surrealistic manner, befitting the blend of history and legend that comprises the basic plot. The action takes place on three different planes, and the characters enter and exit on all three and move back and forth among them. Considerable temporal displacement and intensive lighting are also employed, and both Padre Bernardo and Branca leave their roles on occasion to speak to and about the audience.

The action begins, presumably in the present, with a woman telling her child the story of Branca Dias. Presented in verse form and accompanied by the mournful sound of wind in the trees, this scene provides an aura of legend and fantasy. Padre Bernardo appears on stage and attempts to defend his actions before the audience, and then Branca enters to take her own part. There follows a shift to the past and a scene from Branca's trial, in which the terrified girl attempts to explain her own manner of loving God and states that if she had been possessed by the Devil she would not have saved Padre Bernardo from drowning. At this point the anguished cry of Padre Bernardo is heard, and there is a second temporal shift, this time back to the day when Branca pulls him out of the water and revives him by placing her lips on his and applying mouth-to-mouth resuscitation.

The action then proceeds chronologically to the time of the trial, and during this period we witness Padre Bernardo's growing sense of guilt, resulting from the lingering sensation of Branca's lips, and his subsequent shift from confessor and protector to accuser. The Padre's change is accompanied by increasing confusion and frustration on the part of Branca, as she finds herself unable to make anyone understand that her zest for life is a manifestation of her love for God.

As it turns out, both Branca and Augusto, her boyfriend, die at the hands of the Inquisition, he through torture and she at the stake. Branca's father escapes by bearing false witness, an act to which neither Branca nor the young man will stoop. When Branca learns of her father's actions and of his failure to release Augusto from the rack when the two of them were alone together simply because he did not want to "get involved," she accuses him of complicity in her friend's death. The father professes innocence, however, as does the guard when Branca accuses him of not accepting his responsibility to man.

At play's end, Branca extends this accusation to the audience, after first questioning the guard once more:

Branca. —E você?

Guarda. —Que posso fazer?

Branca. —Eu sei, você nada pode fazer. (*Referindo-se à platéia*) Eles
também acham que nada podem fazer e que nada disso lhes diz
respeito. E dentro em pouco sairão daqui em paz com suas
consciências, em seus belos carros e irão cear.[22]

She is then seen contorting in flames while Padre Bernardo, also contorting, watches her die and then falls to the ground crying, "Finalmente, Senhor, finalmente posso aspirar ao vosso perdão!"[23] As the curtain is about to fall, the stage effects of the opening scene are again employed, and the spiritlike Branca is seen as if she were floating through space.

Numerous threads link *O Santo Inquérito* with Dias Gomes's *O Pagador* and *O Berço do Herói*. In terms of character, there is a close resemblance between Branca Dias and Zé-do-Burro; both are simple but courageous persons whose innocence and forthrightness make communication with complex forces of society impossible.[24] Branca's love for ants, a lowly form of life, is in striking parallel to Zé's devotion to his burro, and, in fact, both the burro and the ants are deemed evil beings by the church authorities. Zé, nonetheless, is essentially a tragic figure, whereas Branca, though with certain tragic overtones, suffers the death of a martyr.

Like *O Berço*, *O Santo Inquérito* questions military and political controls over the individual in present-day Brazil, but in the latter work this criticism is couched in an indirect and metaphorical fashion—hence its success in reaching the stage. In terms of technique, these two plays share a wide use of expressionistic devices. However, *O Santo Inquérito*, by virtue of the surrealistic mode in which it is cast, is set apart from the rest of Dias Gomes's dramas, even though it shares with them common themes and concerns. This mode, which is employed with great effectiveness, makes *O Santo Inquérito* a highly successful dramatic work.

Following *O Santo Inquérito* and representing yet another experiment in structure and technique is *Dr. Getúlio, Sua Vida e Sua Glória*, a piece in two acts in which verse and prose are mixed. This play, written in collaboration with the poet Ferreira Gullar, dramatizes the period of ultimate crisis in the life of the Brazilian president-dictator Getúlio Vargas—the crisis that precipitated his suicide in 1954. However, rather than presenting their story in a straightforward historicopolitical frame, the authors have availed themselves of the play-within-a-play technique and permitted the story of Vargas to be the *enrêdo* (plot) for a *carnaval* performance by a samba club. Through the medium of this club, an institution steeped in the popular tradition in Rio, a fusion of the historical and the legendary Getúlio Vargas is effected, and there emerges a figure of poetic, mythically real proportions.[25]

What affords the play depth, nonetheless, is not just the creation of a mythical Getúlio Vargas, but also the fact that the samba club itself is undergoing a crisis that parallels the one in Vargas's regime and hence serves as a dramatic metaphor for it. Thus, Simpatia, the president of the club, at once symbolizes Getúlio Vargas and portrays him in the *enrêdo*. In similar fashion, the three Birds of Prey and Tucão, who is Simpatia's chief rival for control of the samba club, represent the foreign powers and their supporters in Brazil who for financial reasons opposed Vargas. The other members of the club, by extension, both represent and portray the Brazilian citizenry of the early 1950s.

As the play begins, Simpatia comes forth and tells the audience that they are about to see a rehearsal of the *enrêdo* his club is to perform during *carnaval*. He then alludes to the financial difficulties that have beset the club since Tucão, whom Simpatia defeated for the presidency, withdrew his support:

> Nossa Escola tem problemas
> que não vamos esconder,
> porque estão no jornal.
> O principal é dinheiro.
> Tucão nos abandonou
> e Escola sem bicheiro,
> minha gente, se dá mal.[26]

At the end of his address, Simpatia also informs the audience that he will play the role of Getúlio: "Sou presidente da Escola, / exigi a regalia: / afinal, somos colegas..."[27] They are, of course, much more than just colleagues, for Simpatia, as previously stated, is himself a symbol for the very man he is portraying.

The rehearsal then begins but, in good Pirandellean fashion, is continually interrupted by actors who leave their roles in the *enrêdo* and become involved in the club's crisis. The outcome, as one might suspect, is the same as that which befell Vargas: Simpatia, largely for financial reasons, is deposed and ends up dead. He, however, is actually shot and killed by the symbolic Birds of Prey, an action that clearly suggests that Getúlio Vargas's death, though nominally suicide, symbolically is at the hands of real birds of prey—the foreign powers and their ploys.

In the final scene the characters, in their roles as members of the samba club, scream that Simpatia has been killed. Almost simultaneously, in their roles as characters in the *enrêdo*, they shout that Getúlio Vargas is dead. In the latter case, however, the meaning is double, for Getúlio here refers both to the character in the *enrêdo* and to Simpatia, who as president of the club serves as a metaphor for the historical Getúlio Vargas. Thus, the dramatists achieve, at the end of the play, a unification of the various levels of action and, through this unity, a mythification of the figure of Vargas.

While the two major plot lines—the crisis in the samba club and the portrayed crisis in Vargas's regime—are not fully merged until the end, they do run parallel throughout and in various instances the two are momentarily joined. Perhaps the best example of this parallelism comes during a demonstration against Vargas in which the protesters enter carrying placards that state, "MORRA GETÚLIO... ABAIXO GETÚLIO."[28] At that moment an actress rushes in and advises Simpatia to flee because the other actors have turned against him and he is in danger for his life.

Three components of the samba club are successfully woven into the *enrêdo*, and hence into the play, as technical devices: the *bateria*, or orchestra, the *passistas*, or dancers, and the *Comissão de Frente*, which is a sort of popular chorus. The first two dramatize the different moods in the play through music and dance, while the third, in the tradition of classical chorus, presents in chant a synopsis of the plot at various moments during the performance. Near the end of the play, yet another device is skillfully employed: Getúlio takes out a letter and begins reading silently. As he does so a recording of his voice, presumably reading the same material, is heard on a loudspeaker. This use of mixed media, effective in its own right, takes on added importance when the amplified recording is again heard in the final moments of the play, after the death of Simpatia-Getúlio. Here, moreover, the message becomes that of both men.

As one would expect with the use of the samba club, the tone of *Dr.Getúlio, Sua Vida e Sua Glória* is light and often festive. The language is quite colorful, and the predominant verse form employed is the eight-syllable line, which, of course, is the ballad line most frequently used in popular poetry. A generally light satirical humor, which is almost always directed at the foreign powers involved in the economic exploitation of Brazil, also pervades the play. At one point, for example, the U.S. Ambassador exclaims that his country's marines defend democracy and have full respect for the principle of self-determination. Getúlio then asks him to explain their invasion of the Dominican Republic, but the Ambassador contends that the question is not valid because that invasion does not occur until 1965 and their conversation is taking place in 1952. The criticism, through this temporal game, thus remains light in tone even though the point is made. At another moment in the drama, three sailors from a powerful squadron of cruisers paying a "courtesy visit" to Brazil enter onstage "com chapéus de *cow-boy*, armados até os dentes, cada um dêles girando dois revólveres nos dedos e mascando chicletes."[29] Once again, the biting sarcasm inherent in these stereotypes is evident, though the trappings remain festive.

Because of its light, popular tone, its innovative structure, and its generally balanced view of the figure of Getúlio Vargas, *Dr. Getúlio, Sua Vida e Sua Glória* stands far from Dias Gomes's generally realistic thesis plays, *A Invasão* and *A Revolução dos Beatos*, and equally distant from his highly satirical *O Berço do Herói* and his tragic *O Pagador* and *O Santo Inquérito*. It ranks, nonetheless, with these three latter works as the best of Dias Gomes's theater.

Anatol Rosenfeld, in his penetrating study of Dias Gomes's theater, concludes that the dramatist's two latest works, *Vamos Soltar os Demônios* ("Let's release the demons") and *O Túnel* ("The tunnel"), do not measure up to the seven earlier ones. He further suggests that the political climate in Brazil may have had a somewhat stifling effect on these two pieces (I, xliii). While Rosenfeld's estimation of their relative merit is certainly accurate, one must, I think, recognize that these two plays do represent continued experimentation on Dias Gomes's part. They may, therefore, prove to preface more polished creations in their same veins.

Dias Gomes's eighth play, *O Túnel* (1967), is a thinly veiled satire in two scenes on political and military controls in Brazil and on the Brazilian citizenry's submissive acceptance of them. The veil, an absurdist plot situation, provides the piece with considerable humor but does little to blunt the pointed satire. Like *O Berço do Herói*, *O Túnel* was banned from performance by the censors and, given the targets of attack shared by these two works, it is highly unlikely that either will be played in Brazil until a significant change in political climate takes place.

The setting for the drama is a tunnel, within which cars have been trapped for about two hours. There are four principal characters: a young woman named Loura, and three men, each of whom is identified and in part characterized by the car he drives (Homem da Mercedes, Homem do Fusca, Homem da Kombi).

The first scene portrays the reactions of the three men to the traffic jam. The impetuous Homem do Fusca wants to protest the situation by blowing his horn, even though the effort may prove fruitless. The Homem da Mercedes, whose car has air conditioning, television, and other luxuries, prefers to remain silent and hope that the traffic commission will find a solution. The Homem da Kombi, meanwhile, is the pseudointellectual who tries to analyze and rationalize all aspects of the dilemma but whose remarks at first seem confused and virtually pointless. For example, he determines that, if all the cars' engines are turned off, the motorists will have enough air in the tunnel to survive for about six months. When asked if he plans to be there six months, he responds: "Estou apenas analisando a situação. Temos que assentar a cabeça e examinar tôdas as hipóteses. Começo a pensar que um desastre de enormes proporções deve ter ocorrido e que devemos nos preparar para uma longa permanência dentro dêste túnel."[30]

Four years later, the time of action of the second scene, the people are still trapped in the tunnel. By now, however, each has a gas mask, and there is an elaborate communications system by which the Traffic Director can both speak to the motorists and hear everything that they say. A kind of futuristic society has sprung up with beauty parlors, laundries, a black market, a postal service, and with births, baptisms, and deaths by asphyxiation. The Traffic Director insists, of course, that no deaths have occurred, claiming that what the motorists thought had been deaths were merely hallucinations caused by the neurosis of the tunnel. He also proudly proclaims that automobile accidents in the vicinity of the tunnel have been reduced by 93.5 percent.

The Homem do Fusca still tries to rebel by shouting into the microphones and by building a bomb with which he hopes to clear one end of the tunnel. The Homem da Mercedes, as submissive as ever, warns him that these acts are against the rules, but he responds: "Pro inferno com os regulamentos. Em cada um déles nós deixamos um pedaço da nossa liberdade."[31] The Homem da Kombi wants everyone to sign a letter of protest, but the Homem da Mercedes, while agreeing with the intent, says he never signs petitions, and the Homem do Fusca refuses because he prefers to act alone. As the play ends, the Traffic Director, via loudspeaker, congratulates the motorists on the fourth anniversary of their stay in the tunnel and informs them that an American technician who specializes in unclogging tunnels will soon arrive and begin to remove the vehicles. He further announces that the tunnel, once cleared, will be filled with dirt and turned over to the Ministry of Agriculture, for: "Precisamos pensar no Agricultura! Aterrar os túneis, e aproveitar a encosta para plantar café, cacau, algodão, cana-de-açúcar, banana—e por que não dizer—batatas! . . . Nisso está nosso futuro! Com isso estaremos livres para sempre dos engarramentos e cumpriremos o nosso destino de país essencialmente agrícola..."[32] With these words, the motorists all begin sounding their horns in protest, and the deafening noise marks the end of the play.

The motorists trapped in the tunnel are obviously symbolic of the Brazilian people who are entrapped in a closed, tightly monitored society, and the range of reactions of these motorists is representative of those of the Brazilian citizenry: some prefer violent rebellion, others seek nonviolent means of protest, and still others choose to remain silent and "hope for the best." The Traffic Director, of course, symbolizes the government, and the fact that he is three times referred to as "general" makes it clear that this government is a military one. The act of rebellion—the blowing of horns—by the motorists at play's end may be taken as the dramatists's recommendation of a course of political action, but more than likely it is not profferred as an answer but as an expression of extreme pessimism, just as is the outcome of *O Berço do Herói*.

The humor in *O Túnel* falls between that found in the farcical *Odorico, o Bem Amado* and the type encountered in the highly satirical *O Berço do Herói*. In intent it is clearly allied with the latter piece, but in tone it is closer to the former. This humor, as mentioned earlier, springs chiefly from the absurdist plot situation but also abounds in the dialogue, which is often witty and sarcastic. The account of the trials and tribulations, past and present, of the principal characters is also quite comical. The Homem da Mercedes, for example, seeks advice on how best he might murder his nagging wife, who for twenty-two years has sent his dirty laundry from Rio to São Paulo because as a *paulista* she believes their laundries are better. The Homem do Fusca refuses to offer any suggestions, however, stating that: "Isso é problema seu. Mulher, cada um deve matar a sua."[33]

In *O Túnel*, then, the humor is well wrought and the satire pointed and crisp. Message or thesis predominates throughout, nonetheless, and, as is so often the case, character and plot development suffer accordingly. Thus, while the play stands as a rather good example of *théâtre engagé* in Brazil, it falls considerably short of the level of artistry achieved in Dias Gomes's best plays.

Vamos Soltar os Demónios (1969), the last work by our playwright to date, is a psychological study of an "intellectual" whose inner fears and weaknesses, normally hidden behind a rigid mask of superiority, are forced into the open in a period of crisis.[34] The setting is an erotically decorated apartment in Rio maintained by several prominent men for their extramarital adventures, and the time is the present, specifically just after a successful military coup. The two principal characters are Sérgio Pontes, the intellectual, and Nara, his wife. The former is an egotistical journalist who contends that he has sacrificed personal wealth and status to stand by his political convictions and who shows great contempt for such things as the domestic brand of whiskey and the pedestrian sexual mores of his countrymen. His wife, on the other hand, is a woman deeply resentful of her husband's superior attitude and is, in fact, the stronger of the two.

The play is nominally in two acts, but its structure is actually tripartite. The first segment, which takes us to near the end of act I, serves to introduce the characters and to set forth the two crises that confront Sérgio during the play. The first, obvious from the beginning, is political: his editorials against the new regime have associated him with the previous government, and he, dressed as a priest, is hiding in a friend's apartment—the aforementioned mini-*garçonnière*. The second crisis, his personal relationship with his wife, emerges more slowly, even though her resentment toward him for his condescending attitude and for his overriding concern with self is evident immediately.

As the play begins, Moura and Vera, the businessman and his secretary who are the two minor characters in the work, enter the apartment, set for an amorous interlude. They leave in consternation, however, upon encountering Sérgio, whom they take to be a libertine priest. Nara then enters, and the rest of the segment involves a conversation-argument in which the two crises unfold. Nara, at one point, forces Sérgio to admit that, all his high-sounding statements notwithstanding, he is in hiding because he is afraid. Sérgio attempts to excuse his sense of fear in much the same terms as those found in O Berço do Herói. He states, "Todo herói é ridículo,"[35] and adds, "Só os irresponsáveis e os inconscientes não sentem mêdo."[36]

The second part of the play begins near the end of act I when, through a sudden burst of passion, Sérgio and Nara cease to argue and enter into a ritualistic game. Sérgio, assuming the role of a priest, hears Nara, as a woman come to him for confession, profess her passionate love for him. As the stage darkens, the two, still in their roles, are undressing each other.

The ritual continues in act II, which begins with Sérgio (as priest) reciting the Apocalypse. He and Nara have just finished making love, and the religious trappings have obviously served as a sexual stimulant. Nara (as the penitent woman) asks Sérgio if he believes in "o Demônio," and then she confesses: "Eu acredito mais no Demônio do que em Deus. Sério. Deus é uma idéia vaga, abstrata. O Demônio, não. E concreto... Está dentro de nós."[37] She then adds: "Quando a gente faz amor, como nós fizemos agora, liberta um bando dêles.

Mas é só nessa hora que a gente tem coragem de soltar nossos demônios. Normal-
mente, guardamos todos muito bem guardados e sujeitos à mais severa vigilân-
cia."[38] These last lines, which contain the essence of the play's title, are highly
significant in that the depicted moment of sexual crisis and the resultant effect
on the psyche represent metaphorically the two moments of crisis through
which Sérgio is passing and suggest what their effect will be.

Nara, in keeping with her statement, takes advantage both of the period after
sexual intimacy and of her assumed role to express to the "priest" her deepest
feelings about her husband, something she had never been able to do before.
Sérgio, though trying in his role as priest to react impartially to her remarks,
finds it very difficult not to defend himself:

Sérgio.   —. . . E seu marido...

Nara.   —é . . . um homem muito fraco!

Sérgio.   —(*Ferido em sua vaidade, mas levando avante o seu papel*) Ele não
me dá essa impressão. Ao contrário, parece um homem de
grande fôrça moral e mental.

Nara.   —E é justamente isso que o torna vulnerável. Ou melhor, a
consciência que éle tem dessa fôrça. Isso o torna auto-suficiente,
egocêntrico, vaidoso, cruel e covarde, ás vêzes.

Sérgio.   —Um monstro!

Nara.   —Não, um intelectual, apenas. Capaz, talvez, de gestos maiores,
mas também das maiores fraquezas. Frequentemente indeciso
entre morrer por uma causa e viver pelos pequeninos e muitos
prazeres de uma existência acomodada. Enfim, um ser admirável
e desprezível ao mesmo tempo.[39]

Segment two then ends with another outburst of passion in which the two seem
to achieve orgasm through the recitation of biblical verses.

Following a brief silence, the doorbell rings, and Moura and Vera enter to
retrieve the latter's coat. Sérgio berates them for their hypocritical attitudes toward adultery, contending that it should be open and aboveboard. He is, nonetheless, struck virtually dumb when Nara then tells him that she has had various
affairs and has now decided to leave him for another man. This moment of
spiritual crisis for Sérgio, like the political and sexual crises earlier, forces him to
"release his interior demons" by admitting that he is guilty of the same hypocrisy
he criticizes in others and, thus, that he is actually not superior to any of them.

As the play nears its end, Sérgio discovers that police are searching the building. Nara goes out to seek help but soon returns stating that she could not bring
herself to leave him in such a predicament. She then talks him into making love

while they await the police. And, in fact, six heavily armed policemen do enter and find them lying on the bed reciting scripture. The stage becomes dark as the six stare perplexedly, but Sérgio's recitation continues to be heard.

Vamos Soltar os Demônios, with its sexually oriented atmosphere and its use of a twisted game-ritual, constitutes yet another theatrical experiment on the part of Dias Gomes, an attempt to incorporate features prominent both in concurrent Brazilian drama and generally in the theater and cinema of the late 1960s. The ritual, which Anatol Rosenfeld has aptly described as very Buñuelesque in its religious overtones, is quite effective symbolically. The playwright's commitment to the creation of a sexual framework or atmosphere in which to present his story is excessive, however, and it is here that the play fails. Sérgio, for example, is a very credible protagonist in many respects, particularly in his moments of painful introspection, but his sexual prowess in time of crisis lacks verisimilitude. Rosenfeld poignantly comments, "Also surprising is the excessive—and dubious—sensuality of the intellectual who, not inhibited by the extremely precarious situation (it would diminish the potency even of a bull), reveals himself a supermale governed by genital supremacy" (I, xli).

Yet another aspect of the play that does not measure up to Dias Gomes's best works is the dialogue; the speeches are often long and ponderous, and Sérgio's conversations with Moura and Vera, which appear to be designed in part for shock value and in part to emphasize Sérgio's disdain for provincial customs and values, at times seem redundant. Thus, even though the segment with the game-ritual is quite strong and effective, the play generally suffers, at least in terms of traditional evaluation. If, however, Dias Gomes has here adopted the tack of the absurdist playwrights and sought to portray by his play the "intellectual" rather than merely describe or analyze him within it, he has done a masterful job, for the work has many of the same negative qualities it ascribes to Sérgio—wordiness, obsession with sex, and generally weak character.

Of Dias Gomes's four best plays (*O Pagador de Promessas*, *O Berço do Herói*, *O Santo Inquérito*, and *Dr. Getúlio, Sua Vida e Sua Glória*), the first three treat the same basic theme—the problem of individual freedom in modern society—and the fourth attempts to present, through mythification, a reasonably balanced view of Brazil's president-dictator, Getúlio Vargas. In terms of type, however, all four works differ widely. *O Pagador*, clearly within the realistic mode, is a stark tragedy, while the essentially expressionistic *O Berço do Herói* and *O Santo Inquérito* are, respectively, a mordant satire and a historico-legendary drama staged in a highly surrealistic manner. *Dr. Getúlio, Sua Vida e Sua Glória*, also basically historicolegendary, is presented as a play-within-a-play and is light and carnivalesque in spirit. *Odorico, o Bem Amado*, though with less depth than the four plays above, is a well-made farce and, thus, successful in its own terms. *Vamos Soltar os Demônios*, the playwright's one attempt at psychological drama, is less successful, as is the absurdist-tinged "political parable" *O Túnel*. Both of these works have their moments, nonetheless, just as do his earlier *A Invasão* and *A Revolução dos Beatos*.

Alfredo Dias Gomes is, as mentioned at the outset, already one of Brazil's two most important contemporary playwrights, and there is every reason to hope for continued production and experimentation on his part. One can expect his role in the theater to grow accordingly, both in Brazil and internationally.

NOTES

1. For other studies on the theater of Alfredo Dias Gomes, see Francis A. Dutra, "The Theatre of Dias Gomes: Brazil's Social Conscience," *Cithara* 4, no. 2 (May 1965):3–13; Richard A. Mazzara, "Alfredo Dias Gomes: Social Commentator and Artist," *Latin American Theatre Review* 2, no. 2 (Spring 1969): 41–59; and, particularly, Anatol Rosenfeld, "A Obra de Dias Gomes," in *Teatro de Dias Gomes*, 2 vols. (Rio de Janeiro: Editôra Civilização Brasileira, 1972), I, xi–xliii.

Both the nine plays discussed in the present study and critical introductions to the six of them published in separate editions are included in the two-volume *Teatro de Dias Gomes* cited above. Subsequent references to and quotations from these introductions will therefore be identified in the study by volume and page number in parentheses and translated by me. Quotations from the plays will be identified in the same manner in footnotes and there translated by me.

2. Flávio Rangel, in his "Notícia sôbre Dias Gomes" (I, 121–122), mentions five of these works—*Pé-de-Cabra*, *Amanhã Será Outro Dia*, *Zeca Diabo*, *Um Pobre Génio*, and *Sulamita*. O. Vasilieva-Schvede and Anatólio Gach (*Antologia da Literatura Portuguesa e Brasileira* [Leningrad: Leningrad University Press, 1964], p. 247) refer to two additional titles and comment as follows on Dias Gomes's early years in Rio: "At the age of fifteen he arrived in Rio de Janeiro, where he premiered with the play *Pé-de-Cabra*. In 1943 *Amanhã Será Outro Dia* was carried to the stage by the Teatro Brasileiro de Comédia. The following year *Doutor Ninguém* and *Zeca Diabo* appeared. Between 1944 and 1954 Dias Gomes dedicated himself to radio broadcasting. Not until 1954 did he write the following piece: *Cinco Fugitivos do Juizo Final*" (my translation). Dias Gomes, in a letter dated 29 November 1973, explains that *Sulamita* and *Doutor Ninguém* refer to the same play, the latter title being adopted in 1945 when the work was staged. He also states that he wrote four other plays during this period: *João Cambão*, written and staged in 1943, and *Sinhazinha*, *Eu Acuso o Céu*, and *O Homem Que Não Era Seu*, none of which were staged but all three of which were done for radio (Dias Gomes to Leon F. Lyday, personal files).

3. Dale S. Bailey interestingly suggests that *O Pagador* can also be interpreted as a modern morality play ("*Pagador de Promessas*: A Brazilian Morality," *Latin American Theatre Review* 6, no. 1 [Fall 1972]: 35–39).

4. Dutra employs this term and discusses at some length its role in *O Pagador de Promessas* (see Dutra, "The Theatre of Dias Gomes," pp. 3–13).

5. See Mazzara, "Alfredo Dias Gomes," p. 45.

6. Satire of the cult of relics and mementos is also found in Dias Gomes's *O Berço do Herói*, in which a button, supposedly from Cabo Jorge's underwear, is offered to a woman seeking help with her pregnancy.

7. *Odorico, o Bem Amado* was apparently not widely known, at least outside Brazil, until its inclusion in the two-volume *Teatro* in 1972. It was, nonetheless, originally published in 1962 and later rewritten as a movie script. Dias Gomes says of it: "*Odorico, o Bem Amado* was published early in 1962, coming after *A Revolução dos Beatos* and before *O Berço do Herói*. Initially, it appeared in a special Christmas issue of the *Revista Cláudia*, and later it was rewritten as a movie script. The authorial rights to the script were granted to a production company, but the company never actually filmed it. Based on this script, I rewrote the play in the form that it is now published" (Dias Gomes to Leon F. Lyday, 23 February 1973, personal files, my translation).

8. "A good governor, my people, is one who governs with his eyes on the future. And the future for all of us is the cemetery" (I, 358).

9. "The band and the entire population of the city. Even the businesses closed. Odorico decreed a municipal holiday. And if what they're saying were true, it would be the only holiday in the world commemorating an act of adultery" (I, 417).

10. *Chorus*. Dudu in the cemetery! Dudu in the cemetery!

Cotinha. Long live the Municipal Cemetery!

Everyone. Vivaaaaa!

Odorico. And law, and liberty, and Christian civilization which is in question. Either we bury Dudu, or we bury ourselves.   [I, 424]

11. ". . . backward city, where there are no crimes, disasters, robberies, where women don't even deceive their husbands" (I, 364).

12. "The inauguration of the cemetery is a great victory, even though it has cost the life of one of our group" (I, 420).

13. "Works that are enduring are always constructed with tears and blood" (I, 420).

14. "No one builds a highway without sacrificing many lives. That's the price of progress" (II, 564).

15. "You understand that when two powers, the Executive and the Judiciary, are at odds, it's prudent for the Church not to get involved" (I, 430).

16. A more detailed commentary on the element of satire in *O Berço do Herói* can be found in Leon F. Lyday, "Structure and Theme in Dias Gomes' *O Berço do Herói*," *South Atlantic Bulletin* 37, no. 2 (May 1972): 10–15.

17. "Ah, but the hero profession is very demanding. If I had died, it would have been easy. Or if I had been a hero by accident, without willing it, like many. But I am a hero by conviction. A career hero. Therefore I have to be a hero twenty-four hours a day. It's exhausting" (II, 549).

18. "Of course, I don't go so far as to think that my comportment merits a statue. But even so, can it be that I'm so repulsive? Just because at one moment in my life I thought that I was a free man and could use my freedom as I saw fit. Then, why is a man free, if not for that, for being able to choose his own path?" (II, 536).

19. "The honor of the Army cannot be dependent on the fate of one man" (II, 552).

20. For more on the relationship between these two plays, see Leon F. Lyday, "*O Pagador de Promessas* and *O Berço do Herói*: Variations on a Theme," *Romance Notes* 14, no. 2 (Winter 1972): 275–282.

21. George W. Woodyard, "A Metaphor for Repression: Two Portuguese Inquisition Plays," *Luso-Brazilian Review* 10, no. 1 (Summer 1973): 68–75.

22. *Branca*. And you?

Guarda. What can I do?

Branca. I know, you can't do anything. (*Referring to the audience*) They also think that they can't do anything and that none of this relates to them. And shortly they, at peace with their consciences, will leave here in their fine cars and go have dinner."

[II, 664–665]

23. "At last, Lord, at last I can hope for your forgiveness!" (II, 665).

24. Yan Michalski, in his preface to *O Santo Inquérito*, considers at length the many parallels between Branca Dias and Zé-do-Burro (II, 574–578).

25. It is interesting that Jorge Amado, in his novel *Tenda dos Milagres* (São Paulo: Livraria Martins Editôra, 1969), also avails himself of the samba-club tradition to create a total, mythicized portrait of his protagonist, Pedro Archanjo.

26. "Our Club has problems / which we aren't going to hide / because they're in the newspaper. / The main one is money. / Tucão abandoned us / and a Club without a bookie / my friends, is in bad shape" (II, 682).

27. "I'm president of the Club, / I demanded the privilege: / after all, we're colleagues" (II, 684).

28. "DEATH TO GETÚLIO... DOWN WITH GETÚLIO" (II, 741).

29. ". . . with cowboy hats, armed to the teeth, each one of them twirling two revolvers and chewing gum" (II, 716).

30. "I'm just analyzing the situation. We have to put on our thinking caps and examine all the hypotheses. I'm beginning to think that a disaster of enormous proportions must have occurred and that we should prepare ourselves for a long stay inside this tunnel" (II, 769–770).

31. "To hell with the rules. In each one of them we leave a piece of our liberty" (II, 777).

32. "We need to think of Agriculture! To fill in the tunnels and take advantage of the hillside to plant coffee, cacau, cotton, sugar cane, bananas—and why not say it—potatoes! . . . Therein lies our future! With that we shall be free forever of traffic jams and shall fulfill our destiny as an essentially agricultural nation" (II, 784).

33. "That's your problem. A wife, each man must kill his own" (II, 769).

34. Peter J. Schoenbach, as respondent to a paper by Leon F. Lyday entitled "*O Túnel* and *Vamos Soltar os Demônios*: Dias Gomes' Two Most Recent Plays" (XVI Congreso del Instituto Internacional de Literatura Iberoamericana, 28 August 1973), has posited that in Sérgio, Dias Gomes has created what is in many ways an autobiographical character: "I believe that he is, indeed, an absurdist portrayal of the intellectual as a type, and by extension, of the playwright. The dilemma of the artist in Brazil today is lived by Alfredo Dias Gomes. As Sérgio worked for the system, earning his living as a journalist, Dias is the author of several extremely popular television 'novelas.' There is little time for him to write and even less chance of having his work produced for the stage in view of the problem of censorship. There are further parallels. The playwright's wife, under his tutelage, has become even more successful as a writer for television than he, and they, like Sérgio and Nara, have two children, a boy and a girl."

35. "All heroes are ridiculous" (II, 810).

36. "Only the irresponsible and insensitive don't feel fear" (II, 810).

37. "I believe more in the Devil than in God. I'm serious. God is a vague idea, abstract. The Devil, no. He's concrete. He's inside of us" (II, 822).

38. "When people make love, as we just did, it releases a band of them. But it is only in that hour that we have the courage to release our devils. Normally, we keep them well guarded and subject to the severest vigilance" (II, 822).

39. *Sérgio.* . . . And your husband—

Nara. He is—a very weak man!

Sérgio. (*His vanity wounded, but carrying on in his role*) He doesn't give me that impression. On the contrary, he seems a man of great moral and mental strength.

Nara. And it's precisely that which makes him vulnerable. Or rather, the awareness that he has of that strength. That makes him self-sufficient, egocentric, vain, cruel, and cowardly, at times.

Sérgio. A monster!

Nara. No, just an intellectual. Capable, perhaps, of great deeds, but also of the greatest weaknesses. Frequently vacillating between dying for a cause and living for the many small pleasures of a comfortable existence. In short, a being who is at the same time admirable and despicable." [II, 823]

15. Plínio Marcos: Reporter of Bad Times

Peter J. Schoenbach

On December 16, 1966, the theater world of Brazil was both shocked and moved by a low-budget production held in a café. *Dois Perdidos numa Noite Suja* ("Two lost men in a dirty night"), produced and acted in by its young author, Plínio Marcos de Barros, took São Paulo by surprise.

The author was not new to the theater. An ordinary man whose plays are written in the crude and simple language he learned on the piers of his native Santos, Marcos had been associated with drama there since 1956, when he joined the Clube de Arte, an amateur organization, as an actor. Shortly thereafter, in 1958, Pascoal Carlos Magno, father of student theater in Brazil, met him at one of the periodic Student Theater Festivals, sponsored in the different cities by the then Minister of Education. The aspiring playwright explained that his play *Barrela* ("Gang bang") had been banned by the censors. Carlos Magno had the play approved, and it went on to win prizes in that and other amateur festivals.[1]

Before his success with *Barrela*, the controversial dramatist had had a varied, albeit undistinguished, career as an office boy, factory worker, soccer player, and sometime soldier.[2] Of humble origins, he had not gone beyond an elementary school education. His contact with many segments of the lower classes provided him with abundant material and developed his extraordinary ear for the language they spoke, larded with slang and profanity. His wife, the actress Walderez de Barros, whom he met in 1960, has aided him and served as an inspiration in his career. They married shortly after he moved to the capital in order to work as a street vendor. Two of his lesser plays date from this period: *Os Fantoches* ("The puppets") and *Enquanto os Navios Atracam* ("While the ships moor"). After parts as an extra in *Caesar and Cleopatra* in Cacilda Becker's Company, he appeared as an actor in Lauro César Muniz's *O Santo Milagroso* ("The miraculous saint") and in the same year (1963) in *Onde Canta o Sabiá* ("Where the sabia sings"). After a successful television play, another of his works, *Nossa Música, Nossa Gente* ("Our music, our people"), was closed by the censors in April 1964, shortly after the military coup. The next year *Reportagem de um Tempo Mau* ("Report of a bad time") was also prohibited. Nonetheless, he was administrator of the São Paulo production of *Opinião* ("Opinion"), a show with political overtones, for Nídia Lícia's Company. There he was to direct another of his works, *Jornada de um Imbecil até o Entendimento* ("Journey of an imbecile toward understanding"), but it, too, was stopped by his old nemesis, "a censura," the censors. When Walderez bore their second son, he set out on his own with borrowed money to do *Dois Perdidos*.

Plínio was not interested in the clichés of the theater of the "Festive Left."[3] Instead of the heroic workers and evil capitalists who tended to dominate Brazilian plays of the time, he chose to record the brutal facts of the life of society's lowest classes. The protagonists in his dramatic world are the *marginais*—the underworld of criminals who were produced by the social injustices of Brazil in the sixties. He was in agreement with the ideology of the Arena Theater, which was the center of social drama, and was personally friendly and professionally involved with its chief proponents (Augusto Boal and Gianfrancesco Guarnieri). However, Marcos expressed his personal theatrical goal in the following manner: "The theater was the form that I found to testify about the bad times in which we are living. I speak about people that I knew and I know, people that are made petty by people . . . My theater is just that. I present the facts like a reporter. I know the facts, and I don't know the solution. The message that I have to give is just this: there are people living in hell out there. My ideal is to get the audience to think about what should be done."[4] He therefore focused on the victims of the explosive urban situation in the fastest growing city in the world, São Paulo.

The working class had been seen on the stage before in Brazil. Nelson Rodrigues had dealt with it, especially with members from the "zona norte" of Rio de Janeiro, the working-class district. His *Vestido de Noiva* (1943, "Wedding dress") had incorporated the spoken language of Brazil and had presented modern techniques of direction. Despite the new importance given to the working class, social problems were secondary to Rodrigues. His was a psychological theater, and the censorship obstacles that caused *Album de Família* (1945, "Family album") to be banned for twenty years were a result of Rodrigues's preoccupation with Freudian themes. Treatment of incest and other taboo sexual activities were unacceptable to the bourgeois audiences of the time. Like Marcos, Rodrigues had patterned his dialogue according to the origin and class of the characters. Marcos was to carry this technique to its ultimate by employing slang almost to the exclusion of traditional literary vocabulary. The debut of *Vestido de Noiva* had also marked the arrival of the currents of European stage techniques to the national theater, and the expressionistic direction of Zbigniew Ziembinsky underlined the psychological emphasis of the playwright.

The censors objected to the themes and language of the new dramatist, as they had to those of Nelson Rodrigues. As they stated when prohibiting *Navalha na Carne* ("Knife in the flesh"), there is "a profusion of obscene scenes, indecent terms, anomalies and morbidity exploited in the play, . . . which is void of a constructive, positive message."[5]

The fact that such social elements exist and speak just as Marcos portrayed them, and that the government does nothing to correct the injustices while crushing such criticism, is ironic. As critic Yan Michalski stated, rather than blame the playwright and the Brazilian theater, those who permit such conditions to exist should be brought to task.[6]

The battle of the *palavrão*, or "cuss word," as the confrontation between theater and government came to be called, centered on the underworld slang and off-color language that constituted in itself a large part of Marcos's dramatic breakthrough. It was necessary for the characters of *Navalha* to speak naturally in order to create a convincing dramatic ambience. The language thus functions as an important factor in plot development, even though the shock impact is not unintentional. Used by one character against another, it becomes a weapon of degradation. At other moments the very surprise of its crude descriptiveness elicits a laugh.[7] Just as all the language is reduced to the lowest common denominator, emotion and conflict are also at the most basic level.

Marcos does not subscribe to formal theories that would make him a Naturalist or a Neo-Realist. His philosophy lacks the sophisticated determinism of the former and differs from his Brazilian contemporaries in the latter, because his vision is one of participant, not observer.[8] The relative lack of success of the later works can be attributed to diminished authenticity, since he was dealing with social strata with which he was not as familiar. As a result, these plays slip into melodrama, as in *Quando as Máquinas Param* ("When the machines stop"), or political naïveté, as in *Jornada de um Imbecil até o Entendimento*. In the latter, the stylization inhibits the dialogue. However, these works do demonstrate a versatility that, after *Dois Perdidos* and *Navalha*, was necessary to keep Marcos from repeating himself artistically.

All his dramaturgy is concerned with the political and social realities of contemporary Brazil. In the first of his plays, the protagonists are members of the underworld, not hardened criminals, but the poorest element whose desperate plight keeps them on the fringes of society. They are unskilled, not members of organized labor, yet they aspire to the middle class and the accouterments of bourgeois life. Marcos's characters are not like the romantic protagonists of the theater of Guarnieri, who are concerned with unions and strikes (for example, Tião in *Eles Não Usam Black-tie* [1959, "They don't wear a tux"]). Instead of having his characters work in concert as a Marxist writer would wish, Plínio portrays them as turning on each other. They are hopeless individuals venting their frustration and anger on fellow sufferers. Such acts of violence against the bourgeoisie as there are in his plays are irrational and counterproductive.

Plínio Marcos's first produced play was originally conceived for television with the title *O Terror*.[9] Based on a short story by Alberto Moravia, it was adapted for the stage and was favorably reviewed under its new, evocative name, *Dois Perdidos numa Noite Suja*.[10] Undoubtedly the original had to be changed because the same term was applied to the urban guerrilla movement in Brazil during the late 1960s.

By means of two symbols, shoes and a flute, Marcos develops the theme of social isolation or "marginalization." Striving for these objects, which represent means of upward mobility, the characters Tonho and Paco propel themselves toward the tragic denouement. Tonho sees the shoes as a key ingredient of bourgeois respectability, which society denies to him. Paco had obtained a shiny pair as a present from an admirer for his beautiful flute playing.[11] Through his musical talent, he had achieved a higher status. However, he is victimized by another member of his class, as he is to be by Tonho. The flute, which he played in bars and gardens to get free drinks, is stolen while he is in a drunken stupor.

The protagonists are residents of a São Paulo flophouse. Before Tonho's entrance, Paco busies himself by shining and admiring his own shoes. He also desultorily plays a harmonica, an indication of his musical inclination. Paco ridicules Tonho because of his worn footwear, provoking a violent reaction from his burly companion. They circle each other like strange dogs, taking each other's measure. Tonho tells Paco to stop playing and is so infuriated by the derisive laughter about his shoes that he attempts to throttle the weaker man. The attack leaves Paco gasping for breath and foreshadows the ending. Paco is sensitive and nervous. When accused of stealing the new shoes, he breaks into hysterical sobs, quickly followed by more mocking laughter. While Paco is masochistic and gives the impression of below-average intelligence, Tonho, on the other hand, is defensive, insecure, and quick to anger, earning the sobriquet of "Sr. Zangado" ("Mr. Angry"). Another beating follows, but peace is finally made as Paco manages to placate Tonho with his harmonica playing. He admits that the shoes are at the root of his resentment. Tonho produces a revolver for which he has no bullets and frightens Paco, who reiterates his fear that his companion will kill him for the shoes. They eventually do establish a certain comradeship and reveal their daydreams to each other.

With Tonho in command, they decide to hold up a pair of unsuspecting lovers in the park. In the second act, as dusk approaches, they enter a "lover's lane" where Paco is more interested in watching the couples kiss than in preparing an ambush. Finally he grabs a stick, and, as prearranged, the "dois Perdidos" approach an amorous twosome, claiming to be policemen. This is of no avail, since the boy infuriates Tonho by immediately seeing through the ruse because of his old, worn-out shoes. They seize watch, wallet, ring, and shoes from the hapless victim. Paco ridicules him when he discovers that the shoes have lifts because the boy is shorter than his date. Then, without provocation, Paco strikes him on the head, knocking him unconscious, and they flee.

In the third act, Tonho is terrified that the police will catch them, while Paco fantasizes that he will become the "terror of São Paulo." They set out to divide the booty equally. Paco insists that he be given the pair of new shoes, although he is aware of Tonho's obsession. He relents only when granted everything else.

In an ironic twist, the shoes prove to be too small for Tonho's feet. Out of desperation he offers to sell or exchange them for Paco's. The latter enjoys seeing Tonho squirm, teasing him unmercifully before finally agreeing to the switch. The offer comes too late, however, for Tonho greets the overture by striking his companion on the head with the revolver. Furiously, he tears off Paco's shoes, only to discover that they, also, are too small. Tonho throws himself at the dead Paco and beats his prostrate body, which even then seems to smile mockingly. The other men in the hotel are awakened, and the desk clerk calls the police. He replaces the shoes on the corpse with the comment, "Já. Está pronto para o entêrro."[12]

These two lost souls are impelled by the harsh rejection of society to vent their frustrations on each other. They superficially resemble characters in the absurdist theater, but "they differ from Beckett's model to the extent that they do not spend themselves in silence, but rather opt for violence, which consumes itself in useless noise."[13] If the force of their anger and resentment were turned on others in an organized manner instead of striking out blindly, as did Paco against the robbery victim, a meaningful confrontation might occur between haves and have-nots. Marcos shows that flutes and new shoes, the means to a better life, are not available for the latter in Brazilian society. Paco knows this intuitively, and so he opts for real criminality. As critic Tite de Lemos concludes, "If one cannot be powerful, because one was not born powerful, no recourse exists except that of attacking the powerful by means of crime."[14] Those who are not powerful are as lost as the protagonists of the play.

The text is extremely terse, completely stripped of any excess verbiage. The central feature, the powerfully realistic dialogue, reveals command of the language and an understanding of the psychology of the characters. The message communicated is so socially relevant that the controversial Archbishop of Olinda and Recife, Dom Helder Câmara, has said that the play was worth several sermons.[15] This liberal prelate was referring to the function of the theater as a social document to awaken the public's conscience to the existence of poverty and injustice in Brazil.

The next play to be produced by this Brazilian "angry young man" is his best known, *Navalha na Carne. Dois Perdidos*, although full of slang, had relatively few *palavrãoes. Navalha* was daring in theme and language, so it was prohibited by the censors in May of 1967. Undaunted by such obstacles, the late Cacilda Becker and her husband, Walmor Chagas, staged *Navalha* in the private theater, Centro de Estudos Teatrais, which they operated in their residence. By September of 1967 the battle was won, for the censors reversed their previous decision and productions were staged in Rio and São Paulo with excellent casts.[16]

The question of *Navalha* was related to a general confrontation between the authorities and the "classe teatral," as the theater people call themselves, which led to a strike less than a year later. Early in 1968 the Teatro Oficina of São Paulo was prevented from presenting Leroi Jones's *Dutchman*, and actress Maria Fernanda had to close her company's production of Tennessee Williams's *A Streetcar Named Desire* when she was banned from the stage for thirty days. Jorge Andrade's *Senhora na Bôca do Lixo* ("Lady in the slums") was also prohibited, even though it had just enjoyed a successful, uncut run in Portugal (hardly noted for its tolerant theater censors). In response, all the theaters of Brazil were closed for three days, and demonstrations by the major figures of the national stage took place in Rio and São Paulo from February 11 to 13. Finally, Minister of Justice Gama e Silva agreed to accede to the strikers' demands. Feelings still were running high, however, and in June the newspaper *Estado de São Paulo* ran an editorial urging moderation, which was interpreted as supporting the government's position of censorship.[17] All the recipients of the Sacy prizes in theater for the best performances of the year returned their statuettes en masse in protest to the sponsoring newspaper. Décio de Almeida Prado, dean of the drama critics, who had always supported the theater world, resigned from the *Estado*, because he felt caught between the paper's position and that of his theater colleagues.[18]

In a sense, *Navalha* is an extension or elaboration of *Dois Perdidos*. In this *Huis Clos* of the poor, we delve into an even lower social class. The theater of cruelty in the manner of Artaud and Genet is relieved by a lyricism and ritualistic magic that are not present in *Navalha*. In forceful language three unhappy souls tear at each other. Only the prostitute, Neusa Suely, reveals a touch of humanity, a desire for communication—hence, the pathetic and moving, "Será que somos gente?" Searching for a grain of human dignity, she tells Vado, "As vêzes chego a pensar: puxa, será que eu sou gente? Será que eu, você, o Veludo somos gente?"[19] Her vulnerability provides an opening for her gigolo's sadistic maltreatment of her. He, Vado, is in turn manipulated by the homosexual, Veludo, who has the effect of threatening his strutting *machismo*.

The purgative impact of the violence and aggression, reflected especially in scatological language, is a veritable knife-thrust into our own flesh. The reader-theatergoer vicariously participates in the world of these almost subhuman beings, reduced by circumstances to the most elementary passions. Marcos shows them dealing with each other as objects. Pleasure is negotiated, not exchanged, in the search for a little warmth. As Anatol Rosenfeld observes, "The money earned by the prostitute from those who buy her, and which serves to buy the pimp, is stolen by the homosexual in order for him to be able to buy, in turn, a little affection."[20] The message is not meant to be restricted just to the tiny minority of *marginais* that the characters represent. By extension, the author is speaking about the falsification of values of the greater society, here seen in a grotesquely deformed and primitive microcosm.

The play is written in one act, and the action takes place in a fifth-class hotel. Neusa returns to her room to find Vado in bed, reading a comic book. He had not been able to go out because the money she was to have left for him was missing. Veludo, the *bicha* ("homosexual") janitor, admits taking it to obtain a marijuana cigarette and arrange a liaison with a boy in the neighborhood bar. This is revealed in a sadistic interrogation carried out by Vado, who takes the cigarette away from Veludo. Veludo pleads for a "toke" on the "grass," which Vado alternately denies him and forces on him. In the struggle of wills, in which the question of honor among thieves is contested, Veludo is manhandled, almost killed. Yet his cries, worthy of a soap opera, "Ai! ai! ai! Meus Deus, que loucura! que loucura divina!"[21] could refer to his contact with the gigolo during the struggle. His masochism matches Vado's sadism and makes him invincible, since any rough treatment, verbal or physical, becomes sexual in his strange world. The use of force, which is so successful in the pimp's intimidation of Neusa, fails when applied to the ambiguous Veludo. Vado is left disoriented, doubting his own virility.

Neusa senses the attraction between the men and interrupts, expelling Veludo from the room. She is then debased and humiliated by Vado. He forces her to look at herself in a mirror without makeup. In desperation, she produces a knife and tries to force him to make love to her. Vado dissuades her, explaining that he treats his women badly to drive them wild ("Judio de mulher p'ra elas gamarem").[22] In the pathetic final scene, Neusa calls out after the exiting Vado and sits eating a cold sandwich alone as the curtain falls.

In *Navalha na Carne*, Marcos proves himself a master in delineating psychological relationships, such as in the case of Vado and Veludo. The dialogue consists of two levels: that of the words themselves, which are as elemental as the mental processes of the characters, and that of the much more subtle and complex emotions that lie at the root of the play. The action is moved forward by the dynamic tension created between the two levels.[23]

We have indicated that the relationships revolve around each character achieving a position of superiority relative to the others. They attack to prevent being attacked and react aggressively. Nonetheless, each has false pride according to his self-determined role: the gigolo as a self-important manipulator of women, the homosexual in his defiant inversion that disturbs the relatively simple relationship between Vado and Neusa, and the latter with her moving plea for understanding and her need to feel young and attractive. Each is unmasked during the course of the play. Vado feels the stirrings of doubt stimulated by the insinuations of the exhibitionistic Veludo at the play's end. Veludo finds himself threatened by Neusa at knife point. He manages to extricate himself with a verbal smoke screen, but he is momentarily placed on the defensive by her recourse to violence. Besides being humiliated by the others for stealing the money, Veludo is thrown out of the room by a jealous Neusa. She, also, is reduced to the realization of her aging loneliness by Vado, who unfeelingly strips her of her last illusion.

An examination of language in *Navalha na Carne* indicates a careful selection of words for their dramatic impact. There is not a mere outpouring of epithets and street expressions. As Joel Pontes has stated, a studied elaboration of these terms is employed to characterize the three souls.[24] Besides the strongest expressions *merda, trepar* ("shit," "screw"), and the inevitable *puta, viado,* and *bicha* ("whore," "queer," "homo") to refer to the characters, there are many words that are strong, but not necessarily relevant only to a prostitute, pimp, or homosexual, such as *vaca, nojenta, vagabunda, cachorro, sem-vergonha, sacana* ("cow," "disgusting woman," "tramp," "son of a bitch," "shameless one," "pederast"). These are combined with the former, for example, *puta nojenta,* in a great number of variants. In addition, other insults are used that are acceptable even for the most conservative audiences, such as *desgraçado, miserável, paspalho,* and *canalha* ("wretch," "miserable one," "fool," "rogue").

On some occasions, words are used for dramatic impact with ironic effect. Thus, when Neusa suspects another "lady of the night" of having betrayed her, *filha da puta* ("daughter of a whore") is the insult that she uses, simultaneously affronting herself. She curses out of desperation as she explodes against the injustices of her lot. Veludo's speech is that of the homosexual, full of diminutives and words usually reserved for use by women ("Adoro," [I adore]; "Que homem bruto, meu Deus," [What a brutish man, my God!]; "Deus me livre," [God save me]; "São Jorge Guerreiro," [Saint George the Warrior]). He also uses a more sophisticated language of verbal aggression. Vado, who can only express himself in epithets sprinkled liberally in the *gíria* ("slang") of the underworld, uses the *palavrão* as a symbol of virility.

Certain subjects employed by the language are developed within particular scenes. In the tense scene in which Vado refuses to allow and then forces Veludo to smoke, the most violent language is absent as it would detract from the action. The verbs *querer* ("to want") and *fumar* ("to smoke") are repeatedly used ("quero fumar," "quero que fume"). Later in the play, Vado perceives the impact of Veludo's vindictive line "galinha velha" ("old hen"), and he, too, seizes on Neusa's age to torture her. Variants such as *coroa* ("hag") abound as he abuses her mercilessly on the sensitive subject of her fleeting youth. The extraordinary effect of the masterful language is to underline its function, not as a means of communication but as a means of aggression.

Although the atmosphere and characters are more stereotyped than those of *Dois Perdidos*, once again in *Navalha na Carne* Plínio Marcos achieved a moving and highly theatrical indictment of injustice in Brazilian society.

His career since these plays has been less successful. He has experimented with a great variety of themes and styles. Since many of his works had already been written and put aside awaiting the chance for production, Marcos immediately followed his first breakthrough with several shows. *Homens de Papel* ("Paper men") and *Quando as Máquinas Param* were both staged within a few months of each other in Rio and São Paulo.[25] These plays, while effective on the stage, do not read well. They represent a departure from the first two plays in several ways. There are more characters in *Homens de Papel*, and both works take place in a different social milieu. However, they are less successful, since the psychological intensity and suspense that contribute to the effectiveness of *Navalha* and *Dois Perdidos* are missing.

Homens de Papel is the story of the exploitation of a group of urban poor who earn a living collecting scrap paper in São Paulo. Their leader and tormentor, Berrão, uses their services to obtain the paper that he then drives to a factory on his truck. He rounds off the weight of the sacks brought to him and pays the lowest possible price. The *catadores* ("collectors") do not have the option of selling directly to the factory, since Berrão has bribed the appropriate person there.

The plot deals with an incipient revolt to force Berrão to pay better wages. Chicão is plotting with the help of Tião, whose wife, Maria Vai, is having an affair with the hated leader. By playing on the wounded pride of the jealous husband, Chicão gets Tião to propose a work stoppage to the others. A conflict is created by the arrival of Frido, Gá, and Nhanha, a family that has come to the city from the interior. They plan to earn the money necessary to treat their young girl, Gá, who is mentally retarded. They have gathered six bags of paper, leaving little for the others to find, and consequently are set upon by the "homens de papel." Family loyalty, a sentiment that is nonexistent among the strikers, prevails over class solidarity. Despite the enmity of the others, Frido and Nhanha render the work stoppage pointless by looking after their own interests.

In the degenerate world of these *marginais*, even the love her parents feel for Gá is doomed to tragedy. Côco, an imbecilic member of the gang, shows interest in her from the beginning. He has a broken doll that he lends on several occasions to the retarded girl. At the play's end, he kills Gá when she resists his advances. The group manages to act with solidarity first to kill Côco and then to force Berrão to pay Nhanha for her daughter's burial. In the pessimistic conclusion, however, everyone returns to work, intimidated by Berrão.

Homens de Papel is set in the streets of São Paulo, among the poorest of its inhabitants. The theme is similar to that of *Dois Perdidos* and *Navalha*. The members of the lower classes exploit one another rather than organizing and confronting the society that oppresses them. Berrão exploits the *catadores* as a parasite of his own class, just as Vado had used Neusa in *Navalha*. The *marginais* cannot improve their lot while they prey on each other.

Although related by theme, the artistic value of this and the later plays is inferior to *Dois Perdidos* and *Navalha*. There is, for instance, a constant slipping into the sort of pathos characteristic of the Brazilian television *novela*, or soap opera. This is the result of an overly ingenuous characterization of the rural family, especially of Nhanha, the mother. As Décio de Almeida Prado observed, "Its heroine is overly perfect, containing an almost romantic element of idealization—the country seen by a city man like Plínio Marcos—who conflicts with the raw realism of the other characters."[26] The other characters are also exaggerated and fall far short of the complex psychological verisimilitude of Neusa Suely or Tonho. The end is particularly contrived and unconvincing.[27]

The other hit of 1968, *Quando as Máquinas Param*, deals with a slightly different social ambience: that of the working class. Zé and Nina belong more to the world first brought to the Brazilian stage by Gianfrancesco Guarnieri in his *Eles Não Usam Black-tie*.[28] Zé is a working-class family man who aspires to the security and perquisites of the middle class (a television set and season tickets to see the Corinthians play football). Nina wants nothing more than a happy husband and a child born of their love. He is roughhewn, free with four-letter words, while she is more refined and seemingly from a higher social class.

Unfortunately Zé, an unskilled worker, has been laid off, and throughout the play he unsuccessfully searches for work. In fact, Plínio Marcos is undertaking a study of the process of "marginalization." The protagonist, who begins fully incorporated into society, is driven by economic injustices to increasingly desperate straits.

Despite a lively dialogue, an idiomatic authenticity, and an exceptional eye for the details of the life of the Brazilian urban poor, the plot is quite banal. The struggling young couple seems excessively stereotyped. The ending, which illustrates to the maximum the shortcomings of the play, slips into the cheapest sentimental melodrama. Nina reveals that they are to have a child, but Zé insists that an abortion must be performed because he is unemployed and their creditors are hounding them. She refuses, and in the quarrel that follows, he strikes her in the stomach, causing her to lose the baby. This denouement is more suitable for a television *novela*, or soap opera, than for a serious social drama.

The next work of the 1968 season, *Barrela*, as previously mentioned, had been the first play by Plínio Marcos to be performed. Carlos Magno had managed to have the amateur production presented in Santos, despite censorship problems. Ten years later the Teatro Jovem in Rio undertook to stage it professionally (in a slightly modified version) and had completed rehearsals when the censors banned it definitively in March of 1968.[29] Although produced later, it belongs to the early plays in tone as well as subject matter.

The author produces a striking indictment of the Brazilian penal system by dealing with common criminals in prison. The language is as strong as that of *Navalha na Carne*, and the violence and ugliness are on a par with that of such works as *The Brig*, which was shocking American audiences at about the same time. The theme is again the struggle for domination between the weak and the strong. This candid picture of life behind bars is highly schematic. The development of the story line is predictable. Marcos draws on his personal experiences as a prisoner to communicate the degradation of a homosexual *curra*, or group rape.

Bereco is *xerife*, boss of the cell block. He intervenes to prevent the other prisoners from picking on one of their number, Portuga. The latter, in turn, mercilessly teases inmate Tirica for having had relations with another prisoner while still in the reformatory. A new arrival is introduced into the tension-charged atmosphere. He is a young man charged with disturbing the peace in a bar. A battle for his favors culminates in a gang rape, and Tirica takes advantage of the confusion to stab his tormentor, Portuga, to death. The boy is released with the changing of the guard and the murderer sent to solitary confinement.

In *Barrela*, Plínio Marcos has written a direct and powerful comment on Brazilian houses of correction and the society that produces them. The central theme in his dramaturgy, the disadvantaged turning on each other rather than on their tormentor, is clearly delineated here as well.

In June of 1968, Rio audiences were treated to an outstanding production of *Jornada de um Imbecil até o Entendimento*.[30] It represents a radical change of style if not of theme. Instead of a realistic approach, Marcos utilized a stylized combination of the *auto popular* and the circus farce—the two most essentially indigenous forms in Brazilian theater.[31] While following the example of Ariano Suassuna with regard to style, Marcos continues to study the relationship between oppressor and oppressed, a constant throughout his work. He is clearly speaking in allegorical terms about capitalist society. The dramatic expression of the exploitation of workers by owners with the connivance of the Church is not new to Brazilian theater. The "Seminário de Dramaturgia" at the Arena Theater in São Paulo (c. 1958–1962) produced such social playwrights as Augusto Boal, Guarnieri, and Roberto Freire, who wrote about this subject. In the strict censorship that prevailed after 1964, however, such material was acceptable only when cloaked in the language of a parable. "Since he did not mention Brazil and agrarian reform, and just talked about one man having many hats and others having no hat at all, apparently the censorship didn't get it."[32] Although Marcos contended that the new mode marked a move toward a more popular theater, it can be argued that *Navalha* speaks more directly to the workers and common people.[33]

Originally titled *Chapéu sobre Paralelepípedos para Alguém Chutar* ("Hat on the cobblestones for someone to kick"), *Jornada* uses the symbol of the hat to represent power, affluence, and capital. Mandrião, the leader, and Teco, the "religious" authority, manipulate the dissidents, Pilico and Manduca, who wish to have their own hats. They earn their living by borrowing Mandrião's *chapéus* and using them to beg. He also forces them to buy their food from him, and Teco aids authority by creating the image of a horrible hell that awaits hat robbers. The revolutionary potential is destroyed by Mandrião's ability to set his opponents off against each other, to divide and conquer. Pilico is bought off and Manduca eliminated. Even so, the ending is meant to offer a spark of hope. The most conformist character, Popo, is shocked by these totalitarian methods into thinking for himself for the first time. The play is politically naïve and lacks the lively and spontaneous repartee of the other works. Although his stylization detracts from the dialogue, Plínio Marcos reveals in *Jornada* that he is capable of writing good, theatrically convincing drama other than social realism.

His most recently produced play, *Balbina de Iansã* (1970), draws heavily on the Afro-Brazilian cult of *Umbanda* (the São Paulo version of the *candomblé* of Salvador and *macumba* of Rio). Marcos utilizes the setting and customs of a *terreiro* ("voodoo locale"), that of Pedra Branca, to weave the tale of Balbina and João. The extensive incorporation of music and dance from real *escolas de samba*, as the carnival clubs are called, gave the production authenticity. Marcos directed and produced the show, which received relative critical success in São Paulo and Rio. The lovers belong to rival *terreiros* and are a sort of Romeo and Juliet à la *brasileira*. The evil *mãe de Santo* ("sorceress"), Zefa, has Balbina severely beaten when she feels threatened by Balbina's challenge of her leadership. She tries to keep Balbina on the *terreiro* by intimidation and deceives her by telling her that João is dead. Balbina loses faith in Iansã when informed of the rumor. In the denouement, João comes to save Balbina and joins her in renouncing the African gods, exclaiming, "Minha fé é a gamação que tenho em Balbina."[34] The play is more picturesque than profound. Although authentically Brazilian in language and setting, the work seems trite in comparison with his best.

There is no doubt that Plínio Marcos has made a major contribution to the Brazilian theater. The themes and language of the first plays alone would guarantee him a place among the most important Brazilian playwrights. The later works show him never to be satisfied, always searching for new dramatic forms. He revolutionized the Brazilian theater just as Nelson Rodrigues had done twenty-five years before. *Vestido de Noiva* was the first Brazilian play in which the language employed was not a literary, peninsular Portuguese. The speech was filled with idioms and regional expressions and did not use the second person of the verbs, an affection that kept the landmark *Deus Lhe Pague* (1934, "God bless you") by Joracy Camargo from being a truly Brazilian play.

Plínio Marcos employs the language of the underworld. His knowledge of *gíria* and scatology leads to a convincing realism that enables him to re-create the pathetic and repugnant ambience of Brazil's criminal element. Marcos's innovations in technique, presenting the inhuman conditions of the poorest, disenfranchised Brazilians without romanticizing, make a direct conflict with the censors inevitable. Nonetheless, many of his works have been performed virtually intact and serve as an accurate social document, which heightens the public awareness of these problems by means of his art. With his relative youth and despite his limited education, there is reason to expect that he will continue to play a leading role in the national dramaturgy. Most significant in his work is its essential Brazilian character, which illustrates his desire "to create a regionalism and through it achieve the universal."[35]

NOTES

1. See Sábato Magaldi, "O Proibido Plínio, Antigo Frajola," *Jornal da Tarde*, 10 May 1967, p. 9; and Yan Michalski, "*Barrela*, a Peça que Conta a Vida como Ela é," *Jornal do Brasil*, 20 March 1968.

2. According to Marcos, he lasted ten months in the air force and spent time in prison on three occasions as guest of the army, navy, and federal police. The navy found him innocent, the army did not proffer charges, but the police case is still pending. Taped interview, 21 December 1970.

3. "A Esquerda Festiva" is the term applied to the dissenters from the Left who used their political action for social activities—e.g., participation in a strike was a good way for a girl to meet exciting new people.

4. Jefferson del Rios, *Fôlha de São Paulo*, 19 March 1968. This and all other translations are my own.

5. "Edict of 14 June 1968, published in the *Official Daily of the Union* on the 19th," cited in Sábato Magaldi, "Documento Dramático," *Estado de São Paulo*, n.d., as reprinted in Plínio Marcos, *Navalha na Carne* (São Paulo: Senzala Editôra, 1968). This is the only published play of Marcos and is an exceptionally beautiful edition. It consists of photographs of the Grupo Opinião (São Paulo cast) and imaginative graphics. The volume has no pagination but contains reprints of the following major critical articles (undated) on the play: Anatol Rosenfeld, "Navalha na Nossa Carne," *Estado de São Paulo*; Sábato Magaldi, "Documento Dramático," *Estado de São Paulo*; Décio de Almeida Prado, "A Prospecção de 'A Navalha na Carne,'" *Estado de São Paulo*, and others.

6. Michalski, "*Barrela*."

7. See Joel Pontes, "Plínio Marcos: Dramaturgo da Violência," *Latin American Theatre Review* 3, no. 1 (Fall 1969): 26; also published in the *Revista de Teatro*, no. 375 (May–June 1970), pp. 17–22.

8. Pontes calls him a *primario* ("primitive"), while Marcos prefers to apply the term *realismo crítico* ("critical realism") to his work (Pontes, *Latin American Theatre Review*, p. 22, and previously cited interview, respectively).

9. Manuscripts of this and all other plays discussed are in my possession. The original of *O Terror* contains detailed stage directions for television cameramen.

10. Alberto D'Aversa wrote seven articles on the play in the *Diarios de São Paulo*, which projected Marcos into the spotlight. A fine director as well as critic, the late D'Aversa encouraged many young talents. Also see Sábato Magaldi, *Jornal da Tarde*, 2 January 1967.

11. Both Paco and Tonho earned enough money to pay the lodging in the hotel as *biscates* ("handymen"), doing odd jobs. Any possessions had to depend on the generosity of others.

12. "O.K. He's ready for the funeral" (*Dois Perdidos numa Noite Suja*, MS.).

13. Sábato Magaldi, "Dois Perdidos, um Achado,"*Jornal da Tarde*, 28 December 1966.

14. Tite de Lemos, "O Teatro Vivo de Plínio Marcos,"*Jornal do Brasil*, 4 June 1967.

15. Pontes, "Plínio Marcos: Dramaturgo," *Latin American Theatre Review*, p. 20; Djalma Bittencourt, "Plínio Marcos," *Revista de Teatro*, no. 372 (November–December 1969), p. 6.

16. Tonia Carrero, Nelson Xavier, and Emiliano de Queiroz; Ruthineia de Morais, Paulo Villaca, and Edgard Gurgel Aranha, respectively.

17. *Estado de São Paulo*, 11 June 1968.

18. For representative documents and an appraisal of the Brazilian theater of this time, see "Teatro e Realidade Brasileira," *Revista de Civilização Brasileira* (Caderno Especial 2), July 1968. This special volume contains studies by a large number of authors on the Brazilian theater and has no designated editor.

19. "I wonder if we are people? Sometimes I think: gee, am I a person? Am I, are you, Veludo, people?" (*Navalha na Carne*).

20. Anatol Rosenfeld, "Navalha na Nossa Carne," *Estado de São Paulo*, as reprinted in the above-cited edition of *Navalha na Carne*.

21. "Oh, my God, what madness! What divine madness" (*Navalha na Carne*).

22. "I mistreat women because they love it" (ibid.).

23. Décio de Almeida Prado, "A Prospecção de *Navalha na Carne*," *Estado de São Paulo*, 1 October 1967; and in *Navalha na Carne*. He employs the term *dramatic transparency*, meaning "the capacity to reveal thoughts not explicit in the dialogue."

24. Pontes, "Plínio Marcos: Dramaturgo,"*Latin American Theatre Review*, pp. 24–26.

25. The former starred Maria della Costa under the direction of Jairo Arco e Flexa; the latter featured Miriam Mehler and Luis Gustavo. Not discussed in this study is the play *Dia Virá* by Plínio Marcos, which received an amateur performance at the Catholic Colegio des Oiseaux. It dealt with Jesus as a social revolutionary. See Sábato Magaldi, "Crítica,"*Jornal da Tarde*, 16 September 1967. Also see Marcos's one-act play *Verde que Te Quero Verde*, in *Primeira Feira Paulista de Opinião*, a collection of plays by such contemporary social playwrights as Augusto Boal, Jorge Andrade, Gianfrancesco Guarnieri, and others (MS). For a review of *Primeira Feira Paulista de Opinião*, see A.C. Carvalho, "Crítica," *Estado de São Paulo*, 1 September 1968, p. 21.

26. Décio de Almeida Prado, "Plínio Marcos Apresenta 2 Peças em São Paulo," *Estado de São Paulo*, 28 October 1967. See Yan Michalski,*Jornal do Brasil*, 13 and 25 November 1967, and 5 December 1967.

27. Michalski calls it "a dismal and totally untenable ending" (*Jornal do Brasil*, 13 November 1971). He also was increasingly critical of *Máquinas* from its premiere through its restagings. See *Jornal do Brasil*, 24 January 1968, 11 May 1969, and 1 April 1971.

28. Décio de Almeida Prado sees in the class setting the "little Italian of Brás [a neighborhood in São Paulo] in [the works of] Antônio de Alcântara Machado," referring to the modernist author of *Brás, Bexiga e Barra Funda*. Alcântara Machado was the first to deal with the new, urban Brazilians who were emerging from the neighborhoods of São Paulo, such as those of Italian descent who lived in the working-class neighborhood of Brás.

29. Yan Michalski did review the dress rehearsal in "*Barrela*."

30. See Yan Michalski, "Jornada de Plínio Marcos para o Teatro Popular," *Jornal do Brasil*, 26 June 1968. The cast included the excellent black actor Milton Gonçalves, Ary Fontoura, and others associated with the Rio Opinião Group under the direction of João das Neves. An earlier version had been banned. The Group took its name from the first show, *Opinião*, staged in 1965, and it functioned as the Rio branch of the Arena Theater.

31. For a discussion of the *auto*, see L. H. Quackenbush, "The *auto* Tradition in Brazilian Drama," *Latin American Theatre Review* 5, no. 2 (Spring 1972): 29–43.

32. Bárbara Heliodora, "Theatre in Rio de Janeiro: 1968," *Latin American Theatre Review* 3, no. 1 (Fall 1969): 55.

33. Michalski doubts that the play can "establish a more intense and direct communication than the bourgeois naturalism of *Dois Perdidos* and *Navalha na Carne*" ("Jornada de Plínio Marcos").

34. "My faith is the love I have for Balbina" (*Balbina de Iansã*, MS). The speech is reminiscent of Calisto's declaration of faith in Melibea in *La Celestina*, a work that shares many parallels with *Balbina*.

35. Marcos, taped interview cited in note 2.

Notes on the Contributors

SANDRA MESSINGER CYPESS* has taught at Duke University, Point Park College, the University of Kentucky, and Carnegie-Mellon University. Her literary interests include narrative technique and Latin American drama. Her publications, some of which investigate the relationship between the theater in France and in Latin America, appear in *Hispania* and the *Latin American Theatre Review*.

FRANK DAUSTER* is professor of Spanish at Rutgers University. His nine books include the *Historia del teatro hispanoamericano: Siglos XIX y XX*, which reappeared in 1973 in an amplified edition. His articles have appeared in numerous professional and literary journals. In addition to editorial work for *Hispania* and the *Revista Iberoamericana*, he has served in various administrative and consulting capacities for the SSRC-ACLS and the MLA. He prepares the Latin American theater section for the *Handbook of Latin American Studies*.

ALYCE DE KUEHNE* earned graduate degrees at the University of Mexico. Formerly with the Universities of California and Brown, she has been directing theater in Spanish at Wayne State University since 1972. She has been devoted to the theater as actress and director in New York, Mexico, and California. Her publications on Pirandello, Brecht, and classical myth in Spanish American theater appear in *Hispania*, *Revista Iberoamericana*, and *LATR*.

MERLIN H. FORSTER* is professor of Spanish and Portuguese and director of the Center for Latin American and Caribbean Studies at the University of Illinois, Urbana-Champaign. His research interests are twentieth-century Latin American poetry and drama and the history of the decades between the two world wars in Latin American literature. Recent publications include a book on death in Mexican poetry, an annotated index to *Letras de México*, and several articles on contemporary poets and dramatists.

TAMARA HOLZAPFEL holds degrees from the University of North Carolina and the University of Iowa. A U.S. citizen since 1957, she has been teaching Spanish American literature at the University of New Mexico since 1964. Her articles and reviews on contemporary Mexican and Argentine fiction and theater appear in *Hispania*, *Modern Drama*, *Modern Language Journal*, *LATR*, and *Revista Iberoamericana* and in *Festschriften*.

JOHN K. KNOWLES has spent his adult life reading, studying, and teaching about Spanish America. His special literary interest in contemporary Mexican letters is the generation of postwar dramatists. Under his direction, the Modern Language Department of Salisbury State College (Maryland) has developed a strong cross-cultural approach in the teaching of languages and literature.

LEON F. LYDAY* is associate professor of Spanish at the Pennsylvania State University. His special interests are the Latin American drama and Colombian literature. His publications on several Spanish American and Brazilian playwrights appear in various professional journals. He is a member of the editorial board of *Modern International Drama*, and co-editor (with Frank Dauster) of *En un acto*, an anthology of Spanish American plays.

RICHARD MAZZARA is professor in the Department of Modern Languages at Oakland University (Michigan). His interest in Portuguese has led to programs in Portuguese and Latin American area studies at Franklin and Marshall College and Oakland University. He continues to teach French and Spanish, but his principal areas of research and publication are the modern Brazilian novel and theater.

MARGARET SAYERS PEDEN* is professor of Spanish at the University of Missouri, Columbia. She is the author of various articles and reviews on Spanish American theater and the contemporary novel appearing in *Hispania*, *LATR*, and *Modern Drama*. Her translations of works by Emilio Carballido and Egon Wolff will soon be followed by others of Horacio Quiroga, Octavio Paz, and Carlos Fuentes.

DONALD L. SCHMIDT is assistant professor of Spanish and Portuguese at the University of Denver, where he has been active in the humanities program on contemporary Mexico. His interests have focused on Argentina and Mexico, with publications on novel and theater appearing in *Hispania*, *LATR*, *The Americas*, and *Graduate Studies on Latin America*.

PETER J. SCHOENBACH is a Hispanist and professional musician and, since 1973, the dean and administrative coordinator of the Curtis Institute of Music in Philadelphia. A year's research in Brazil on a Foreign Area Fellowship led to his dissertation on the modern Brazilian social theater. He has taught at Temple and Minnesota and published in various professional journals.

EUGENE R. SKINNER is assistant professor of Spanish at the University of Iowa. His special interest is Cuban literature, stemming from a doctoral dissertation on the novels of Alejo Carpentier. His articles on education and theater in post-Revolutionary Cuba and in Mexico have appeared in the *LATR*, *Hispania*, *Southern Humanities Review*, and others.

GEORGE WOODYARD is chairman of the Department of Spanish and Portuguese at the University of Kansas. Editor of the *Latin American Theatre Review* since its inception in 1967, he is the author of articles and reviews on Latin American theater appearing in *Comparative Drama*, *Theatre Documentation*, *Luso-Brazilian Review*, and *Hispania*. His anthology of plays in English translation is titled *The Modern Stage in Latin America: Six Plays*.

*In addition, member of the Editorial Board of the *Latin American Theatre Review*.

Source Materials on Latin American Theater

Under each of the categories below is a select list of works or references. These lists are by no means complete, but they should serve as a useful guide to those interested in further inquiry into the contemporary theater in Latin America. Items listed under "Brazil" are national in scope, while those under "Spanish America" are international. Studies on individual playwrights and on the drama of specific Spanish American countries are thus not included. These, however, can be found through the bibliographies.

BIBLIOGRAPHIES

Hebblethwaite, Frank B. *A Bibliographical Guide to the Spanish American Theater*. Washington, D.C.: Pan American Union, 1969.
Rela, Walter. "Contribución a la bibliografía del teatro brasileño." *Cebela*, no. 1 (1965), pp. 109–129.
Woodyard, George W., and Leon F. Lyday. "Studies on the Latin American Theatre, 1960–1969." *Theatre Documentation* 2 (Fall 1969–Spring 1970): 49–84. [Spanish America and Brazil]

CRITICAL STUDIES

SPANISH AMERICA

Dauster, Frank N. *Historia del teatro hispanoamericano: Siglos XIX y XX*. 2d ed. Mexico City: Ediciones de Andrea, 1973.
———. "An Overview of the Spanish American Theatre." *Hispania* 50, no. 4 (December 1967): 996–1000.
———. "Recent Research in Spanish American Theater." *Latin American Research Review* 1, no. 2 (Spring 1966): 65–76.
———. "Social Awareness in Contemporary Spanish American Theater." *Kentucky Romance Quarterly* 14, no. 2 (1967): 120–125.
Green, Joan Rea. "Character and Conflict in the Contemporary Central American Theatre." In *Contemporary Latin American Literature*, edited by Harvey L. Johnson and Philip B. Taylor, Jr., pp. 103–108. Houston:

Latin American Studies Committee, Office of International Affairs, University of Houston, 1973.

———. "The Hero in Contemporary Spanish American Theatre: A Case of Diminishing Returns." *Latin American Theatre Review* 5, no. 2 (Spring 1972): 19–27.

Jones, Willis Knapp. *Behind Spanish American Footlights*. Austin: University of Texas Press, 1966.

———. *Breve historia del teatro latinoamericano*. Mexico City: Ediciones de Andrea, 1956.

Neglia, Erminio G. "Temas y rumbos del teatro rural hispanoamericano del siglo XX." *Latin American Theatre Review* 5, no. 1 (Fall 1971): 49–57.

Rojo, Grínor. *Orígenes del teatro hispanoamericano contemporáneo*. Valparaíso: Ediciones Universitarias, 1972.

Saz Sánchez, Agustín del. *Teatro hispanoamericano*. 2 vols. Barcelona: Editorial Vergara, 1963–1964.

———. *Teatro social hispanoamericano*. Barcelona: Editorial Labor, 1967.

Solórzano, Carlos. "The Contemporary Latin American Theatre." Translated by Rafael Sánchez. *Prairie Schooner* 39, no. 2 (Summer 1965): 118–125.

———. *Teatro latinoamericano del siglo XX*. Buenos Aires: Editorial Nueva Visión, 1961.

———. *El teatro latinoamericano en el siglo XX*. Mexico City: Editorial Pormaca, 1964.

Woodyard, George W. "The Theatre of the Absurd in Spanish America." *Comparative Drama* 3, no. 3 (Fall 1969): 183–192.

———. "Toward a Radical Theatre in Spanish America." In *Contemporary Latin American Literature*, edited by Harvey L. Johnson and Philip B. Taylor, Jr., pp. 93–102. Houston: Latin American Studies Committee, Office of International Affairs, University of Houston, 1973.

BRAZIL

Ayala, Walmir. "Brasil: Teatro de Hoje." *Cadernos Brasileiros*, no. 2 (April–June 1962), pp. 82–89.

Fernández, Oscar. "Brazil's New Social Theatre." *Latin American Theatre Review* 2, no. 1 (Fall 1968): 15–30.

Figueiredo, Guilherme. "Atuais Tendências do Teatro Brasileiro." *Revista Interamericana de Bibliografía* 15, no. 3 (July–September 1965): 209–225.

Gordon, Fortuna L. "The Theatre in Brazil Today." *Kentucky Foreign Language Quarterly* 13, no. 4 (1966): 229–236.

Hecker Filho, Paulo. "Teatro Brasileiro." *Revista do Livro* 6 (1961): 109–130.

Heliodora, Barbara. "El Momento Actual en el Teatro Brasileño." *Mundo Nuevo*, no. 3 (December 1968), pp. 79–83.

Jacobbi, Ruggiero. *Teatro in Brasile*. Bologne: Cappeli, 1961.

Magaldi, Sábato. *Panorama do Teatro Brasileiro*. São Paulo: Difusão Européia do Livro, 1962.

Martins, Wilson. "The Theater in Brazil." *Theatre Annual*, no. 20 (1963), pp. 20–40.

Pontes, Joel. "Agora, Brasil, Teatro." *O Tempo e o Modo do Brasil*, pp. 142–147. [*Caderno* published concurrently with *O Tempo e o Modo* (Lisbon), no. 50 (July–October 1967).]

————. "Dramaturgia Contemporânea no Brasil." *Luso-Brazilian Review* 3, no. 2 (Winter 1966): 25–42.

Prado, Décio de Almeida. *Apresentação do Teatro Brasileiro Moderno: Crítica Teatral, 1947–1955*. São Paulo: Livraria Martins Editôra, 1956.

Quackenbush, Louis H. "The *auto* Tradition in Brazilian Drama." *Latin American Theatre Review* 5, no. 2 (Spring 1972): 29–43.

Scarabótolo, Hélio Alberto. "Evolución de la Dramaturgia Brasileña." *Revista de Estudios de Teatro* 2, no. 5 (1962): 40–51.

————. "El Teatro Brasileño de Nuestros Días." *Ficción*, no. 39 (September–October 1962), pp. 43–50.

Thomas, Earl W. "Protest in the Novel and Theater." *In Brazil in the Sixties*, edited by Riordan Roett, pp. 379–421. Nashville: Vanderbilt University Press, 1972.

ANTHOLOGIES

SPANISH AMERICA

Colecchia, Francesca, and Julio Matas. *Selected Latin American One-Act Plays*. Pittsburgh: University of Pittsburgh Press, 1973. [10 plays]

Dauster, Frank N. *Teatro hispanoamericano: Tres piezas*. New York: Harcourt, Brace & World, 1965.

————, and Leon F. Lyday. *En un acto*. New York: D. Van Nostrand Co., 1974. [9 one-act plays]

Jones, Willis Knapp. *Men and Angels: Three South American Comedies*. Carbondale: Southern Illinois Press, 1970.

Lamb, Ruth S. *Three Contemporary Latin-American Plays*. Waltham, Mass.: Xerox College Publishing, 1973.

Luzuriaga, Gerardo, and Robert S. Rudder, eds. and trans. *The Orgy: Modern One-Act Plays from Latin America*. Los Angeles: UCLA Latin American Center, University of California, 1974.

Oliver, William I. *Voices of Change in the Spanish American Theater*. Austin: University of Texas Press, 1971. [6 plays]

Rodríguez-Sardiñas, Orlando, and Carlos Miguel Suárez Radillo. *Teatro selecto contemporáneo hispanoamericano*. 3 vols. Madrid: Escelicer, 1971. [20 plays, including 1 from Brazil]

Solórzano, Carlos. *Teatro breve hispanoamericano contemporáneo*. Madrid: Aguilar, 1970. [16 one-act plays]

———. *El teatro hispanoamericano contemporáneo*. 2 vols. Mexico City: Fondo de Cultura Económica, 1964. [14 plays]

———. *El teatro latinoamericano actual*. Mexico City: Ediciones de Andrea, 1972. [8 plays, including 1 from Brazil]

Woodyard, George W. *The Modern Stage in Latin America: Six Plays*. New York: E. P. Dutton & Co., 1971. [Includes 1 Brazilian play]

BRAZIL

Martins, Wilson, and Seymour Menton. *Teatro Brasileiro Contemporâneo*. New York: Appleton-Century-Crofts, 1966. [5 plays]

Index